THE APOCALYPSE OF LOVE:
MYSTICAL SYMBOLISM IN REVELATION

By
Richard Shiningthunder Francis

Bookman LLC
Publishing & Marketing
Providing Quality, Professional
Author Services

www.BookmanMarketing.com

DEDICATION:

To Maria Francis, my lover, my Soulmate, my "goddess," and my best friend,

And to Pat Fields, the sweet, lovely giver of life,

This book is dedicated, with joyful Love. May you both live forever in brightest Love and deepest serenity.

ACKNOWLEDGMENTS:

This book was created due to the kind and loving support of the following superfriends, without whom it would not have been possible:

Dennis Bailey, who aided and worked with me to come up with the original idea for this much-needed book, lo, many years ago, way back in 1979!

Ann Blufeather, the giver of this life, a tender, kind, compassionate lady with very much patience, who lived well and died like a peaceful warrior.

Barbara Cole and Jim Plants, who have made much beautiful educational work possible due to their kindness.

Dominic and Noeleen Ellickson, who gave so generously to aid and support our voyage to their home in the Emerald Isle.

Pat Fields, who leaped at a chance to save her brother's life, and who has granted me, by divine grace, more time on earth.

Maria Francis, whose humility and deep Love arc an exceptional example of true wisdom-- a giver of joy and peace.

Tom Gustin, who has worked to make himself the servant and messenger of Love; no better path exists anywhere.

Gene Janning, whose kind compassion and generosity have enriched life and have been used by Love to facilitate our work. Love will use your great heart to improve our world!

Frank Merriman, whose solidarity and stability allow for a wide "family" of loving, adoring "children," and who is also a masterteacher, filled with kindness and very much generosity.

Greg Sexton, he of the sharp mind and skills and great talents, used for aid and comforts of other people.

Shirley Sexton, whose heart of gold is also the heart of God, full of Love and sweet kindness.

Isaiah Toran, my long lost brother, with whom we work every day to make a better world.

To you all, may you live forever in peace and Love.

May whatever merit is created by this book be shared with all sentient beings everywhere, and may all hearts find happiness.

CHART OF MIND

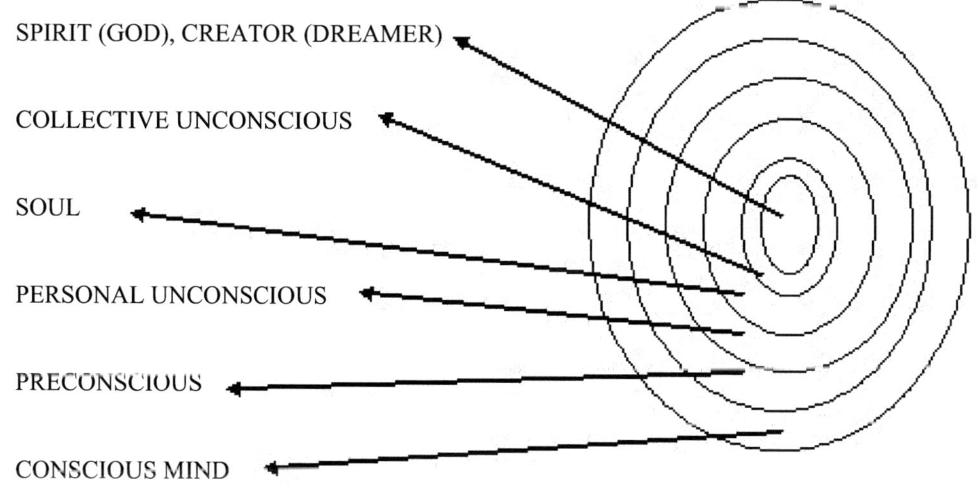

LEVELS OF MIND
ACCORDING TO APOCALYPTIC SYMBOLISM

Cosmicmind [Goddessmind; Godmind; Lovemind (agapopsyche); Coremind; ultimate Mind; Spirit; Absolute]. Also, Supermind, Superconscious, Christmind (blissmind), "Heaven," Sourcemind, divine Mind.
Dreamer/Creatormind
Inner Light (lampstands, stars, sun)
Controlmind
Jerusalemind
Edenmind
Crystalmind, Stillmind
Surrendermind (lambmind; altarmind)
Goldmind
Angelmind (spiritual Mindarea)
Neopsychicmind
Michaelmind (Positive, but still in duality)
Silvermind
Seamind (the Unconscious, often including the subconscious, the "moon")
sandmind
Soulmind
Omegamind
starmind
cavitymind
Desolationmind (created by darknight of mystical path)
coppermind
Mosesmind (religionmind)
Arkmind (illusiongod)
Human mind (intellect; human forms; alphamind)
Egomind
Stonemind (claymind)
woodmind

cavemind (subconscious)

Earthmind (animal-mind; sense-dominated mind; materialistic mind; bodymind; bionature; locusts, horses, etc.)

desertmind

illusionmind

Jezebelmind

scarletmind

Wildbeastmind (animalmind; leopardmind.)

Preface

Apocalypse as Nightmare: A Psychotic Monster God

Lightning flashes and slashes through the gray skies, ripping them into wet ribbons and soggy cotton balls. It sizzles, sending slender silver slivers and streamers sliding suddenly through the shining sky. A dazzling tongue of flame licks out quickly from the graphitic cloud, and lands squarely in the face of a young woman who, a microsecond ago, was an Aphroditic beauty. As the skies roar at her, the bolt rushes jaggedly through her nervous system, frying and tearing it apart viciously and causing her brain to explode. Where a nanosecond before stood the visionary, somehow ethereal, form of a delightful, delicious, slender nymph-goddess now is an acrid, putrid heap of burning, smoldering flesh. She has been vaporized.

This is happening concurrently all over the world. Inexplicably, the lightning has become not only vicious, but angry. And it is not just the lightning, but all of nature, that has gone mad. Those who are not pulverized by cruel, crushing hailstones suffer from agonizing and terminal diseases. At least a thousand new disease organisms have appeared during the last month. Each creates a ghastly set of violent and hellish symptoms. And medical science has not a clue. The hideous new viruses and superbacteria have decimated entire populations. They make the Black Plague look like a sneezing competition.

Those who manage to escape the fates of lightning and disease might be bludgeoned by hailstones the size of beach balls. Nature has released her fury. Little girls and old women drown in their own vomit. Bright-eyed teen girls writhe in agony before perishing. Boys whose biggest worry a week ago was trying to grow their first mustaches collapse into pools of their own blood.

Earthquakes tear through continents as through tissue, and their resulting chasms swallow entire cities, mercilessly crushing thousands at a time. In some areas, lakes of blood have pooled.

Nuclear devices have spontaneously gone off all over the earth, covering tens of thousands of square miles in deadly, lethal ash. Men and women are raping each other in the public streets. Little children are murdered in public. The government has totally collapsed, and order is only a vague, evanescent memory reflected in the tear-soaked eyes of hapless, despairing victims. Chaos and panic reign everywhere. And no end to the ghastly nightmare is in sight. Brutally savage thugs have taken over entire blocks, entire territories. They demand fullest, unquestioning subservience to their will and whims-- or else, they will use those knives (in ugly tortures) and machine guns. Local "warlords" have raised personal armies to quench their horrific lusts and psychopathic greed. Their "soldiers" battle it out on every corner, in every city, on every hill.

What utter madness is this? It is the scenario of the future dreamed up by assorted nut-cases, survivalist freaks, psychotics, losers, and bizarre religious fanatics. But what kind of nightmarish mind causes an otherwise ordinary person to view the future as such a grisly and horrific atrocity? When her fear-ridden eyes contemplate tomorrows, why does the religious fanatic panic? Why do the fundamentalist and the survivalist freak out when the future is visualized?

This grotesquery is the dark insane fantasy of a group of crazy religious and political extremists called "Armageddonists." For them, this monstrous portrayal of the "near future" is not mad, loony sciencefiction, but "prophecy." They call their grotesque vision "Armageddon" or "Apocalypse." These wild speculations come down to unimaginably hellish grotesquerie, atrocity, and absurdity.

At this moment, someone is greedily hoarding, in frenetic panic, food, weapons, or both. He (leaders among these sad lunatics are almost always males) cares only for his own personal survival; to hell with everyone else. He would gladly murder you -- and ten thousand other people-- to save his all-important, selfish skin. In fact, he has vivid, sickening plans actually to murder his neighbors if and when it becomes "necessary." (This will be when they try to steal his dried bananas.) His derangement is wildly out of control at the start of the twenty-first century.

For these psychopaths were hugely disappointed when their beloved "end of the world" did not come, as they all had predicted, with savage glints in their eyes, in the year twenty hundred. These brutal savages rerun monstrous visions, such as the one just presented, every day. Some relish the gore and madness several times a day. This makes them very sick puppies. They carry a crushing and shattering mountain of stress and anxiety on their backs. It is magnified by restless and tormenting fear. They are selfterrified by their vision of the future.

Nearly as horrifying to them, however, is the possibility that this hell will never come to fruition in reality. It might be just a nutty illusion. For that would prove them laughable, the butt of everyone's jokes. And they would rather see the streets soaked in blood than for them to be exposed as sadly amusing loons and losers. They continue to review visions of disaster to "remain strong."

In the "battle of Armageddon," all order will collapse into utter chaos. Government authority will disappear. Animals in human bodies will rape and rampage on the streets. They will kill in their hideous hordes. So, the pathetic survivalist or fundy collects dried bananas and practices using an ak47 to protect his dried bananas from the "marauding hordes." These lawless mobs are just over the horizon. Do his visions trouble him? No, astonishingly, he finds them gleeful! And he is going to be damn' good and ready, with two pistols, two knives, and a machine-gun! He can barely wait! His bloody prognostications confirm that he, a perennial jerk and loser, has the wisdom and foresight to prepare. This, in turn, proves that he is smarter than anyone else. He is one of the elite "chosen few." In fact, in his sick delusion, he can draw a kind of horrible "happiness" from his pathetic "prophetic" visions. Blasting away with his machine-gun to protect his bananas, killing the "evil" mobs, he sees himself as Rambo.

But he is much more. Because of his "special and great understanding" of "prophecy," he is like Jesus Christ! He is part Jesus and part Rambo! He is impressed to death with his fantasy-self! So, he is his own childish image of Superman wrapped up with the greatest mind in history. Lost in this perennial unrealistic fantasy, he barely allows his feet to touch the earth. He is the star of his own show! And the worse the world becomes, the more that it needs him as its "savior."

He is an intellectual and spiritual giant among men. He is one of the few "insiders" when it comes to the "secret plan" of God, whom he usually calls, "Gawd." Great if hazy and obscure, "truths" have been vouchsafed to him. They are the province of mysteries hidden from the average person. Indeed, they have been hidden from the greatest minds for ages!

Usually uneducated, he has the inside track on many of the deepest, darkest secrets. The mysteries of the ages, long hidden, he now understands. He clearly sees all the magnificent truths hidden from the scholarly and wise men. If God has not spoken to him personally, He has revealed in "Bible-study" the solutions to complex mathematical and historical conundrums and ancient mysteries.

These are so incredibly complex and difficult to understand that only one in several billion ever sees them. Fortunately for everyone in the world, he is that one in several billion! He is the world's greatest hero! He is the "white knight" that will "gallop in" and bring the entire world to a new level of Biblical understanding.

And when civilization does fall apart, and people are bludgeoning each other, and raping, in public, he will be proved "right"! (In his delusion, it is far more important to be "right" than to be compassionate, or even sane!) He finds "hidden meaning" in the words of Jesus. Jesus was not all about only Love; only fools, he says, believe that. No, he says in a conspiratorial if dramatic whisper, Jesus was all about prophecy. That's the magic word! Like Nostradamus, Jesus knew the future-- not only his, but ours!

The troubled man, with all his secret knowledge and ancient God given wisdom, has a serious psychological problem! He will dance as fast as he can to hide it, but he is seriously mad. Deep down, he feels worthless, and loathes himself. He is sickened by the awareness, buried deeply, that he is a loser. That is why he practices overcompensation (he smirks smugly) in selfpresentation. For he presents himself as the greatest person who has ever lived. For he is one of the special elite, one of the "chosen ones," the illuminati, although he might object to that term.

He can read with special understanding the ancient Hebrew prophets, for he is in on their greatest secret-- they were really writing about the twenty-first century! (A few years ago, he would have argued just as vehemently that they were really writing about the twentieth century!) What a man!

But good news! These false prophets of gloom and doom are nothing new. There is absolutely no reason why their lame-brained panic-attacks should disturb us. For sane and balanced people, even wise people, still exist. The sane outnumber the worldenders, and the wise counter their religions and politics of selfterrorism with truly reasonable alternatives. The worldenders have been predicting the collapse of civilization into violence and flame for thousands of years. Centuries before the birth of Jesus, there were fanatical groups predicting the "end of the world" just "around the corner."

Hundreds of times throughout history, cults and extremists have steeled themselves for the end of civilization. Indeed, they have panted after it, longing and yearning for the absolute catastrophic end of everything. Like the Marquis de Sade, they have been nihilists, but closet nihilists.

They have done this so often that reading about them-- even listing them-- can be an intolerably boring task. So, we will not burden the reader with it. Let's just say that thousands, belonging to dozens of cults, have sold all their possessions. They have quit promising marriages and careers, refused to have children, or to save money, and fled to the mountains awaiting the end. Or they have holed up in caves, waiting for the skies to catch fire and the world to be consumed. Or they have meandered off to the desert, carrying crates of dried bananas and the machine-guns with which to defend them.

This is the craziest idea in the history of the world. Yet it underlies very much in fundamentalist and "right-wing whack-o" propaganda. In fact, the "fundies," who are no fun at all, have been called "allegorically challenged," because they take everything so literally!

Yet this fanatical literalism is by no means limited to the limited mindsets of fundies. Newagers are also notorious if gullible victims of the panic-response. In 1992, the followers of the "I Am" cult conjured up by a couple who called themselves "Prophets" gathered in the desert to await the "end." Other groups, every few months, gather together on a mountain to await the "Mother Ship." This is a ufo that is going to rescue them and take them to a perfect planet. Heaven's Gate, the infamous cult, was not alone.

There is something grotesque and savage, in the subconscious mind, that causes some people to indulge in these worldender perversities in a sick cyclic pattern. For every few years, some group(s) cannot seem to resist predicting the "end"-- yet again. Excuse me if I yawn. Worldenders, with all their screaming false predictions, have managed to make the "end of the world" a major snore. They have "cried wolf" a thousand times.

A strong cult-history marks this trend in America. As an example of a single line of this kind of pathetic "prophetic" tendency, we need look no further than the notorious Millerites. They pinpointed October 1844 for the "end." This specificity was based solidly and squarely on "Biblical chronology," often ungrammatically called "Bible chronology."

It seems that a fool named Miller, with nothing better to do, calculated the creation of the world to have occurred around four-thousand something BCE. (Details are just annoying, not necessary.) This had already been done long before, although Miller never had a clue, being a historical illiterate. Archbishop James Ussher (1581-1656), to be exact, had calculated that the world had been created by God in the year 4004 BC.

How did the bishop achieve this amazing feat? Simple. He added up all the life-spans of all the people descended from Adam. (These are listed in a dull lists of "begats," in the Hebrew Scriptures, misidentified as the "Old Testament", a term that reveals Christian bias). So Miller, retracing steps already well-worn, "discovered" a very exciting fact: The end was just around the corner! (It always is.)

So, he got out his old reliable pad and paper, and opened to the lists of life-spans in the book of Genesis. With one or two (some say three or more) errors, he reckoned that in the year 1844, human beings would have been on the earth exactly six thousand years. Now, since the "reign of Christ" is predicted to last a thousand years, and since all really good spiritual stuff happens in sevens, this time of Christ's reign would have to be included in a seven-thousand-year period that also included human history. Confusing? You bet! Dubious? Indubitably!

But this tidbit of pseudoscholarship was enough to get Miller and his followers incredibly excited! (These are people who could be turned on by the fascinating art of watching paint dry!)

After October 1844 came and went without moving an allegorical blade of grass, Miller desperately, quickly set up another date-- 1845. But he had already lost his steam, and it was a very halfhearted effort. Understandably, members of his cult abandoned him in droves. They could not wait to get out of his humiliated cult!

But this desertion by no means ended the deep psychological need to feel special, as the "chosen people" of God. It did not end worldender fever. The Millerites, a very minor cult, fragmented and fractured, and regrouped into other cults following other gurus. One cult that sprang up from the hopeful but hopelessly misled Millerites was the Russelllites.

A showman/haberdasher named Russell picked up Miller's false and stupid "prophecies," and started tinkering and fiddling with them. Although Miller had been spectacularly wrong, Russell reckoned, maybe the idea was right that the "end" was near, anyway! Miller had simply, tragically "miscalculated". Russell sensed a great opportunity for a smart operator to start a money-making cult of his own. Russell did not say that Miller was on the right track out of courtesy, but because he himself was a determined worldender. In fact, in the mid- to late nineteenth century, worldenders were coming out of the woodwork. You could not lift up a rock without finding one, or swing a dead cat without hitting one! Many best-sellers of that time-period often were obsessed with worldender themes.

It struck Russell as a great idea, very exciting, and potentially profitable, to declare that the "end" was so near. So, performing his own razzle-dazzle sleight-of-hand, he convinced his own desperate (hence, gullible) followers that Miller had been right, after all. Many ex-Millerites were very desperate to believe Russell anyway. Miller had simply made an "error" in his calculations. The end, announced this quirky little man, was "really" coming in October of 1874. Incredibly, this questionable fanatic got a small following. For nearly thirty years, from 1844-1874, his followers were able to entertain and sustain their own little fantasy, with breath-taking and breath-holding suspense.

Nothing, of course, happened in 1874. All those complicated, confusing and confused calculations and charts laboriously constructed by Russell went straight where they belonged-- into the trash. But they did not rest in peace there.

Belief in worldender speculations has nothing to do with reason. It is tough for us to get our minds around this bizarre concept. We are accustomed to using reason to choose our styles, occupations, interests, and yes, even our religions. But the shocking truth is that *much religion has nothing to do with reason!* So the utter disproof of all these little theories by the nonevents of 1874 had little impact on Russell's followers. Logic, validation, and observation have nothing to do with absurd speculations about the "end of the world." They are embraced not from intellectual cerebration or conviction, but out of knee-jerk fears, longing, desperation, and dark fantasies. This worldender worldview appeals to people who have discovered an altered state that has turned into a steady state. The altered state is a desperation so highstrung, so tense, that it crowds out everything else from the mind. The steady state to which this yellow brick road leads is studied and cultivated hopelessness. They say that human beings are hopelessly stupid, and so "need" the "end of the world" to get rid of unsolvable problems! (People who "sell" this are likely to have some deeds to Florida swampland lying around!)

Russell knew, smugly, that his followers had been gullible enough to follow him. So, despite his humiliating failure with the 1874 debacle, he still wanted to control them. He then reinforced his cult and made it official. Miller, Campbell, and Wilbur had also done this before him. Many people at this time were at spiritual loose ends, and cults proliferated. (Both the Christian Science cult and Theosophy, among others, got their starts in this period.) Russell, not a terribly bright man, announced that there had been yet another "error" in his arithmetic! (This was getting old!) Maybe, he thought cunningly, it would be worth a calculated risk to try the ploy again. So, Russell started teaching that the end was coming in 1914. Astonishingly, his mesmerized followers didn't bat an eyelash at the dramatic forty-year change in course.

With bated breath, they looked forward to 1914. That year would bring in the "kingdom of God." (The illusion of the end was based upon another misunderstanding, that the "kingdom of God" was a literal earthly government.)

This snafu, as ignorantly launched as the previous attempts, dovetailed with a "lucky" synchronicity. As we all know, nothing did not happen in 1914. But clearly, the end did not come either. World War 1 broke out. Russell and his followers were exhilarated by this hideous outbreak of stupidity and savagery. Wide-eyed in wonder, they seemed to say, "Close enough!"

Russell had been dead wrong again. But he was determined to make the best of a terribly embarrassing situation. So, he benignly neglected his stupendous error, quietly hoping that everybody else would do the same. He put the most positive spin on his blunder.

Russell had predicted the end in that year. People conveniently forgot that he had been totally wrong. They started to say that he was "nearly half-right," which was just "right enough" for his duped, sheeplike admirers. World War 1 was just too good a coincidence to let it pass by. So, Russellites did not die out. They continued to thrive as a fringe microminority. (Later, they even claimed that the "kingdom of God" did indeed "come" in 1914. But it was "invisible" and "heavenly"!) They repeated the "half right" slogan until it, in time, evolved into a message that Russell had somehow been "right" all along. Although dead wrong, he was hailed as a prophet by those determined, in the face of contradiction, to believe him. After 1914, after the inevitable dwindle of enthusiasm, his followers got the bright idea of setting a new date for the end. 1925 seemed as good a year as any, and so they began to proclaim that the end was indeed coming then. (They even built a house in California where the "resurrected patriarchs" could live; no one ever lived there but the Russellite president!) The nut jobs that came up with this bright idea are mercifully lost to history, but it was an unusually stupid strategy. It was almost as if the Russellite leaders were trying to sabotage the cult by setting another date for the "end". Actually, they had just the opposite in mind: They wanted to give it a shot in the arm, to renew it with new vigor.

This dumb strategy can never work for long. Why? Because, sooner or later, the date that you have predicted must come. If the end does not come in that year, you have proved your cult wrong, ignorant, in darkness. Then, all reasonable people will leave your group. Strangely, though, cults have never been at all interested in keeping reasonable people in their ranks. They prefer gullible "sheeplike" followers incapable of independent thought. These are not better people, but they do make "better" cultists. They play "follow the leader" without a murmur.

 Cults make predictions that are so far in the future that they can put off explaining why they were wrong. It is a terrible idea to predict the "end" next week or even next year! And no one ever does!

At the time of this writing, there is a small but growing frenzy that, since the Mayan calendar ends in the year twenty-twelve, so will the world as we know it. That date is just far enough in the future to stir up some momentum and short-term excitement for people who really need to get lives! But if the cult is to survive, people must actually believe its predictions, at least for a while.

So, many shady cultleaders predict the "end," but they've learned to keep the blessed event at least five to ten years in the future. Otherwise, they know, they wouldn't get much "mileage" out of the exciting, enthralling lie! In time, cult-leaders become so cynical, jaded, and egocentric that they can become careless. If the modern, resurrected Russell-cult needs a shot in the arm, they might yet again make the horrible mistake of setting a specific year-date for the "end." This is incredibly shortsighted. At best, it is good for only an immediate boost, a shorterm fix (as in a "heroin-fix").

As noted, no one joins a cult for reasons of reason. People do not follow cult-ideas because they are seeking wisdom. They do not join because they are particularly smart, bright, wise, enlightened, or educated people. They join such groups as the Millerites and Russellites due to a deep feeling of alienation and of unworthiness. The need to belong to a cult is unaffected by the objective truth of its teachings.[1]

---

[1] For a more indepth but informal psychosocial understanding of cult psychology, see my *Jehovah Lives In Brooklyn: Jehovah's Witnesses as a Model of Fundamentalism* (Liberty Township, Ohio; Love Ministries, Inc., 2000)

Stubborn and ignorant cultists will even reverse a teaching and march forward as if nothing has happened.

They are blissfully oblivious to the fact that yesterday's "truth" has become today's error. They respond in this "Stepford" mindless pattern even when a core-doctrine has just been disproved and demolished.

In 1931, the cult called the "Russellites" changed its name to "Jehovah's Witnesses," claiming the name of the ancient wargod of the Hebrews. This primitive god was notorious for hot tempered barbarities, and atrocities, including genocide.[2] Anyone seeking a realistic appraisal of truth (reality) should have taken a warning from this turn for the worse. (The embracing of the name "Jehovah" as a trade-mark) Almost all the doctrines of Russell were abandoned en masse. In fact, the new cult damned most of Russell's teachings as "evil," and so labeled anyone who remained faithful to the original teachings. Even this gargantuan, shameless flip-flop had zero effect on cultist die-harders.

But incredibly, astonishingly, the cynical leaders repeated their most crucial, short-sighted, and stupid blunder. When enthusiasm for the cult began to waver and to vacillate, it needed a booster. So, in 1966, cult-leaders repeated the crazy last resort of setting a definite year for the end. They declared that it would occur in 1975. In 1966, that was far enough in the future to allow the cult to get a real rush from the dogma. (Of course, now it is official policy to lie and deny that the end had ever been predicted for that year. The leaders blame the members, as if the latter had just made the whole thing up on a boring Sunday afternoon!) Now, about thirty years after the "end," the subject is never mentioned in polite company.

Fundies always get all worked up about the "end." They rave like lunatics about it! The vision of all that blood brings a terrible glint of glee into their eyes! Some become virtual animals, completely devoid of all compassion. After all, only the "bad" guys are going to perish in

---

[2] For an unmasking of the myth of the psychotic "macho-monstrosity" god see my *Jehovah Goodbye. the New Theism of Love* (Liberty Township, Ohio; Love Ministries, Inc., 2004)

pools of their (and their beloved family's) blood! ("These are the ones who refused to join our church!")

But of course, their comic-book ideas never upset reputable scholars. Their god, fundies say, has turned the tables on educated and intellectual types. He has revealed his greatest truths to the uneducated. Some ministers shamelessly, a bit absurdly, boast about their lack of education! Not that this is at all necessary! It simply cannot be hidden, under even the largest "bushel." So, they decide to make the best of it, and put a positive spin on it, turning it to their advantage.

But why do fundies and fanatics see the grisly nightmare of Armageddon as an event to celebrate? What on earth has caused some ministers to declare that a universal nuclear war would be a "God-given blessing"? They are obsessed with themselves, having abandoned care for others. As long as they "survive," who gives a care about the rest of the world?

Besides, before the end, the rest of humanity has the option to "repent." This means to join the worldenders' cult or church. Only those who do will be "saved." The "good guys" are only the people in their cult/church/religion. They have a "monopoly" on truth! Worldenders teach that even other worldenders are going to be murdered by their god. Of course, they would object to the use of the word "murder." It makes them sound like jerks. Well, get a clue! For this mass slaughter, this gargantuan massacre, is the nuclear teaching of all Armageddonists! And there is just no polite way to say "murder"!

The rule of the Prince of Peace does not come peacefully. It begins with the most horrific bloodbath. It is so horrendously nauseating that its visualization is enough to turn the stomach. It will make all of Hitler's concentration camps, plus his miscellaneous and innumerable cruelties, look like a Sunday in the park. It will make binladen's atrocities look like a joyful gift. It will make the horrific tortures of the Inquisition look like harmless fun and games!

For the Prince of Peace comes breathing fire. He is presented as a psychotic mass-murderer! He makes Ted Bundy look like a reasonable saint! He will mercilessly "execute vengeance" or "judgment" upon his "enemies." He slaughters the human race in a megagenocide. Perhaps "pangenocide" is more accurate, for the gentle Jesus kills all but the members of the cult. This is the most gargantuan and absurd anti-human action conceivable.

It demands a totally new incarnation of Jesus, not as teacher of Love and forgiveness, but as a monstrous and psychotic murderer. *Christ becomes the antichrist!* This new, reinterpreted Jesus is the very worst in human psychology: vindictive, vengeful, vitriolic, vituperative, vicious, venomous, he comes breathing fire and splashing human blood with a giant sword. He is so insane that he is the polar opposite of all the qualities by which we recognize sanity and inner peace in a person. *He is the polar opposite of the Jesus whom everyone knows and loves! He has mutated horribly into a sadistic fiend, a blend of the sickening hitler, manson, saddam, binladen, and all the other losers and weaklings of history!*

He is a no-nonsense damnation-machine without a particle of patience, and even less forgiveness. The temptation to see this Jesus as a mere reflection of nutty cultleaders is irresistible. He is brutal, the creator of atrocity and genocide so great that they are straight out of hell. This vision of Jesus fits the most damnable mind of the lowest demon, but can have no place in the sane and balanced mind.

This dissonance is enhanced if one has any familiarity with the Jesus of the Gospels. Worldenders have made a travesty of the Jesus of Love. A mockery and caricature of the devil himself stands in the place, and bears the name, of "Jesus."

With the empty-headed concept of an insane god, fundies teach that nature will be whipped into vicious and evil frenzy! It will be used as a weapon against young girls and old women, by a heartless, vicious god.

How did the God of purest Love preached by Jesus ever mutate into a psychotic monster? How was his tender compassion replaced by bloodlust? How did the Fountain of forgiveness become a savage, unforgiving sadist? How did the Lord of Love and Light come much more to resemble a god in need of major medication instead of a God of tender mercies and sweet forgiveness?

Much responsibility lands squarely on the back of a single book in the Bible. It is the final book of the Christian Scriptures. The Greeks called this book "Apocalypse." This is a transliteration, not a translation, of the Greek word used in ancient texts. It is used in Catholic Bibles. The translation of the word appears often as the name of the book in Protestant Bibles-- "Revelation."

"Apocalypse" need not strike terror into our hearts. Originally this harmless word meant only "revelation," implying nothing bad, harmful, or negative. It is a simple "lifting of the veil," an uncovering or "dis-covering." So, when God reveals that His/Her Love is bottomless, and His/Her forgiveness inexhaustible, this is also a revelation or "apocalypse."

Let us abandon, then, the superstitious fear and ignorance that strike our hearts with horror at the word "Apocalypse." Instead, in sweetest tranquility and Love, let us open widely our warm hearts to embrace it as the matchless gift of the Lovegod.

But there is nothing particularly sexy about God's Love. Horror and sickening atrocity are much more captivating to the human psyche and imagination. For the human mind has a perverse and compelling fascination with nightmarish evil. Witness the popularity of violence and evil in fiction and in the news. Most interpretations of Revelation are like something out of a badly written tabloid! (And they're just about as credible!)

The mind has two sides-- a lower, hypersensual, "materialistic" part and a higher spiritual part. [3] Some actually suffer from a mental disorder which could be called "apocalypsosis." This does not refer to the healthy apocalypses of Love, joy, and peace received by people from the beginning of time. This is the true "revelation" of God as Love, peace, forgiveness, etc.

But "apocalypsosis" indicates unhealthy obsession with blood and guts. It focuses pathologically on a monstrous god who gets his jollies by murdering people, often in the messiest and most agonizing ways! This psychotic god could give lessons to serial killers and to serial rapists. He is a study in ultimate brutality and unfeeling insanity. [4] In the

---

[3] For the full story of the Enlightenment Tradition or mysticism with psychological, philosophic and historical highlights see my *Journey to the Center of the Soul: Mysticism Made Simple* (Liberty Township, Ohio; Love Ministries, Inc., 2002)

[4] For a more indepth look at the history and philosophy of the nightmarish Jehovah-image of God, see my *Jehovah Goodbye, op.cit.*

apocalypsotic, violence, waste, and stupidity are compulsively rerun in nightmare visualizations of Armageddon. (By contrast, there are "subconscious armageddonists" who believe in the atrocity, but will never permit themselves to imagine it in any great detail, lest their sanity be irrecoverably wounded.) Apocalypsosis is a sick obsession with brutality and atrocity. It is blamed on, projected onto, "god."

Victims of apocalypsosis are armageddonists or "worldenders." They are also fanatics who have gone so far off the deep end that they come to celebrate the end of civilization, and the death of billions, because it is actually seen as a positive event. These fundies would *delight* to hear of the start of international nuclear war! This is why the mythology of Armageddon is not a joke. It would make us laugh if it did not make us cry.

Fundies would be double-delighted to hear of nuclear war, for it would also "prove" that they were "right"! And, in their severely disturbed view of history, their bloody, psychotic god massacres the human race to give them the planet. For apocalypsotics generally believe that, after all the "bad guys" (people outside their church) are slaughtered by their god, this god will give them everything. "Yes Billy, you really can have every lollipop in Texas. So, greed and an abysmally low selfesteem combine synergetically as one root of the complex disease. A deeper, more serious breakaway from reality would be hard even to imagine.

This pathology is fear. Part of that is the fear of not, or never, being good enough, or competent enough, to earn an honest living. Worldenders are always masking a pathetic sense of inadequacy. You don't have indefinitely to earn a living if God is going to give you everything on a silver platter. Receiving requires no skill or talent at all!

Greed and laziness have reached new heights among true believers! They thrive on the unhealthy illusion that they will not have to work for anything. Like spoiled brats, they will be given all the world's wealth, dropped into their laps. For these, "God" is like an unpredictably friendly uncle who is completely bonkers. After he murders everyone else, he will distribute all the world's great abundance to the members of the elite chosen people (members of the exclusive cult or church). So, no matter what these fundies say, their core-teaching belies their claims to nobility and compassion. Material things are far more important, in their religion, than are people. All the gold, jewels, homes, cars, and miscellaneous "toys" of the dead "bad guys" will be theirs. This requires cultivating a sense of entitlement which parallels that which belonged to the Nazis.

The enormity of the murder of the whole human race as the most immorally obscene act imaginable is carefully neglected. (Here, "enormity" is used in its correct sense, meaning not "enormousness," but "horror.") These worldenders are seriously mentally ill. People tend to become like, imitate, the god(s) that they worship. And their god is a psychotic monster.

This god reflects the Jehovah-myth of the earliest Hebrew Scriptures. To believe the Armageddon-horror, you must first buy into the Jehovah-horror. You must embrace this deity of anger, spitefulness, jealousy, genocide, and ferocious madness. You must then reject the gentle, tender God of Jesus and early Christians. And you must choose: It is just not possible to accept both polarities as representing reality.

This is a stunning revelation: The god of the earliest Hebrew Scriptures is completely incompatible with the God of Love. The two godimages are polar opposites. Many Christians, but especially fundies, blithely and carelessly assume that the Jehovah of the Hebrew Scriptures is the same as the God of Jesus. But viewed objectively, this simply cannot be. Why?

Because the "faithful" or "loyal" people of Jehovah were the ones who engineered the murder of Jesus by the Romans. If Jesus had agreed that their religion-- including their god-- represented truth, he never would have been murdered. He was murdered because he threatened the status quo. He rocked the boat, and threatened the dissolution of an entire religiocultural system, by teaching the "dangerous heresy" that "God is Love." His disciple John wrote these lifechanging words. (1 Jn. 4: 8, 16) *Early Christians forcefully rejected Jehovah as repugnant and repellant! Many very early writers among Christians did not hesitate to label him an "evil spirit."*

The view that God is Love is the highest of which the human mind is capable. It is the zenith of enlightenment and awakening. The legalists of Jesus' day were fundamentalists. They were simply unable to rise to this elevated mystical vision of God.

This book is not antisemetic. Nor is its author. No one is responsible for the behavior of her ancestors. These ancient Jews just illustrated a particularly virulent and dangerous facet of fundamentalism. Judaism is a fine religion filled with beauty. It is fundamentalism, not Judaism that poses a danger to mind, soul, and society.

Fundamentalism is the opposite of mysticism. The state of mind encouraged and reinforced by fundamentalism actually supports apocalypsosis. This mental disease goes directly against all the finest principles of social justice, peace, and wisdom. Its "god" is an angry beast.

It also devalues those who believe in it. This is the last thing that fundies need, for they already see themselves as ultimate underachievers and losers. And the more that the "end" keeps "not happening," the deeper grows their mental illness.

But, viewed logically, what can we expect from a person who builds her entire worldview upon the words of antisocial crackpots, and her entire religion on the blood of innocents? For many of the so-called "prophets" were themselves suffering from various mental imbalances and illnesses. They were not only condemnatory and antisocial, but crazy. Half-naked "prophets" living in the desert and shouting about the stormy wrath of God are not exactly credible sources. More educated and intelligent people of the twenty-first century demand more sophistication-- not to mention simple balance, sanity, and wisdom-- from the people who influence their lifedesigns. They also rightly demand more compassion. Yet fundies consider it completely normal to construct an entire worldview on excerpts from selfstyled "prophets" who, living centuries in the past, were "really" writing about the twenty-first century!

How reasonable is that? Worldenders are people who have given up on life. They suffer from serious selfesteem disorders. Many secretly, unknown even to themselves, loathe themselves. This emerges as a half-hidden hatred for humanity. The insides of their minds, where they live, are torture-chambers and chambers of horror! This nightmare-mind seriously deteriorates selfimage.

For the value of a person is related to the contents of her mind. The visionary spectacle of the worldenders is a horrific, violent, wasteful view. It degrades God seriously. But it also degrades the believer.

****

It is impossible to embrace the most antihuman beliefs imaginable and still to maintain a positive selfimage.

****

The belief in Armageddon is antisocial to the max. Can you imagine a more antihuman belief than that God is going to murder all His children? Can you even come up with an idea that is more murderously psychotic?

****

People become like the god(s) they worship.

****

So, the apocalypsotic buys into a belief that is both psychologically catastrophic and also socially disastrous. To get people to believe that God regards human life as of no more value than an ameba is the first step to a full negligence of the value of all human life, including yours. When carried to its logical extreme, apocalypsosis forces people to believe that human life has no more value than that of the average cockroach. Worldenders shout with sick pride that their dogmas are indeed more important than human beings. It was precisely this pathological mindset that allowed "Christians" to burn innocent women alive at the stake. It allowed and created the most grotesque sexual and other tortures! Some of them are so malevolent and sick that they will not even be described here, to spare the readers several nightmares!

God is the supreme Role-model. If God is going to "solve problems" by murder, then it must be a good and valid idea! This hideous path of pseudo-reason has led Jews, Christians, and Muslims down the bloodiest, most horrific paths possible. It has led them to rape, torture, and murder. It has been used to support sickeningly animal behavior.

****

An "evil god" is the world's most harmful, painful, and dark oxymoron.

****

It makes it easy for believing fundies to rationalize killing, torture, and rape. This behavior is okay as long as it is directed at the "bad" or "lost" people, towards "infidels." This view makes them all subhuman anyway.

The ancient Israelis claimed, for example, that their god Jehovah commanded them to slaughter women and helpless infants. The Moslem sacred book, the Quran, also justifies the murder of "infidels," using the same vicious argument. Christians have also justified massacres many times in their history. In these cases, the excuse is even better than, "The devil made me do it." It is, "God made me do it."

Indeed, in very primitive faiths, it is challenging to tell the difference between their god and their devil. At any rate, their devil could not possibly behave worse than their god. For them, murder just might be a viable solution to problems with "enemies." And nothing is easier than to become the "enemy" of the dangerous, unbalanced paranoiac!

They, in their social psychoses, believe that "God is always right." So, it follows, it must be "right" to murder people. It must, in fact, be "good" to kill them if they are "your enemies" or the "bad guys." *Killing people is "good" if the people are "bad."* This was the dangerous course followed by such morally bankrupt fools and moral morons as hitler, manson, saddam, and binladen. Can't we do better? Should these violent idiots be actual models upon which we construct the Mind of God-- the best in all creation?

Those who defend the massacre of the human race are giving their approval to the same attitudes held by these human monsters. They unite themselves philosophically with the hitlers and binladens of the world. Their stamp of approval makes it "okay" to solve social problems by killing people. It is no surprise that the god of right-wing extremists, created in their image, displays attitudes and actions similar to their own. The neonazis, for example, insist that their god is "Yahvch," "Yahweh," or a similar name of the ancient Hebrew wargod "Jehovah."[5] And because this "god" is so violent and stupid, they actually use the Jewish god to justify and defend the most ridiculous antisemitism, and other moral monstrosities. But, examining the actions

---

[5] The more correct form of the name of the ancient Hebrew war-god is "Yahweh" but it has been twisted and distorted into the incorrect form "Jehovah".

of God/Jesus at "Armageddon," you would expect better, saner behavior from a drunken sex-pervert, or a killer high on heroin.
****

To pretend that God is a psychotic monster is the most sickening of blasphemies.
****

To defend mass murder in the name of the Lord of Love is simply nuts. There is no way that it can be made reasonable. And it sure as hell can never be made palatable to a civilized human being. What would we think of a strong man who beat his cute little daughter to death, or electrocuted her, or infected her with smallpox, because she had "disobeyed" him? There is no way that such a giant injustice can be made just-- no matter how much you talk about God's "right" to "do anything." You can blab all day about his "power." You can blah-blah all night about his "higher vision." But the bottom line is that if you try to make God out to be a monster, you have made Him/Her subhuman. We have a full right to expect at least as decent a behavior from God as that which we demand from fellow human beings. The "monstergod" is considerably worse, exponentially more savage, than our worst human psychotics. If your "god" is a brute, an animal, you need to become more fluid. You need to open yourself to new visions and perspectives!

For Armageddon is a mockery of God. It reduces Him/Her to less than the worst human crackpot or moral moron. Should we not ask from God at least the behavior that we would demand from an average man? How do we, as civilized people, view human leaders who use murder or war to get their way? Do we not see them as simpering and infantile spoiled brats, throwing temper-tantrums and stomping their feet? Are they not nutty to the point of being almost amusing?

Suppose you knew an ordinary man who lived down the block from you. Let's suppose that this man was extraordinary in one way only: He and his wife had produced ten beautiful kids. What if he took a machete and started hacking to death his screaming, bloody little girl? Or what if you saw him beating his five-year-old son, over and over, while the kid's voice grew raw from screaming? What if he took hot insulated wires and forced them upon the tender flesh of his little girl, until the skin burned and began to smoke, while she shrieked her sheer horror? What if he forced the wires into her mouth? What if he forced them into the most tender areas of her body? These scenarios make sensitive people literally sick. Their skin crawls, and they feel creepy, just imagining the hideous barbarity! But even all this *is nothing* compared with the nightmarish atrocity of Armageddon!

Would you nominate this guy for the "Father of the Year," award? or, Time magazine's values notwithstanding, could you bring yourself to reward him as "Man of the Year"?

No, I think that you would probably be more comfortable if he were shackled in a rubber room somewhere. I know that I would. Certainly his kids would.

But you can't put God in a rubber room. Fortunately, as almost all people know, God does not belong there. In our society, despite the Armageddon madness, most people are too reasonable to fall for the lie that God is infinitely meaner and immeasurably nastier than the devil.

God as bestial maniac must be rejected by decent people. For God is better-- more loving, more forgiving, kinder-- than any human being. The absurdity/atrocity of the Armageddon/Apocalypse nightmare arose from the minds of psychotic religious leaders. (Brought to you by the same fellows that created the idea of the barbecue orgy of everlasting hellfire, the delightful Inquisition, the Crusades, and the witch hunts!)

****

Religious doctrines are only as sane and compassionate as those who create them.

****

But is not this doctrine of Armageddon taken directly from the Bible? Do the main ideas of Christianity not originate with God Himself? This naive and simplistic view does not at all countenance the multifarious hydra-headed complexities of history, or the mutability of the human mind or of religion. It naively ignores textual changes made over centuries. This is just ignorant literalism, and has not worked for most people with half a brain since the middle of the Dark Ages.

For everything depends on how you define "Christianity." Its simplest meaning is to be "like Christ." In fact, at its deepest mystical level, Christianity is the art of becoming another "Christ," or perfect mirror of Love in this world.

This is the Christianity of Jesus. It is not organized Christianity. It is not orthodox Christianity. It is not even historical Christianity. It is the Christianity of unstained Love. It could even be defined as "Love plus nothing." It is a very far cry from "Christianity" as the word is usually used today. This is the pristine form of crystalline, unstained, bright activities of "Christ" in the heart. Christ always creates Love. It is impossible for Christ to create hatred. For that arises from fear. And, "Fear and Love cannot coexist. Where Love has been made complete, fear is thrown outside." (1 Jn. 4:18)

So, we must define "Jesus-Christianity" as a different historical entity from "traditional" Christianity. For this latter form contains many ideas created long after the life and death of Jesus. These include a ton of excess baggage, including dogma, doctrines, hierarchies, and institutions. The most twisted of errors is the transformation of the simple Way of Love into a complicated system that requires libraries to understand. Throughout history, incredible, innumerable distortions have slipped in, or have been engineered.

The most extremist fundy believes that the King James Bible was handed down from a cloud by the hand of God. It contains no error. It is the infallible, letter-perfect Word of God. But even the uneducated literalist has major problems with Armageddon. For in the entire Book of Revelation, it is mentioned only a single time, in 16:16. Clearly, it was a microscopically unimportant teaching to the writer of Revelation. In subsequent centuries, it has ballooned and mushroomed into one of the most blasphemous, atrocious, outrageous teachings of a depraved, hate-based "Christianity."

The text itself says simply that God "gathered together" a number of important characters in the Revelation. It does not describe the terrors usually associated with the end of the world.

The phrase "end of the world" is not found a single time *in the entire Book of Revelation!* In fact, *it is not found a single time* in the original Bible. In the King James Version of 1611, it is found, for example, in Matthew 24:3, but the Greek word translated "world" is not *kosmos*. Now, *kosmos* is the Greek word for "world," in the language of the ancient manuscripts of the Greek Christian Scriptures, commonly called the "New Testament." So, this is the word that would have been used if the disciples had been asking Jesus about the "end of the world." Many modern translations get this right, but King James blew it.

But this is not the word used in this verse. The word used is *aion*, a Greek word that means "age." So, the disciples were actually asking Jesus about the "end of the age," not the "end of the world."

Many mainstream Christians are not Armageddonists. They do not buy into the ghastly, gory predictions so close to the hearts of worldenders. How do we explain the fact that so many Christians, including professional scholars, are not Armageddonists? The answer is simple: The whole idea of Armageddon, as the mass slaughter of all people but Christians (and only the "select" among them) is simply not a clear teaching of the Scriptures. It is an interpretation. And these are notoriously unreliable.

But these violence-minded fundies are not the only ones suffering from a bad case of apocalypsosis. The sick, destructive idea has infected a wide spectrum of independent selfstyled teachers. Still influenced powerfully by the fundamentalism that they believe that they have escaped and transcended, some "newage" teachers still cling to a universe ruled by madness. In this worldview, human life has zero value. This is a grotesque cosmos in which people are disposable. Some of the wildest, zaniest predictions for the end of the world in the year twenty hundred (or even before) originated not with gullible Christian fools, but with gullible fools outside of Christianity. These whackos bought into some of the scariest scenarios for the end. They swallowed hook, line, sinker, and half the pole the predictions of loony prognosticators. They enjoyed, in a sick way, either being scared or scaring others.

With goofy predictions about miscellaneous horrors that threatened millions, these fortune-tellers made radical fools of themselves in public. Hal Lindsey has been doing this for decades, so he should be used to being wrong by now. But he was joined in the late 1990's by Richard Kenninger, who was so absolutely certain that the end was coming in twenty hundred. Even a community was started, called "Adelphia." It was a bunch of newage survivalists who made emergency preparations to use airplanes to insulate them from the mass destructions predicted to plague the surface-dwellers. Since the late 1980's, predictions of the dreaded "polar shift" started showing up everywhere, whetting the appetites of endmongers.

Endmongers get a terrible look of something like evil combined with glee in their eyes when they discuss the end. Is this simple subconscious hatred of the human race? It is at least that. Still, it is astonishing just how many traditions seem to embrace this hatred of all humanity. Many who claimed native American descent, or at least, inspiration, jumped upon the terrible "endwagon." It was not long before they too were seeing the year twenty hundred as the year of the end. A guy named Scallion got a little overheated with his own demented visions: He predicted the break-up of the North American continent for the year 1997. One of those run-of-the-mill "newage channelers" was also fooled completely. Lori Toyes said that the "ascended masters" were confirming that the end would arrive in twenty hundred. The planetary line-up on May 5 was said to be a sure and certain mark, a sign given by the cosmos itself, that the end was coming on that very day.

The truth is that the "end of the world" scenario is nothing but a metaphysical soap-opera. It is badly-written metaphysical sci-fi. It is an absurd jumble of harmful, often ridiculous, superstitions completely unrelated to the writings of Christian, Native American or any other truly spiritual traditions.

Nor is this comic-book theology related to any other major world-tradition. It is "entertainment" of a psychotic kind. It appeals to those who are very sick. Normal human beings, and certainly those with Love in their hearts, could never find anything gleeful or attractive about the bloodiest and stupidest megamess of all time. It appeals to only those who are completely hopeless.

But, back in twenty hundred, with the news of computer crashes, the fire was whipped into a gasoline-fed frenzy. People absurdly began to tie up their earthly lives as if these were over. As the Jehovah's

Witnesses had done as early as 1975, they changed even major life-plans. Jobs were lost, marriages cancelled, money wasted. (After twenty hundred, money will be worthless, so might as well spend it all now). Even desperately needed medical treatment was put off or cancelled. Some went so far as to sell everything and head for the hills of the desert, living out of rv's. In short, for a few extremely scary and hilarious moments, a portion of the world went berserk. Religious and metaphysical fanatics showed up to feed the frenzied fire with more gasoline.

Can you, then, be a real Christian and not believe in Armageddon? Certainly and absolutely you can. The whole Armageddonist nightmare is embraced by fringe-groups. It has nothing to do with solid (academic, text-based, or sophisticated) Christianity. It appeals only to extremely unhealthy people who desperately long to say, "I told you so!" Their childish motive? To prove themselves superior to everyone else.

But the bizarre teaching has no place in a well-adjusted, normal, happy, or productive life. You can live as a good Christian every minute of every day without ever having a single thought about Armageddon. In fact, to be the best person you can be, it's a good idea to scour your heartmind completely clean of this horrible fantasy.

Not surprisingly, the idea has always appealed to borderline fringe-groups, as well as to those who were recognized as extremists and lunatics. It, together with the supporting monstrosity of the Jehovah-myth, has strong appeal to neonazis and other mentally ill, right-wing extremists. They lust for the vicious, disastrous breakdown of society, so they can take over with their machine-guns and dried bananas, robbing and raping at will.

Now, of course, to say that the ancient Hebrews, living in a society filled with violence, worshipped an ignorant wargod says nothing about modern Jews. Everyone's ancestors behaved in ignorance, often atrocity. So, no Christian-- indeed, no person-- can ever justify any bigotry against the Jews.

In the real world, outside of fundamentalism, views and interpretations of God grew and evolved with the human race. Many primitive peoples, not just the Hebrews, believed in more barbaric and ferocious deities. These were wargods created within and by warcultures. These were people who, twenty-four seven, engaged in vicious, nonstop warfare. They would have scoffed at a God of Love. What they demanded was the "biggest, boldest," toughest god on the block. All the gods, including Jehovah, carried swords, and were bloody, stupid wargods. Their only purpose was to win wars for their little nations. The more ferocious the god, the more intimidated the enemy. So, the ancient gods were not beings of peace, Love, or forgiveness. They were all storm, violence, and fury. They could be described, without fear of exaggeration, as abysmally ugly and evil beings, out-of-control. They were savages worshipped by savages. They had the emotional maturity of four-year-olds, and threw temper-tantrums if they did not get their way. They hated viciously, and murdered their enemies. They were pathetically jealous and insecure. (Jehovah is notorious for having said, "I am a jealous god.") They thrived on creating fear-- and this they did with both their own people and with the enemies of their people.

The old gods of the Middle East were ghastly, grotesque, nightmarish beings of pure evil, fashioned not to comfort, but to terrify. They were designed to intimidate the "enemy." So, they had to be as ghoulish and unpredictable as possible. In the history of the various "Jehovahs," however, this image applies to only the "protojehovahs." These were the earliest images of Jehovah. As the Hebrew culture grew and matured, a number of revised Jehovahs appeared, some less chaotic and monstrous than others.

But the very highest vision of God is not simply that God has Love, although divine Love is immeasurable and illimitable. Instead, it is the revelation (apocalypse) that God is Love.

The monstrous visions of a Hal Lindsey have no place in the relationship of a peaceful, loving Christian with her God. The vicious and horrible visions of the worldenders have no place in the Christian life of Love and forgiveness. In short, Jehovah has no place in the life of honor, wisdom, and peace. It is time that, as a society, we outgrew the myth of the capricious, petulant god of our ancestors, who obsessed about the political machinations of a minor tribal group on a tiny desert.

But if Revelation is not about the gory horrors with which it is associated by the worldenders, what is it all about? In the present detailed, in-depth commentary, we will approach Apocalypse as a metaphorical allegory. Indeed, in the first century, allegorical writing was immensely popular and common throughout the known world. Gnostic teachers such as Valentinus and his student Ptolemais were superb allegorizers. They were, in fact, pioneers of allegorical exegesis (explanations of Biblical texts).

In other words, we deny and repudiate all the literalists. Remember that people have struggled for centuries to figure out the "historical meaning" of Revelation. Every book ever written from a historical perspective has ended up in the trash-heap. Books from ancient times and the Middle Ages have predicted the "end" in certain time-periods. When those times came, the theories were proved wrong, and the books fed the fires. The same thing will befall the many false prophets of gloom and doom in the twenty-first century. This is what happened to books of that *genre* written during the twentieth century. All their terrifying, hair-raising predictions will be nothing but amusing anecdotes, as we now view flat-earthers: Quaint, but totally lost in ignorance.

They insist that Revelation is a book of prophecy, defined as dealing with nations and calendars. They have also demanded that it be interpreted solely in terms of geopolitical activity. Various symbols have been interpreted to symbolize a wide spectrum of leaders, starting with early Rome, when some symbols were erroneously identified as representing Nero or another Roman emperor.

Such abysmal moral monstrosities as nero, napoleon, and hitler have been identified, for example, as the "Antichrist." But-- and this is a fascinating proof of the ignorance of worldenders-- the word "antichrist" *is not found a single time in the entire book of Revelation.* This proves just how much confusion has accumulated over the book, over the centuries. Modern preachers inevitably include references to "antichrist" when discussing Revelation. No doubt they believe that Revelation mentions this. It is the center-piece of most apocalyptic horror-stories, including entire novels. But "antichrist" is completely absent from the text of Revelation!

Here is a paradox: Even those literalists who believe that Revelation is about nations and calendars use symbolism. So, even they are not at all consistent. For they insist that some of the events and images of Revelation are literal. Others, however, are accepted as symbolic.

Which is which is arbitrary. This "pick and choose" approach is blundering. Whenever it seems convenient to interpret something as a symbol of something else, it is accepted as symbolic. But especially when an image is more exciting when interpreted literally, it is then literalized.

Old interpretations which literalized everything have ended up in their well-deserved places in the trash-heaps of history. Some modern interpretations turn Apocalypse into a badly-produced Godzilla movie. But even in accepting it as a symbolic work, most students (they are not "scholars") of Revelation have so hyperelasticized the symbols that virtually any symbol can mean almost anything.

But here is what is suggested in this work:

****

Revelation has nothing to do with history, or calendars. It is not about geopolitics, or international events.

****

For if you believe the tale-tellers and agree that Revelation is all about history, you must gulp down the fantastic premise that writers of the first century were writing about the twenty-first. How unlikely is that?

It takes only a tiny bit of common sense to realize that a book-- any good book-- must be relevant to the people reading it. Since Revelation was written in the first century, then, was it about the nations of the first century?

No; Revelation is not about nations. What is it about? We suggest that it is all about those people who read it in the first century. And the same is true for those who read it in the second, third, fourth, and succeeding centuries. Revelation is remarkably relevant to life because

****

Revelation is all about you.

****

It is about all people. It is about every individual who has ever lived, and how she explores the deep Mind. In exploring Mind, she comes across "demons," "dragons," "animals," "angels," and many other potent Mindforces. For the entire collection of symbols used in Revelation has nothing to do with calendars or nations. Instead, Revelation follows a very common form of writing, as a part of the great body of literature called "allegory." This kind of symbolic story was often used by mystics (writers of the Enlightenment Tradition) to describe their long, hard inner journeys to God or Love -- the nucleus or Core of all Mind.

One of the most common themes in all mystical allegories, from the most ancient times, is that of "marriage." And in Revelation, this motif also appears. In fact, the marriage involves two major characters-- the "lamb" and "New Jerusalem." The use of the common marriage-motif seamlessly links Revelation to other mystical allegories, adding evidence that it is also a mystical allegory.

****

Revelation or Apocalypse has nothing to do with the end of the world.

****

That is why every attempt to interpret the book as a book about history and/or governments has ended up in the trash. For every interpretation of Revelation as a historical book has been disproved by the simple passage of time.

How have these older ideas and systems been disproved? Because every time that a future event was predicted from Revelation, it failed to materialize. Worldenders really got up a head of steam way back in the 1960's. Some were foolish enough to make precise or detailed predictions for what would happen in the 1970's and 1980's. Those books are all now completely worthless. You can buy them on the "twenty-five cent" table at any bookstore! You could learn more from a book whose pages are all blank.

The "prophecies" all and always failed. But worldenders learn slowly. And many learn not at all. So, each year is cursed with a new batch of "prophecies," greedily lapped up by desperate, but not very bright, worldenders. Often, these books about "apocalypse" say just what the true believers want to hear: The end is coming this year (no matter what year it is). Or, the "end" is in sight: Only a vague "few more years," and the end will come! It reminds me of the cartoon of the long-haired, long-bearded old man, dressed in rags, carrying in public a sign that reads THE END WAS NEAR. James Penton has written a book about Jehovah's Witnesses called Apocalypse Delayed.

Who are these loopy people called "worldenders"? They share qualities with binladens: They are fundamentalists. They are on a "mission from God." Their shabby "theology" demands the violent death of all "infidels," or unbelievers. Their god, violently stupid, solves problems exactly as a Middle Eastern dictator: He's got the biggest bomb. They believe certain teachings for no reason better than that they appear in a book (just about any book will do). Secretly, deeply hidden even from themselves, they hate humanity with a vicious ferocity. They have no respect for environment or ecology. (Environmentalism is a scheme of satan and his liberals!) They are losers, who have failed to make a successful life. They are jerks, who worship a god of imagination who is an even bigger jerk! They want to "get back" at the socioeconomic system, and even at the universe itself. It has badly "abused" them in their paranoia. They are perennial "victims" who will "get even" by seeing "god" destroy the whole thing. They are alienated from real feeling and thinking people. They feel a false sense of "belonging" with other extremists who embrace a worldview that is as crazy as their own. These factors create a terrorist-- or a worldender.

Since these factors are unhealthy, they do not support real spirituality. But they can very enthusiastically support religion. The most important lesson that we are all supposed to learn from the tragedy and horror of 9-11 is:

****

RELIGION, WITHOUT SPIRITUALITY, IS A DANGEROUS MONSTROSITY!

****

Revelation does not support worldenders. But it is validly recognized as a foundation-document of early Christianity. It is also a classic in mystical literature. It must have something to offer. It must have something valid and valuable to say. This is the approach that we will take in this commentary:

****

Revelation is a psychological commentary presented in symbols.

****

It describes the events that have taken place in your own mind. It is a tour of the roller-coaster oscillations, vacillations, changes, phases, and cycles of the psyche as it moves from despair to Love. But it is not simply the story of the bodymind. Instead, it tells the very long history of the Soul. It is symmetric with the book of Genesis. Many of its symbols are the same. But

****

Genesis is the story of disintegration and division; Revelation is the undoing of Genesis, the story of reuniting and reintegration.

****

In the beginning, in Genesis, all is one in God. Then, heaven is separated from earth, light from darkness, sea from dry land, animals from human beings, Eve from Adam.

Genesis is an allegory of the apparent primal "separation" of the "material" cosmos from the unified and singular Mind of God. Revelation is the story of how, apparently "separated" from God, the human Soul finds its way back to Unity with Lovemind (God). This is the nucleus of the intercultural Enlightenment Tradition, called "mysticism." So, Revelation is filled with mystical symbols and ideas. Revelation is a book for all times, for all people.

THE ENLIGHTENMENT TRADITION, THE WAY OF LOVE: WHAT IS MYSTICISM?

"Mysticism" is seriously abused! Even to many professionals, the word means nothing more than "occult," with flavors of the parapsychological. It is spooky and scary, like something out of the X-Files. Mystics practiced sorcery. Or they sat in caves and focused on their navels, for years.

Wrong! No way! These bizarre activities have nothing to do with mysticism, the *passion to understand Reality.* It overlaps with theology, psychology, and religion. But it is more!

What is the big mystery? Isn't it obvious what "reality" is? It is what is happening right here, right now! That is the "short and sweet" answer, and mystics would agree.

But mystics want to probe more deeply. They want to ask what relationship the cosmos has with mind, and what relationship mind has with "God." They explore inquiries such as, "Does the Soul live forever? If It does, what on earth does it do? Does evil really exist? Does justice? Is anything, in this fluid cosmos, really dependable? Does anything really last? Is anything *absolutely* real?"

Mystics have come, over centuries of study and meditation, to see *Love as the most important pursuit in the cosmos!* They believe that, in your Unconscious, Love is what you most deeply need, the satisfaction of all desires. Work, money, reputations, cars, sex, entertainment, books, and intellect are all just "Love-substitutes." That is why *they can never satisfy* for more than a brief period. Love is the answer!

Mysticism is the "Way of Love." Despite the fact that it asks the big questions, it is not a religion. Historically, luminaries of the Enlightenment Tradition have been Catholics, Protestants, Moslems, Jews, Buddhists, Hindus, Taoists, earth-religions, no professed religion, or agnostics! Mysticism is a lifepattern. Mystics are normal people. Schoolteachers, accountants, artists, librarians, doctors, cleaning-people, or cops can all be mystics! The mystic has *traded in religion for spirituality.* Spirituality is Love. So the mystic is the most compassionate person that she can be. She is committed to goodness, honesty, morality, ethics, kindness, and compassion. She probably spends extra time every day focusing on her inner Self-- practicing meditation-- but she does not make a big deal of it!

A mystic once said, "Kindness is my religion." So, the mystic seeks to cultivate Love in two practical forms-- service and friendship.

But she is usually marked also by the fact that she holds a very different worldview than does the average person. She sees herself as a mind, not a body. She believes that she is a mind, or "Soul," playing a "role" in this world. A mystic, for example, named "Mary Smith" does not believe that she *is* Mary Smith.

Instead, she takes literally the immortal words of Shakespeare, who wrote, "All the world's a stage, and we but actors." *For the mystic does not see the world as absolutely real.* Not that she is psychotically unable to distinguish reality from hallucination. But *mind is more real than world.* In fact, she believes that *Mind has ultimate reality.* In the final analysis, *Mind is the only factor of which we can be sure.*

So, "God" must be Mind Itself. Since you also have a mind, you are directly "plugged in," at unconscious levels, to this infinite Mind. And the true Mindmystic has actually experienced a few moments when this luminous, ecstatic, Lovefilled, Lightfilled inner Mind was breathlessly, breath-takingly touched directly. It ascended or floated up from the Unconscious and was made completely conscious.

The world is not as important, or as real, as the mind. Why? Because it is the *mind that dreams up the world.* Seeing the world as dream, the mystic does not take it with utter, deadly finality, or with grim, taciturn, humorless seriousness. The world is a very complex game, and we are here to learn to play!

Not that nothing is serious. Many things are, and the mystic is not a ham-handed fool who laughs at funerals! But nothing in this world is *utterly, totally, absolutely* serious! Why? Because nothing is final; everything is in transition, and everything changes.

So the mystic named "Mary Smith" is actually an invisible, powerful, deathless, birthless Mind (Soul) *pretending* to be "Mary Smith." When Mary mystically realizes this, her selfesteem shoots through the roof! She knows herself to be a being of enormous wisdom, gargantuan tranquility, bottomless bliss, and immeasurable Love! For just as her "mind" is really a Soul, so this Soul is really "Spirit." That is, it is the immediate expression of the best and biggest Mind of all-- what we call "God."

Mystical vision is described by the mystic John of Facan (990-1078), who wrote of "mind enkindled with heavenly desire." Of God, he wrote, "...He now and then allows His very Self to be seen suddenly,..." In the mystical event, he continues, to God, "the heart burns,... the memory grows strong, the intellect shines, and the whole Spirit is lit up by... Your beauty..."

Probably the most famous theologian ever to have lived, Thomas Aquinas,(1225-1274) said that all of his work in theology was so much "straw" compared with a single mystical glimpse into the actual nature of God. Although this revelation was transcendent, it was not irrational or selfdelusive.

Mysticism is the study of the deepest Unconscious as Love. (In this book, that Mind will be called "Lovemind.") (It is "God.") To touch this Mind results in a supremely elevated spiritual state! *Up to half* of all ordinary people have touched a mystical state! And, surprisingly, in most, there was *no religious component; it had been entirely spiritual.*

The Revelation describes the various states of mind involved before, during, and after the mystical experience. It is a Christian document. An astonishing number of mystics arose in the Christian tradition. Indeed, at its very beginning, the followers of the Christian Way used the Greek word for mystical "knowing" (*gnosis*) to call themselves "gnostics."[6]

The word "mystic" goes back to the Mystery-school of Eleusis in the fifth century BC, whose initiates called themselves *mystae*. (The other great "mystery religions" were those of Dionysius, Orpheus, Demeter, Magna Mater, Isis, and Mithras.) But were they really "mystical"?

Their underlying philosophy certainly was: Their core-teaching was the "death" to the ordinary world, and being "born again" into a spiritual Self or Soul. Then, this Soul would itself have to continue to Its "death" into ultimate Spirit-- a yet higher, supreme, Self.

Later, in the fourth century BCE, there was a period of widespread disaffection with the traditional gods, and many turned to mysticism. The feeling was, "The gods don't work anymore." Widespread cynicism exploded.

---

[6] The brief introduction to mysticism here was adapted from Bernard McGinn, *Foundations of Mysticism: Origins to the Fifth Century* (New York; Crossroads Publishing, 1995) and from R. A. Gilbert, *The Elements of Mysticism* (Boston; Element Books, Inc., 1991)

Many followers of the reworked Plato, a group called "neoplatonists," adopted the "Chaldean Oracles," as much-needed guides, in the second century. Even more important were the *Hermetica,* ascribed to Thoth-Hermes (between the first and third centuries CE). These texts had much to say about the nature of God. They discussed conflict between the "god of this world" (called the "cosmic" god, from *kosmos* or "world") and the primary God.

Mysticism begins by inwardness; you begin by examining your own mind. The ultimate reality of the material world is denied. The mystic Ye-She-Gyal-Tshan wrote, "All things, within and without, like an echo, appear, and yet, are nothing." He spoke of the rejection of "the spell" of "fear, lust, and hate." He went so far as to define "bliss" as "no-thing-ness."

In another tradition, Sankara (c. 800) was a monist. (He argued that only supreme Mind is real.) He called this ultimate Mind, this absolute Reality, "One without a second." The classics called the *Upanishads* teach that the whole cosmos is Mind (Brahman).[7]

But how can all the things around us-- cars, buildings, computers, birds, rocks, books, and an immeasurable spectrum of other items and objects, be "mind"? There is only one Way: If they are all dreamimages within the Mind, then, they are also "mind."

This Mind is the Absolute that is called "God." But mystics have even better news, the best that can be imagined: This Mind is Love.

All mysticism glows with Love. But this is not mere sentimentality or mere sexuality. Love is a cosmic force that is ignited at the very core of Mind, the central flame of which is Lovemind (Spirit or God; see "Chart of Mind.") Love is the force of upward spiritual evolution. It creates essential goodness, kindness, and compassion. The mystic's aim is to be literally "absorbed" by Lovemind. She begins by trying to "absorb" It.

The dual heart of mysticism is surrender and renunciation. (The latter is not a rejection of the world as evil-- an extremism-- but the rejection of the world as your master.) When, indeed, the self is

---

[7] For a more detailed analysis of the *Upanishads* see my *Luminous Jewels of Love and Light,* Volume 2, Part VI (Liberty Township, Ohio; Love Ministries, Inc., 2003)

merged with God, the world is seen as filled with stunning beauty and peace.

The mystic poet Rumi wrote, "I am the rose, and the nightingale drunk with its fragrance. I am the chain of being, the circle of the spheres. I am the Soul in all." The mystic realizes that she is mind, not body. As mind, she does not have the membranes of flesh that seem to divide her from greater Mind. She seeks Union with the Dreamer or Creator; then, she, because It is the world, *becomes the world,* as Rumi did here.

In the West, much in Judaism, Islam, and Christianity was anti-mystical.[8] The oldest Western faith, Judaism, was obsessed with the transcendental greatness of Yahweh and the microscopicity of human beings. (This is true as a material view.) But still, the "Song of Solomon" remains a classic in mystical literature. There are also two other great mystical Jewish classics: *The Book of Formations,* or *Sepher Yetzirah*, and *Bahir.* These were matrixworks of the mystical Jewish system called Kabbalah. And, despite centuries of persecution by the mainstream, Jewish mystics managed to maintain their enthusiasm.

The greatest revival of Jewish mysticism occurred with a group called the *Hasidim,* in the sixteenth century. Their motto was, "All is God, and all serves God." God must be met both within the world and in the mind, beyond the world. Jewish mystics reached the pinnacle called "Union." But they never went as far as other mystics into actual *identity shared with divine Mind.* Human beings were usually seen as a part of God's creation, but not a part of God Himself.

Some mysticism was evident in an entire *genre* of Jewish literature called the "Apocalypses" (revelations). Early Christianity also had a whole spectrum of literature called "apocalypticism." The Revelation to John, in the Bible, was only one specimen of an entire *genre* of allegorical accounts. Most were seriously infected with dualism.

In one of the Jewish apocalypses, a "throne" was seen whose appearance was "like crystal." (These same symbols appear repeatedly in Revelation.) It was a kind of chariot, and had wheels "like the shining sun," another repeated Revelation-symbol. (The same symbolic ele-

---

[8] See my *One With the One: Mysticism and Fundamentalism in Judaism, Christianity and Islam* (Liberty Township, Ohio; Love Ministries, Inc., 2004)

ments appeared in Greek, Roman, and Arabian literature.) In some of these Apocalypses, the visionary author was taken on a "heavenly journey," much as "John" is, in Revelation.

These are *purely allegorical.* (This is true even though many of them were "eschatological," or dealing with the "end times," or "end of the world.") Among the Jews, interpretation of these and other written texts became a fundamental religious activity.

The ancient scholar Philo (20 BC-50 AD) brought Greek influence into Hebrew textual analysis. (The Hellenistic or Greek period was from 332 to 167 BCE.) The Greeks had a powerful effect on Hebrew literature, resulting in the "wisdom tradition." This produced such works as "The Wisdom of Solomon," and "Ecclesiasticus" (both between 200 BCE and 40 CE). The wisdom literature was much more optimistic than Apocalyptic writings had been.

But the Apocalypses of Judaism are a side-road to the history of mysticism. They covered a wide spectrum of themes, and, unlike the Revelation to John, did not concern themselves with the discovery of the Coremind or Lovemind. Many mystics saw *the totality of the Hebrew Scriptures* ("Old Testament") *as allegorical.* In the second century, early Christians called these interpretations "mystical."

The Apocalypses were thought to have a degree of inspiration equal to that of the Bible. (The Biblical Daniel is an example of an Apocalypse.) Another Apocalypse was First Enoch (third century BCE).

This literature proliferated at a time when contact with God was thought to have been lost. Some originated with Persian mythology. Others were Greek. In the Greek myths, nonphysical Souls ascended through seven planetary spheres, and in the Hebrew variations, through seven "heavens."

Older Jewish traditions held that Jehovah was represented in the Temple by the Light of *Shekinah.* But many were geographically so far from the temple, another Way of touching or contacting God was needed. For Jehovah or Yahweh was seen to be limited to one location.

This is, in fact, when wise Hebrew mystics began to differentiate between the Lord of Love Who dwelled in the heart, and Jehovah, who dwelled literally "in" the temple. So personal experience (mysticism) arose.

Ezekiel was an example of this need to contact God outside of the temple. He was not a mystic so much as a visionary. In vision, he saw the "chariot" (*merkabah*) of Yahweh. This, much later, gave rise to a whole school of Jewish mysticism called "*Merkabah* mysticism, also called, "palace mysticism" (since the "palace of Yahweh" usually appeared).

This did not appear until the second century, by which time, Jews and Christians had fully developed their mutual rejections and bitterness. So, *merkabah* had no influence on Christian mysticism. The central theme, at any rate, of the whole of the Jewish Apocalyptic literature was the Soul's survival of bodily death. This is a premise with which intercultural mysticism agrees.

In mysticism, Lovemind is seen as both transcendent (a Mind greater than Its creation) and immanent (dwelling, as dreaming Mind, within its dream, the cosmos).

The goal of mysticism is *not cessation of being, but transformation of being, by divine Union. The mystic is "lost" in the great Mind as a snowflake is lost in a blizzard, or a dewdrop in the shining sea.*

The history of Christian mysticism is rooted largely in Jesus, Paul, and John. But it was also an outgrowth of Greek philosophy. It is a grecochristian synthesis. At the risk of being overly obvious, Christian mysticism shifted to a near-obsession with "Unity with Christ," or with "God through Christ." It was *completely Christocentric.*

By the later second century, much of the matrix groundwork had already been laid, which would influence Christ-focused mysticism for centuries to come. A significant literature had evolved, usually referred to as "Christian Gnostic" writings. Among both generic ("small g") gnostics (mystics) and cultic (capital "G") Gnostics, these had the authority of Scripture.

Debates over the exact meaning of *gnosis* occurred. This was the most crucial word in the history of Christian mysticism. It meant the direct, immediate, experiential knowing of the Presence of God within the heart, as Love.

Two early teachers, Clement and Origen, from the Alexandrian school of Christianity, wrote about this gnostic nucleus of early Christianity.

Clement (150-215 CE) thought the Soul intrinsically divine, as did the gnostics, and wrote of "Union." He makes free use of other gnostic (mystical) ideas, including divine "unknowability" and "deification." Gnosis is fundamental to Christianity, although, reasonably, not a precondition to "salvation."

Some of the cult like "cap G" Gnostics taught that the "seed of Light," or potential for enlightenment, was restricted to an elite. Clement is more reasonably universalist: He claims, like the early Gospel writer Thomas (c. 110), that this "seed" is within everyone. He puts gnosis in a Platonic context.

Clement broke away from the hardline "cap G" Gnostics. But he still saw them as superior to average Christians. In time, Clement came to believe that belief, not gnosis, was the key to salvation. He fell in line with, and fell for, the illusion of orthodoxy. Still, he felt that the gnostic lifepatterns, severely disapproved by orthodoxy, reflected the "tradition" of Jesus.

The special knowing of God directly by actual experience, gnosis, he wrote, "is the gift of Christ." Love was perfected in gnosis, and gnosis in Love. He saw Plato as nearly inspired by God.

In Clement, the phrase "vision of God" occurs eighty-four times. "The goal of life is vision." Only gnostics actually "arrived" at this "goal." Perfection is "Union with God." This moves the Soul through a state of being passion free (*apathea*), an idea borrowed from Stoicism.

Origen (born c. 185) was an orthodox exegete (teacher of Scripture). He wrote commentaries on two great Scriptural mystical classics, the "Song of Solomon," and the Gospel of John. His work gave birth to so much in the later monastic tradition that it has been called "protomonastic."

He emphasized literal virginity. He leaned towards the antisensual and antisexual, as an ascetic. Oddly, he felt that the Self could be known only through the Scriptures. This was in perfect conformity with unenlightened orthodoxy.

The Logos, he taught, was created by the "selfemptying" of the Father. In turn, when Logos became the Christ, in Jesus, he "emptied Himself."

Origen wisely saw the Hebrew Scriptures as allegory. God, he says, is the only "Being"; the world, and all others, are only "becomings". His God was transcendent. But he also writes, "Our Mind... is also itself Spirit."

Before "material" creation, there was a "spiritual" creation. Ideas precede objects, as mind precedes world. But he does know that the material body and world are not "evil."

The job of the Logos is to rescue fallen intellects. Hebrew history, which entangled so many Christians, is thought to have allegorized the ascent and descent of the mind. (This "ascension" theme would affect later mysticism.) The three books of the Hebrew Scriptures ascribed to the mystic Solomon are examined: Proverbs is the Purgative Way of mysticism; Ecclesiastes is the Illuminative Way, and the Song of Solomon is the Unitive Way.[9]

Origen, like Gregory, is the "mystic of Light." He is the first of a long line of mystics to use mildly "erotic" language to express the intensity of mystical Love.

We get our word "erotic" from the Greek *eros*. In its limited use as "erotic" Love, it was not denied, but transformed, by mystics. Origen agreed with Plato that *eros* was not just sexual Love, but also was a "heavenly" force. Good sex, of course, can be heavenly, but this is not exactly what Origen had in mind.

For he went so far as to say, "God is *eros.*" (Of course, the original, in John's epistle, said, "God is *agape,*" a related form of Love.) So, for Origen, *eros* could be an expression of *agape.* (Generally, the latin *caritas* is *agape,* and the Latin *amor* is *eros.*) Origen suggests that God might also be "passionate Love." Indeed, Plotinus(205-274 BCE) and Proclus (410-485) both gave *eros* a divine meaning. And the Gnostic teacher Marcion took the idea of God as *eros* very seriously. Love was "implanted" in us to find God, but it must be "removed" from other objects, and "all turned toward God."

---

[9] For a discussion of the three traditional "Ways" of mysticism, see my *Journey to the Center of the Soul: Mysticism Made Simple,* op. cit.

Origen indeed thought that literal virginity was "purity." He saw human nature as divided between the "inner," created in the image of God, and the outer, created from dust. This dualism not only divided God from creation, but human nature from itself! The gnostics said that "God" created the higher nature, in Genesis 1:26, but that Yahweh created the lower nature of "dust" in Genesis 2:7.

This duality divided even Love. For one must love God, and not creation. This implicitly rejected monism, in which you love God *by* loving creation, and so, Love is one.

Origen, like Clement (C. 150-215) and Bernard (1090-1153), writes repeatedly, although not always clearly, about the inner spiritual "senses" of the Soul. This is "spiritual sensuality." This is how sensual passages in the Song of Solomon were explained. Origen spoke of the Soul as "bride" of Spirit-- a very common motif in mystical writing, found also in Bernard, other mystics, and in Revelation.

He says that Love can express as "knowing." So, contemplative life, in perfecting Love, was seen as superior to the active life. (This is the old Martha/Mary dichotomy.) God is seen with, and within, the heart.

Like others, Origen was indifferent to altered states, even ecstasy. He knew only that contemplation led to divinization or deification of the Soul, "becoming like God."

It was "by fellowship (Greek, *koinonia*) with divinity" that "human nature might become divine." Platonists and Gnostics believed that the Soul was intrinsically divine. Origen denied this, and spoke instead of Union by grace. Like the later pagan neoplatonists, he spoke often of Union (*henosis*). But he did not see this as *a union of identity or indistinction*. The "Father" was linked with creation, including the mystic, by means of the Logos.

Was Origen, then, a real mystic, or simply a writer of mystical speculations? If he was a mystic, *he was not a "full" Mindmystic*. For he still bought into the illusion of dualism. Perhaps he did have real but periodic episodes of mystical experience, but *they effected no permanent change in him*. For example, he saw his Christianity as making him an "enemy" of nonchristians. A real mystic would have been lifted above and beyond such polarities.

The Stoic Marcus Aurelius (121-180) was not a mystic. But he recommends a type of practical Love-- service-- and holds it to be compatible with the overall philosophy of Stoicism. He also recommends detachment (*apathea*), to remain free of the tyranny of being controlled by the world. Love and detachment are the twin-cores of mysticism. This *apathea* was not "apathy," in the modern sense of complacency, but closer to Lovebased detachment. This appeared in the lives of those who called themselves "apathetic gnostics." These were actively energized by Love, but detached from the world. Like Jesus their Master, they were "no part of the world."

Christian gnostics worked to combine the best of both worlds-- *theoria* (contemplation) and *praxis* (practicality). They sought to engineer a type of *agape* (Love) both mentally profound and useful. Christian "perfection" was "divinization"-- becoming "like God." (The very word "Christian" means "like Christ.")

Later, it was taught that "the Logos became man so as to learn how man can become God." This was even later expanded to the teaching that "He who obeys his Lord... becomes God."

The vital question of the time: What did it mean to be a "Christian"?

One thing that it definitely meant, after the year 70: If you were going to be a Christian, you could no longer be a Jew. By that very early year, the different philosophies of the two groups had radically diverged. It was evident, *as Jesus had intended,* that Christianity had evolved into a wholly different faith. Being a new religion, it had its own Bible. Having different Scriptures, it also had a different God, although even religious teachers still get confused about this. [10]

In fact, for centuries, the two religions tended to be mutually polemical. Even though they both had mystical traditions, *even these were solidly independent.* Early Christians clearly and strongly *rejected Judaism.* It was a "false religion," with a "false god." Later, attitudes were to become more confused, and "neojudaizers" among Christians would win the day. They would for years thrive on the lie that Christianity evolved from Judaism, and would erroneously regress

---

[10] For the many and important distinctions between the Jewish Jehovah and the Christian God of Love see my *Jehovah Goodbye: the "New Theism" of Love*, op. cit.

to the Hebrew Scriptures ("Old Testament") when discussing the Christian God. This monumental error still occurs, all the time. Obviously, the Hebrew Scriptures *never said anything about the Christian God, for among the Jews nothing was known about this God until after the time of Jesus.* Their god-theme was only Jehovah.

The Gospel of John proves that, by about the year 110, Christians had a new identity of their own, seeing the Jews as outside of their faith. It is no coincidence that the one Gospel that is clearest in its rejection of ancient Jewish theology is also the most mystical of the Gospels. Although repelled by much in Judaism and its presentation of a primitive, anthropomorphic god, Christians were not trouble-makers. So, they accommodated the Jews as much as conscience would permit. They even quoted from the Hebrew Scriptures. But this was only good teaching, not full agreement. It was much more effective than absolutism or stark rejectionism. Had Christianity arisen in India, early Christians would have quoted from the Vedas and Upanishads

Early Christians also graciously accommodated to the Hellenistic world all around them, including its strong mystical streak. *They did not condemn it.* In fact, in the Christian Scriptures, Paul even quotes from "pagan" sources. From about 125 till about 200, an apologetic Christian *genre* appeared. It argued forcefully that *Christianity was the sum of all wisdom-traditions that had preceded it.* The wise thinkers of Greek philosophy, for example, were seen to have stated "Christian" truths in prechristian terms. Socrates and Plato had an especially receptive audience among the earliest Christians. At any rate, the enormous weight of Plato can hardly be denied-- especially in its later, resurrected form, called "neoplatonism." It strongly influenced mystics.

Greek religion took two forms: Olympian, based on the gods and their activities, and mystical, based on inner experience of the Real. In turn, Plato had been influenced by Heraclitus, Pythagoras, Parmenides, and Orphism. These writers were pushed by "mysteriosophical" influences. Plato says that the Soul is "beatified" through *theoria* or "contemplation." This, as in later mysticism, occurs through purification (Greek, *catharsis;* Latin, *purgatorio*). This is the Purgative Way of the mystic. The divine Mind (*nous*) within the Soul is assimilated to its divine Source. This is mysticism in a nutshell.

Plato called the Absolute "the One." It was also "the Good and the Beautiful." He distinguished between the outer world of appearances and the inner world of ideas-- very mystoid. Mind is seen as an "exile" in the timeworld, exactly as mystics also saw it. True *eros* is "Love for the Good." A unitive vision with the Beautiful-Good was not impersonal. A "Form" ("god") takes possession of the lover. This was the "indescribable supreme moment."

Nor was it entirely intellectual; both knowledge and Love acted. This was a "sudden, immediate vision of true Being." It was the "union with the supreme Good." This is "superior Reality."

Socrates had taught that the Soul had "fallen" from a higher state. It was, ever after, unable to participate in "divine nature." But after a while, all Souls are destined to return to this lost Nature. Socrates remembers a time when his Soul "rose up into real Being." It was then "initiated into perfect mysteries," a reference that is irresistibly mystical.

With Plato, the Way to happiness begins with awakening. The zenith of human growth was climaxed by the sudden appearance of its "transcendental Goal"-- again, very mystical. This summit, analogously to grace, was not achieved by mere human effort.

Plato goes so far as to speak of "taking flight from the body in which the Soul is imprisoned." Implicit in Plato is a transition from a merely material to a spiritual mode of knowing and loving. And what appeared suddenly, after preparation, was "the One"! Plato agrees with later mystics that the Absolute is "unknowable." It is a real Reality! Timaeus spoke of the "Maker and Father of the universe."

The Soul is of divine origin, and like is attracted to like, which drives the Soul relentlessly into the Mind of God. So, Plato's philosophy is what later mystics would call "deification" or "divinization" of the Soul. And the Soul, he said, was not just "divinizable," but was intrinsically, inherently already divine! It just had to remember! *Theoria* (contemplation, a form of meditation) is the activation of this natural divinity within the Soul. This is precisely what the later mystic Plotinus (205-70 BC) taught. In his work, transcendent levels of Mind or Reality were called "hypostases." The presentation of Reality through the analysis of Mind is called "metapsychology." Plotinus wrote, "The One is all things." For him, *eros* was never selfish, but creative. (In Plato, it is deficient, not divine.) The whole cosmos is "erotic" with a desire to return to the Source. The role of Love in this "return" is a constant theme in Plotinus. In time, he said, *the Soul becomes Love.* "Nothing like things exist in true Reality," he wrote. The "metasubjective" understanding of the One underlies all of Plotinus. He refuses to use any adjectives to describe the One; hence, his writing is "apophatic" (negative theology, saying only what God is *not*). This God is unreachable, beyond even *gnosis*. But It does have activity (*energia*). But its activity is the same as Its essence (*ousia*). It is clearly identified as Love. This begins with selflove. (This is also called "superintellect," *hypernoesis.*) Selfdirected, it does not *have,* but *is,* the knowing (gnosis) of Love. In seeking the One, you seek "what is within all things."

The intellect (mind) both is, and is not, the One. It is, because It is the cognitive mind, thinking *through* you, but It is not, for It cannot be limited to mere intellect. For Mind is projected to "outside" the One, as the material universe. Because It is Mind, Reality is called "transcendental subjectivity." The Mind that is the Source of "The All" is in everything."

Plotinus rejects particularity (the self existence of many separate objects.); Everything is just unified dream. "You have become all," he writes, reminding us of the *Upanishads* and their "Brahman." "All things are one." And, we might add, all are *the* One. The One is Mind and everything is the dream of the Mind. So the One is all. To attain to the One, as in later Christianity, the Soul must strip Itself of all "other" things.

Thus does the Soul find "transcendent communion (*synnousian*). We are, can be, never separated from the One. The person of "communion" fuses with, melts into, the One. "She ceases to be himself" and becomes immensely greater. She "retains nothing of herself" as she slides into the inner Other, Lovemind.

The cosmos is Mind. "All things ... are contemplation." But Plotinus is a mystic, not merely a pantheist. (He does not say that the physical cosmos *is* God, or is all there is to God.) The One is always the Soul. But the One is *more than* the Soul. So, with the cosmos: The One is it, but more than it. The One is the Mind behind it.

So, *the soul and the One can be the same in nature,* but not *in totality.*

Throughout the years of Christian history, Plotinus has been interpreted by many Christians, and so, he has influenced them. He presented the "true Self" as the "undescended" Soul, still one with, unified with, *nous,* or Mind. This was a much deeper Self, in the Unconscious. (See "Chart of Mind.") It was the "higher Self" of metaphysics, and the "deeper Self" of mystical psychology.

And even despite the Soul's intrinsic divinity, the concept of "grace" (Spirit-Soul Love) does apply! For it is grace, or Spiritlove, that draws the Soul into Union with Its deepest Self. And its deepest self is Spirit or God.

Does Plotinus teach "autosalvation," in which, by the Soul's own intense efforts, divinization is "achieved"? Does he even teach "salvation"? Liberation does occur, analogous to "salvation." But is there an "external" Liberator?

The "oneness" of Plotinus does not culminate in Union with a God who is another "person." To understand Plotinian mysticism, we must shake off the trappings of Christianity, Islam, and Judaism. For this pure form of mysticism has *nothing to do with history, or, hence, with religion.* Enlightenment is *completely a "here and now" process, and is not rooted in history,* culture, or religion.

In that sense, it is a "purer" experience than the tradition-bound mysticisms of the historical religions. Plotinus says, of the deepest Self, "It is eternally present." He does not have to carry the complicated and heavy burden of history.

Nor does he hypothesize an "external" God to aid in liberation. Something about this strikes the mind as very adult, as contrasted with the childishness of crying out to a "daddy."

****

For *nothing and no one can ever be "external" to Mind.*

****

Aid does arrive through grace from the "inner Other," the "Beyond within." This God certainly *seems* like another being, but literally, cannot be so, and so, is called a "Self." As in the mystical classic, the *Upanishads*. Still, it is megagalaxies away from anything that we have ever considered a part of our "selves." Also, in Plotinian mysticism, the only thing from which you need "salvation" is ignorance, including the lower mind and its multitude of fears.

NEOPLATONISM. Platonic teaching is divided into three types, from three periods of history: 1) the "Old Academy," his immediate teaching (350-100 BCE); 2) Middle Platonism (100BCE-200 CE), and 3) neoplatonism (after 250).

MONASTICISM originated about 370. It was an attempt to create a kind of "gang-mysticism," shared by groups, or to institutionalize the practice of mysticism. Arguably, it never really succeeded. Because they were ostensibly fulltime mystics, both male and female monastics came soon to be seen as the ideal Christians. Their goal: To combine ascetic selfmastery with knowledge of God. But an arrogant elitism developed in which monastics thought of themselves as a special "elect," or the only "real Christians." Pride was inevitable, and attempts to counterbalance it through humility enjoyed only partial success. (Humility naturally marks the genuine mystic.)

This put Christianity in the double straight-jacket of elitism and esotericism. But once it found its footing, monasticism resisted these tendencies. The monastics insisted on public accessibility of truth-teachings.

Still, monasticism taught "flight from the world," and, for weaker persons, became an escape and avoidance. It was social denial and renunciation. The best among the monastics insisted that Christianity was not a matter of solitude, but of kindness, charity, and Love.

In 330, Eusebius, the court-theologian of Constantine, praised monks. The new lifestyle was rapidly accepted. Monasticism originated not with Judaism or Hellenism, but, in Eastern Christianity, with simple village Christianity. By contrast, in the West, it was heavily promoted by bishops. Among those in the West who formed or supported monastic communities were Eusebius (c.360), Ambrose (c. 370), and Augustine (c. 390). Jerome (c. 380) was never a bishop, but he spread monasticism among the Roman aristocracy. One aristocrat,

Paulinus, sold everything that he owned, and started a monastery in 395.

Martin of Tour (317-397) was this kind of archetypal monk. Even after his appointment as bishop, he continued to live in simplicity, as a hermit. In his monastery, everything was held in common. No one owned anything, and buying and selling were forbidden. (This group came to welcome many converted nobles.)

Predictably, pure mysticism was highly tinted by the converging streams of monasticism and asceticism. Late fourth-century mystical writers included Hilary, Jerome, and Ambrose. Augustine (354-430) wrote on the subject, even though he was not an active mystic. He was much more fascinated by the technical hair-splittings of theology, and indeed is the founder of Western theology. He wrote two massive and dull volumes, *Confessions* and *The City of God*.

Hilary (315-367) was a Roman aristocrat turned bishop. He too was more theologian than true mystic, and wrote a twelve-volume set *On the Trinity*.

The most powerful influences on mysticism at this time were three: the ideal of virginity, monasticism, and neoplatonism (the resurrection of Plato's ideas). Microbius was a famous pagan neoplatonist. His school (c.350) was tightly packed with the mysticism of Plotinus.

Marius Victorinus (285-365) was powerfully influenced by both Plotinus and Porphyry (c. 232-303). Converted to Christianity, he wrote the first speculations on the trinity in the Western Church. About 363, he wrote a series of commentaries on the Pauline epistles. He integrated the Plotinian Being, Life, and Wisdom into the Christian trinity. His view of the Spirit was feminine, and he called her a "mother." She played a key role in the "ascent to God."

He explored the neoplatonic idea of the Soul's fall and return. First created in God's image, the Soul reflected the supreme life, the Logos. But it fell into the "love of the world." This was the illusion of hyper-sensuality (biomind) and materialism.

But it was destined to rediscover its final Union with Logos, and thus, with God the Creator. It was Victorinus who actually began the Christianization of the neoplatonic tradition.

Virginity appealed to many. Some monastics retreated from the world out of fear, and it is likely that the fear of sex or intimacy was part of the equations of their lives. But celibacy was not at first recommended for priests. That did not come along until a Council decided it in Spain in 309.

Jovinian was an interesting monk, who stood up and denied that virginity was superior to marriage. He publicly doubted the perpetual virginity of Mary. He drew the fierce lightning of Ambrose, Jerome, and Augustine, who were quite touchy about this subject. For virginity was championed by the whole official Church from 370 to 430.

How much of this was motivated by a fear of sex and/or women? That is unknown. But what is known is that very much of the Church was misogynist, and where misogyny prevails, gynophobia (terror of women) is usually not far behind. Did church fathers suffer from performance anxiety? Or did they suffer from simple fear of intimacy? Or both?

Julian of Eclanum also argued for marriage. He questioned Augustine's interpretation of "original sin." Not surprisingly, the possibly unbalanced Augustine argued that this sin was "concupiscence." Despite all the sexual fears and hatred boiling among Christians in the fourth century, celibacy did not become mandatory for the whole clergy until the eleventh century.

Ambrose (died 397) was notorious for his solid-rock stance at the Nicene Council against the Arians or nontrinitarians. He had been influenced by Plato, Plotinus, Porphyry, and Origen. He Christianized much of Plato, and made the Song of Solomon a center of mystical speculation.

He hammered away incessantly about the importance of virginity. He wrote, "The Treatise on Isaac or the Soul," an allegory of Genesis, and one of the first recognized works of Western mysticism. (This was an allegorical reading of the lives of the patriarchs.) He also wrote, "On Death as a Good," and "On Flight from the World." He wrote about the descent and ascent of the Soul, and a lot of miscellaneous exigetical stuff. His writing is not easy to read, and not as profound as that of others. He also changes the Platonic "identity" with the divine to a mere pursuit of the divine. He does agree that the "supreme Good" is in the inner world. "Let us strive for the Eternal, and fly up to the divine on the wings of Love." "The Soul that cleaves to God entered into the garden of the mind."

The "mysticism" of Ambrose is seriously diluted and weakened by its ecclesiology. In other words, he insists that mysticism occur within the organized Church. This feeble "mysticism" is a pale reflection of the universalist, more true, variety of the Enlightenment Tradition. His support for virginity also tends to enfeeble his mysticism; but we must remember that many very wealthy noble Roman women had donated their goods to the Church.

Jerome (born c. 340) lived as a hermit for a time. It was he who made something of a "fad" of monasticism among wealthy Roman aristocrats, especially women. It was he who created the standard Bible of the Western Church, the Latin translation called the *Vulgate.* Although he later translated Origen, still later, he turned against him. A heavy promoter of virginity, he was not a mystic. He is marked by an obsessive, pathological fear about how easily virginity can be lost.

John Cassian (born 360) interviewed many desert-dwelling monastics. He wrote *The Conferences.* The "Eastern fathers," Anchorites,[11] and general interior work were subjects of his study. He did much to connect Eastern and Western monasticism. Monasticism was "Christian perfection." In fact, the Church was supposed to be only a monastic institution. Monasticism supposedly repressed the ultimate purity of Christianity in its solitude and asceticism.

But, "purity" is nothing but Love. He taught a paradoxical idea about "earning grace". The goal of prayer is *Unity with the Father,* the same Unity as enjoyed by the Son. The prayer recommended was mantric: The repetition of a short verse. *Theoria* (contemplation) is Love. It is the "vision of God," and this "vision" is Love.

Augustine (born 354) was not a mystic, but a doctrinal polemicist and intellectual who longed for mysticism. Even his writings are over ninety percent intellectual, and only a tiny percentage mystical. He never even mentions the major theme of mysticism, Union through Love. He was dogmatic and disputatious. In his usual exclusivism, he

---

[11] These were people, mostly women, who practiced, as far as possible, a totally solitudinous life.

insisted that true mystical experience could occur to only Christians. So, his "mysticism" was not only blunted by intellect, but dulled by ecclesiology and dogma. It turned out to be quite a tasteless thing. He did recognize the human mind as the key to beginning study of the great mysteries. He also did mention Love for all, "good and evil" as the only Way to "draw near to" God. To go within was to go "above," in the "instatic" movement. It could lead to the "ecstatic." Still, he insisted on the old traditional dogma of the forever and insuperable distinction between God and the Soul. He also saw Christ as some kind of "third entity" standing between God and humans. In a burst of true insight, he did teach that only in loving your neighbor do you truly love God. He also hit the nail on the head in teaching that, if you cling to goodness, you will "find" God and be happy! Christ, who "prays in us," is also "prayed to." But his noblest spirituality was crippled by his blind faith that every action of the Church was an act of God. He has no explanation of the hundreds of mystics who lived before there even existed an organized Church. Love, he says wisely, leads to the "fullness of knowledge," and is the "glue" that binds us to God.

In the Eastern Church, monasticism started with a move into the desert, when people wanted solitude to pray and to practice undisturbed mysticism. They searched for the inner God in silence. Like-minded people started to come together in small groups.

A form of the word "monastic" first appeared in 324. (It means "solitary ones," and comes from the Greek *monos,* "one.") In fact, as early as 274, withdrawal into the desert had already begun. In Christian history, the monk was the successor to the martyr as the "ideal Christian." Many went to unhealthy extremes in asceticism (selfdenial and selftorments).

The prototype of the ideal monk was Anthony (250-356). His is a story of withdrawal, purgation, and transformation. He was converted by the message of "voluntary poverty." After adopting a fellow villager as mentor, he moved into the desert and barricaded himself in an abandoned fort. There, he continuously fought his "demons." In time, the primitive people began to recognize him as healer and exorcist. He tried to talk others into the pursuit of the solitary life.

In time, people fleeing from ordinary life (which left much to be desired) started to make the desert look like a city. Many became visionaries, and claimed easy contact with the "other world" (the inner world of mind). This form of life later came to be called the "heremetical life," or the "hermitic life."

To be solitary and silent was regarded as the very root of salvation, or enlightenment itself. Monasticism was rapidly organized in the service of the economic, political Church, and lost its original innocence and idealism. Soon, monasteries developed tensions with each other, over rules and beliefs.

Soon, they divided into two camps: The Anchoritic, who were relatively independent, and those which lived under a "rule." A major conflict also occurred between ordinary desert-dwellers and those who insisted on following Origen.

Three famous, mystical writers appeared: Gregory of Nyssa, Macarius, and Evagrius Ponticus.

Gregory (335-395) presented God as boundless. He created the first negative theology (describing what God was *not*). The goal of life was "divine nature." The Soul progresses gradually, in stages. God is visible in the "mirror of the polished Soul."

Macarius (died 390) affected a mystical "heresy." Called the "Enthusiasts." They shunned manual labor, gave their lives over to sleep, and interpreted their dreams as "revelations." (This did not always attract the most responsible people.) They prayed continuously. They suffered from the odd idea that the devil's influence could be removed by getting rid of bodily excretions. They were a snobbish elite. They referred to themselves as the "true spirituals." Generally, they made fools of themselves, and were more a source of amusement than of spirituality.

Macarius did not see the Soul-body separation of Origen. He has been called a "Gestalt mystic."

Evagrias Ponticus (died 399) was a desert-dweller who later became the nucleus around whom a number of legends coalesced. His mystical classic was *The Great Trilogy*. He wrote aphorisms collected in groups of one hundred (called "centuries"). At times, he seems deliberately ambiguous, and at other times, rigid. Some of the teaching is closer to Buddhism than to traditional Christianity.

Eventually, everything leads to the inevitable "return" to God or Godmind. Before this universe, there was a prior creation. It was populated by spiritual beings called *logicoi*. The first creation enjoyed absolute Unity with God. Christ was an "unfallen *logikos.*" The goal of spirituality is to "restore" *nous* or "Mind."

In the physical, Mind is "in all things." The best prayer was gnosis. This leads to "unmediated contact" with God. One should cultivate perfect *apathea*. The Soul becomes divine through "reception." Of creatures and God, he says, "all those become this One, forever."

This is discovered by developing an "empty" and clear mind. "Blessed is he who has attained unsurpassable ignorance." Intellect could interfere with perfect Union.

The body was not evil. Grace was necessary for contemplation. The monk is "separated from all but united with all."

One of Plotinus' students, Porphyry (232-304), although not a mystic, was a neoplatonist.

There were two kinds of "being." Theologians couldn't just let it be! They had to split hairs, and try to figure everything out! But, anyway, they claimed that "being" came in two varieties: pre-existent being, and produced being. Only the One was the "true existence." Only He was "being" (*hyperxis*). [The One was also called "mind" or "intelligence" (*noesis*), and "life" (*zoe*).]

When the One "emanates," It shines, disperses, nebulizes Itself into "being." But when It returns to Itself, after having experienced countless lives, It is a finished product, much richer for having acquired new experience and intelligence.

Proclus (410-485), a late neoplatonist, was the last great pagan philosopher. (His major work was *The Platonic Theology*.) He hypothesized that all the Greek gods were actually forms of the One. But unlike Plotinus, Proclus never says that the *divine One was eros*. Still, Mind produced Goodness, Wisdom, and Beauty; from these arose Faith, Truth, and Love. This "love," *eros*, was a force that bound together all levels of reality or mind. Its major job is to draw all towards, and into, the One.

Proclus teaches that the One is so far above comprehension that nothing positive and meaningful can even be said about It. Love activates "the One's image in us." He called the inner interface with the unknowable One the "Flower of the whole Soul."

A core of Proclus' work is "Union" (*henosis*). Later, Christian Procleanism became one of the many varieties of Christian mysticism.

It was almost inevitable that mysticism would converge with monotheism and give rise to specifically theistic (based on a personal God) forms.

It was the Hebrew-Greek Philo (20 BCE-50 CE) who used the idea, later co-opted by the Christian mystic John, of the *Logos*. Much earlier, Platonic cosmology had confirmed the centrality of the Logos in creation. Philo defined this as an "intermediary" between the unknowable God and humanity. Logos was the manifestation of the "hidden" God. This was the "face" or facet of God's infinite being turned towards creation. Logos is immanent in all things, but especially the human mind. Progress towards Logos would demonstrate the "absolute nothingness" of created being. You had to lose faith in yourself in order to know Him.

****

Logos is the highest manifestation of God that can be experienced by the human mind.

****

It is the highest upper reaches of the Soul, where the Soul interfaces with, fades into, infinite Mind.

Very mystically, both Plato and Philo hold that this transition from Soul into Logos can happen suddenly. The master teacher Jesus was held to be the absolute and purest incarnation of this Logos, God's perfect, flawless Lovexpression.

JESUS. Until the twelfth century, Christian mysticism was exclusively exigetical (Scripture-based). Some Christians used the Hebrew Scriptures, but when they did so, they preferred the ancient Greek Translation, called the *Septuagint*. They always insisted on seeing and interpreting even these prechristian texts through Christological filters. *They completely changed the intent and meaning of these texts.* Some Judaizers, who were not mystics, portrayed Jesus inaccurately as striving to mold his lifepattern along the lines of these ancient texts. The idea that these ancient texts were talking about Jesus, although written centuries before his birth, represents a seriously improbably bias.

The historical truth is that *Christianity did not evolve from Judaism.* Christianity was something brand-new in the world. It arose from the mystical experience of a single man, Jesus. And so, *Christianity was*, like Buddhism, Hinduism, and Taoism, *a mystical faith from the time of its inception.* For his words make it abundantly clear, indeed, undeniable, that *Jesus was a mystic.*

Just as obviously, Paul and John were both mystics. Indeed, during the first entire century of the new religion, there is good evidence to infer that, *every Christian studied mysticism,* which they called by its Greek name, "gnosticism."

For example, Jesus said, "You must be perfect, as your heavenly Father is perfect." (Mt.5:48) This might have been a simple statement of mystical fact: Since the heavenly Father who dwells in you is perfect, you must (or, will) also be perfect. Seen this way, it was not a loathsome, burdensome, impossible demand.

The Christians of the first century were the first to give mystical interpretations to Jesus. It is possible that *all original Christians were "small g" gnostics.* [The "capital G" Gnostics who came later had odd ideas, and operated almost like cults. Here, we refer not to them, but to generic gnostics (mystics).] [12]

The supreme place of *agape* or Love in Christian teaching supports the idea that Jesus was a mystic. So does his anti-orthodoxy relative to the respectable mainstream religious community. (They saw him as a dangerous heretic!) *Gnosis*, a technical Greek term for mystical knowledge, is used in John 17:3, where Jesus says that "timeless life" is to "know God." It is also used in Romans 11:33 to describe God's own knowledge! Second Corinthians 2:14 refers to the hidden mysteries of God--words commonly used by mystics. (Compare also 10:5) Christ "lived in the hearts of believers" and knew of a hidden Self. (Eph. 3:16-19) Paul's famous term "in Christ" appears 164 times in the Epistles! He spoke of "Christ who lives in me." (Ga 2:20) He wrote,

---

[12] For the whole story of the evolution of Christian mysticism in the first two centuries, see my *One With the One, op. cit.*

"You have clothed yourselves with Christ ...All of you are one in Christ Jesus." (Ga 3:27) Believers lived "in Christ," and He "in them." (Php 1:21) "The Spirit of God has made His home in you." (Rom 8:9) "Anyone who is joined to the Lord is one Spirit with Him." (1 Cor 6:17)

The fourth Gospel is marked by a powerful Johanine mysticism that is pervasive throughout the words of Jesus.[13]

John speaks quite explicitly of a very odd "oneness" with God-- a theme that *makes* sense *only in a mystical context.* Also, mutual Love, the perennial theme of all mysticism, is the "new command" given by Jesus Christ. Jesus prays, "Father, may they be one in us, as You are in Me, and I am in You... that they may be one as we are one, Me in them, and You in Me..." (Jn. 17:21-23) This makes absolutely *no sense whatsoever* except in the context of mysticism. As in the Way, the Enlightenment Tradition, Jesus makes plain that *the only valid barometer of our Love for Christ is our Love for other people.*

Early Christians wrote and spoke of "Communion" (*koinonia*) with Christ or God. *This word is* explicitly *mystical*, since it breaks down to "common union," which, in turn, means the famous "oneness" of mystical philosophy. Here, divinization of the Soul is implicit. It is, to use mystical language, a "sharing" in "divine nature." (2 Pet 1:4)

By about 200 AD, the Christian Scriptures had reached their final form. (Composition had been completed about 140 AD.)

Until the formal "Bible" had solidified in concrete, there were other writings considered to have been equally inspired. As an example, "The Shepherd of Hermas" was an early quasi-apocalyptic writing.

The seven epistles of Ignatius, murdered around 110, were also candidates for inclusion in the Bible. He also wrote mystically, speaking explicitly of the "Union of flesh and Spirit." He, like Paul, often speaks of being "in Christ," and of Christ's being "in us." He also uses the term, "in God." The word "Union" (*henosis*) occurs regularly in his work, a word that often identified mystical writings in the larger field of spiritual literature. He also speaks nineteen times of "attain-

---

[13] See my *Luminous Jewels of Love and Light,* Volume 2, Part III, "The Gospel of Universal Love," *op. cit.*

ing" God. *What could this possibly be but the mystical ideal of Union with Lovemind?*

Another ideal of second-century Christians was martyrdom. Only after death could the Soul enjoy fullest Union with, "marriage to," the Spirit. (In the Kabbalah, of Jewish mysticism, full Union with *Shekinah*, the Light of Yahweh, was also possible only after death.) Christians, like mystics generally, did *not regard death as a "bad" occurrence.* It was, in fact, the beginning of a new and better life "in God." Research has shown that *the death-experience is a mystical event.*

What happened to all this mysticism? Mystics never die; they just go underground, and/or blossom into polychromatic splendor. As early as 200, a ferocious battle was brewing between the orthodox, largely intellectual "doctors" of religion, and the mystics-- largely kind, good but simple people. The Church gritted its teeth at the thought of being regarded as a bunch of bumpkins. The intellectuals, especially educated Romans, at first, looked down on the church as a pack of uncivilized, uneducated peasants. Church leaders were horrified at this lack of respect. So, gathering together and strategizing, the Church *decided to make it an intellectual institution.*

The Church suffered from serious Plato-envy. More than anything else, its leaders longed to be respected and "respectable." To do this, Christianity would have to struggle to become a highly complex intellectual system. This was a nightmarish and disastrous error, from the spiritual perspective. *For it all but stripped the Church of all Love.* Since God is Love, this meant that *the Church all but abandoned God.* In fact, since God or Love was not very stylish, God was gradually nudged out of "official" or orthodox teaching almost altogether.

Now, of course, there is nothing wrong with intellect. But *the very definition of your Christianity came to be judged by intellect.* You were not a "Christian" because you had more Love in your life, but simply because *you believed the "right" things about God, Jesus, and the Bible.* (This was a thinly disguised "works" doctrine, but now salvation depended upon conscious choices and beliefs, rather than solely on God's Love.)

The bottom line: Now, in the orthodox Church, you could rape, murder, torture, and lie, and *still be a Christian* if you believed the "right" doctrines. (These were the official dogmas of orthodoxy.) By the same token, you could live a life filled with kindness, goodness, respect, compassion, tenderness, and Love, *but you could not be a Christian* if you believed the "wrong" things.

"Christian" shifted from a moral/ethical/Lovebased definition to a merely conformist and intellectual one. Christianity was robbed of its goodness, stripped of its Love. This had to occur if it was ever to become the political and economic giant that it was destined to become. For a group of soft, tender, loving men could never have taken over the whole world, and ruled it, as formal, official Christianity was to do. That required an iron, sometimes cruel, hand.

In embracing mind-definitions, and throwing out the heart, Christianity also absorbed much of the hardness that marked the martial Roman character. Now, religious challenges were political, and vice-versa. So, before it stormed the world, and took over, it had to cultivate the warrior-spirit that marked its two historical predecessors-- the Hebrews and the Romans.

This religiopolitical mess got a gigantic shot in the arm when the secular emperor Constantine called the Council of Nicea in 325, to dominate the Church and to define orthodox belief. These beliefs were not optional, but mandatory; failure to conform could mean death!

This immense economic and political institution and complex *had nothing to do with the simple teacher of Nazareth. It was a caricature, and later a denial, of equality and brotherhood.* There were still many very good men and women within the Church, but its leaders found the whole teaching of Love to be a nuisance and inconvenience. The orthodox Church rushed to cultivate greed and dominance.

In its quest for total absolute power over the people, it had to convince them that *a personal relationship with God, outside the Church, was impossible.* Since mysticism is all about this warm link-up, personal and intimate, between God and the individual, mysticism had to be doctrinally resisted and administratively discouraged. So, by the year 200, "Christians" were raping, torturing, and cutting the throats of other Christians. To be accused of "heresy" was to be as good as already dead.

Mysticism taught the reality of individual relationship with God outside the formal Church. It also upheld that God could, as He had always done, reveal Himself. This teaching, called "progressive revelation," also threatened the official Church.

Mystics were damned as heretics. This made them subhuman in the eyes of their tormentors, and hence, fair game for torture and murder. The orthodox would torture you, your kids, or wife to death, but it would all be "for God," or "for the sake of your eternal Soul."

Not surprisingly, it was not long before the Church was ruled by the toughest, meanest, and cruelest men. Roman politicians, never famous for tenderness, took over positions within the politicized Church. Monsters took over administration.

Doctrine and dogma were designed by men who did not have a clue. Dogma was designed by fools and lunatics for their own purposes. In designing such power-serving doctrines as everlasting hellfire, they remade "god" in their own hideous image.

About 160, a selfstyled "prophet" named Montanus began to teach the idea that revelation continued after the writing of the official Bible had been completed. Mystics of the time declared the same idea, calling it "pneumatic inspiration."

This, of course, flew in the face of a militarized, authoritarian, rigid Church. It was the mystics' loss of this struggle that led to *Faith in human authority and institutional authority.*

"Revelation" was declared impossible. The last genuine revelation was given to Jesus and his first, earliest, followers. After about 140 AD, revelation, said the Church, never occurred again. God went into hiding, and deep silence.

A teacher named Marcion taught a Pauline form of Christianity, about 140. He *totally rejected the Hebrew Scriptures,* as indeed Paul had implied in Galatians. The gnostics were much more flexible, elastic, and open-minded than the orthodox. Some were "philohellenic," compelled by Greek mysticism, although less receptive of Judaism with its wargod Jehovah.

Also, the mystical texts of gnosticism were, in essence, the *same* as Hellenistic mystical texts. Many gnostics did not hesitate to say clearly that the god of the Hebrew Scriptures ("Old Testament") was *not the God of Jesus or the God of the universe.*

Later cultic groups called "capital G" Gnostics fell into dualism, seeing the material world as a "mistake." Jehovah, the god of the Hebrews, was an ignorant spirit. (These groups had been influenced by the ignorant dualism of Zoroastrianism.)

Nevertheless, "small g" gnostic groups tended to be very Love-based and eclectic. They believed in the equality of women, and doctrines and "administrivia" were not very important to them.

The whole of "cap G" Gnosticism cannot be clearly defined, for they split into so many sects and texts that no one definition fits all. Even among "small g" gnostics, many varieties of mysticism flowered, as freedom was sacred to the gnostics, and each was free to develop her own philosophy.

Still, "cap G" Gnostics, like the generic "small g" gnostics, did teach that the higher parts of the Soul were inherently divine. One wrote, "Elevate your divine element as being God."

The "whole Journey" to God is said to be "interior." A part of this Journey is revelation, "the vision of the eons." "Beholding" is the first step to "unification." They believed in salvation through gnosis, or enlightenment, a grace of God.

The gnostic view was one of "immanence," which meant that God, as Mind, indwelled everything in His dream-universe. A major theme is "awakening" to the intrinsic divine Spirit (Christspirit) deep within the Soul.

"Containment" is another important theme: The "uncontained Father" contains all things and persons within Himself.

"They discovered Him within themselves. The inconceivable Uncontained, the Father ...the entirety was within Him.." (Gospel of Truth 18:31-39)

The aim is to escape "forgetfulness," which brings "the fullness of Love." The believer is asked to "recognize the nonexistence of the material world." She then "becomes aware of the unchanging permanence of spiritual Reality."

"People cannot see anything in the real Realm unless they become It." "If you have seen the Spirit, you have become the Spirit." (Phillip 30:8)

Both the famous Gospel of Thomas and the gnostic "Hymn of the Pearl" emphasize the *divine identity of the Soul.* Deep down in Mind, *Soul is Spirit.* That is why gnostic texts speak of the believer "becoming Jesus." (Thomas 108)

Justin Martyr (died 165), a former Platonist, was an orthodox Christian opponent of Christian mysticism. He rejected the Platonic intrinsic divinity of the Soul. According to Origen, an orthodox teacher, the Soul might be capable of "divinization," but did not possess it intrinsically.

The Valentinian Gnostics treasured Love above all else, as did all other "small g" gnostic groups. So, the orthodox were simply lying when they went to the extreme of accusing the Gnostics of rejecting faith and Love, in favor of gnosis. (Actually, gnosis grew out of faith and Love.)

What set orthodox teeth on edge was that gnostics recognized several sources of revelation, the most important being the attentive heartmind.

A gnostic exegete (explainer of Scripture) was Heraclion. He thought, as did all gnostics, that he was guided by the Spirit in creating exigesis (Scriptural commentary). The gnostics, and some Gnostics, believed that the traditional Scriptures contained an "esoteric message." The gnostic explanations were big on metaphor and allegory.

In fact,

****

allegory was the spiritual language of early Christian mystics.

By stark contrast, it was strictly limited in orthodoxy, which favored literalism.

About 180, Irenaeus formulated the antignostic orthodox positions in his unoriginal and dull writings. This man was clearly no genius, and had a knack for unclear writing. He was an early "heresiologist," or specialist in "damnable heresies." He quotes a gnostic named Saturninus as teaching that Christ came "for the destruction of the god of the Jews."

The orthodox Church had a problem with the "peaceniks" called "gnostics." The orthodox had every reason to want a god of cruelty, toughness, and even barbarity, atrocity, and injustice. It needed this kind of god to justify its bloody horrors.

The gnostics' "God of pure Love" would never do! So, the Orthodox turned away from the Lord of Love and forgiveness taught by Jesus. They sought to revivify the archaic Jehovah of the Hebrew culture.

Valentinus (c. 175) was a famous Gnostic teacher. He implied belief in a Gnostic apostolic tradition going all the way back to Paul.

Origen had a fully developed "mystical theology." By the sixth century (in 553), he was condemned for heresy. In fact, two strains or paths of early Christianity soon evolved, the ascetic and the contemplative. The latter was the mystic. Their personal "visions of God" became their vehicles to happiness and contentment. But to earliest Christians, the zenith of the mystical event was not simple "absorption" into an undifferentiated Source. It was full Union with the wise Lovespirit, the Lovemind at the Center of life and Mind. (See Chart of Mind)

God is, like the old candy-bar, "indescribably delicious"!

But God did not settle arguments. After the fourth century, divisions among Christians would be settled with the sword, not the pen. When the Empire split between East and West, Christianity also split.

In the West, after considerable squabbling among several bishops, the bishop of Rome proved to have the most muscle, and bullied his way to the top to become the "papa" or "pope." Conflict exploded between Rome and Constantinople.

The institution of the papacy had nothing to do with its flimsy, transparent cover-story, that Peter had been the first "pope" appointed by Jesus. Jesus and Peter knew nothing of administration or organization.

This was *purely a political move*. It was all about power and influence, a contest of popularity expressing as a mad chess-game. Secret strategies and lies abounded. God was not even consulted! Yes, there were peripheral murmurings about the Bible, but they were drowned out in the cacophony of greed and power-plays.

Dionysus (about 500), in the midst of this hurricane, resorted to, and resurrected, the quiet interior life. He created the term, "mystical theology." Both neoplatonic and Christian, he wrote in arcane, indecipherable, esoteric language. He taught that divine *eros* (Love) reflects itself throughout the cosmos. Universal *eros* was divine goodness. Plato had defined *eros* as "acquisitive longing." It was something not possessed, that created yearning. *Eros* could be *agape*, a related form of Love; it could be ecstatic. At its zenith, it is transcendental and cosmic.

In time, all the universe is to "return" to God. Beauty is emphasized. Dionysus wrote no Biblical commentaries, but has complex links with both Origen and Platonists. He wrote about a "hidden" and a "manifest" God.

God was Being, Life, and Wisdom. "Everything is a reflection of the divine Mind." So, in knowing Himself, God knows everything. We are returned to Union with God through an "anagogic" or uplifting process. He uses the two metaphors of "ascent" and "journey." Union can come in "darkness" and "silence."

The mystic "knows" (gnosis) by "knowing nothing" (intellectually). (This is the clearmind or still mind called *agnosia*.)

God is "hyperagnostic," or unknowable to the intellectual mind. "God is love, God is all love, God is all nonlove..." Why? Because *God is everything!* "Leave behind everything perceived and understood."

God is known through "unknowing inactivity." To know the Fountain you must "unknow" all the waters that flow forth from It. Union is divinization (*theosis*). It is a gift, not a birthright, bestowed, not intrinsic.

"All things both reveal and conceal God." "God is therefore known in all things, and as distinct from all things."

Jesus is a supreme example. The Incarnation was from Love.

To "negate the world" is to "return to God."

****

LATER MYSTICS

Not all that is called "mysticism" is the real thing. Unbalanced ecstatics and ascetics are often mistaken for mystics, but are not. Genuine mystics love, and never abuse, their bodies. It was a mystic who wrote the fourteenth-century English classic *The Cloud of Unknowing*. Throughout history, ideas collide and merge, and do not always conform to our neat categories.

So, some were quasimystics, and some semimystics. But the genuine article can be recognized because of her insistence on the practice of Love above everything. [Lady Julian of Norwich (died 1416) wrote the classic *Revelations of divine Love*. She was a mildly ascetic solitary. Her fifteen "revelations" were accompanied by illness. "Love was our Lord's meaning," she wrote.]

Mysticism was seen as "heresy" by the mainstream Church. This was the case with Meister Eckhart (died 1327), who was charged with "pantheism." Pantheism is not mysticism; pantheism says that God is nothing more than the material cosmos itself; mysticism agrees that God dwells in all, but is the Dreamer behind the great dream of the cosmos. So, mysticism says that God is Mind, while Pantheism reduces God to mere matter. Eckhart wrote, of his Lord, "I must really become He, and He I." He defined God as "a sheer, pure, limpid One, detached from all duality..." He says, "The very best and noblest attainment in this life is to be silent, and let God work and speak within."

Two of the most famous mystics, St. Theresa of Avila and St. John of the Cross, both lived in the sixteenth century. They worked jointly to renew and expand the Carmelite Order. Theresa, passionate and eloquent, was quite ill when her first "revelation" came to her. It was "a sweetness impossible to describe." St. John wrote two classics in mysticism, *The Ascent of Mt. Carmel* and *The Dark Night of the Soul.* Of God, he writes, "He...caused all my senses to be suspended. I remained lost in oblivion." This was a prelude to revelation.

There are also well known Protestant mystics. This is true even though Protestants traditionally resisted the discovery of mysticism in the Christian Scriptures. Jakob Boehme (died 1624) began his Journey depressed about evil. He became "caught up in love." "My Spirit suddenly saw through all and in... all creatures,... it knew God." He described the external physical world as "a substance manifested forth out of both inner and spiritual worlds." In other words, the material cosmos flowed out of Mind.

Mystics are famously orthodox, and many reject any organized religion. Some are completely nonreligious. These might be called "nature-mystics." Their mystical awakening is often triggered by natural beauty, or by being in Love.

Carl Jung described "the ecstasy of a nontemporal state..." similar to the mystical. He felt that this was rooted in a Power or Reality behind the human Soul. Mystics would agree.

Nature-mystics feel at one with the cosmos, but do not refer to a divine Being. Mystics would say that this is because *the experiencers are themselves that divine Being.* For, in mysticism, *God is Mind, and all Mind is one.*

****

Anyone who has any mind is capable of sinking into all Mind.
****

Cosmic Mind can never be found *within* nature, because It is *behind* nature.

****

That is why the pantheist Richard Jeffries was right when he said that there was no God in nature. At the same time, paradoxically, he was also wrong: God is everywhere in nature. God simply cannot be limited by the boundaries of nature.

But like Jeffries, others called "mystics," such as Walt Whitman and Edward Carpenter, were not true mystics, but pantheists.

Mystics are truly guided by the maxim, "Nothing exists that is not God." This is because God is Mind, and the entire cosmos is the dream of that One great Mind. So, mystics have described the whole physical cosmos as the inscrutable "veil of the Mystery," and "re-velation" means literally a "removing of the veil." This is to "see" the Mind behind creation.

65

Mystics have also made attempts to express their truths in literature. This is the case with the literary mystic Thomas Traherne, in the seventeenth century. Of his mystical event, he writes, "All things were spotless, pure, and glorious." Imperfections fled from his mind. "I knew not that there were any sins,..." Poverty, tears, and quarrels disappeared. So did sickness and death, as he caught a view of a higher, more real, Reality.

There are also mystics who are not either religious or literary mystics, not so easy to classify. It is due to some of their efforts that mysticism has survived, sometimes as a "secret" tradition, down through the ages. They have left an encrypted literature, which teaches that the fall from Godmind was humanity's greatest loss, and that there is a Way back.

One example of this kind of mysticism is symbolic alchemy. Alchemists knew that the "magic substance ("philosopher's stone") that could turn all things to gold" was Mind. They knew that "gold," as in the Revelation, signified earthly enlightenment. In 1651, Thomas Vaughan wrote *A New Magical Light*, in which he said that Spirit is "in all things." "Salvation" was "transmutation" into higher Mindstates.

The French St. Martin wrote, of the Way, "It is simply to seek for God within the self." He said, "We enter into the heart of God." By this, we cause "God's heart to enter into us."

Real mystics usually reject ritual or ceremonial approaches to the One, as they are far too stiff and formal. Mystics see God as friend, lover, or spouse. It was the Mind of God within that produced the *mysterium tremendum* or interior Power that forcefully pushed them into the Mind of God, and It into them.

But even when entered, or even possessed, by Spirit, *phenomena do not necessarily occur*. Mystics tend to discount psychic or supernatural occurrences. What *they themselves say* truly identifies them is only Love-- which is Itself supernatural. *Mysticism occurs due to internal changes within the mystic, not due to divine intervention.* Psychic phenomena have no necessary place in real mysticism, but are inferior and "parasitic." Mystics dismiss and neglect them as completely unimportant.

In the past, both psychics and psychotics have been mistaken for "mystics." But usually, *mystics have very ordinary lifepatterns,* and are never paranoiacs. And visionaries are not always mystics, nor mystics visionaries.

For example, the mystic does not claim that the world is *unreal,* but only secondarily or relatively real. The world is "real" in the sense that it is a real dream being produced by a real Mind. Was that dream that you had last night real?

All that the mystic denies is the *absolute* reality of the world. Mystics are moderate, balanced, and well-adjusted. Most importantly, they give their lives to healthy and healing Love.

The mystical event does utilize alterations in neurochemistry. Many of these become permanent, but, far from being confusing, like drug-changes, the mystical gives one solid guidelines and powerful answers. It elevates morals and ethics, and boosts positive selfimage.

It is healthy by every measurable parameter. Verbal expressivity is heightened, and skills sharpened. Will unites with lucid emotional clarity in positive and productive synergies. This shifts the *quality* of your thought. Meaning floods everything. During the event, the world, and the self, grow flawlessly beautiful. Ultimate freedom results.

Mystical events span a very broad spectrum, and come in an astonishing multiplicity of varieties. Still, they all do have certain features in common: 1) A sense of oneness dawns, that the many things and events of the everyday world somehow share a single Source, known clearly as Mind. The Rootmind is the only factor in creation that has intrinsic, absolute, nonrelative existence (a philosophy called "monism").

2) This Mind is recognized as nontemporal ("timeless") and nonspatial (unlimited to one location). 3) There is an irresistible subjective sense that this experience is "more real by far" than the everyday world. It constitutes a new "objectivity." 4) The event is marked by "blessedness," "ecstasy," "rapture," and related very high states. 5) The feeling is overwhelming that the Object of this event, the Mind, is sacred or holy. Because you are an expression of this divine Mind, you are also sacred. 6) Paradoxicality often marks the ineffable knowing.

7) Indescribability of the Infinite. These seven factors are the core of a generic mystical experience.

Mysticism is "holistic" as well as holy. Body, mind, and Soul are all equally involved. The result of the mystical experience is that the true mystic "returns to the ordinary world" with a passion to serve life, as an expression of practical Love. So, mystics do not live as stereotypic hermits in caves, but become active in many areas of education, healing, and even leadership.

Triggers for the transcendental event can include great natural beauty, including flowers or their fragrances. Mystical awakening can also be triggered by music, art, friendship, special "Kodak" moments, intimacy, intimate communication, silence, symbols, churches, temples, or sexual Love. More rarely, it can be triggered by extreme sorrow or distress. Most become mystics after voluntarily seeking "God," and the mystery of spiritual meaning.

The mystic Zu Yun wrote, "The nature of Mind, when understood, no human words can encompass or disclose." The mind is Soul; it is Spirit. *The Mind is Love.*

Although the mystical event cannot be reduced to, captured by, mere words, it can be indirectly indicated. It can also be fruitfully discussed. That is why we have whole libraries filled with the luminous classics of mystical literature. That is why this book was written.

But this hinting at the mystical must take place peripherally to the actual experience. That is why almost all mystical literature comes in the forms of metaphors, parables, symbolism, representation, and allegory. Here, Revelation is no exception. For *the mystical event has no true sensory counterpart.* Words were made to describe sensual experiences and objects, and cannot reach the mystical heights of knowing.

This is also where paradox enters: "I am one with God, but distinct." Such statements must be understood within a larger overview. So must, "God is in the Mind, but in the world." "God is all things, but all things are not God." "The world is real, but unreal." These are not merely illogical, but translogical, statements. *Meaning is not the province of logic;* it is not up to the task.

Mysticism is not irrational; it is nonrational or metarational, often best expressed in poetry. One of the best examples of quasipoetic mystical literature is Lao Tzu's *The Book of the Great Mind and Its Expression,* the classic often called, *"The Way of Virtue."*[14]

Our world is one of things, numbers, logic, and relationship. This is the world for which language was designed. But there is another world, an inner world of Mind which Buddhists call the "transcendental world." It, too, is real, but is quite beyond language. That is where allegory and vision, as in Revelation, can lift the mind into a whole higher level of communication.

The word "mysticism" has been hideously abused by misdefinition. This verbal assault marks even religious leaders and journalists, whose job it is to know better. Whenever they want to describe something a little weird, scary, creepy, unscientific, occult, or fuzzy, they will grab the word "mystical." To most, it means something vaguely paranormal or parapsychological, with a little otherworldly creepiness thrown in. But the supernatural or parapsychological has nothing to do with its correct academic, historical definition and proper usage. (In fact, the famous mystics Origen, Meister Eckhart, and John of the Cross were downright hostile towards visible supernatural "phenomena.")

A "mystic" is one who has directly realized certain major truths (realities). The "knowing" (Greek, *gnosis*) of these truths arises from immediate experience. It comes from within the deep Mind, the Unconscious. (See "Chart of Mind.")

This important knowing is not just taught by books. What are some of the bright truths (realities) known by the mystic? They include: 1) "God" is not a "big daddy in the sky." He/She is not a "person" in outer space. The infinite Mystery called "God" is Love Itself. 2) As Love, God indwells the human being and guides her mind. 3) Her highest goal is to turn her life over completely, surrendering, to this higher Power. She yearns to express Love as perfectly as possible. She wants, in fact, to become the temporary "incarnation" of Love, or God.

****

---

[14] See my *Luminous Jewels of Love and Light,* Volume 2, Part IV, "The Book of the Great Mind and Its Expression, *op, cit.*

NOTE: Revelation is an extraordinarily complex document, as might be expected from any work that seeks to describe the human mind, and then, to indicate an infinite Mind. This is made exponentially more complicated because it discusses many levels of Mind, each consisting of many layers. (See "Chart of Mind" at the beginning of this book.)

Even more confusingly, the narrative is almost never chronological or sequential. Happy ecstasies are wrapped up, entangled with, moments of anxiety or depression. It is, in short, like the mind that it describes-- never laid out in predictable, neat geometricities, but stormy and chaotic.

Still, after you have read it, it is hoped that you will decide that it has been worth the reading. For it can greatly enrich your life!

THE APOCALYPSE OF LOVE: MYSTICAL SYMBOLISM IN REVELATION

Chapter 1

Verse 1. "A revelation of Jesus Christ. God gave him this revelation to show to his slaves. It is about things which are bound to occur quickly. He showed these things by signs. He showed them to his servant John through an angel."

COMMENTARY: What on earth-- or elsewhere-- is Revelation all about? In the history of the world, no more baffling, bewildering, confusing package of words has ever been accumulated within a single cover. No book has ever appeared more mysterious, haunting, or just plain frightening!

The very first word, "apocalypse," is a clue! Upon hearing this bombshell of a word, the heart races. The mind is flooded with images of Godzilloid creatures, disasters, catastrophes, and the unraveling of the entire world as we have known it! It means to many the notorious, scary "end of the world," to come in fire and hail and blood!

Yet the word really means nothing more than "re-velation," or "unveiling," "uncovering," or "dis-covering." So, a revelation is about removing the cover from a Mystery which is hidden. The Mystery is already there, but simply veiled. Implication:

****

The Book of Revelation is all about a deep inner Mystery awaiting exposure to the light of conscious awareness!

****

The Intro is quiet, serene, in stark contrast with its later ferocity and intensity. The mind (John) climbs so gently aboard the warpspeed rollercoaster of bottomless Mind that all seems placid. But storms, hurricanes of Mind, lie just around the corner!

Revelation is not a "revelation by Jesus Christ," or "a revelation given through Jesus Christ." It is "a revelation *of* Jesus Christ." This means that the "Christ" is what is revealed to the mind! Your definition of "Christ" will, then, shift the meaning of Revelation!

Those who see "Christ" as interior starkly contrast with those who see Christ as compressed into the historical man Jesus. Mystics have always emphasized that "Christ" is an interior Mystery, a potential for Love that *all people* have hidden deeply in the mind, in the Unconscious. It is an everlasting Spirit, and did not die when the man Jesus died. Deep down, you partake of Christnature. Christ is God. And God is Love. So, your Essence is Love. At the very core of your unconscious Mind lies Lovemind (Spirit or God).

****

So, Revelation is all about you.

****

Revelation describes the terrifying, blissful path to the inner Christ. It is a heaven-to-hell voyage into the hidden and ugliest, as well as the most gorgeous, depths of your own mind. Within you are savage beasts, dripping with blood, and glowing angels, smiling with Love. At the Core of your Unconscious lies a lightfilled jewel wrapped in the flower-petals of mind. This is perfect, flawless, stainless, bottomless Mind. This is Lovemind. (See "Chart of Mind," at the beginning of this book.)

Revelation uses the language of symbols ("signs"). It doesn't mean what it says-- not literally.

The events described must occur soon ("quickly"). This denies all zany ideas that John could have been writing about the twenty-first century.

Verse 2. "He gave testimony to the Logos of God and to Jesus Christ, as many things as he saw."

COMM: The mind (John) blossoms with the perfect flower-expressions of Love ("Logos"). This Logos is God. (Jn. 1:1) But while Lovemind can be God in *potential or God static*, the Logos is *God expressed or manifested*. It is the perfect, symmetric mirrorexpression of God (Love). They are one. Like two clouds merging, the natures of God and Logos are interspersed within each other. As minds, they have no boundaries to separate them. They are one seamless Mind. Logos is Love.

It can incarnate in flesh. Usually, It does this as the "Soul." (Compare 19:13) [The Greek word (*sarx*) for "flesh" did not mean only a physical body. It meant an entire world-outlook. So, it was a mindstate starkly contrasting with Spirit.] Incarnation of the Logos occurred in Jesus Christ. But there is no valid reason to assume that It happened *exclusively* in his case.

The mind ("John," "beloved") is beloved by infinite Lovemind. *All minds are beloved.* Both Gospel and Revelation (written by "John") are about this Lovemind-- bottomless, luminous Mind. Both are about transcendence, and the mystical path that carries you to that ultrahigh state.

John's Gospel is accurately celebrated as that of the mystic (gnostic). It is the "Gospel of Universal Love."[15] Love and Unity between "Christ" and human nature shine from Jesus' every word, in the Gospel of "John." This truth is an essential mystic-matrix. God's direct, immediate, overwhelming Presence in the heart is revealed. (See "Chart of Mind.") [The gnostic (mystic) knows this directly by the special "knowing" called gnosis.]

During a mystical event, you touch like an electrically hot wire the Logos deep within your own mind. This is the same Logos that Paul wrote about (Rom. 10:8): "The Logos is... in your own heart."

God, then, is in you.

****

To discover this is the meaning of life!
****

Inner growth/transformation is the platinum of revelation.

"John" never once said, or even indicated, that Apocalypse concerned geopolitical struggles in the twenty-first century. Swept away by omniscience, he could have. But he conspicuously did not. Instead, he says that "Christ" ("Logos") is the amazing subject of the whole book.

"John" records what he "saw." To "see" is to be given insight, usually by the Spirit, or deepest Unconscious.

---

[15] This is the name that I have given it in my *Luminous Jewels of Love and Light*, Volume 2, Part III, op. cit.

Verse 3. "Happy is the one reading aloud, and those who hear, the words of the prophecy. Happy is the one who observes the things in it. It was written for the select time, which is near."

COMM: Politics and calendars do not drive you. They do not "inspire" you. They cannot be implemented in everyday life ("observed"). The revelation refers to an *intensely personal* process, within mind. It tracks an action. A dance between the Observer and deepest inner Mind (Lovemind, God within) is implied ("observe"). (The "inner Observer" is the special part of your Unconscious which records and evaluates your every thought, word, and action. These are evaluated by standards of perfect justice.) This is all about selftransformation.

Revelation and its observance are not about large groups or nations. The goal is to absorb/reflect ("reading") it publicly ("aloud"). The next aim is contentment ("happiness"). How could reading about politics make you "happy"? This can never come from reading about conflicts among nations, or about dry chronologies. To create happiness, a message must have personal, relevant emotional impact. To have that kind of hearteffect, it must reach deeply, intensely within. *If it is to have maximum emotional effect, it must be about you!*

Apocalypse was written about a special prechosen time ("select time"). Some claim that this phrase applies only to international events, predestined by God. But the mysticsage Solomon wrote, reflecting perennial and ancient wisdom, "For everything there is an appointed time." (Ecclesiastes chapter 3). Solomon lists a number of *personal* events: birth, death, peace, trouble, laughter, weeping. So "select time" does not apply to only international events. It can also describe personal ones.

True, cosmic Mind does have "select" or "appointed" times for geopolitical earthquakes. Certain historical events, such as the fall of the Berlin Wall, occur when the human mind, and its societies, are ready for them. The same is true of major scientific breakthroughs: Love creates them at Its own time.

But events in personal life are also "appointed" by the Unconscious Lovemind. The Soul, working with Spirit, predetermines some conditions and events. This plan, in your life, was largely formulated, by your Soul, before your birth, and parts of it were even encoded into your genome (genetics). These most important conditions and events occur in "select times." Your Soul implements a limited "predestination." A few *major* events in a given life are preselected and predetermined, although ninety-plus percent of all actions are the result of free will.

For example, your moment of birth was chosen, before your birth, by your Soul. So were the major contents of your genome (genetics). So was your death-moment. Until that moment arrives, nothing in the world can kill you. But when it does come, nothing can keep you on earth.

What are the most important events in your life? Periods when you are plunged naked into the deep abyss of your own mind are among the "top ten." Only then do you come face-to-face with glaring, unblinking, inignorable Reality. (In the Enlightenment Tradition, this Absolute, Reality, is Mind; but more on this later.) Predetermined by your Soul are major moments in spiritual development. The text says that the time for ultimate inner awakening is about to occur ("near"). Again, John could not have been writing about the twenty-first century.

Verse 4. "John, to the seven ecclesias in Asia: Grace to you, and peace, from the One Who is, who was, and Who is coming, and from the seven spirits which are in sight of his throne."

COMM: It is the holy parts of Mind (Greek, *ekklesias;* "Churches") that now receive attention. An elaborate, ostentatious building that costs thousands of dollars is *not* a "church." In fact, "church," in the Scriptures, never refers to a building at all. Instead, a "church" was a group of "brothers and sisters." They were not marked by conformity of doctrines. What did mark them? They had turned their lives over completely to Christ. They knew Him (Greek, *gnosis*) in a relationship of personal and intense Love.

Revelation targets spiritual ("seven") Mind. Like a laser, it focuses intent and energy [16] on the sacred areas of Mind ("churches").

---

[16] The word "energy" is used throughout the Commentary. It is thought-potential, or "pre-thought" that has not yet formed, or crystallized, into actual, consciously recognizable thought. These pre-thought "psychemes" must incubate before they coalesce

So, the parts of your psyche set aside for the service of Love ("churches") attract like a flash of lightning the attention of cosmic Mind!

Holy teachings exist within Eastern mysticschools ("Asia"). Turn your attention to the cultivation of peace (tranquility), Love (compassion), and joy (bliss).

These qualities are chief among the "fruit of the Spirit." (Ga 5:22) They are not produced by the conscious mind, but only by Lovemind (Spirit, God). They blossom with the discovery of ultimate Reality (God, Lovemind). In many ancient Eastern traditions, as well as early Christianity, the lifepattern of Love-cultivation was called simply "the Way." (This is reflected in the Chinese *Tao* or Sanskrit *dharma*.) Eastern ways are introspective. They are all and always about the inner Self. This is also the theme of Revelation.

The "churchmind" is deepest, interior mind. This is the first of many times that John uses a group to represent a mental aggregate, a collection of related thoughts.

These holy mental patterns are carefully monitored by Lovemind [(God); "in sight of the throne"]. God's "eyes" are allseeing. This deepest Mind knows your every thought.

Verse 5. "And from Jesus Christ, the Testifier, the faithful, the first-born of the dead, the ruler of the kings of the earth, he who loves us and loosed us from sins, in his blood ..."

COMM: The poor teacher from the humble slum town of Nazareth is not the bright Center here! No, this is the glorified, spectacular Spirit of Love (This is not just "Jesus" but "Jesus Christ". *The "Christ" makes all the difference!)* This is an incomprehensible Power! It lives within your mind in this very moment! It is as far from normal mind as the Andromeda galaxy is from earth! It is quite beyond everything that the mind knows intellectually.

---

as thought. This "energy" is spiritual, i.e., a potential to activate Love-thoughts. It originates in the Core of Mind, Lovemind.

 Also, one way that "thought-energy" can be visualized is as the neuroelectrical or electrochemical energy used to create the circuitry of the brain. [The brain is the organic (physical) transmitter of the nonphysical "mind."]

It is lightyears beyond anything that the mind *has ever known! It is far* beyond anything that the mind *can* know! The only Way to know the Christ of Lovelight is through the miraculous, supernatural revelation of Itself (gnosis). This occurs through Love, not learning. This "Spirit" is "truth" (Reality).

But how can a "Spirit" be "Reality"? Is not "reality" a complex set of innumerable physical objects and conditions? The Enlightenment Tradition says no. The entire cosmos, this teaches, is a great dream of an illimitable, immeasurable, incomprehensible Dreamer Who lives in the very Center of your Unconscious. (This is God, Christ, or Lovemind; See "Chart of Mind")

All the "material" and "external" cosmos is really neither. Everything exists within the Mind, as Its dream. Only Mind is absolutely real; Its dream is not. So, in mystical tradition, "Absolute" is synonymous with "Reality." (Both are synonyms for "God.") All three terms mean "cosmic Mind."

The unconscious Observer is the inner Judge, the part of your mind that watches, records, and evaluates everything ("Testifier"). This is a part of the larger, inner "Christ." It monitors your life through your own mind. It is accurate ("faithful"). It doesn't miss a thing. It weighs every action, thought, and word in the scales of perfect and absolute justice. This is to design your future based upon your own actions (karma). This inner Observer/Testifier is interwoven with conscience. It is an indispensable inner Guide.

The Christspirit is within the Soul like the seeds within the apple-- the Core. The mystic Bernard of Clairveaux said, in the twelfth century, "The Spirit dwells within the Soul." By nature, in most, Spirit is dormant, potential, or deactivated ("dead"). But "death" is funny in Revelation. It is only a temporary condition. It is both survivable and reversible! When something descends so far into the Unconscious that it is indetectable to the conscious mind, it is "dead." This is the state of Christmind.

When, at long last, it ascends back into the conscious mind-- when you become aware of It-- it is brand-new ("born") from its hiding ("dead"). *Nothing spiritual can happen* until a conscious connection with this Spirit of Lovelight is made. So, *it must come to the aware mind first* ("firstborn of the dead").

The Enlightenment Tradition says that the Soul (deep in the Unconscious) is the Actor. The ego ("Mary Smith") is just a role that this Soul is playing. "Mary" is just a mask being worn by the great Soulmind. It is a game, played on a cosmic scale. Only when the person, the role, "mask," or ego dies is Christ fully born in us.

Before you can be reborn as an enlightened being, you must *first* know that the Christspirit lives within you. You can't get there if you don't know where "there" is, where you are headed. That is why all the compasses of spirituality point straight to Lovemind.

The Christ is the first and the last. Your spiritual Journey begins with the Christ, for it begins only after you have found this Lovespirit within. And it ends with the Christ, with the final fusion or melding/merging of "your" mind with His. (The great Mind of Love is the only final, absolute Reality in the cosmos.).

Christmind controls ("ruler") the most influential, powerful matrix-thoughts ("kings") of the whole Mind, including hypersensual mind ("earth"). His kingdom is *within the mind.*

How do we know that the Christ does not want to become president Bush, saddam, or to imitate some other literal politician? We can study the incarnation of Christ in Jesus. Jesus refused the political office of the Jewish "Messiah."[17] The Jews were, and are, right: Jesus was not the "Messiah." He never made this claim for himself. The idea of a "Messiah" arose from ignorance and desperation. It was but a superstition; but it did bring a lot of comfort to the Jews. Their Messiah was to be a violent, powerful political and military leader who would throw off the yoke of Rome and liberate the Jews as their ruler. This leader would be a study in psychotic brutality and ghastly violence. He would thus reflect the primitivity of the Jehovah-myth. [18] Jesus did none of this. So, reasonably, the Jews had no interest in claiming him as their Messiah, and he, no interest in claiming the title.

---

[17] The complete story of Jesus' refusal to play any political or religious games is expanded in my *The Mystic Gospels of Jesus the Christ* (Liberty Township, Ohio; Love Ministries, Inc. 2002)

[18] See my *Jehovah Goodbye, op. cit.*

He was the "Christ." [But the Greek word *khristos* ("Christ") was much more than a mere translation of the Hebrew *mashiahh* ("messiah").] More about this later. *Jesus was not just a modified Jew* He was a full mystic. This is why he was criticized, ridiculed, tormented, and finally murdered. *He was no "harmless" member of the respected religious establishment.* Respectable people rejected him as a rebel and renegade. The elders and leaders could not stand the sight of him! He was hated, not respected, by the most religious people of Jehovah.

By the first century, in Christian circles, the word "Christ" had come to refer to a level of spiritual awareness, or what the Eastern masters called "enlightenment." The meaning of "christ" is "anointed one." This refers to a rather messy ceremony in which oil was smeared all over the head. But later, the word "Christ" evolved into a rough equivalent of "Buddha." It was a title of respect, and designated a being who had fully found Unity with the Lovespirit within. The word had lost all connections with the Hebrew "Messiah".

Originally, "Christ" did not refer to only one man. All who followed the Christ were to become the Christ of Love incarnate, with the passage of time. They were to be perfected by grace. It might sound quirky and alien to our ears to hear the phrases, "Kevin Christ," or, "Jessica Christ," but each Christian was supposed to become an incarnation of the same inner Lovespirit that manifested in Jesus!

Christ is unarguably interested in changing the world. This he does one person at a time.

He has no literal government, no "theocracy," such as those atrocious specimens that murdered people and ruined lives throughout history. ["Theocracy," which places human rulers in the place of God (Love) is one of the most despicable ideas of history, in Islam, Judaism, and Christianity.] Christ reasonably uses techniques that work. Laws cannot legislate spirituality.

Christ is Lovemind, and this God sees all of His/Her children as perfect. This Mind is too pure to behold "evil." Being perfect Mind, it can create (dream up) only good, and so lives in an "allgood" cosmos. This view is called "monism." ("monism" is the philosophy that only one Mind truly exists.) According to the monistic Enlightenment Tradition, you are perfect for your niche right at this moment. Though your "sins" be black as coal, Mind will see them as white as snow ("loosed us from sins"). In the perfect vision of perfect Mind, we are already forgiven of all sins, and so, we have been liberated from them! *It is as if they had never existed!* Only forgiveness is real!

Christspirit is the part of God that dwells in the human psyche. Even It must give up any idea of "separate" existence! For *nothing can exist outside the one real Mind.* Even the great Power of Christ can be limited until It "dies" into God, vanishes or evaporates into Lovemind, leaving not a trace; a person must give his/her entire life ("his blood") to God. For ultimate liberation comes only in the sequence: 1) the traumatic death of ego into Soul, 2) Soul "dies" into Christ, and 3) Christ "dies" into God (Lovemind).

Verse 6. "And he made us [a] kingdom, priests to his God and Father. To him [be] the glory and the might into the ages. So be it."

COMM: A "kingdom" is the domain rules by a "king." God, in Christ, is the King, not of geographical areas, but of hearts. We are the heartminds regulated by Lovemind ("kingdom") only when we learn to follow the Way of Love. This is not a religion, but a lifepath.

Our minds then blossom into fulltime servants of Love ("priests"). These thoughtgroups are pristine and pure to the Core, each thought a cosmic Lover!

This calling is no office, but a thought-career! That is, these thoughts become "priests" not by "appointment." Nor is it because they are recognized by other thoughts. They actively manifest Love! That is their only necessary qualification! All thoughts of Love are "priests of God."

In the everyday world, the local priest, elder, minister, rabbi, or imam might not have the calling to this inner "priesthood" of thought. But a girl five years old might. God (Love) chooses.

God (Love) is our tender, gentle Father/Mother. For all Mind, yours and mine, originates with Him/Her. He/She is also the Source, and Recipient, of all power.

The Greek word for "age" (*aion*) can also be extended to mean a condition or "state." Life in the 3-d spacetime world is one "age," and the afterlife another. (Both are dreamworlds or Mindworlds.) Psychology is all about "states." Mysticism is all about *altered* states. So, the word "ages" refers also to states of Mind. The rendition of the New Testament by Campbell (1835), indeed translated the Greek *aion* consistently as "state." God's (Love's) pervasiveness in all levels, layers, stages, and areas of Mind ("ages of the ages") is evident. It states His/Her "psychomnipresence." He/She is ubiquitous in Mind, "here and now," always. He/She exists fully in "ugliness" as well as beauty, in the Soul of "evil" as well as good people. The Mind, "your" mind, is immersed in Godmind. It is saturated with it. Infinite Mind is at every level-- subconscious, preconscious, conscious, and Superconscious. (See "Chart of Mind")

Verse 7. "Look! He is coming with the clouds. And every eye will see him. And the ones who stabbed him [will see him,] and they will strike themselves upon him, all the tribes of the earth. Yes, so be it."

COMM: The sky has always been, in all ancient cultures, the "abode of the gods." But it is sheerest superstition to think that God is really "out there," above the clouds, or in outer space. (For this reduces God to an extraterrestrial.) Sophisticated and wise spiritual people realize that God is *within*. So, "sky" or "clouds" represent "higher" (deeper) Mind.

Also, as another symbolic interpretation, clouds obstruct clear vision, and symbolize mental factors, such as ignorance, evil, or materialism, which block inner vision of the Christmind (deep within the Unconscious). Christ appears amidst these foggy conditions of mind.

So, Christmind is not at first "seen" clearly.

We need not be rigid or dogmatic in our interpretation. So, a third possible meaning of "cloud": Water is the unconscious mind, and air intelligence. Clouds combine both. Christmind arises from deeper Mind (water), but is recognized by cognition (air). Intelligence created by the Unconscious ("cloud") supports the vision.

Every part of the psyche understands through the gift of inner vision ("every eye"). Each mindarea recognizes ("sees") Christ. Christmind re-emerges into conscious awareness. For Mind has known Christmind for all eternity.

The sense-dominated mind ("earth") will know him. Its "antichrist" ideas (thought-clusters; "tribes") will be shattered ("strike themselves") if they resist his Love. Hypersensual mind, in the past,

has tried to kill ("stab") the Christnature or Lovemind. The relationship has been stormy and violent: Lovemind continuously entreats and
seeks to seduce mind to Love; this is just an annoyance to hypersensual or biological mind ("earth"). The biomind of hypersexuality, territoriality, competition, and greed has always resisted the gentle goodness of Lovemind.

Verse 8. "'I am the alpha and the omega,' says the Lord God, 'the
One Who was, and is, and who is coming, the almighty.'"

COMM: Ultimate Mind is the beginning and end. This means that
all life and Mind began with the One, and It is to the One that all will
ultimately return. All Mind was created by Lovemind, and all is destined to become Lovemind.

This Mind has always existed ("was"). It is the only Reality that is
absolute ("is"). It promises that, at the end of Its revelation to Its children, it is "coming" to the mind.

It does not serve time-sequences. Always, It has been, irrespective
of time altogether. It is, like the enlightened Soul, "timeless" (outside
the flow of time). [19]

It is "almighty." Its mental power is illimitable and immeasurable.
Jesus said, "Nothing is impossible with God." That summarizes omnipotence.

Verse 9. "I, John, your brother, and cosharer of both tribulation
and kingdom, as well as the endurance in Jesus, came to be on the island called Patmos, through the Logos of God and the testimony."

COMM: The conscious mind ("John") is a loving "brother" to all
subsections of mind, which it organizes. As a mind lost often in ignorance, he has shared the troubles and perplexities ("tribulation")
known to the whole limited mind.

But, also, he is aware that the Power and Spirit of infinity live
within him ("glory"). All mindelements ruled by Love ("kingdom")
are known, but imperfectly, to mind.

John means "beloved." The deepest Mind (Lovemind; God) loves
the mind. But this mind must learn this. It comes to this hard-won

---

[19] The Greek word *aionian* is usually translated "everlasting", but its literal meaning
is "timeless". (Compare Jesus' words in my *Luminous Jewels of Love and Light*,
Volume 2, Part III, "The Gospel of Universal Love," *op.cit*)

knowledge by facing challenges ("tribulation") and the cultivation of strength ("endurance"). It requires divine aid, in a higher state of spiritual Mind ("in Jesus"), to grow spiritually. In fact, it requires grace to finish its path. (The Christspirit is the Godhuman interface.) Human spiritual passions are set ablaze by the ignition of Love.

Love is the interface between human and divine Mind. For Lovemind is Christmind, and is also God. All revelation originates with the part of the psyche that is Love, and then is given to the part that knows Love.

Revelation stuns you while you are still in the human condition ("Patmos"; "mortal"). It hits your Soul while It (your deeper Self) is locked and strapped into the straightjacket of the "material" world and "physical" body. Infinity reveals Itself to mortal mind, which is an island. It is immersed within, and engulfed by, the ocean of illimitable Mind, limitless as the sky.

The human mind can serve animal and bestial mind, or Lovemind. It can serve madness or tranquility, greedy lust or Love-- a decision that we make every second of our lives, with every thought. We can choose to serve pornoflicks, or to see divine beauty; we can choose sex or Love, or their blend; we can choose violence or reason; we can choose religion, or spirituality, or their blend; we can choose generosity or miserliness, etc.

This revelation comes through the Logos, or perfect Lovexpression in the heartmind, emanating from the infinite Unconscious. (Later, we will study the identification of the Soul with the Logos, forming "Soulogos." See 19:13-15.) This apocalypse comes to the intellectual mind.

Revelation is much more than gigantic monsters climbing out of the sea and attacking. It is no cheap "Godzilla" flick! It is more than stars falling from the sky. It also carries and hides an encoded message for the mind. It is truly revealed to the intellect, but is also shown to even lower mind, the "biomind." (This is hypersensual or sense-dominated.) This secret is hidden within the symbolism of "island." For an "island" is made of "earth." ("Earth" is the archetypal symbol for hypersensual mind and bionature-- all mind controlled by senses or biology.) This shallow biomind is immersed within a much greater Mind, the Unconscious, as an island is within a "sea."

Verse 10. "I came to be in Spirit, in the day of the Lord, and I heard behind me a voice as great as [the sound of a] trumpet."

COMM: Revelation comes only when we are introspective, not focused on the world or senses, in a deeper state of mind ("in Spirit"). It is heard only when we are listening. This is the first of a multitude of understandings ("I heard") that occur. It comes to us when we are turned towards the inner Lovecenter.

Revelation does not usually register. We are almost always focused exclusively on the senses or the world. That is why the high-powered executive is an unlikely candidate for the mystical experience. There are exceptions-- dramatic ones. Mystical literature is replete, filled to overflowing, with accounts of people who have been blasted awake by the Spirit when It was the furthest thing from their minds.

But the mind ("John") was, like most mystics, already "in Spirit" (an introspective, receptive mode, touching deepest Mind) when he "heard" the inner "voice." The message blasted him awake by a loud, possibly annoying or obnoxious, inignorable signal ("trumpet") from interior Power.

A gigantic shift of attention towards inner Mind occurs. Then, we know that all time ("day") belongs to, originates from, cosmic Mind ("Lord"). No time is really ours. In fact, no time *really* exists. What is time? It is an organizing factor that allows Mind to know the world a little "bite" or "bit" at a time. The witticism that time was created so that everything did not happen all at once comes near the truth! The genuine life, the authentic life, is "timeless" (to use the Greek adjective usually mistranslated as "everlasting").

Communication comes from the Unconscious ("behind"). (For "behind," like "below," is an archetype of the Unconscious.)

Verse 11. "It said, 'What you are looking at, write in a small book, and send to the seven ekklesias: Ephesus, Smyrna, Pergamum, Thyatira, Sardis, Philadelphia, and Laodicea.'"

COMM: Mind is warned to remember ("write")! Ephesus means "desirable," Smyrna, "lamentation," Pergamum, "closely knit," Thyatira, "incense," Sardis, "precious stone," Philadelphia, "brotherly love, and Laodicea, "justice."

Possible symbolic meanings for these cities are: Ephesus, personal desire, too much of which prevents the Flow of Love; Smyrna, sadness; Pergamum, matrix of reason (logical, intellectual, analytical thought); Thyatira, beloved or elevated activity; Sardis, stable and beautiful ideas; Philadelphia, brotherly lovemind; Laodicea, the decision making part of mind, seeking justice by balancing and analyzing thoughts.

Verse 12. "And I turned to look upon the voice which was speaking with me and, having turned upon it, I saw seven golden lampstands."

COMM: The mind changes its direction ("turns"), and gets into a receptive mode. It becomes introspective. Three symbols of inner Light converge. So Revelation begins with a very bright promise! The number seven, light, and gold all symbolize spiritual en-lightenment: "Seven" is highest spirituality. "Gold" is enlightenment while still linked to the human state or material world. And "Light" is transcendental enlightenment of the inner Mind, unaffected by material or even ordinary mental considerations. (This is the "tranquility in a hurricane" which marks the mind of a selfmaster.)

These miraculous beauties are revealed ("seen") only after the mind changes orientation ("turns") and faces them. So, full enlightenment requires the cooperation of the mind.

Verse 13. "And in the midst of the Lampstands [was] one like the son of man, clothed with a garment that reached to his feet, and having around his breast a golden girdle."

COMM: A true human mind ("son of man") this *is not!* It is *"like"* the human nature. Since it is surrounded by symbols of transcendence, we would hardly expect it to be fully or only human! It is the human nature transformed and glorified by Lovelight!

****

It is the Soul!

****

It is the semi-enlightened Mindstate between Spiritmind and mind. (It is the "higher" Self of metaphysics, and the "deeper Self" of mystical psychology.)

It is "in" the Light ("in the midst of the lampstands"). But does this mean that the Soul is fully enlightened? Not necessarily. It is much closer to the Coremind of Spiritlight than is the merely human mind. It has so much more Lovelight! But It still peers through the murky and cloudy darkness of "separate" existence. (It believes Itself "separate" from the One.) Soul-- although brilliant and wise beyond human comprehension-- is still imperfect, still a victim of illusion. And this delusion of separation (dualism) hangs around its neck like a millstone! So, despite its fantastic, astounding beauty, It is not fully enlightened. This is not Lovemind (Coremind, Christmind, Spirit, or God). But it is the illuminated Soul. (To see the difference between "Soul" and the deeper "Spirit," see "Chart of Mind.")

This very vision is a verification and validation of the original bright promise. The mind ("John") has had a dazzling and uplifting vision of the future of his own mind, in this Lightfilled Soul.

Selfimage ("garment") is not identified re its color. (Affiliation with the deeper Self is always represented by a "white garment.") Selfimage is rooted in your spiritual level. At the lowest level, that of biomind, you are locked into the dreary and depressing, "I am only an animal." If, on a higher level, you say, "I am this body only," you are still way off track! But in saying, "I am Mind in limited manifestation," you are in the ball park! You are catching on! You are getting it!

The garment goes to the point of real progress ("feet"). (Feet are symbolic of inner movement or progress.) So, selfimage extends only to the beginning of progress on the path. To enter real progress, to accelerate it, selfimage must not stop at the self as ego. As it now stands, this selfimage is inadequate! It is like mistaking your earlobe for your "self." That lobe is *part of you* only. Your egoself is also *only a part* of your deeper Self. So, this selfimage must dissolve, or end at the "feet" (beginning of progress). It is a "role" being played by your Soul. It is a "mask" being worn by your Soul! When *real progress begins, selfimage as a separate ego ends* ("garment" ends at "feet"). This is because "self" disappears into Soul.

Selfimage must reach for help. Original selfimage is always the ego-- the socially defined self. In psychology, this has been called the "looking-glass self." It is the self that you see reflected in society, and in the "mirrors" of others' eyes. This is the selfimage designated by your name: It is the self called "Bill," "Jack," "Mary," or, "Jane."

We will here refer to this shallow (ego) identity as "Mary Smith." For in the Enlightenment Tradition, this "self" is a lie. So, although we, and the people all around us, believe ourselves to be egos, we are really Souls-- birthless, timeless, nonphysical, and deathless. We are invisible beings, for we are minds! The Soul is also brighter, clearer, and capable of enormous Love and wisdom.

****

The path to enlightenment, the Way of Love, is all about the transformation of selfimage.

****

So, this is the nucleus of the Way. You must grow to see your "Self" not as a human being, but as an immortal mind! You are a very deep Soulmind. (Since you are generally unaware of this, It is a part of the "Unconscious.") You are not "Mary Smith." (See "Chart of Mind.")

The heart is the most ubiquitous archetype of Love. Those who have been wounded by Love, who know only its agonies, tragedies, and severe blows, might not agree with this, but:

****

It is Love that lifts you into a Self (Soul) that cannot be harmed by the world.

****

The Soul is materially invincible. Being Mind, it cannot be affected by anything material. It is invulnerable to environments. Realizing this is heartlove protection. In Eastern tradition, Love flows through the fourth *chakra* (energy-center), right over the heart. The "girdle" covers it. So, it protects the Love within you, and brings it earthly enlightenment ("golden").

Lovemind, of course, does not need any protection or enlightenment. So, this phase of blossoming is all about Soul, not Spirit. Spirit is purely invincible, stronger even than Soulmind. While the Soul can be harmed by nothing physical, It might still be vulnerable to psychic stresses. But Spirit is a wall of steel twelve feet thick, and the "bullets" of emotional damage bounce from Its surface like droplets of summer rain.

Verse 14. "His head and hair were as white as white wool, white as snow. His eyes were like a flame."

COMM: The Soul is a virtual snowstorm of dazzling white. This state arises through a purified ("white") intellect ("head"). Even small egothoughts that affect selfimage ("hair") are purified.

Surrender of your will to the One ("wool," implying "sheep" or surrender) is a form of this purgation. At the Soulevel, you are "purified" of personal will or desire.

"Snow" is also purification. It occurs at deeper Mindlevels, in the Unconscious ("water"). The Way begins with three Mindphases: 1) the intellectual ("a higher Power exists"), 2) inner metamorphosis ("This Power is within me."), and 3) dramatic action ("I'll turn my desires over to this higher Power.")

Understanding ("eyes") dawns through purification by pain ("flames"; compare 2:18; 19:12; see "fire" in the Glossary). The mystic Ambrose (died 397)wrote that the Soul was "cleansed like gold by the fire of Love." So, Love can teach through even pain. ("Fire" is purification through pain.) Gregory, the "mystic of Light" (died 604), spoke of the "fire of tribulation" necessary to purify the mind before the contemplative (mystical) experience could occur. The mind uses pain as its educational tool. Whether this is sensory pain or not, the senses are used to understand it. The Soul screams in agony. It bursts open with tears. It is racked and wrecked by illusion. It is plagued with anxiety and restlessness. But that's okay; this is all a part of Its growth. This is purgatorio ("purification"). And this occurs only in the beginning of the Journey. So, you must be "purified" in intellect ("head") and in understanding ("eyes").

Verse 15. "And his feet were like fine copper, as if from a fired furnace. And his voice was as of many waters."

COMM: You are bolting down the Lightpath at warpten! Your progress ("feet") is ablaze with Love ("copper")! You are mind, headed directly for the target of Soul! You have begun the path of knowing (gnosis)! You are not just a body, an ego, but a Soul! You've had things blow up in your face, and you've been temporarily crippled, by obstacles, agonies, and suffering ("fired furnace"). These have knocked you off your feet, but you have arisen to walk again!

"Copper," is the metal of Venus/Aphrodite. This is not highest earthly mind ("gold"), and so, not perfect Love. But, as "coppermind," you are midway between that exalted "golden" state and toddlermind ("iron"). Here are the levels of mind, starting with the lowest:

Animal
Hypersensual ("earth"; "clay")
Toddlermind ("iron")
Loving mind, but partial ("copper")
Mind merging with Unconscious ("silver")
Highest earthly enlightened mind ("gold")
Spiritmind ("light")

Still, although only partial or incomplete, this Love is the real thing! (Copper, when gleaming and polished, looks golden.)

Copper can secondarily represent sexual Love. Lovemind can truly express Itself beautifully and joyfully in sex. But all sex is not Love. It can be a phony copy, a counterfeit. But sex can also, of course, be the real thing. So, "coppermind" is headed in the right direction, with or without sex.

Sex is its own "furnace" of purgation. It can be baffling, bewildering, vicious, and cruel. It can create massive, immense pain, especially without Love. Indeed, the rest of Revelation describes many painful experiences. These arise as you grow from "Adam" ("iron" of human nature) to "Christ" ("gold" or full divine nature known while still human).

The communication within the self ("voice") is as the stirrings of the Unconscious ("many waters"). It is calling for the conscious mind to sit up and take notice! "Your attention, please!" says the Unconscious. ("Water" is the Unconscious.) So, deeper Mind is starting to "talk."

Verse 16. "And he had in his right hand seven stars. And from his mouth came out a two-mouthed sword, a sharp one. And his countenance was as the shining sun in its power."

COMM: The black velvet midnight sky of mind begins to glow with radiant luminescence. Light appears in darkness ("stars"). Light phosphoresces into the subconscious.

In Apocalyptic numerology, numbers are not quantities but qualities. So, the Light within is spiritual ("seven") rather than merely conscious or intellectual.

This Light is not merely theoretical. It is applied in a practical way, guided by the mind ("right hand"). ("Right"=conscious; "hand"=activity).

A nightmarish war ("sword") is sparked within the psyche, which explodes. The mind expresses ("mouth") anxiety and frustration. The mindforce behind this ghastly conflict is illusion. For the mind has clearly fallen into the illusion that is the mother of all delusions-- duality ("two-mouthed").[20] [Dualism teaches that something, anything, outside the Lovemind has real existence. Actually, the entire cosmos is the One, the one Mind, emanated. Lovemind is immanent in all things and persons ("monism"). It has no real opposite.] All the worlds are Mind, and Mind is God, and God is Love. *Nothing exists that is not Mind modified.*

The self as seen by others ("countenance") can be genuine, as it is here. (Compare "face," in the Glossary.) Here, the Soul, as viewed by the mind ("John"), shines and scintillates in the Splendor of Spirit, as pure, very bright "Lovelight," ("sun"). At the deep Mindlevel called "Soul," you are immersed in Lovelight, as in an ocean. Despite all the clumsy stupidities and foibles of the egoself, the deeper Self (Soul) is usually in harmony with, reflecting, Lovemind (Spirit). This Lovemind shines at the Center of Mind. The Soul is also similar to ("as") the spirit ("sun"), but itself is not, until enlightenment, that Lightsource.

Verse 17. "And when I saw him, I fell towards his feet, like a dead man, and he put his right hand upon me. He said, 'Do not fear; I am the first and the last.'"

---

[20] This sword is, in the ancient Greek text, "two-mouthed." This does not mean simply "double-edged," as often implied by various English translations. Its symbolism is deeper. It means duality of expression, even conflict. As long as we are in mental darkness (ignorance), we remain in dualism ("two"). This is what dualism means: "Evil" is just as real as good. Separation seems just as real as Unity, hate as Love.

COMM: Egoself collapses. Soul spurts ahead into a new growth-cycle. When it first glimpses the mindblasting glory and beauty of Soulmind, egoself is paralyzed. It is petrified by fear and wonder. Still, it is making progress; it is moving ("at his feet").

It is de-activated ("dead") during the moment of knowing (gnosis). The Soul drains the ego of energy. Often the first effect of an entheognostic (inner God-knowing) event is the weakening of the stubborn egomind.

But Soul is not the enemy of ego. For after creating its deathlike trance, this same Soul then voluntarily ("right hand") reactivates it, so that it can begin the Journey within. If the Soul did not do this, you would forget the mystical awakening, like a wonderful, beautiful dream.

The Soul's message is: Chase all fear out of your mind! ("Do not fear") As Love's apparent opposite (Love has no real opposite), fear can put a major kink in the Lovestream from the Unconscious. It can eclipse, like nothing else, inner divine Splendor.

The Soulspirit (Soul having realized that It is Spirit) then educates the lower mind: This Coreself (Lovemind) is Soul's origin and destiny ("the first and the last"). Soul originates with Spirit and that same Spirit is its final destiny.

Here, as earlier, the definition of "Soul" becomes blurred. It is almost liquified in its elasticity. There is no clear demarcation separating the Soulmind from the deepest Spiritmind. When the Soul is fully ignited with the flames of intense Love, It voluntarily loses Its boundaries and identity in that greater Mind of Spirit. Like a piece of wood in a fire, that *becomes* fire, so Soul, in the crucible of Spirit, *becomes* Spirit. For, as the Soul lives deeply within the mind, so Spirit lives deeply within the Soul. So, as here, the words of the Soul can be inseparable from those of Spirit. (See "Chart of Mind.") Soul can be completely assimilated into Spirit. Rebirth occurs in this sequence: Ego awakens to the fact that it is really a birthless, deathless, timeless Soul; then that Soul awakens to the fact that It is really Lovemind (Spirit; God).

Verse 18. "'[I am] the living One. I became dead, but look! I am alive! And I live into the ages of the ages. And I have the keys of death and of Hades.'"

COMM: Soul implies Its apex. Like a house ablaze, which actually turns into the energy of fire in which it is immersed, Soul becomes the energy of deepest Mind (Spirit). Its passion, Its Love, draws it into the bright Love that consumes It. It becomes the same as the deepest Self (Spirit, Lovemind, God). For Spirit also Loves the Soul, and the "two" Loves are like two flame-throwers pointed at each other, consuming each other! They mingle in the heat of passionate Love.

The Soul derives Its being from Lovemind. This mystical coretruth is summed up in the Upanishadic formula, "*Atman* is *Brahman.*" ("The Soul is the Spirit.") This is talking about you, right now: For you are Mind, Mind is deeply Soul, and Soul is deeply Spirit (God).

For years before enlightenment, Soul was continually suppressed, repressed, and eclipsed by the dominant egomind. It then lay dormant, latent, deactivated ("dead"). From the view of the mind, It was buried so far in the Unconscious, so deeply, so inaccessibly, that it was "dead." All the time, It was the only "true" (real) Mind. The egomind was a disguise-master, a phony, a counterfeit "mind."

But now Soul has reemerged into awareness. This is the Unconscious manifesting Itself, by revelation, to the egoself.[21] Soul commands egoself to use the senses ("look"), and to turn them Soulward. This is how mind knows Soul to be alive. Soul is more alive than the fake self. It is alive in all states ("ages"). It enjoys seamless continuity, unbroken identity, with the deepest Self (God).

Let us be clear: Soul is not God in totality. Soul cannot dream up the cosmos on Its own. Realizing that it is God does not turn Soul into the ultimate "computer" or "magician." For *God is Love.* Soul is God

---

[21] The egomind and the conscious mind are not equal, technically, in the metaphysics of mysticism, although closely linked. The conscious mind is that mind that is aware, as contrasted with the Unconscious, of which we are unaware. The egomind exists within the conscious mind, and is the "role" or "mask" worn by the Soul as its "play-self" on the "stage" of the earth-play. It has no ultimate reality, but is more similar to a very complex game.

in nature[22] only. *It does not become "God" in totality.* When It awakens to Its truest identity, It knows Itself to be Love in incarnation. It is Lovemind pretending to be a limited and separate mind.

Soul treasures Its secret knowings ("keys"). These are Powers. Although these ideas are unenlightened, they still can "unlock" secrets of the Mind. These unexplored canyons of Mind lie either in the subconscious or the larger Unconscious of which it is a part. Soul can unlock the mysteries of mindeath ("death"). Even when egomind undergoes "mystical death," Soul knows exactly what is happening. Though the mind is petrified, terrified, and confused, Soul understands all. It knows that this "death" is only pruning, not the end of anything real.

Soul also has a knowing ("key") to understand "hades." Hades is translated "hell." But in Greek writings, it was never the torture-pit of a psychotic god. No monstergod laughed gleefully while his beloved children, the center of his heart, were roasted like so many marshmallows. In fact, the original hell of Greek mythology (Hades) was a rather dull, neutral, and, well, dead place. There, "shades" (Souls) went after death. It was "boring as hell." This is a part of the subconscious, the mind's garbage-heap. Hades is the collection of thoughtareas that are sometimes trashed ("dead"). It does not imply that a person is "dead from the neck up." But it is an area of Mind that is deactivated. It is a "dead zone" in Mind. It is the symbolic equivalent of a "numbskull." The area of mind called "hades" is the depository of suppressed, repressed, ugly and useless thoughts. Understanding it ("keys") means recognition that even this part of mind still can support spiritual growth. How? By returning unused mindenergy to the rest of mind, supporting creative, constructive, positive, happy thoughts.

Verse 19. "'So, write what you saw, and what is, and what is about to occur.'"

COMM· Mind is commanded to remember ("write") three vital memories:

---

[22] Even this mild claim scared some more traditional and timid mystics. For example, Erigena (810-877) carefully distinguished between the claim to be "God in nature" and becoming "God" by "adoptive sonship." The latter, he felt, was the only viable goal of the Christian mystic.

1) what insight revealed ("saw"), 2) its present state ("is"), and 3) strangely, the future ("what is about to occur").

Verse 20. "'The mystery of the seven stars which you saw upon my right hand, and the seven golden lampstands: The seven stars are the angels of the seven ekklesias, and the seven lampstands are the seven ekklesias.'"

COMM: Spirituality ("seven") is key. Angels/stars hit the mind like fireworks, exploding into Lovelight that fills up the whole Mind. Inside the psyche, angels/stars create and support the holy thoughtgroups called "ecclesias/lampstands." ("Ecclesia" is a transliteration of the Greek ekklesia, "church.") So, both "churches" and "lampstands" are sacred Mindareas glowing with illumination.

"Stars/Angels" light the subconscious, as Lovenergies that are directly plugged into the Spirit of Lovemind, the Source of their Lovelight.

The church/lampstand is the collection of thoughtgroups that consistently serve Love. This is a great "mystery." This word unites Revelation with many ancient traditions of *mystos*, or inner enlightenment. So, this allegory was not simply "prophetic," foretelling the future of geopolitics. It was a document predicting ("prophesying") interior growth. For this has always been the meaning of *mystos* in the Enlightenment Tradition.

Chapter 2

Verse 1. "'To the angel of the ekklesia in Ephesus write only the things that he is saying who holds the seven stars in his right hand, the one walking about in the midst of the seven golden lampstands.'"

COMM: Soul holds "stars/angels" in Its Power or control ("hand"). It progresses as the center of ("walks in the midst of") sacred areas ("lampstands/churches") in the Mind. These are all about spirituality ("seven"). It is on the great Journey of enlightenment.[23]

Its first message is about desire ("ephesus"). In every form of the Enlightenment Tradition, renunciation of egodesire is a major core-teaching. Personal desire keeps mind locked into the hypersensual (sense-dominated/human) nature.

Verse 2. "'I have known your works, your labor and your endurance, that you are not able to carry bad men, and you put to the test the ones who are saying that they are themselves apostles. But they are not. And you found them false.'"

COMM: Personal desire creates temptation. But the Spirit has wrestled desire to the ground. It has conquered it. More, It has brought it into humble subservience. Like a tiny puppy, egodesire feels powerless. For it cannot resist the Light.

Desirenergy drains the mind of spiritual force. But when it has been appropriated by Spirit, this energy metamorphoses, like a soaring butterfly emerging from the cocoon, into Lovenergy. All desirenergy is turned over to God (Love).

The person on the Way to enlightenment transforms this massive energy into cathartic force that cleanses her inner Self. She turns the desirenergy into analysis, and turns the spotlight on her inner Self, hunting down the last "criminal fugitives" of egodesire. When her in-

---

[23] For a very complete, indepth psychological, philosophic and historical study of this inward Journey see my *Journey to the Center of the Soul, op. cit*; Compare also my *Falling in Love with Yourself. Love and the Inner Beloved*, (Liberty Township, Ohio; Love Ministries, Inc., 2002)

terior being is flooded with bright Light, there is no place for them to hide.

Of course, even in temptation, these secretly serve the Lord. For no other mind really exists. They serve Love by demonstrating their pitiable inability to bring real satisfaction.

When, by contrast, desirenergy begins voluntarily to serve Love, it produces good actions ("works") that follow Its positive thoughts. These are Love-actions for self and others ("labor") and tenacity in following and doing good ("endurance"). Committed to the labor of serving living creatures, Mindenergy does not want to be wasted or scattered in serving egodesire. It wants to bring forth Love. This it does in practical and helpful ways.

As the mind becomes purified, it cannot tolerate ("carry") harmful intellectual concepts ("bad men"). Some of these ideas claim, to the mind, to be created by God. They appear to be even holy. These are concepts "sent forth" as teachings of God ("apostles"). But they are frauds! Still, their chicanery does not fool the Spirit. The desire of Love ("will of God") roots them out. It exposes them as false.

Verse 3. "'You have endurance. And you have carried [your load] through My name, and you have not labored [in vain].'"

COMM: Mind is tough ("endurance"), "armor-plated," against fear. But in its incarnation as "Mary Smith," it is powerless. For the ego, or "person," is not real; it is just a "mask" being worn by Soul.

But from Soul, it draws and derives its energy. This makes it possible for Mind to get through the day ("carry... load"). For Soulmind is a deep well of wisdom and energy. It is ancient, timeless, highly spiritual. It is a reservoir of vast experience, immeasurable knowledge, and an ocean of wisdom. Mind replaces ego-identity with the identity ("name") of Soul (deeper Self). Mind is no longer egomind, but Soulmind.

It lives in and through Love. Love is the only activity ("labor") that lasts for eternity. It is *the only occupation that is not futile* ("in vain").

Verse 4. "'But I must criticize that you let go of your first Love.'"

COMM: Mind has progressed. It is willing to sacrifice itself in the terrible agony of egocrucifixion. Then, it will do the desires of Love exclusively. But it is losing the fresh novelty of the Way. It no longer strikes mind as a vibrant, exciting path of discovery. The mind is starting to get bored. And this is on the threshold of victory!

It is also on the verge of hellish peril! Why? Because it is losing its first burst of enthusiastic Love for Love.

Verse 5. "'Keep in mind, therefore, from where you have fallen. Repent, and do the works [that you did at] first. If not, I am coming to you, and I will move the lampstand from its place, if you don't repent.'"

COMM: Mind was on its Way! It approached very close to perfect merging with Soulmind! Later, Union with Spiritmind beckoned with its haunting siren-call! This sweet state filled mind with Love at the beginning of its Journey. But it suffered a setback, and even reversal.

It still remembers, nostalgically, deliciously, the high state from which it has regressed ("fallen"). It is warned by Soulspirit to screech to a sudden stop, and reverse its trajectory ("repent"). The flame of passion, of Love, has gone out. Fires of enthusiasm have died, leaving not an ember. Its Way is plain, dull. It is wrapped in a brown mental bag, all color sucked away.

This might be even worse: The Way is threatening! If the mind does not straighten up, recoup its losses, the Soul threatens to steal away with Its Light! It will tear away from mind Its jewels of Lovethoughts ("Lampstands"="ecclesias"). This means that it will actually tear away the sacred areas of mind, leaving it devoid of spirituality.

Verse 6. "'But this much you have: You do hate the works of the Nicolatians, which I also hate.'"

COMM: Nicolatians were sexually obsessed. As nymphomaniacs and satyrs, they indulged their vicious, merciless animal lusts, and then, dared to claim that this sexual frenzy was "spiritual"! Fornication (sexual betrayal) was their stock-in trade. But why was this so important, scandal aside?

Because it masked a deeper disease and evil: betrayal of Love. Sex is not Love, always, but it is as close as many ever come. *And sexual betrayal is always Love-betrayal.* So, it was the betrayal ("fornication") of Lovemind or God that ruined mind and infected Soul. This virulent infection infests mind when it mistakes sex for Love. The warning is: Turn your passions away from obsession with sexuality! Don't funnel all desirenergy into hypersensuality! "Love" is not just biosex! Come back to cosmic Love!

The mind is mesmerized by, compellingly attracted to, sex. That is a good and natural thing. It is a sweet, pleasurable gift of God through nature. But when it begins to eclipse Love, it is "too much" of a good thing, which makes it a "bad" thing.

But don't forget: This verse is about the abuse of sex, but its symbolic theme is larger: It severely, seriously warns against the betrayal of Love!

Sex can be a terrible betrayal of Love, although good sex is Lovexpression. But sex is not the only way that Love is betrayed. Religious activity without Love also betrays It; so do intentional acts of violence, harm, injury, dishonesty, or hurt towards any sentient being. If these acts are intentional, voluntary, or deliberate, then they are "fornication" in the spiritual sense!

Verse 7. "The one who has ears-- let him hear what the Spirit is saying to the ekklesias: 'To the one who conquers I shall give to him to eat of the tree of life, which is in the paradise of God.'"

COMM: Unstop your capacity to understand (inner "ears")! Understand ("hear") Love's communications ("saying")! Overcome ("conquer") fear!

In bold parallelism with Genesis, the motif of spiritual enlightenment, Union with Lovemind ("tree of life"), blossoms. (Genesis is a parallel allegory to Revelation.)

Trees produce fruit. ("fruit", implies, symbolizes action.) The "fruit" of this tree is the behavior/action created by Love. In Galatians 5:22, Paul called this the "fruit of the Spirit." It includes Love, joy, and peace.

Action-potential ("tree") is a function of Mind. It translates thoughtfeelings into practical actions. As the famous aphorism reminds us, "By their fruits ye shall know them."

The Spirit does not here speak to the whole mind. It speaks to only the "ecclesias." (Parts of mind devoted to the surrendered and holy life).

The Garden of Pleasure in the heartmind ("paradise of God") beckons! (In the Genesis allegory, Eden means "pleasure.") This is the state of Mind that arises only from touching Lovemind, and from drifting out weightlessly and floating on the smooth untroubled surface of Love's inner ocean.

The state of utter tranquility and bliss ("paradise") is personal Mind disappeared into Spirit, mindfusion, mindmelding, or mindmergence. It is cosmic inner Union. It is enlightenment, liberation, *moksha* and *nirvana*.

Verse 8. "'And to the angel of the ekklesia in Smyrna, write: "But the things being said by the first and the last, who came to be dead, but lived..."

COMM: Christspirit is Soul made one with Lovemind, the Source of all Mind and life ("first"). It is also the Goal of all Mind and life ("last"). We emerge, as Souls from God, into the stormy world of confusing illusion. Then, after overcoming that illusion, we again lose ourselves in God. We merge and meld with It. Lovemind begins the inner Journey to Lovemind. Lovemind is the Source of Lovemind. Lovemind is also the final Aim of Lovemind.

Lovemind acting through the mystic is the seeker, and, as the cosmic Unconscious, is also the "buried treasure." It is the Finder and the Found. The Soul knows that It is secretly, deeply the Spirit. But it knows this stunning, incredible reality only by discovery. *Enlightenment is not an achievement; it is a discovery!* God is the secret identity of every Soul. (Atman=Brahman.) This Soul spent most of Its early time, at the beginning of the Journey, buried very deeply in the Unconscious ("came to be dead").

When Spirit is finally realized, it is not at all unusual for the first conscious response to be utter despair and regret (sadness or "Smyrna"). For Soul sees with clarity Its past regrettable behaviors. Or, it might also be sad that so much time has elapsed already, and that It has taken this long to awaken into the Light. To maximize the benefit from this apparent tragedy, It must remember ("write") what It has learned.

Verse 9. "I have known your tribulation and poverty. But you are rich. Blasphemy arises from those who say that they are themselves Jews, but they are not. [Instead,] they are a synagogue of satan.[24]"

COMM: Mind sobs ("Smyrna") because of challenges ("tribulation"). But none is as deep and hopeless as the darknight. Insufficient spiritual, intellectual, and esthetic substance to sustain the mind ("poverty") dogs it. It is dressed in tatters and rags. It is skinny and starving. But this is only the lower mind, deceived by the illusions of a space-time "external and material" world.[25]

A favorite paradox in the literature of the Enlightenment Tradition (mysticism) is that the "poor" are really "rich." Those who do not waste timenergy accumulating "material" possessions have the timenergy to look inward. They have timenergy to cultivate rapport with the inner Lovespirit. They possess infinite, immeasurable, and unfathomable riches. Often, then, it is through conditions of "external poverty" that you are internally and truly "rich."

Certain thoughts arise from good motives ("Jews"), but miss the entire point of Love ("say that they are Jews"). What mistakes do these make? There are three: 1) They believe that "Love" is interchangeable with mere religion. They think that all that they have to do is the "right" actions, that *motives,* which are allimportant, do not matter. 2) This crazy idea leads to mechanical, legalistic, or ritualistic behaviors that have *nothing to do with goodness.* These are called "religion." 3) They also believe that Love can be an exclusive "personal possession."

These are the three delusions that bind inner "pseudo-Jews." The whole Spirit of Love and compassion is lost in the following of rules, laws, regulations, rituals, etc. Formal religion replaces spirituality. During the time of the writing of Revelation, Christians repeatedly

---

[24] The word "satan" is used here as a common, not a proper, noun, and hence, begins with a small letter. If, as common superstition has it, "satan" were the name of a person, it should be capitalized. (This would, btw, show respect for "satan.") But, as a synonym for fear, it need not be. Many early Christian gnostics understood that "satan" was not a separate being created by God, of which God then lost control. This satan is not a "person" gone crazy, flying out of control, out to "possess" people and make them sin. People are quite capable of a wide spectrum of evils without invoking supernatural influences. Fear is the only "satan".

[25] See my *Journey to the Center of the Soul op.cit.*

pointed this out to the Jews, insisting that salvation was not due to religion or culture, but to God's Love only (grace).

This is the very essence of the conflict that, in the first century, irretrievably tore Christians apart from the traditional Jewish community. The poor "salvation" or "enlightenment" analog among the Jews was "pleasing" their wargod Jehovah. This has nothing to do with genuine "salvation" (enlightenment), of course. (That is why we call it an "analog.")

Christians insisted that the Jewish god Jehovah was not the cosmic God. Salvation arose from the Love of God alone, not from obedience to rules and religion. We are saved by "love plus nothing." (They called this teaching *charis* (Greek), or "grace." Later Christian writers, such as Thomas Aquinas, Augustine, and St. Catherine, were grace-obsessed.) Grace was the very crux of the Christian message, its nucleus or core.

"Jews" symbolize thoughts that seek to honor and worship God. They also symbolize harmony with legalistic rules. But these are misled. For, in the first century, Christian writers believed that Judaism, while good, was nevertheless a "false religion." Jews of that time-period were corrupted with pride in the delusion that they were specially "chosen" by their god Jehovah, and hence, superior. They considered their god to be their personal possession.

So, the symbolism of "Jews" is complex. They are thoughts with good and positive motives. In fact, they are *all thoughts in harmony with the good rules, laws, and regulations of religion.* But even they are misled, having fallen for the lies of religion rather than reaching for the more profound and difficult spirituality. Thoughts that pretend to be Jews, then, are those which, with the best of intentions, do not lead people even as far as religion.

If the Jews missed the entire point of grace, and they had, those who "say that they themselves are Jews" would be even less spiritual! These would be thoughts without even good intentions. Religion can be good, *if it is a step towards spirituality.* But, as an end in itself, it can be lousy. For it leads to only arrogance and pride. These thoughts claim to know God, but they do not. So, these represent sheerly intellectual "understandings" of God. But of course, *God belongs to no particular religion or culture.* He/She is by definition universal.

[When Jesus presented a universal God for all people, this went far beyond the abilities of the traditional Jews to conceive. For, since ancient times, gods had been the exclusive possessions of nation states. These tribal and primitive communities too often played the silly, childish game, "My god is bigger than your god," or even, "My god can beat up your god." This horrific misunderstanding of the definition of "God" resulted in vicious violence. Each culture or nation thought it was a divine mission to cut the throats of others. Each tiny nation in the Middle East was a "theocracy," ruled by priests, religion, and temples.

Each microgovernment honestly felt that its king was a god, or a representative of a god. The healthy concept of church-state separation never occurred to these ancients. Most gods were the bloodiest war-gods. Despite our mountains of prejudice and historical bigotry, the god of Israel was no exception. In the Hebrew Scriptures, this god was vicious and merciless against "his enemies," and *almost everyone* was his enemy! It was he, Jehovah, who actually *ordered warfare,* and he who *ordered the unfeeling slaughter of women and children.* Many Christians and Jews in the modern world are still locked into the worship of this monstrosity of a god. This is the source of so much modern religious schizophrenia!]

Beliefs that you have the whole "truth" are hopelessly unrealistic. They mark only the unthinking fundamentalist, of Judaism, Islam, or Christianity. They reflect the bold but brash arrogance that you fully understand Reality in its bottomless depths. Mechanical ways, obeying and following sacred books, *can never make you a microparticle more spiritual!* (This was the essence of Paul to the Galatians, in the Christian Scriptures.) This mindset is a pathetic substitute for certainty in the midst of an infinite universe. Usually, it expresses as dogmatism. It is the arrogance to claim that you actually possess all the answers, and that they are all "right," all the time! Of course, this is incredibly unrealistic, not to mention hopelessly selfinflated.

Mechanical, legalistic thinking sets up an antiagapic (counter-Love) system of fear. It is organized and complex. It is likely to express itself in formal religious systems or organizations, theologies and beliefs. This fearsystem is supportive of fearmind or satanmind ("synagogue of satan").

Verse 10. "Do not fear the things that you are about to suffer. Look! The devil is about to throw [some] of you into prison, so that you might be tested. You will have tribulations for ten days. Become faithful until death, and I shall give you the crown of life."

COMM: The Soul is bluntly, harshly honest. The Way is not all peace and roses. The spiritual apex is bliss, but getting to the top of Bliss Mountain requires walking barefoot over jagged rocks and searing volcanic lava. What is the solution? Become fearfree! ("Do not fear...").

The "devil" is fearnature. Cast it out! This ultimate exorcism frees you! Fear is utterly deadly to Love. Its lethality is fear's absence of faith.

The root of faith is perfect relaxation. It is the unshakable conviction that Love is in ultimate control of everything. This is most tested when very "bad" things happen to very good people. Fear totally restricts. It petrifies. It paralyzes. It stagnates. It kills.

Love requires a free Mindflow. It requires some trust, some relaxation. This demands belief in the invisible, in the Power of the deepest Unconscious.

Fear rips away your sacred freedom ("prison"). This is just a stress-trial ("test"). Its purpose is not to wreck you, to crush and shatter you irrevocably. It is to try the strength of the surrendermind. The fearmind includes sadness ("Smyrna").

Although an ecclesia (holy Mindarea), Smyrna is temporarily in bondage to illusion. That is why it is sadness. "Satan" (fearmind) has it locked firmly within its iron grip. It must suffer until it finds total freedom in earthly enlightenment ("ten"). Its agony is time-limited ("days"). It will not last forever. For the only timeless Mind is the Soul; and this sadness strikes only the shallow mind. This is that of the spacetime world. It is egomind. It is illusionmind! Suffering-time will be neither too long nor too short.

When the personal egoself is loyal ("faithful") until its spiritual extinction ("death"), the reward for the deeper Mind is true spiritual life.

This is a life of Power ("authority"). This is due to conscious Union with Lovemind, blossoming in eternal bliss. This can come only after egodeath. So, this verse is a prophecy about the state of unbroken bliss still to come.

Full Mindcontrol ("crown") is granted Soulmind after Its victory over fearmind. Still later, this "crown" will be turned over to Lovemind. Enlightenment fully blossoms only with the complete opening and activation of the "crown" chakra. (This is the energycenter at the top of the head.) This is full awakening, complete enlightenment.

Verse 11. "The one having an ear, let him hear what the Spirit is saying to the ekklesias: 'The one who does conquer should not be harmed by his second death.'"

COMM: Egomind is killed ("conquered") by Soulmind. It perishes into the higher Self, without a trace. This is the "first death." It implies a "second death." This death is positive and constructive ("not be harmed"). This "second death" is the end of hypersensual dominance.

In fact, this first death is a real blessing. For the awakening that follows this death is the direct knowing (gnosis) of the Self as deeper Mind (Soul).

The second death is a higher Mindprocess. It is the death of deeper Self (Soul) into deepest Self (Spirit, God). It is a resurrection. You come to know your Self as deepest Mind. This "death" is actually a deeper life!

Verse 12. "And to the angel of the ekklesia in Pergamum write: 'But the things which the one is saying who has the long sword of two mouths, the sharp [one]...'"

COMM: Here, Mind warns against the dangerous-looking Being (Soul) addressing the rational intellect ("Pergamum"). His expression ("mouth") feels perilous, full of hidden, bloody conflict ("sword"). Horrific oppositions verging on insanity are threatened by dualism ("two"). Trouble looms on the mental horizon.

For the Soul is very advanced, but not perfect. Indeed, some Souls have been locked into the *maya* of "separation" from Mind (dualism) for centuries! This worldview is catastrophically reflected in the rational mind ("Pergamum").

Verse 13. "I have known where you are dwelling, where [is] the throne of satan. Yet you are holding My name. You did not deny My faith in the days of Antipas, My testifier, My faithful one, killed beside you, where satan is dwelling."

COMM: Logical mind ("Pergamum") staggers and vacillates when hit by fear ("satan"). Many fears are cleverly disguised as "reasonable cautions." So, logical mind is the logical place for fear to establish a foothold. Its goal is mindcontrol ("throne of satan"). (This "fear" is often mere uncertainty.) Logicmind pendulums between Love and fear.

Soulspirit is familiar with ("I have known") its methods. Love is not a fully conscious activity. So, logicmind cannot reciprocate: Love is far beyond the control ("kingdom") of logicmind. So, at this point, mind receives love from God (universal Lovemind) but cannot love fully in return.

Knowing (gnosis) produces Love. It does not flower from logical thought. Only fears do. Such psychogames as, "What if...?" multiply the fears. They always present themselves as protective. They pretend to be even spiritual. Logicmind, then, can support fearmind. It can lie, and, lost in the fog of illusion, give fear a "logical matrix." It says, "You'd be nuts if you were *not* afraid in this circumstance. Fear is only natural, and logical."

Still, the Mind, deep down, retains Its knowing that it is Christmind. This realization remains in the deepest Unconscious, Lovemind. There, It always knows Its truest identity ("holding My name"; "name"=identity).

Logicmind falls for the tricks of fear. But it does not become fully enmeshed in them. So, it retains the Power to resist and reject fear. It need not reject the idea that a greater Mind runs the whole show ("deny My faith"). "Faith" is relaxation. It is knowing that you do not have to control the cosmos. For that "job is already taken." The cosmic, everlasting, bottomless Lovemind already does that. It works its magic subtly, invisibly, through the Unconscious.

Simply trusting that this is so ("faith") is not any more cogitative or conscious than Love. It is an entire change of attitude and approach, not a conscious attempt to force or trick yourself into believing something. Like the birds, flowers, and nursing infants-- all three recommended as models by Jesus-- faith is "acognitive." It is simple being. It is free of most conscious thought, and hence, it is free from all worry and other fears.

The entire mind that exercises this simple trust ("faithful") lives in acognitive relaxation. There is another part of your mind ("testifier") that explains all this so that you can know it consciously, using only logicmind ("Pergamum").

The "faithful" and the "testifier," are alternative names for Christ-supporting thoughts. The testifier is also a part of the Mind that observes and records everything. In its depths, it is one with It. This same group of thoughtfeelings is also called "Antipas."

"Antipas" is a shortened form of "Antipater." This means "against the father." These positive, enlightened thoughts deny that God is a literal "father in the sky." So, "Antipas" is the whole collection of thoughtideas that deny the Jehovah-myth of an "external" god. Antipater-mind is repulsed by the archaic primitivity of a violent wargod! Antipater-mind recognizes, and insists, that God is Love!

The idea of the Supreme Principle of the cosmos being a childish "big daddy" is illogical. Still, the mind goes through a temporary phase: After denying the literal "parenthood" of an anthropomorphic "father," it begins to doubt. For a time, it might even deny the existence of any supreme Principle or ultimate Reality, any Absolute. This atheistic phase throws the mind into increased panic-- more fear.

So, "Antipas" is deactivated, or forced into the Unconscious ("killed") for awhile, from fear. This fear is never far from any of us ("beside you, where satan is dwelling"). Why?

Because, as children, we were reared with the very comfortable, extremely attractive lie that "God" was indeed a literal "father" in the sky! We grew accustomed to this childish myth as children. As adults, our "inner children" still have an iron grip on the fairy-tale. It is excruciating to let go of this pleasing fantasy. We are so familiar with the idea, reinforced for millennia by the ignorant, that we cling like barnacles to the idea that God is indeed "out there," watching, and watching over, each of us. As the old song says "God is watching us... from a distance." We hypnotize ourselves even into the silly belief that if ever anything "bad" should threaten us, this external God will save us, maybe at the last minute.

This idea holds that God is some kind of "good guy," a cowboy with a white hat, or a great, caring cop, or a superhero who has allowed billions to suffer throughout history, but will never permit this to happen to "me." Can you see how miserably egocentric, and thus, antispiritual, is this greedy, selfish, fearbased view?

Objectively, this is obvious. Yet fear is so terribly powerful that, if we try to jettison this concept, we feel shaky, uncertain, and nervous. You long and yearn to believe that *you personally* are so very special that God will act interventionalistically to save you, despite the fact that this kind of "external" interference *never has occurred* within the millennia of reliable history.

Verse 14. "But I criticize a few things: You have among you ones who hold to the teachings of Baalim, who taught Balak, to throw a cause of falling in the sight of the sons of Israel-- to eat things sacrificed to idols and to commit fornication."

COMM: A story is recycled from the Hebrew Scriptures: Balak was an ancient but dull king of Moab. He hired a sorcerer named "Baalim" to curse the ancient Israelis. But by the magical spell of their god Jehovah, Baalim could only bless, not curse. So, "Baalim" represents the Mind's collection of antiagapic (counter-Love) thoughts and thoughtgroups. This part of mind is victim to superstition, and thus, to illusion.

Also, note: "Baalim" is a Hebrew word meaning "lords." It often referred to Middle Eastern gods other than Jehovah. All but Jehovah were regarded by the ancient Hebrews as "false gods," and hence, illusion and "evil." Baalim is an archetype of "evil."

"Balak" also represents "evil." But it's thoughts have greater influence. While Baalim contains hints or tints of the supernatural, and alien gods, Balak was a "king." So, Balak represents a controlling matrix-thought ("king"), guiding and influencing many others. Balak is the thought which recognizes anything but Lovemind as supreme. Other thoughts coalesce around it, and grow into ideas, until it has a personal inner "kingdom," consisting of thousands of thoughtideas.

"Balak" is the illusion that career, money, sports, religion, politics, or something else is the most important thing in life.

The "Baalim Balak complex" symbolizes all thoughts caught in illusion and ignorance. Hence, they are subject to the core-illusion that underlies all others. This is, of course, "separation" from Lovemind. (This is "dualism.")

Paul okayed the eating of foods sacrificed to idols ("meat"), although it was still disgusting. Symbolically, this "meat" is deactivated ('dead') animalthoughts. It was formerly funneled into naked, animal sex, territoriality, vicious brutality, rape, murder, and other "animal" behaviors. But now, it is all dead.

These are thoughtenergies which should have been devoted to Love. But they were wasted, instead, on false animal "gods"-- money, violence, greed, materialism, inappropriate lust, etc. To "eat" these is to absorb their toxicity into the mind-- a catastrophe!

The betrayal of Love ("fornication") is what this verse is all about. It is the most serious "sin." It is this against which we are being warned.

Verse 15. "So you also have those holding to the teachings of the Nicolaitians."

COMM: Sexual betrayal was justified, even celebrated, by the first-century cult called the "Nicolaitians." They, without an eye-blink, or a second of hesitation, betrayed Love! Most of us "commit" this "spiritual fornication" every day! This we do in ways both large and small, deliberately or inadvertently.

This is often supported by the cognitive logicmind ("Pergamum"). For the analytical mind is notorious for its ability to justify any behavior, no matter how despicable. (That is why the loserusers, the nazis, and witch-hunters of the Middle Ages, were able to convince themselves that they were "human," in the midst of subhuman, bestial atrocities.)

Mind fornicates in a plethora of other ways. How? By giving Love to money, fame, career, intellect, material things, religion, politics, or other "false gods."

Verse 16. "So, repent. If not, I am coming to you quickly, and I shall war with them in the long sword in My mouth."

COMM: This is no threat to war with "*you.*" So, Love has no bone to pick with the whole conscious mind. It is a warning about war ("sword") against "them." Egomind is just deluded, not evil. The mind is not Soul's enemy. Through ignorance, it is an arresting force. But there is a galaxy of difference between ignorance and voluntary evil.

Mind contains plethoras of "spaces," and is multi-leveled. (See "Chart of Mind.") Mindfunctions vary in strength and autonomy.

Christnature's only foe is fear-ignorance. Lovemind, expressed as Soul, threatens war against the "Baalim-Balak complex" (all deluded mind). It is wisdom against ignorance, light against darkness.

If the mind does not turn around from its selfcreated nightmares ("repent"), the consequences will be agonizing and terrible. It must knock itself out, work diligently, to discover clear truth (Reality). Soul threatens ferociously to turn against the ignorance-components of screwed-up egomind ("them").

It will viciously conflict ("war") with them ("in the long sword"). The division of the Mind's energies ("war") can rape and terrorize the whole conscious mind. This hideous conflict will be one of expression ("mouth"). It will be an interior "war" of thoughtexpressions. One Mindelement will bludgeon another. They will be mercilessly pitted against each other as a house divided. This is a war of angrily, fiercely polarized thoughts and ideas!

Verse 17. "The one who has an ear, let him hear what the Spirit is saying to the ekklesias: 'To the one who conquers I shall give hidden manna, and I shall give to him a white pebble, with a new name written on it, which no one knows but the one who receives it.'"

COMM: Dramatic victory over nightmarish slavery to fear is blissfully anticipated! Illusion is overcome ("conquered")! She who transcends the lower mind ("conquers") receives a gift from the deep Unconscious ("hidden"). What is the gift? It is spiritual, interior nourishment ("manna"). When she dives deeply into the ocean of Love, she imbibes its sweet nectar in secret. Like making Love, this feeding is very personal ("hidden").

Being "manna," it exudes from Love. Secreted by Lovemind, it is licked from the surface by conscious mind. The inner Spirit is made as ecstatic by her feeding as she is.

Although an inside job, it is neither a brainthing nor a product of emotive outburst. Mind is granted sweet purity ("white"). It is given a piece of the "Rock," or Christnature ("pebble"). The Soul is just beginning to realize its interior gemlike stainless condition-- that, through Love, it is one with Lovemind.

This is a tiny gift, only symbolic, to give a clue about Reality within. (Lovemind is the only Reality.) This "pebble" of graceful purity is only a token of things to come.

The compelling illusion is losing its grip over the mind. The mask or role of ego has begun to fade away. For the mind receives a new identity ("name"). The "new name" is the transformation from, "I am this egomind and this body," to, "I am a timeless, invisible, eternal Soulmind." This secret identity is sunk so deeply into the Unconscious, where it is guarded, that it is known only to the mind of the person ("one who receives it").

Verse 18. "'And to the angel in the ekklesia of Thyatira, write: "But the things that the son of God is saying, the one who has his eyes as flame, and feet like fine copper...""

COMM: Love-action ("Thyatira") is worship. For *every act of Love is adoration of Lovemind.* The Soul ("son of God") envelops a divine nature. The words remind us again of insight, resulting in understanding ("eyes"). This is discovered only through suffering ("flame"). Again, progress ("feet") occurs in stages. It forms within, through passing through phases and types of imperfect Love ("copper").

Verse 19. "I have known your works-- Love, faith, service, and endurance. And your later works were more than your first ones."

COMM: Beautiful Love-treasures appear. These jewels are: 1) supreme Mind ("Love"), 2) total relaxation into and trust in Love ("faith"), 3) compassion expressed by helping others ("service"), and 4) tenacity in continuing to do good ("endurance"). This kind of activity is *real worship*! True worship is not Bible-study, attending meetings or church-going, hymns, public prayers, or the "right" doctrinal beliefs. *Real worship is service* (Love).

Verse 20. "But I have against you that you are letting the woman Jezebel go [freely in your midst]. She calls herself a prophetess. She is teaching My slaves, and causing them to err, to commit fornication and to eat things sacrificed to idols."

COMM: The mind of dark perversions and degradation ("Jezebel") springs from abuse of hypersensuality-- complete tyranny by the senses. This drives mind to orgies of selfindulgence, making it sloppy and careless. It is teaching mind the same two errors as the "Nicolaitians": 1) Supporting "false gods" ("eat things sacrificed to idols"). This is assimilating unclean "meat." Meat is dead. So, the parts of mind that serve the gods of materialism, hypersensuality, ego, and fears are already dead. (Compare verse 14.) They are devoid of energy.

2) betraying Love ("fornication"). So, Jezebelmind resists the imperative of goodness. She is chaos and immorality. She is thought-aggregates that mislead other, Lovesupporting thoughts ("My slaves").

Astonishingly, even this horrific activity creates, not deliberate "evil," but error ("to err"). The mind is, again, more sick than voluntarily evil. For *true "evil" must be intentional.* It must not be simply psychopathology (mental illness or weakness). All evil cannot be explained away or denied as "illness," however, for this unhealthy extreme creates irresponsibility. Still, a great deal can be.

Jezebelmind is ostensibly in touch with Lovemind ("prophetess"). But its commission of gross errors betrays Love. So, acting against Love, it claims to serve Love! It is filled with rotten hypocrisy! When this is deliberate, it is arrogance and pomposity. (It can be even ego-obsession.) But even when it is inadvertent (selfdelusion), it drags mind down into the dark, murky, stinking, filthy depths of ignorance.

Verse 21. "And I gave her time so that she might repent, but she is not willing to repent of her fornication."

COMM: Jezebelmind thrives within the disgusting chambers of horror of satanmind. It clings to chaos and ignorance, even when Lovemind grants it time to heal. It stubbornly refuses to yield to the sweet nectar of Love.

Verse 22. "Look! I am throwing her into bed, and the ones committing adultery with her, into great trial, if they do not repent from her works."

COMM: Amazingly, "she" is not destroyed by Lovemind! In "his" great and tender mercy, "he" only forces her to rest ('throws her into bed')! Anger does not drive Lovemind, which is *always free of all anger*. Lovemind desires only the healing of Jezebelmind. For It wants her to integrate with the rest of peaceful Mind. It recognizes her valid need for rest, and seeks to accommodate her.

But she has already, sadly, infected other thought-groups. These will have to suffer ("trial") for having blindly followed their lusts, sexual and others. Their "error" was betrayal of Love ("fornication"). Whenever Love is voluntarily betrayed, cosmic Mindmechanisms guarantee suffering. This is not imposed by any "external" deity. It arises as nightmare within your own mind. And there is nowhere that you can possibly hide from your own mind. This is the unfolding of natural law, called "karma".

Lovemind does not slay Jezebelmind. Anger, ferocity, or humiliation will not facilitate recovery. But a period of rest ("bed"), an "inner vacation," might be just the ticket.

Verse 23. "And her children I will kill, and all the ekklesias will know that I am the One Who searches kidneys and hearts. And I shall give to each of you according to your works."

COMM: God does not prance and strut around, like the old archaic and primitive Jehovah, to impress trivial and petty Middle Eastern rulers. God is no pathetic Saddam! The people of Jehovah made him out to be a petulant, spoiled little dictator without much brainpower. This was the pattern of their kings, after all. Jehovah did a lot of peacocking and bragging! Why? Because his followers had no idea that the entire earth was but a dustmote in the galaxy, and the galaxy but a pebble in an infinite universe.

Jehovah, in pathetic bragging that he was more powerful than earthly kings, behaved like a toddler boasting that he is "smarter than the doggie." It is like a "pipsqueak" who compensates for his impotence by crushing ants! "I'm stronger than any ant," boasts the pathetic and sick self-hater.

But Jehovah is even more pathetic; he has to boast that he is "smarter/stronger than a dustmote."

Actions of the Lovegod are strikingly different: He/She alters psyche in mindboggling ways! He/She moves *only in Love*. Mind loves

Mind, in all Its structures ("hearts" and "kidneys": "Hearts" are emotional parts of mind, "kidneys" those which help purify the psyche.)

God, unlike Jehovah, is not interested in dazzling insignificant egocentrics with tricks! His/Her only interest is to prove to the holy mind ("ekklesias") that He/She cares for it, loves it deeply.

Jezebelmind has produced crazy, hateful, unruly thoughts/ideas ("children"). They are independent but severely arrested. The Soul deactivates ("kills") them.

Soul searches deepest thoughts. Each will receive 'according to its works.' (This is "intrapsychic" karma. Good thought creates good energy. Every "bad" thought engenders a counterproductive force. Cumulatively, these create inner states of "heaven" or "hell." And when you create heaven or hell, that is where you must "do time," until perfect justice and balance are fully satisfied.

Verse 24. "But I say to you, to the ones left over, to the ones in Thyatira not having this teaching, who never knew the deep things of satan, as they say. I am not throwing upon you another heavy burden."

COMM: Much of intellect is diseased and infected by the boils and sores of Jezebelmind. But not the whole Love-actionmind ("Thyatira"; ones left over"). Jezebelmind is terrified, filthy, degraded, and perverse ("deep things of satan")! 'She' is a subsystem within "satanmind" (fearmind).

Lovemind, and Soulmind, both want Jezebelmind to turn around, and away from her ignorance ('repent'). But the Soul does not want to overload ("burden") mind with too much input.

Verse 25. "Hold on until I come."

COMM: Intellect hangs on to its brightest ideas. This is what Soul commands. It will have to hang in there until the Soul flashes up like a supernova into the mind. This occurs the moment that you realize that, in the deep Unconscious, there does exist a Soul.

Verse 26. "And to the one conquering and observing My works to the end, I shall give authority upon the nations."

COMM: The mind will completely overcome ("conquer") the foul, disgusting, repellant darkness of fearnature, including Jezebelmind. This it will do with the kind, friendly aid of the Soul within it. Then mind will study ("observe") the lovely, enticing, compelling Soul

("My works"). This it will do until the ego is, in time, gulped up by the Soul ("the end").

The sense-dominated (hypersensual; "earthly") mind merges with, slips into, Soulmind. This is implied by rulership ("authority") given the Soul over large thoughtgroups ("nations"). (Later, Soul will slip into Spirit; see "Chart of Mind.") The mind here becomes Soul.

Verse 27. "And he will shepherd them in a staff made of iron, as the vessels of potter's clay are broken, as I have received beside My Father."

COMM: Mind merges with Soul. Soul begins rulership, but mind also tenderly directs ("shepherds"). It starts with the gentle thoughts of selfsurrender ('sheep,' implied). Thoughts are gently oriented towards surrender.

This is tender and soft. But its boundaries are strong and firm, appealing to the undeveloped (toddler-mind; "in a staff made of iron"). Thoughts that unite hypersensual mind with deepest Mind ("staff") begin to draw mind upward. In time, this leads to Fusion, (the vertical "staff").

Supreme Mind uses thoughts of 'toddlermind' ("iron") to nudge the mind towards Union. ("Iron" is the lower metal in the hierarchy of mental states. Starting from the lowest, these states are:

clay
iron
copper
silver
gold

A mindstate below "iron" is the primitive state of mind ("clay") that exists *before* the Journey inward even begins. It includes *all sense-dominated thought.* ("Adam" means "red clay.")

The very first step in spiritual growth is to shatter primitive, "earthly," sense-dominated, or materialistic ideas. ("Clay" is "broken.")

Verse 28. "And I shall give to him the morning star."

COMM: Mind is on the threshold of Lovelight's dawn. The illuminative process that begins very early ("morning star") appears at the start of the inward Journey. It is a collective name for the beginning phases of illumination. (In Zen, lesser enlightenment experiences, preceding *satori*, are called *ken sho*.) Many of the "morning star" transformations occur in the Unconscious, even the subconscious. These are areas that are naturally "dark" (unconscious, outside the "light" of awareness).

Verse 29. "The one who has an ear, let him hear what the Spirit is saying to the ekklesias."

<h1 align="center">Chapter 3</h1>

Verse 1. "And to the angel of the ekklesia in Sardis, write: 'These are what is said by the one who has the seven spirits of God and the seven stars: "I have known your works, that you have the name. You are alive, but dead.'"

COMM: Stable, beautiful thoughts ("Sardis") share identity with the Soul ("have" Its "name"). For convenient shorthand, we will refer to Sardismind as "beautymind," for it is the part of mind that cultivates deep appreciation for spiritual beauty. (Arguably, all that is spiritual is beautiful, and vice-versa.) Beautymind originates with deeper Mind-- Soul, or even Spirit. Concepts of beauty ("Sardis") are deactivated ("dead"), from the egoview. They have sunk below the horizon of perception, into the deep Unconscious (Soul). The ego does not know that this magnificent pool of lovely thought even exists.

Still, beautymind is active ("alive") and well within the Soul. The platonic adage reminds us, "Truth is beauty, and beauty, truth." Beautymind supports all that is good, beautiful, and true.

Verse 2. "Become and stay awake. Fix firmly the things left over, which were about to die. For I have not found your works fulfilled in the sight of My God."

COMM: Beautymind ("Sardis") is on the right track. But it's just getting ready to plunge into the deep sleep-hypnosis of captivating illusion. It must avoid like the plague all lassitude, laziness, apathy, or complacency.

Dynamic, health-giving, lifenhancing Mind ("the things left over")[26], those that reflect Lovemind, are on the threshold of falling into semi-permanent inactivity ("dying").

These positive thoughtgroups (within beautymind) need to be empowered, infused with divine Love. The Soul must complete its Jour-

---

[26] These were "left over" from the "death" of the previous verse. They have survived as "living" thoughts, but are themselves, we are warned, about to "die."

ney to the Center.[27] Soul must become brightly aware ("awake") of the condition of the whole vast mind. It dare not be neutral, but must come into Love and passion for healing and wholeness. It still has a hole in it. Beautymind, within Soul and mind, is not yet complete ("fulfilled").

The mind is seen, analyzed, and evaluated by perfect standards. For it is measured by Lovemind Itself ("in the sight of My God").

Verse 3. "Keep in your mind, therefore, how you have received and heard. Keep [what you have,] and repent. If ever, therefore, you should not keep awake, I shall come as a thief, and you will not even know at what hour I come upon you."

COMM: It's all about 'keeping in mind.' Beautymind ("sardis") has already understood ("heard") many exciting, spectacular truths about bottomless Lightmind (Lovemind). Soul criticizes only its smug selfsatisfaction. It takes for granted progress that it has already got under its belt. For beautymind, these exciting, spectacular sacred aspects might be a big snore, a major yawn!

For when God-- bright, warm, immeasurable Love-- dawns upon the mind, It can be very subtle, more like the touch of a feather than the wallop of a sledge-hammer ("as a thief")! Transformation into the mirror of Lightmind is gradual. Soul ascends to cognition, floating up from the warm depths of Mindocean. In its quiet imperceptibility, it is indetectable. In fact, most of the work of the Soul is entirely unconscious. You cannot get any more silent than that! All the stuff that really counts doesn't even need "you" for it to occur. (Real spiritual growth can occur while "you" are asleep, in dreams.) Much also occurs during meditation which is a Way of tapping this unconscious Mind. So, if the mind isn't alert, its most important transformations occur "without it." The Unconscious says, "All the exciting stuff happened while you were gone!"

This forces a strangle-hold on your Lovexpression. For this divides the psyche. Ego goes one way, Soul the other! The ego, not getting any credit, and not even knowing what is going on, is sure that it wants no part of spiritual growth. It thrives on fear and Love is lethality. It knows that this development is lethal to it, and it goes to extremes to

---

[27] For more information on this complex inner voyage see my *Journey to the Center of the Soul: Mysticism Made Simple*, op. cit.

avoid and resist it! Also, ego asks, What good is it? The splitting of Mind into unconscious worker and conscious analyzer dilutes Lovexpression.

And "you" are not certain even which mind is "you." You still bounce back and forth maddeningly between the old egoname, and the new Soulname.

Verse 4. "But you do have a few names in Sardis which have not polluted their outer garments. And they will walk about with Me in white ones. For they are worthy."

COMM: Selfimage ("outer garment") reflects truer, deeper Mind ("with Me in white...").

Beautymind ("Sardis") enfolds several mental sub-identities ("names"). You can be wife, mother, aunt, and sister. These are "sub-identities." Each is accurate. Analogously, any Mindarea, in this complexity, can be viewed from many angles.

One person is many. And one Mindsector has more than one identity. Beautymind has subsystems that are uncontaminated ("not polluted"). Only a small part is stained by fearmind.

But if you are stained within, it will dirty your whole apparent selfimage ("outer garment"). Pretending to be "holy" does not make you any better. The preacher who dresses in only white, continuously quotes the Bible, and always has "Jesus" on his lips, slips away after the service to find the whore. Or he forms a secret liaison with a young, healthy, pretty girl whose physical charms have captured not necessarily his heart. "Outer righteousness" can be worthless, only a game. But real purity cannot be faked.

Mind possesses thoughtideas of true cleanness. As a reward, the mind will be provided with a new selfimage ("garments") of stainless purity ("white"). It will move in resonant harmony ("walk") with the Soul ("with Me"). So, it will know joy and peace, or bliss and tranquility.

Verse 5. "The one conquering thus will throw about himself white outer garments, and I shall not wipe out his name from the book of life. But I shall confess his name in the sight of My father, and in the sight of his angels."

COMM: Selfimage is pure ("white"); Mind is pure. As awareness of your secret identity, as Soul, grows, naturally your selfimage will become one of great pristinity. Here, the Soul says "I am this person and this person is Me" ("I shall confess his name...")

Soulmind promises to retain the memory ("book") of personal activities ("life"). Thus, the Soul is enriched when It incorporates the ego within Itself. In this context, ego is not the "enemy," but a teacher and a gatherer of experience. *Ego is the part of Soul that learns.*

Identity ("name") is unconscious. For the conscious ego is only a tiny part of total identity. *Most of your identity,* most of who you are, is submerged in the deep sea of the Unconscious mind. Your Soul is much more of your *true* identity than your ego (social self, social name). Mind rockets from egomind into Soulmind. It is blasted out of the old straitjacket of ego into another identity ("new name"). This identity is much vaster, freer, and more glorious.

The Soulmind recognizes the Soulminds within others. The mind has risen above its lower nature-- slavery to the senses, and to ego ("conquering").

It has run ahead of hallucinatory identities. These lies are, "I am my body," and, "I am my mind," and "I am Mary Smith." It has bolted and shot ahead in the spiritual race, to, "I am a timeless, deathless Soul." And, "I am a nonphysical Soulmind." It has undergone an amazing spiritual transfiguration. It acknowledges ("confesses") Its new identity before Lovemind ("father"). Other spiritual Mindareas ("angels") also validate this new identity.

Verse 6. "The one who has an ear, let him hear what the Spirit is saying to the ekklesias."

Verse 7. "And to the angel of the ekklesia in Philadelphia, write: 'But the holy One, the truthful One, the one who has the key of David, the one opening what no one can close, the one who can close so that no one can open, is saying...'"

COMM: Brotherlylovemind ("Philadelphia") is a major power within Soul ("holy One"). This Soul arises from Spirit, Reality, and so, is real ("truthful"). It is more real than egomind.

The wisdom/understanding of the conscious mind ("key of David") is tested. ("David," like "John," means "beloved." So, "David" is "John." Both symbolize the conscious mind.)

The understanding ("key") to access ("open") or de-energize ("close") the Unconscious belongs to Soul. Why is this, then, the "key of David"? Because it is the *conscious mind* that must take in, and learn, new knowledge, and use it to unlock the secrets. For *the conscious mind is the instrument of Soul's growth.* It is the lens through which Soul studies the world, and learns from the cosmos. So real spiritual development is *a dance between mind and Soul.*

If unconscious mysteries are to be unraveled, the mind requires the Soul's cooperation to gain access. When you have seen something within, it can never be "unseen," and when you know, there is no way to "unknow." So the "open" remains that way, and so can the "closed." Thoughtstructures used to penetrate into the Unconscious ("keys") include wisdom, understanding, and, most important, voluntary Love.

Love is especially crucial for "Philadelphiamind." For its very nature, essence, and substance are Love. This results in cognitive recognition and further exploration.

Verse 8. "I have known your works. Look! I have given in your sight a door, which is open, and no one can shut it up. This gives you a little power. For you observed My Logos, and did not deny My name."

COMM: Mysterious, frightening access ("door") to the Unconscious is opened. The mind trembles in terror; here there be tigers and dragons. The mind moves slowly, with trepidation and reluctance. This passage ("door") to a new Mindarea leads into the deep caves and oceans of Mind. The exploration of Mind has just begun!

An open entry, it beckons the conscious mind to take the plunge! It wants the mind to become a "psychonaut," (explorer of inner space). Christ said similarly in Jesus, "I am the door." (John 10:9) This open door leads to a hall that drops away, letting the mind freefall into limitless Mind (Spirit). Thus do the enlightened "fall in Love" with the cosmos.

The mind is swamped by cascades of sheer, intense Power. It is as if a thousand galaxies had gone supernova within. Mind is able to use only a tiny quantity ("little") of gnosispower.

The mind becomes aware of the Unconscious. The process is irreversible ("no one can shut it up").

Brotherlylovemind studied ("observed") the Logos, the perfect expression of God (Love) within deeper Mind (Soul). We will see later (19:13-15) that the Logos *is* the Soul! Both are roles of deepest Mind (Spirit). The ultimate goal of brotherlylovemind is imitation. It did not reject ("deny") its deepest, truest identity ("My name"). It joyfully embraced the deep identity of Soul with Lovemind (Spirit). More technically, on its human (earthly) side, the Soul is the deepest area of the human mind, but on Its spiritual (heavenly) side, it is the "lower" octave of Spirit. Thus, it is a bridge that links God with humanity. It spans the apparent "abyss" between the "two." It fuses them into oneness. Brotherlylovemind says, "In my truest identity, I am not just Jason or Tom (or Andrea or Michelle), but the timeless Soul unified with perfect Spirit. I am Love incarnate."

Verse 9. "Look! I am giving from the synagogue of satan the ones saying that they are Jews. But they are not. They are lying. Look! I will make them come and do obeisance at your feet. They should know that I loved you."

COMM: The "false Jews" are thoughts that wish to honor God. They have the very best of intentions. But they are unbalanced and confused, bewildered and baffled. They live in agonizing ignorance (duality). So, they are committed to the lie that God "belongs" to them. They also buy into the lie that God has anything to do with mechanical religion. These thoughts are low-end "righteous," in harmony with religious law, but not in alignment with Lovemind. (That's "high-end righteous.") This is true goodness while "righteousness" is only mechanical or ritualistic. But God is repelled by religion as mere ritual.

These ideas felt smugly above the rest of Mind. They are anti-agapic. These demonic ideas trigger insecurity, a virulent form of fear. They serve fearmind (satanmind; "the synagogue of satan").

They infect the minds of those who prance and strut. They mark religious leaders who selfdisplay. Selfdisplay leads to selfdestruct. This is the plague of unrestrained, shameless ego. It glories in accepting special honors from others, adopting special titles and garb. It is the hypocrisy of "serving" without humility-- a clear impossibility.

This religious disease makes people pompous and arrogant. They pontificate, making peacocking fools of themselves.

Enlightenment is deadly to pretensions. With the bright dawning of Love, they fall away like the scabs of old boils. As mind progresses, these ideas will submit themselves to Lovemind. These will then be the pure, wise, agapocentric (Love-centered) and agapogenic (Love-creating) thoughtideas of the Soul purified. Mind gives in, yielding to, respecting the Soul ("doing obeisance") and making real progress ("at the feet'; compare 1:13). The Soul loves the conscious mind. It will be able to share even more Love with the purified mind.

Verse 10. "Because you observed the Logos of My endurance I shall observe you during your hour of temptation. It is coming upon the whole inhabited earth, to tempt the ones inhabiting the earth."

COMM: Exquisitely tender and impressionable, brotherlylovemind is exposed to the gigantic force of a thousand suns, the inner immeasurable Logos! It is forever and very deeply imprinted! It then bears the unutterable likeness of Lightbeing!

Brotherlylovemind carefully studied ("observed") the strong tenacity and durable strength ("endurance") of the Logos. It was mindboggled by what it saw! Like an admiring youngster, it wanted to be "just like" the Logos. As mind, it wanted to imitate Soul.

This Logos makes mind surprisingly, astonishingly strong. So mind will reform itself into the reflective, symmetric image of Light and Power. This it will accomplish by discovery, and with open, honest humility. Brotherlylovemind will evolve towards fullest realization of pure Lovemind. (It is already Its subsystem.) The observation is reciprocal: As mind observes Soul, Soul observes mind.

The transcendence of hypersensual, sense-dominated, egoic desires ("temptations") will require this strength. A test or exam is coming soon upon the entire sense-dominated (bionatural) mind ("inhabited earth"). ["Nations" (compare 2:26) are large thoughtgroups. So, it is consistent to see the "inhabited earth" as hypersensual, sense-dominated mind.]

Just a peripheral re mindlevels: This "let's get physical" approach of hypersensual mind is not as low as you can go! Animalnature ("let's get animal") is lower. Both are "low" on the "totempole" of Mind. But to be biological, sexual, or sensual is not "bad" or "evil." For the sensual/sexual also has its real and sacred place in Love. But the wise, and civilized, does not descend to the "animal." A highly sensual painter or lover, for example, need possess none of the lowest biocharacteristics. She does not have to be greedy, hypersexual, territorial, dirty, belligerent, etc. True, bionature ("earth") is the hypersensual, including the sexual. It is unenlightened. But it still can lack the savagery and brutality implied by animalmind. So, hypersensual mind ("earthly") lies just between animalmind and humanmind (intellect). Here is how various Mindlevels compare (starting with highest):

Spiritmind (Love)
Soulmind
Humanmind (intellect)
hypersensual, sense-dominated mind
Animalmind

A "hierarchy" exists among various Mindlevels. This is the metaphor of "height." (It is the "reverse" of that of "depth.") (Compare "Chart of Mind.")

Verse 11. "I am coming quickly. Hold fast to what you have, so that no one can take your crown."

COMM: Self is Soul, not body. Sexuality ceases to be a master with a whip, and becomes instead a pliable smiling servant. The same amazing transfiguration occurs with all the other sensual appetites. Soul floats up into conscious awareness ("I am coming"). This can occur quite rapidly, almost instantly ("quickly").

But so can its opposite: The leadership authority ("crown") of Soul can be distracted. This is destruction by distraction. Then the "crown" is "taken" from Soulmind and given to egomind. The results are catastrophic! Ego turns to "false gods." These illusion-deities are hypersensuality or materiality. Both are stripped of spirituality.

Verse 12. "'The one conquering I will make a pillar in the divine habitation of My God. And he will not go outside. I will write upon him the name of My God, and the name of the city of My God. [This is] New Jerusalem, the one stepping down out of heaven from My God and from My new name.'"

COMM: A "Mindarea" is a theme-related thoughtgroup. The one that holds Lovemind in its "nest" is also Lovemind! Love lives in Love ("divine habitation")! All areas (subject-related thoughtgroups) in which God dwells become God. When touched by the flame of Love, each Mindarea is ignited, until the whole Mind is alight with one single fire! That is Love (God)!

God is the temple. Lovemind (God) is also "heaven." It is also all areas of Mind in which It dwells. It is also Coremind, Spirit, Absolute, God, Tao, Brahman, Christnature, Christspirit, Holy Spirit, Buddhamind, etc. It is the deepest level of the Unconscious. So, "temple"=God=Lovemind=heaven=Christmind=Spirit=deepest Unconscious.

To be a support of the "temple" ("pillar") is to have found Union with Lovemind. It is to uphold the Love-agenda by thoughts, words, and actions. Everything in Mind that supports Lovemind ("pillar") starts to become your new identity.

The story is told of a master sculptor whose next project was to carve an elephant out of a massive block of marble. Someone in the admiring crowd, watching him work, asked the sculptor, "How do you carve an elephant out of that big block of marble?"

"Simple," he replied. "I just chip away everything that is not 'elephant,' and what is left is 'elephant.'"

This is your assignment: Go into mind and delete ("chip away") everything that is not Love (God). Do this assiduously, tenaciously, continually and repeatedly. In time, all that will be left will be Love (God).

During gnosis, the mind is overwhelmed with ecstasy and bliss. It experiences oceanic tranquility, bottomless serenity. It does not even want to leave ("go out" from) this inner sanctuary.

It spends as much time as possible in that delicious altered state! It loves its deep plunge, up to its neck, in the waters of sweetest Mind! It finds this deepest Mind a great Source of comfort, warmth, satisfaction, and bliss!

Retreats attract during intense periods of growth. Some people even give up greedbased careers. For no other pleasure in the cosmos comes even close to Lovebased ecstasy!

At its ultimate zenith, the identity ("name") of God is recalled from deepest, unconscious memory ("written") by Soulmind. The central memory is the central mystery: You are truly Lovemind in incarnation! This is mindazzling! Your truest identity is God! God is the Mind which has always been "playing" the role of your Soul, which has, in turn, "played" the role of your ego. The Soulmind realizes that It exists "in" God. In nature, although not in totality, the Soulmind is God (Love).

Again, the Upanishads say that Atman (Soul) is Brahman (Spirit)! Scratch any Soul, and there is the Spirit! The Soul is an incarnation of Love.

The enlightened catches wondrous, mind-boggling psychedelic visions of her Soul! She recognizes how very complex, astonishingly interwoven, incredibly multiplex and interactive is its human configuration.

A human-engineered thoughtgroup ("city") is given order by design, and structure by intellect. [The organized and complex human-mind patterns ("city") comes straight out of Lovemind ("heaven").]

Lovemind gifts the conscious mind with intellect. It wants you to study It, learn about It! When mind is given the identity ("name") of the "city of My God," it knows its deeper identity: *It is itself this "city"!* That is, the conscious mind is, deep down, a much vaster Mind! It is the Soul! It is *a* direct emanation of perfect Mind. ("Heaven" is the Source of the city, and Lovemind is "heaven.")

Soul is given the identity ("name") of God. *It knows that it is God in nature.* Captivatingly, Soul is not said simply to have the holy Center within her. But it is actually identified as her secret identity ("name").

A meaning of "Jerusalem" is "Fountain of Peace." In the Enlightenment Tradition, the "Fountain" is God. A "fountain" produces Unconscious thought (water) directed into human-structured ideas. (Fountains are not natural things.) In Union, the mystic becomes the Origin of her own peace.

Peace flows from Lovemind. Spirit-Soul synergy produces tranquility. On Its heavenly side, Soul is God reaching down, but on its earthly side, It is the human mind, reaching up.

The mystic, after Soul-identification, is no longer a fragile material body, subject to death and decay. This remains, but it is only her instrument for dealing with the "material" world. She is now an invisible, invincible Mind, a Soulmind! She is intangible, timeless, untouched by death! Her body still suffers but she lives in perfect detachment[28] and peace. Compared with her human self (ego), the Soul is a dramatic Superbeing. This shift of identity is a vital step on the inward Journey. Because she receives a *single* "new name" from all of these, there must be a unity among these three. That is, God, Soul, and New Jerusalem must represent a cohesive "trinity" in which the three are one. For the mind identifies fully with all three. So, the textual evidence supports fully the oneness of "My God," "the city of My God," and "My new name." These three all symbolize cosmic Mind, at various levels, seen from different angles.

"My new name" is God realized within the Soul; "Jerusalem" is God known intellectually; and "my God" is Lovemind in and of Itself, in transcendental nature.

Verse 13. "'The one who has an ear, let him hear what the Spirit is saying to the ekklesias.'"

Verse 14. "'And to the angel of the ekklesia in Laodicea write: "The Amen, the Observer, the Faithful and True, the Beginning of the creation by God, is saying..."

COMM: Mental organization ("Laodicea") joins hands and hearts with Love! Between Lovemind and Its reflective expression (Logos), there is no practical distinction. They are in perfect, seamless harmony ("Amen"). And since Logos is also Soul (19:13-15), your Soul is nothing less than God (Lovemind)! Expressed in perfect mirror symmetry as interior Logos. It is the "first" of creation because God emanates the Soul before creating anything else in the cosmos. He/She uses that Soulmind to dream up the cosmos.

---

[28] For more information on healthy and balanced detachment, see my *Teflon Mind: Sex, Money, Life and Detachment* (Liberty Township, Ohio; Love Ministries, Inc., 2004).

Soul watches and notices everything ("Observer"). An important subset of Soul is "testifier" or "Observer". It studies the world through the eyes of the enlightened psyche. It notices and records all behaviors, and all intentions. Soulmind perfectly mirrors Lovemind ("faithful," as in a "faithful reproduction" of a painting). The Soul, perfectly embodying Spirit, is also Reality ("true").

It was the first of creation, in John 1:1. There, in the very beginning, It was Itself, as Logos, God. So, here again, we find the equation Mind=Soul=Spirit=God. It has come about, full-circle, and created cosmic closure. Its "end" is Its "beginning."

Verse 15. "I have known your works. You are neither cold nor hot. I possess [the idea that] you [should be] cold or hot."

COMM: The Soul is fiercely disturbed, upset with indecision! Organizationmind ("Laodicea") seeks never to make wrong decisions. So, it vacillates. It is too full of itself, too filled with ego selfconsciousness, to make any crystalclear decisions. It is paralyzed and petrified by fear. (Fearmind is satanmind.) What is this horrible, petrifying fear? It is very simple: The mind is afraid that it might be wrong!

The ability to make crystalclear decisions ("hot/cold" dichotomy) is missing. Laodiceamind lets the mind get away with too much. Its indecision results in weakened boundaries. This compromises it morally. When it is exposed to sexual temptation, for example, it will probably collapse and give in. For organizational skills do not provide barriers. (Compare Commentary on 3:17.)

Organizationmind is smart, but lacks common sense. (Not that there is anything common about "common sense.") It would rather stagnate in inactivity than take the chance of taking a wrong decision. This gray neutrality has left it unstimulating, unexciting, dull, and boring.

Verse 16. "Thus, because you are lukewarm, and neither hot nor cold, I am about to vomit you out of My mouth."

COMM: Organizationmind ("Laodicea") is within the Soul. For how could the Soul threaten to expel ("vomit... out") something that was not? It is not very deep in mind, for it is largely appropriated by the conscious mind. It is found in the *expression* of mind ("mouth"). The Soul is sickened by too much indecision ("lukewarm"). This is especially true in spiritual crises! But we need not swing to the other pendulum-extreme-- inflexible or dogmatic rigidity. That is just another sickness.

But we must decide clearly what works for ourselves, and have faith in that. We must then turn that conceptualization into an active life-pattern.

Verse 17. "Because you are saying, 'I am rich, and I need nothing.' But you have not known that you are miserable, pitiable, poor, blind, and naked."

COMM: Organizationmind ("Laodicea") is upside-down and backward. It is crushed under the laughable illusion that all that you need in life is good intellectual organization, and enough "stuff." (It is under the other hypnotic entrancement of material riches.) Because you are materially or mentally wealthy, ("rich") you can easily assume that you are completely without need.

But this is a lie from hell! The Soul knows your deep, dark secret: Beneath all the "abundance," you can be quite miserable. Material things have added not a nanogram to your inner joy. That is because

****

Changes in the "outer" world cannot create real changes in the inner Mind.

****

So, your wealth has not touched your inner sense of despair and futility. Deep down, you know that working for only material "goods" is "bad." It will bring you only dust and ashes. For that world is unstable and unreliable. Your real treasures, what you really yearn and long for, are the inner jewels of Love, joy, tranquility, bliss, and satisfaction.

Your fantasy that, when you became materially wealthy, you would be the object of envy and admiration, is shattered. For you, and all others, know that you are often desperately unhappy ("miserable").

Others pity you, as you do yourself ("pitiable"). In fact, you are caught in an obsessive-compulsive disorder in your "need" to cling to, accumulate, crave, acquire, collect, grasp, and attach your psyche to, material things. You have become the slave/addict of greed.

Your desire is so insatiable that, no matter how much you get, you see yourself as empty and in need. When it comes to the inner wealth, the "possessions" of a clear, compassionate Mind, you truly do find yourself in need ("poor").

This illusionbased lifestyle robs you of all insight and wisdom ("blind").

Your "external" wealth has made you spiritually barren and empty. You are horrified when beholding the desert of your inner self. You have made the tragic error of having invested all timenergy in the "outer, material" world. So, you have had nothing to put in your inner treasure-trove. It is a cold cave which contains only dust, which never sees the sunlight of Love. It is a desolate wasteland.

You are this way because you are spiritually lost. In your obsession with the "outer" world, you have failed to develop your inner senses. So, you cannot see even the bright "sun" at the Center of your being, Lovemind.

This has left you without any inner defenses ("naked") against the onslaughts of materialism and hypersensuality. You are openly vulnerable to the ignorance of dualism, for you have not a clue that Supermind even exists, and would never dream that It is your deepest Self.

Verse 18. "My counsel is to buy gold next to Me, refined by fire, so that you might become [truly] rich, and white outer garments to throw about yourself. Thus, the shame of your nakedness might not be manifest. And [buy] eye-salve to anoint in your eyes, so that you can look."

COMM: Earthly enlightenment ("gold") gleams with a priceless glow. Because it is Mindstuff, it is everlasting. But it can be obtained only when you are close to your Soul. The mind must give up something ("buy"). Cosmic currency is timenergy. Enlightenment does not just drop out of the sky, falling onto your lap or into your head. So, you are being called continuously, by your Soul, to spend timenergy, to make enlightenment your number one career.

You must use timenergy, tenacity, and strength, to prepare your mind. This is preparing the "Way of the Lord", through regular meditation. But, much more importantly, supreme Mind is touched by a regular and consistent practice of Love. *Only this preps the mind!*

It is not a Journey of great mental distance. Enlightenment is never far away ("next to me"). That is why it can occur in a flash. Eastern mystics say, "God is closer than the breath that you are now breathing in." Indeed, like your lungs themselves, It is within you.

This enlightenment ("gold") is made pure ("refined") only through suffering ("fire"). In ferocious lightning-storms of mind, Love must be held intact.

Then, true inner treasure will be genuine. Your life will overflow with the diamonds, emeralds, rubies, and sapphires of beautiful spirituality (Love). This will be the wealth of the psyche ("rich"). This will not be merely material baubles, shiny trinkets. Pretty, but petty, trivialities.

The Way recommended is the adoption of a stainless Selfimage ("white outer garments"). *This can appear through only good behavior!* It does not imply perfection, but the selflove of selforgiveness. It rises from a genuine selfacceptance deep in the Unconscious.

By sad contrast, the state of mind without awareness of purity ("shame") is common. It arises from a false sense of vulnerability and exposure to harmful forces ("nakedness").

Understanding through vision ("eyes"; insight) is linked with anointing. For "salve" is "ointment," which shares a root with "anointing." This is crucial. (The word for "anointed" in Greek is *khristos* or "Christ," a synonym for "enlightened.") So, you, too, can become a "Christ."

Granted that you might just only have begun the inner Journey, and might still be a "baby Buddha," or "toddler Christ." Still, your ultimate goal is not simply to admire, to adore, to worship the man Jesus, but to strive to become what he had become. He calls people to "follow" him, not to worship him. To be like Jesus is *not simply to use the name "Jesus" a lot; Jesus never used it in public teaching.* Instead, it is to strive for the Lovemind within. This is the most genuine, sincere Way to honor him.

The Mind's capacity for insight and Union ("eye-salve") produces wisdom. This is the ultimate solution to spiritual blindness: Union with the inner Christnature (human-divine interface). It is the place in deep Mind where the two natures meld, merge, blend, and fuse, becoming one single nature.

Verse 19. "I discipline and reprove as many as I have affection for. Become enthusiastic, therefore, and repent."

COMM: The mind gets screwed up in a thousand ways. Soul practices Mind-correction ("discipline and reproval"). But this is alien to technical motives of legalism. It has nothing to do with the shallow, fake mechanism of mere religion. It comes from true Love ("affection"). Lovemind actively dreams into your personal world all those "unpleasant" and "undesirable" factors that will boost your growth into Love!

Change ("repentance") is exciting! Mind should be thrilled by its prospect! Facing Love, you will become a mirror of Love! The perfect response to finding Lovemind within yourself is excitement and energy ("enthusiasm"; this word means, "God within")! Repentance is not to be done mechanically or dully. This spiritual renewal is to be celebrated bumptuously with vibrant, healthy singing, laughter, and action! It is the beginning of inner rebirth!

Verse 20. "Look! I have stood upon the door, and am knocking. If anyone should ever hear My voice and open the door, I will come toward him, and I will have supper with him, and he with Me."

COMM: In the Greek, the Soul does not stand "at" the "door," but "upon" it. That sounds like a tricky and dangerous balancing act! Why does Soul stand "upon" the "door"?

A portrait is "upon" a canvas. In the same way, the deeper Self (Soul) is "upon" the entry into deeper Mind ("door").

This is an equivalency of symbols. The Soul is superimposed upon the door. The Soul is the "door." You must pass *through* the Soul to get to deepest Mind (Lovemind). So, it is an almost literal passageway to the deepest Mind.

At its deepest Mindlevel, "Soul" is "Spirit." (See "Chart of Mind.") This Spirit, or Christ, said through Jesus, "I am the door." Soul is both: 1) welcomed into the conscious mind, and 2) the passage (from Unconscious to conscious). This "door" (Soul) has on its one side the mind and, on its other, Lovemind.

The "closed door" is created by the Soul. This is to test the mind. This testing occurs only until it is the proper time for that Mindoor to be opened. When it is, the Soul signals to the mind ("knocking"). It also then reveals contents of the Unconscious to the conscious mind.

When that door is opened, by mutual consent of conscious and Unconscious, the Soul enters, moving "towards" the mind. It enters the "space" of the mind. Bread is broken together between Soul and mind. (The word "companion" means literally, "bread with.") Spiritual nourishment ("supper") comes from the Soul. She is a "guest" who brings her own dinner. The Soul's "food" is shared with the mind.

Verse 21. "The one conquering I will permit to sit down with Me on My throne, [exactly] as I conquered and sat down with My father on his throne."

COMM: The destiny of mind blazes with glory and splendor. It is perfectly symmetric with, analogous to, the "glory" of the One. The Soul shares Lovemind ("throne") with mind. Sharing a "throne" is sharing also a single identity. Your secret identity is the same as the Soul's: You are the Lovemind in temporary manifestation. At its deepest level, mind is Soul, and at its deepest level, Soul is Lovemind (God). If mind is Soul, and Soul God, mind is the "Father" (Love). Mind is God in nature, in temporary incarnation. This is what the model Master Jesus meant by his enigmatic, "The Father and I are one." (Jn. 10:30)

Verse 22. "The one who has an ear, let him hear what the Spirit is saying to the ekklesias."

Chapter 4

Verse 1. "After these things, I saw, and look! A door was opened up in heaven, and the first voice that I heard was as a trumpet. It spoke with me, saying, 'Step up here, and I will show you the things that are bound to occur.'"

COMM: Mind opens widely, allowing insight ("saw") to flood in! Then, deeper understanding ("heard") mesmerizes it. The Soul ("door"; Compare 3:7,8.) lets mind slide down into deeper Mindlevels. The downward slope opens straight into Lovemind ("heaven")!

An ear-blasting ("trumpet"-like) signal ("voice") screams from the Unconscious. It stuns, and then, invites the mind. It calls it toward Lovemind ("step up"). This is to show the mind what is going to happen next in its spiritual development ("things which are bound to occur").

Verse 2. "Immediately, I came to be in Spirit. And look! A throne was sitting in heaven. And one sat upon the throne."

COMM: The entire rest of Revelation occurs in deeper Mind ("in Spirit"). The mind ("John") was in a profoundly altered state. It sank into a visionary consciousness, deep in Mind. Here, to be "in Spirit" was to be "in heaven." For "Spirit"="heaven"=deepest Unconscious=Lovemind=God. So, all authority over all Mind ("throne") is found in Lovemind ("heaven"). The mind ("John") ascended to the heights (descended to the depths) where mind interfaces with Spirit. The first thing that it saw was the controlcenter ("throne").

This psychocontrolpanel is Spirit (Lovemind, Coremind). It is supported by ("sits on") the "throne," and is that very same throne. (Here, then, three symbols share a trilaterality: God is "heaven," "throne," and "the One sitting on the throne.")

It is Power; It is Master of the psychocosmos, and so, Ruler of both mind and world.

Verse 3. "And the one sitting was like a jasper stone, and like sard, and a rainbow formed a circle around the throne, and it looked like an emerald."

COMM: Searing scarlet and crimson flood the vision. For jasper and sard are red stones. Red symbolizes basic bio-energy. It is the energy that an attacking leopard uses when it pounces upon hapless prey. In mind, it makes movement possible. It is "body-energy".

Thronemind is Lovemind, the Source of all energy. It feeds the body. But this energy is not paralyzed, stuck in this low ("jasper...sard"; red) energy state.

A prism splits sunlight into vivid rainbowcolors. Mindenergy also comes in a stunning spectrum of varieties. Like the sunlight, Mindlight is all one Light. But like sunlight, it can be subdivided into beautiful polychrome. This rainbow is the totality of Mindforces. It is a gorgeous, scintillating reflection of the seven colors of light.

Mind shines as the chakras of the human energy-system. The seven chakras regulate: 1) survival (red), 2) sexuality (orange), 3) intellect (yellow), 4) Love (green), 5) communication(blue), 6) insight (indigo), and 7) enlightenment (violet).

This rainbow is a "circle." Mind beams it in all directions. Since ancient times, the circle has symbolized infinity, eternity, or immeasurable Mind. The ancient winged disc of Assyria and Babylonia is still reflected in the wedding ring. Mind sends thoughtenergy into all the cosmos. This omnidirectionality is symbolized, in plane geometry, by the circle, and, in 3d, by the sphere. A rainbow coruscates with colors that are comparable to the energy-centers of the body (although these "spectrum 2 colors" are invisible to biological eyes): red, orange, yellow, green, blue, indigo (cobalt), and violet.

The fourth chakra, which regulates Love, is green ("emerald"). The whole rainbow is here suffused with and dominated by Love ("emerald"). Emerald is crystal. It is transmission of Lovelight without impediments or blockages. In Its utter lucidity, there are no opacities to cast shadows. This "emerald" is Love as a semi-permanent healing, altered state. It *modifies* Light, but it does not *block* It. Emerald is all factors that transform generic mindenergy into Lovenergy.

So, "emerald" is a state of perfect mental clarity that transmits pure, unimpeded Love. Love shines through stillmind or crystalmind. The mind, in clarity or lucidity, is completely transparent to its transmission into the world. Emerald is a variety of "crystalmind." This proves that "divine" Love is human Love.

The fourth chakra is the luminous green Lovecenter of the bodymind. God is Love. This reminds us that all the hellish events to come, in the darknights of the Soul, lead ultimately to serene Love.

Verse 4. "And in a circle around the throne are twenty-four thrones, and seated upon these thrones, I saw twenty-four old people, dressed in white outer garments and golden crowns."

COMM: Lovemind ("throne") is central to the celestial cosmos. Like the emerald-rainbow light, other thrones("24") are in a perfect pattern of cosmic emanation ("circle"). Circles remind us that *everything, in all universes,* emanates from the single Lovemind, the One. Circles tell us, through sacred archetypal geometry, that Mind radiates in all directions. This is called "cosmic omnidirectional emanation." Everything in Mind "orbits" Lovemind.

The symbolism of twenty-four can also represent twelve, the number of cosmic order, in two sections-- conscious and unconscious. (24=12x12)

Twenty-four equals two times two times two times three. So, the glorious Mindfusion of interior wholeness ("three") is discovered only after having passed through some hellish torments of dualism ("two"). And you must pass through these grueling states of ignorance more than once.

Experienced areas of Soulmind ("old persons") have been "around the block" a few times. They "know the score." Age has brought them wisdom. Many "old persons" come from the Soulmindlevel. They also help regulate the whole mind ("thrones"). (See "Chart of Mind.")

They have already been through the mill. Earthschool has been going on for centuries for some, millennia for others, perhaps eons for still others. They are older than the hills, older than dirt. Each has had some enlightenment. Each has been given some authority ("crowns") over the mind. Each contributes to a pure ("white") selfimage ("garments").

Verse 5. "And from the throne are coming out lightnings, voices, and thunders. And seven lamps of fire are burning in sight of the throne. These mean the seven spirits of God."

COMM: This is Control Central! It is both "throne" and the "One Who sits upon it." For both are Lovemind. Free, unbound mindenergy ("lightning"), inner communications ("voices"), and intuitions of coming psychic storms ("thunders") explode in this Controlcenter.

The Soul is on fire with Love. Spiritual ("seven") enlightenment ("lamps") comes through agony and suffering ("fire"). These sources of inner Light ("lamps") are spiritual Mindareas ("spirits").

Verse 6. "And in sight of the throne was a glassy sea like crystal. And in the midst of the throne and in a circle about the throne were four living creatures. They were full of eyes, in front and behind."

COMM: Mind beholds a beautiful Unconscious ("sea"). This one is like crystal. It is transparent ("glassy"). This is the lucid state of inner clarity, crystalmind, Stillmind. It is "acognitive" or thought-free. It permits Lovemind to come through the mind into the world without impedance. Lovelight shines through this silent, pristine Mindstate with no shadows. The mind is tranquil. It creates no personal thoughts as opacities to block the bright light of Love. This mystical, thought-free, still state is stillmind, or "crystalmind."

This "sea" is monitored by ("in sight of") the fathomless, immeasurable, exquisite Lovemind ("throne").

"Four living creatures" are in two places, and so, have two meanings:

1) In one cosmic perspective, they occupy the same place as Lovemind ("in the midst of the throne"). They are actually a part of God, inseparable from Lovemind ("throne"). They are four because they represent Mind potentially expressed in matter (solidarity; the four ancient "elements"). This is the interior unconscious world of "ideals" in which Mind forms the templates of what is later projected as matter (See below).These are in-sight ("eyes").

2) From another cosmic perspective, they are *emanations* ("in a circle around the throne"). These are divine Mind projected into the world (exteriorized). This is the emanated cosmos. So, they are that cosmic Mind expressed as matter. They are infinite God or Mind, but manifested finitely. They are God as the gurgling brook, the singing bird, the shining rainbow. They are God in the eyes of a puppy or kitten, or of your children, or of your lover.

They are four. This connects them archetypally with the four directions. This, in turn, links them with the equilateral cross-- also a symbol of the emanated "omnidirectional" cosmos. That cross predates Christianity by thousands of years. More dimensionally, the equilateral cross links up with the 3-d cross, whose six arms radiate into the four directions, but also up and down. Mind is the emanating Center where the six arms join, and so, is point seven.

The circle is the configuration that encompasses the 2-d cross. (The sphere imaginatively unites the six arms of the 3-d cross.) These symbols-- cross and circle-- unite. As the equilateral cross is within the circle, so the world ("four directions") is within the cosmic Mind.

Verse 7. "And the first living creature was like a lion, and the second like a young bull, and the third had a face as a man, and the fourth was like a flying eagle."

COMM: These Godcreatures are humandivine (intellect-Love) synergies. Each reflects Supernature. But, being "creatures" (animalforms), they also take their energy and some cues from animalmind. So, they are served by hypersensual (sense-dominated) mind or bionature.

In astropsychology, the animals are Leo, Taurus, Aquarius, and Scorpio. These symbolize particular qualities. The lion is ego, the bull determination, the man intellect, and the eagle farseeing vision.

These signs "square" each other, forming a "grand cross." This reinforces what has already been said about the equilateral cross. In fact, in an astrological diagram, this configuration, amazingly, forms an equilateral cross within a circle (cosmos within Mind).

But a "square", or "cross," in astropsychology, means trouble. Around the "throne" were intuitions of interior Mindstorms to come ("thunders"). The astrological cross is the same message: The spiritual path is not going to be all roses.

This equilateral cross is analogous to the *crux imissa* or "Latin cross," the familiar Christian form, with the longer vertical pole and the short, uplifted horizontal. This symbolizes, of course, the agony of inner selfcrucifixion, in mystical writings. Both crosses, in short, mean trouble!

Verse 8. "And the four living creatures each had six wings. From the circle of their center, inwardly, they are full of eyes. And they have no rest day and night, as they say, 'Holy, holy, holy is the Lord God, the Almighty, the One who was, the One being, and the One coming.'"

COMM: These parts of Mind are in transition between the purely human mind and the divine ("six"). Still, they are truly transcendental ("wings"). ["Six" has a terrible rep. Later, it is 666 (13:18).] The reputation of "six" as a demonic, satanic number is undeserved. A number, which is neutral, cannot be "evil" in itself, unless the mind so designates it. In reality, "six" is symbolic of the condition between the human "five" and the divine "seven." It is a period of transition and growth.

The creatures represent both Love and intellect. But their "wings" give them away: These mark them as transcendental mindfactors. ("Wings" are transcendence.) It is their principle job to synergize in the circled cross. Their mission, in short, is to help the mind understand that the cosmos (cross) is formed by, held within, Mind (circle).

The Godcreatures of Mind get in-sight ("eyes") from the knowing that they are cocreators ("circle"). They cooperate with Lovemind ("of their Center"). This is all done within Mind ("inwardly"). The emanated world comes from a "Center" (Lovemind) and spreads out in an infinite "sphere." Understanding also has a Mindcenter that radiates into all subjects.

The Godcreatures remind us that Lovemind is sacred ("holy"). "Holy" shares a root with "whole" and "heal." Lovemind is that Center that alone is *absolutely* whole. It lacks nothing. It alone has absolutely "real" existence ("monism"). Further, the final "healing" of all Mind occurs only with Union.

It is to this God-- Love-- that we come when we need healing. Lovemind heals us mentally, emotionally, and spiritually.

This "pneumogenic" (Spirit-originated) "holiness" manifests in both "worlds" in which we live. It is expressed in 1) the "outer" world (emanated "circle" of cosmos) and 2) in our inner minds ("inwardly"). These Mindfactors are active in the mind continuously ("day and night"). The Godthoughts never take a break, never stop, even for a nanosecond! Being unconscious, they pervade even our dreamstates.

They remind us, as did Jesus ("nothing is impossible"), that God is illimitable ("almighty"). They also remind us that we are in a perpetual, progressive process of "coming." That might be interpreted as God's coming to us, or our coming to God.

Verse 9. "And whenever the living creatures give glory, honor, and thanksgiving to the One sitting upon the throne, the One living into the ages of the ages,..."

COMM: Cosmic Mind alone deserves, and has the Power, to rule ("throne") all Mind. Lovemind, *the Godforce in Revelation,* is represented again by a redundant symbol. (For both "throne" and the "One sitting upon" it represent Lovemind.)

So, any other being that shares the throne, as the Godcreatures do, must be *a part* of this Lovemind, as the Godcreatures are. These spiritual Mindfactors (insight, understanding) connect us with the supreme Mind within our own minds.

They praise Its splendor ("glory"). It is difficult *not* to be in awe of such a Mind! For Its massive intelligence permeates Its dream, from molecules to galaxies!

They also note the esteem ("honor") with which It is regarded, and regards Itself. *The only Way to honor Lovemind is by loving!* Those who would "honor" God by legalism, mechanism, or Biblicism are going to find, to their shock and horror, that *none of this means anything to the divine Mind.* For It calls us to the Way of Love, not to religion!

The Mind is also grateful ("thanksgiving"). In lucidity, it knows that it owes everything-- from its body and brain to the food that sustains them-- to Lovemind. Besides its everyday life, its eternity rests upon the grace (Love) of Lovemind! All happiness and fulfillment emanate from Love, and It indwells every particle of Its dream. *There can be nowhere where It is not!*

Lovemind is pervasive. It exists in all Mindlevels and Mindsectors ("ages of the ages"). It both immanently indwells and emanates the whole cosmos.

Verse 10. "... then, the twenty-four old people fall in the sight of the One sitting upon the throne, and worship the One living into the ages of the ages, and they throw their crowns before the throne, saying ..."

COMM: It's a party in "heaven"! And there is much to celebrate! Experienced Mindfactors ("old people") voluntarily give up their control ("crowns") over the Mind. They turn over their influences and powers to Lovemind. This is surrender.

Verse 11. "'You are worthy, our Lord and God, to receive the glory, honor, and power, because you created all things, and through your will, they were, and were created.'"

COMM: Cosmos is created because Lovemind wants it ("will"). Knowing this, mind turns Itself over to Spirit. This all occurs megafathoms below the conscious mind. In fact, it reaches all the way down to very hidden Coremind (Lovemind). (See "Chart of Mind.")

A specialized part of Lovemind called "Creatormind" has the job of dreaming up the cosmos. [This specialized area of Mind, besides being called the (traditional) "Creator," or "Creatormind," is also called the "Dreamer," or "dreamind."] Dreaming is "creation." Lovemind is "Creator." It continuously dreams up the "material, physical" cosmos.

The deepest Unconscious has the assigned task of dreaming up the "material, external" world. (Of course, nothing is literally either "material" or "external" to Mind.)

Guess what the Mind uses to dream up the cosmos? Surprise! *It uses your mind!* That Mind pours Itself into everything. When the mind realizes that the whole cosmos is the thought or dream of cosmic Mind, then it becomes as clear as midnight neon that the whole cosmos is sacred, and good! Then, it gives itself over, gladly, in fullest surrender. It is stunned at the complexity and bottomless depths of the Creatormind.

It then realizes, with startling crystalucidity, that Mind is the Source of all thoughtabilities, cognition, cogitation, awareness, and analysis. It is the very fountain of all consciousness ("power").

Chapter 5

Verse 1. "And I saw on the right side of the one sitting on the throne a little book, written inwardly and from behind, sealed down with seven seals."

COMM: Revelation is created to be known in mind ("inwardly"). Full understanding forces us to use the Unconscious ("and from behind"). This Greek phrase, "inwardly and from behind" is widely inferred to mean nothing but that the "book," as a scroll, had writing on both sides. This implies, however, that the words of the text were not made deliberately mysterious. It also implies that Revelation contains no secret wordings hiding deeper truths.

Still, there is a gigantic, massive majority consensus among scholars that Revelation is indeed a "book of secrets." Revelation itself uses the Greek word *mystos* or "mystery" in selfdescription! So, things are not always as they appear to be.

Secret codes might be buried even in the text. Early Christians had to use symbolisms, even plays on words, to hide their true meanings. For their religion was deadly. It was against both Jewish and Roman law to be a Christian. To teach in plain language could be lethal.

So, "inwardly" implies inscription by psyche. Also, "behind" refers to the Unconscious. This is according to the archetypal language of spatial positioning. In this esoteric tongue, as in dreams, anything "behind" is unconscious. So, the phrase has been rendered here exactly as it appears in the ancient Greek text.

We are about to plunge into memory ("book"), moving into dangerous and dark "waters." The flora and fauna at these depths is alien and frightening. Still, we cannot tear our gazes away, for they are also exotically, hypnotically beautiful.

Courage comes from Spirit, and mind decides to explore Soul. The memory ("book") is revealed to the conscious mind ("right side").

But there are still spiritual ("seven") barriers ("seals"). These exist in the Unconscious. They block the conscious mind from deeper levels of the Unconscious. They must be penetrated. They make access to the memory difficult. They are memory-blocks, suppressive, repressive, or other defensive, sneaky maneuvers of the subconscious. They hide the deeper Mind.

It is not just that, with the passage of centuries, Soulmemory grows dim. For some of these "seals" were *voluntarily created* to block memory's floating up from the subconscious, the Mind's garbage-heap. What is forgotten (suppressed or repressed) there is too ugly, too hideous, to behold. The mind *wills* itself to forget. For some ghastly, nightmarish memories can be sheer hell!

But the shackles will be shattered. Then, some of the contents of the Unconscious, including the subconscious and Superconscious, will pour into the conscious mind.

Verse 2. "And I saw a strong angel heralding in a great voice, 'Who is worthy to open up the little book and to loosen its seals?'"

COMM: Spiritmind ("angel") recommends exploration of secrets. Knowledge of these forbidden visions is based on selfevaluation ('worthiness'). Spirit is searching for a Mindfactor that has the courage fearlessly to leap into the black waters of deeper mind.

Verse 3. "And no one, in heaven, or earth, or underneath the earth, was able to open up the little book, or even to look at it."

COMM: The Unconscious is an immensely complex Mindsystem. It is "Superconscious" ("heaven") and subconscious ("underneath"). Even the Lovemind ("heaven") cannot bring all the memories ("little book") to the conscious mind at this time! To do this would be to violate the free will of the conscious mind. Hypersensual mind ("earth") cannot understand ("open") the memories, either. This mind did not know that these memories even existed. Thinking them too horrible, too hideous, other parts of mind do not want even to know that they exist ("look at them"). And none of these mindforces was able to decode them.

Verse 4. "And I was weeping much because no one was found worthy to open up the little book, or even to look at it. One of the old people said to me, 'Don't weep. Look! The lion from the tribe of Judah, the root of David, has conquered, and will open the book and its seven seals.'"

COMM: The mind is devastated ("weeps"). It is in excruciating anguish that it might never penetrate the memories locked in the Unconscious. But its fears are baseless. An old part of Mind conveys a message of hope: The facing of inner danger, with noble dignity ("lion") is required.

Praise ("Judah") is part of the answer. So, Power to overcome ("conquer") ignorance arises from mind's relationship with Lovemind. The recognition of this relationship ("Judah") is the key: Lovemind is Master and mind Its servant. So, it is only appropriate that mind's response to Mind is humble "praise".

Knowing this is a form of gnosis. This knowing is the origin ("root") of the conscious mind ("David"). For without this knowing (gnosis), the mind could not exist as it is.

Verse 6. "And I saw in the midst of the throne and of the four living ones, and in the center of the old people, a lamb. He stood as if he had been slaughtered. He had seven horns and seven eyes, which are the seven spirits of God. He had been sent off into all the earth."

COMM: Surrendermind ("lamb") dominates heaven's court. In an ancient and ghastly, bloody ritual, harmless lambs were mercilessly slaughtered in a primitive sacrifice to the brutal Jehovah. "Surrendermind" ("lamb") is our name for all those thoughtgroups (ideas) and feelings collectively that want to surrender the personal will to the divine will. It is mind giving itself unreservedly and unconditionally to Lovemind.

Surrender deactivates egothoughts. The paradox: To be alive, surrendermind must die as egomind, into Lovemind. At this point in spiritual development, it appears already deactivated ("slaughtered"). But, even when its presence is not obvious, it still lives. Surrendermind is just repressed, not dead. It arises from Lovemind ("in the midst" of the "throne") ("Throne" is Lovemind.) So, surrendermind actually becomes Lovemind by disappearing into It.

These surrenderthoughts are in Lovemind ("center" of the "old people"). So, the impulse to surrender to Love itself blossoms from God. It is Love that moves you to surrender your life to Love. God in you hungers to know God in you!

"Lamb" (animal) forms the energy of surrendermind. So, surrendermind derives energy from animalmind ("horns"). Animalmind is not just the crazy, out-of-control madness of pigs and asses! It can also serve Love ("seven"). This brings spiritual ("seven") insight ("eyes"). Surrendermind manifests the allegory of the "birth of Christ" in a stable, among "animals." It is a mind of wisdom, but with humble animal origins.

Understanding ("Eyes") is Power ("spirits"). Stated variantly, inner vision is knowing Unconscious Mindforces. Even the hypersensual mind ("earth") is pressed into sacred service. Surrendermind infuses Mindenergy ("sent off into") into hypersensual mind ("earth"). This realization shimmers into view when bodymind turns itself over to Love.

Verse 7. "And he came, and he took from the right side of the One sitting on the throne."

COMM: Surrendermind ("lamb") gains access to ("takes") memories ("little book"). He gets them from the conscious part ("right side") of Lovemind.

Mind has plunged deeply and nakedly into meditation and/or inner exploration. But mind does not have to wrench, wrest, and wrestle these memories from a reticent, reluctant, and rebuffing Spirit. For it is the deliberate actions ("right side") of Spirit that willingly give these memories. That is, the memory is transferred because the Spirit actively wills it. Indeed, the Spirit always wants us to grow.

Verse 8. "And when he took the little book, the four living creatures and the twenty-four old people fell in the sight of the lamb. Each had a harp and a golden bowl. These [bowls] were full of incenses, which are the prayers of the holy."

COMM: Surrendermind gets dazzling memories, including great truths. It grows healthier and wiser. It has a shining realization: Surrender is what life is all about. The great "why" of life is at last known.

The entire Unconscious (older parts and Godcreatures) bursts into a new level of knowing (gnosis). This makes the world spectacularly meaningful. Mind realizes that this is why it was created-- to give itself unconditionally to the service of Love!

So, all the "multitudes" of mind feel electrically the awe-struck admiration and adoration ("fall") of surrendermind. They agree, concur, indeed, synergize, with it: Selfsurrender is everything This is what Christian mystics call the "crucifixion of the lower self." This is the end of the kingdom of the conscious mind, or its product, egomind.

The Superconscious Mind (old people and Godcreatures) resonates in harmony ("harp"). Small areas of the Unconscious ("bowls") have experienced earthly enlightenment ("golden"). Here, communications with Lovemind ("prayers") and transcendental thoughts ("incenses") enrich the interior life.

Verse 9. "And they were singing a new song, saying, 'You are worthy to receive the little book, and to open its seals, because you were slaughtered. And you bought for God, with your blood, from every tribe, tongue, people, and nation.'"

COMM: Mind is deliriously joyful ("song") when it surrenders itself! This produces bliss, joy, rapture, ecstasy. In this life, this has never been done before ("new"). Only surrendermind deserves (is "worthy" of) this. Memories ("little book") are revealed in shimmering clarity. Mindbarriers created by dark clouds of suppression/repression ("seals") are penetrated and unlocked ("opened").

At first, surrendermind ("lamb") only appeared to have been sent into the very deep subconscious ("slaughtered"). But here, surrendermind actually does get transferred to the mysterious nether world of the Unconscious. It slips below the horizon of perceptibility, disappearing from sight. The mind can no longer "see" it.

It "dies" as a "separate" entity. Of course, it was never *really* separate from Lovemind. It deliberately vanishes, perishes, or fades into Love. Surrendermind is a puzzle and paradox: The "lamb" itself represents a kind of death into Lovemind. So, when the "lamb" is "slaughtered," the allegorical nature of Revelation becomes even clearer. For literalism, this makes *no sense*. For the lamb appears in the vision to be alive and "slaughtered" simultaneously. This can make sense only if we awaken to the fact that surrendermind goes down into the Unconscious.

In surrendering, it begins with itself. It is alive, but only as a symbol. This living symbol represents a part of mind that has already died to itself. This living lamb symbolizes an interior "death." So it can no longer exist as a "separate" or clearly defined entity within mind.

Surrendermind paid the ultimate price ("bought"); It spent itself entirely for the good of the whole mind, and for even the Soul. Much timenergy was invested in facilitating assimilation of Mindsegments into surrendermind. Very large and multiple Mindareas ("every tribe, tongue, people, and nation") benefited. [These four entities are large complexes, aggregates, clusters, or constellations of related thoughts, ideas, and thoughtgroups. They all originate with hypersensual or sense-dominated mind ("earth").]

He (surrendermind within Soul) "bought" these Mindcomponents by "dying" into Lovemind ("with his blood"). By demonstrating how fantastically, breath-takingly satisfying it was to surrender, surrendermind lured and convinced other large Mindsectors to follow. They, too, began to surrender to Lovemind.

Verse 10. "And you made them, to our God a kingdom, and priests. And they reign upon the earth."

COMM: After surrender, these Mindfactors (peoples, nations, etc.) mushroom into an immense ocean of Mindareas ruled by Love ("kingdom"). This is the famous, exquisite interior "kingdom of God." Jesus identified this very beautiful "kingdom" as "within you." (Lk. 17:21)

They are fulltime servants of Love, like professionals ("priests"). These thoughts are obsessed with God or Love, in a magnificent possession by Spirit. Their occupation is their allconsuming Lovefocus. Yet they are not ripped away from their natural selves, their bodies. They are not taken from the hypersensual mind ("earth"). In fact, they rule "upon" it.

This belies the fanaticism and sick extremism of those who hate all things sensual and earthly. The balanced and moderate enlightened being is always a centrist. *She avoids all extremes.* Even when surrender occurs, the body and the senses are not "evil." Instead, their energies are simply redirected towards the support of Love. The people of Love are not whores and pornographers, but neither are they prudes and prigs.

Verse 11. "And I saw, and I heard a voice of many angels to the circle of the throne, and of the living creatures, and the old people. And there were myriads of myriads, and thousands of thousands "

COMM: Mindcomplexity is unveiled. But numbers represent qualities, not quantities. Still, the Mindportrait is stunning with its immensity and intricacy. This vast galaxy of minds within the Mind indicates many exciting interactive factors. In the Unconscious are not only the old people and Godcreatures, but an immeasurable, illimitable "ocean" of Mind. The Unconscious multiplies and ramifies into millions of expressions.

It is a massive assembly of innumerable ("myriads of myriads") thoughts and feelings. (A "myriad" is ten thousand). So it is a gigantic, amplified number (a hundred million). But even though so fantastically immense, this great number still "reduces," in numerology, to one.

Thus, it is the promise of oneness with the One, the vision of ultimate integration of the whole Mind with Lovemind, Soul with Spirit, mystical completion. It is the primal Undivided, the "One" of monism. It is the one Mind, Reality, outside of ignorant dualism. It is the pristine Mind of God, shared by all minds. Its vast, enormous multiplication increases not its number, but its importance and Power.

At its zenith and apex, Mind is One-- the utter and final meaning of "one." The cosmic Mind exists in a permanent state of pristine, uncontaminated purity and wholeness, allgood. This is Its condition when it is undivided, unmanifested in the world of multiplicity. It is "undifferentiated." But even in that world of "the many," It remains one. It is like sunlight, not made the least corrupt, but keeping stainless purity, when shining upon garbage. All the divisions and separations of the spacetime world (illusion or dreamworld) do nothing to divide It from Its original, undivided oneness. I seem to be a "different being" from you, but that is only because we are within a dream or complex game called "illusion." In Reality, You are Mind, and so am I. And Mind is not separated by skin-barriers. We do not end at our skins. Ordinary mind is inseparable from Spiritmind, for it is Its mask or role. God is "pretending" to be you and me. Infinite Mind is just "playing" a very, colossally complex "game" called "earthlife."

This symbolism implies that the Absolute (God) is within the Unconscious. Here's how that works:

The "Unconscious" defines all parts, areas, aspects, conditions, and actions of Mind of which we are not aware. Thus, the Unconscious does contain the garbage-bin of Mind, the subconscious.

Psychology is familiar with this. It is the inner dank, dark, damp dungeon containing skeletons, rats, decay, rampant sexuality and unregulated violence. Here are all suppressed and repressed horrors too hideous to face consciously.

But there is another area of Mind within the Unconscious. This is the Superconscious. This is Lovemind. It is bottomless, immeasurable, illimitable. Here are the bright rainbows of Love, the flowers of joy, the diamonds of tranquility, and the jewels of every fine, stable, healthy, and compassionate thoughtfeeling.

In sum, the best and the worst, God and devil, Superconscious and subconscious, live in uneasy truce within the Unconscious.

Verse 12. "They were saying, in a great voice, 'Worthy is the lamb, who has been slaughtered, to receive power, riches, wisdom, strength, honor, glory, and blessing.'"

COMM: The message ("voice") is a blast ("great") from the Unconscious. It startles even the dull and lethargic mind. Surrendermind deserves (is "worthy" of) seven rewards: 1) mental energy ("power"), 2) mental abundance ("riches"), 3)mental discernment ("wisdom"), 4) tenacity and determination ("strength"),

5)positive selfesteem ("honor"), 6) recognition of inner splendor ("glory"), and 7) selfimage approval ("blessing").

Verse 13. "And every creature in heaven and upon the earth, and underneath the earth, and upon the sea, and everything within them all, I heard them saying, to the One sitting upon the throne and to the lamb, 'The blessing, honor, glory, and might [are yours] into the ages of the ages.'"

COMM: Animalthoughts [dominance by impure sexuality, hypersensuality, violence, brutality, lack of intelligence, absence of wisdom and understanding, unspiritual and antispiritual thoughtfeelings ("all creatures")] join. Unconscious and conscious factors of mind speak as one. They all recognize surrendermind ("lamb") and Lovemind ("throne").

This is a mystical experience. During its momentary illumination, the whole mind is integrated and unified. It all praises Lovemind.

Despite Mindiseases, such as fear, the entire hypersensual, sense-dominated mind ("earth") unifies with, gets behind, the will of Lovemind ("heaven"). Its positive purpose: to give recognition to, and acknowledge, Lovemind as the Center. For the whole Mind ("everything within them all") is ready to accede to Lovemind.

Mindenergy is true strength ("might"). Mind is the *only Source* of Power. The whole mind agrees: Let God and surrendermind influence the thought-constellations ("nations,") etc. of the hypersensual mind ("earth"). Love starts to convert even body-energy to Its noble service.

Verse 14. "And the four living creatures were saying, 'Amen.' And the old people fell and worshipped."

COMM: The whole positive, luminous Unconscious cooperates in perfect harmony. It is unified in respect for Lovemind, to Which it turns Its attention and reverence. It admits that He/She is the supreme One.

Chapter 6

Verse 1. "When the lamb opened one of the seven seals, I saw, and I heard one of the four living creatures saying, with a voice like thunder, 'Come!'"

COMM: The first barrier to the Unconscious is blasted away by surrendermind. This occurs through a combination of insight ("saw") and understanding ("heard"). Power whisks away the mind in a continuing psychedelic (Soul-manifesting) parade of gorgeous and terrifying imagery. Then, communication between the Unconscious and conscious mind ("voice") begins, eerily, to appear. Intuitions of coming internal storms ("thunder"; compare 4:5) are awakening. Lightning flashes, and slashes, in bright bolts, the inner skies, and thunders roar and rumble. Surrendermind is starting to remember. The mind is invited to shift away, move, from stagnation ("come").

A possible implicit invitation is, "come to," or, "come to awareness," or, "Come to life." But the most amazing of messages is, "Come to God!"

Verse 2. "And I saw, and look! A white horse, and the one sitting upon it had a bow, and a crown was given to him. And he went out conquering, that he might overcome."

COMM: A gallant horse gallops into view. But this is not your ordinary, everyday "Mr. Ed." It is a psychobioforce in service to human will, pure as the driven snow ("white"). But the human mind is thirsty for blood! Conflict ("bow") is in the air! Soul is going to duel with ("conquer") inner dragons and demons! It is going to wipe out fearmind's servants, and make a bold grab for Power ("crown").

Verse 3. "And when he [the lamb] opened up the second seal, I heard the second living creature saying, 'Come!'"

COMM: The invitation comes again: "Please attend ("Come") the play-drama, the dreamgame, of earthlife! An undying, birthless, timeless Soul dons mind as its mask. Remember this allimportant fact of your secret identity!"

Verse 4. "And another horse went out, fiery red, and to the one sitting upon it was given [the power to] take peace out of the earth, so that they might slaughter one another. And a great sword was also given to him."

COMM: A horse the unnatural color of fire bursts upon the scene amidst Mindflames. Red is its coat, and red its menacing eyes! ("fiery red" is also the color of the fierce, angry dragon of 12:3, and represents purification through suffering, working through body-energy.) In the chakral system, redspectrum forces rest like a coiled serpent at the base of the energy-ladder. They are the same Mindforces that support the literal horse bolting through the open plain under lightning-split skies. "Fiery-red" is high stimulation that pushes bioenergy up the chakral spectrum, through agony. It tears the force from the body, and thrusts it into Mind. Then, it blasts it through Mind into deeper Soul, then into Spirit.

Red is the flame in the eyes, the ignition of passion, the warm candle of Love, the fires of hell. The spiritual calling is not all roses and rainbows. Grueling, agonizing ("fire") mental warfare is on the red horizon.

This dangerous threat erases the balance of mental energy ("power"). This knowing steals balance ("peace") from the sense-dominated mind, from the natural brainbody system ("earth"). This pain will, in time, create purity.

In the darknight of the Soul, mind crashes into hopeless bewilderment. Life baffles it, Love Itself seems to flee, and the world feels cold and empty. Mind feels divided from its only oneness-- with Lovemind. Thousands of Mindfactors are deactivated ("slaughtered"). They attack each other ("slaughter one another")! Mind goes stark raving mad! The brutal terror is caused by inner conflict ("sword").

Verse 5. "And when he [the lamb] opened up the third seal, I heard the third living creature saying, 'Come!' And I saw, and look! A black horse and the one sitting upon it had a pair of scales in his hand."

COMM: Directed animalmind ("horse") is black. This represents both the unknown and infinity. This is a promise to mind to plunge it into bottomless Mind. Again, mind is invited ("Come") to take the plunge! The "rider" is human (intellect). It forces biomind ("horse") to serve its will. Biomind, in part, is unknown ("black"). It remains partially hidden in psychic shadows. It flees from the "light" of conscious awareness. Parts of it hide in the subconscious. Others are part of the unconscious Observermind. Their job is to record your every action, so that it can, and will, come right back at you! Exactly as you have deliberately smacked another in the face, so you will be slapped! And exactly as you tenderly loved, you will be gently loved. This is karma balance ("scales").

This is perfect justice. As you do unto others, it is done to you. This parallels, "As you judge others, you will yourself be judged." (Mt. 7:1) Balance and payback (karma) are vital evidences of justice. Without the existence of an extradimensional Soul (outside the 3-d reality in the mind), *justice is a mere illusion.* So, if it does exist, it must be elsewhere than earth. But the very existence of Lovemind strongly implies justice ("scales") even in a universe apparently gone mad.

Verse 6. "And I heard a voice in the midst of the four living creatures, saying, 'A quart of wheat for a day's pay, and three quarts of barley for a day's pay. And don't ruin the oil and the wine.'"

COMM: The jewel-lessons of life are the "expensive" ones. We must pay a very high "price" for each of them. The price is astronomical ("a day's wage"), in terms of timenergy, resources, and sheer agony. We are often forced to pay this "highway robbery" price for spiritual nourishment ("wheat" and "barley"). But without Mindfood, the mind runs out of energy. And everything is about energy.

Food refreshes us. Here, mind is close to starvation. It's ready to eat its belt! It is in panic due to an absence of spiritual "food." You cannot get this from religion. Politics fails to satisfy it. Money cannot touch it. Fame and success are like eating straw. Only Love can fill the bill.

Some Soulfood is more slowly assimilated ("oil"). Many thoughts grow from sense-dominated, hyppersensual mind ("earth"). At times, these are spiritually nourishing ('grapes'), and are crushed, as personal possessions, to create Communion ("wine"). For *all personal mind* must be "crushed" to allow Lovemind to take over.

These thoughts ('grapes') also move from a state of cohesive solidarity, where each has an individual identity, to a much more liquidic state. This is the cooperation, trust, and interblending of perfect faith. It is the attitude of Taoist mysticism, in which worry and other fear-forms are abandoned, and childlike, acognitive trust returns to the mind. For you realize your Unity with all that is! For all the individual grapes literally become one in the wine. This is how you become one with Spirit. This is, in fact, the gateway to the inner Garden of Pleasure ('Eden' in the heart.

All of mind does not liquefy. This would produce a confusing psychocosmos with no boundaries, no guidelines, no ethical limitations. Others would "bulldoze" right over you! The desired state is not, then, full liquidity, but immensely increased elasticity. The mind must become more plastic and yielding. This allows Lovemind to form its contents. A concrete mind, like a "blockhead," is already dead.

(This is also the apex or zenith of mind. Elsewhere, "wine" is disorientation. In still another context, it is "blood," or death of the lower egomind, and thus, again, Communion with deepest Mind.)

Verse 7. "And when he opened up the fourth seal, I heard the voice of the fourth living creature saying, 'Come!'

Verse 8. "And I saw, and look! A greenish-yellow horse, and the one sitting on top of it was named death. Hades followed him. And authority was given to them, in a fourth of the earth, to kill with the long sword, with famine, with death, and with wild beasts of the earth."

COMM: Spirituality is death, to some mind. The ghastly ghostly "rider" on the nightmare-horse is "death." Human-controlled animal mindforces ("horse") move ("greenish-yellow") from intellect (yellow chakra) to Love (green chakra). Cold, linear logic is being gently melted by the warm flames of compassion. This fully occurs as the "lower self" begins to "die".

"Death" is followed by "Hades." It is largely due to these "horsemen" that the "four horsemen of the Apocalypse" have such a scary and bad rep. Hades is "hell." In Greek, the word did not represent the later psychotic fiery torture-chamber maintained by a nightmarish god. (This was a leftover of the Jehovah-myth of the ancient Hebrews.) This eternal hellfire was never a teaching of early Christians, and is not taught in Revelation. (It is a monstrous, ignorant literalization).

What, then, is hades? It is the garbage-bin of Mind, the subconscious. It is filled with those areas of mind that are already deactivated (dead). It is the "dead heads" of people who haven't a clue about spiritual truths. This part of mind is hyperinfluential in those fools who turn their interests away from spirituality and erect "false gods" of sports, money, politics, religion, career, or material and hypersensual pursuits.

When mental deactivation ("death") gets power ("authority"), horrible nightmares appear. Hypersensual or sense-dominated mind ("earth") falls into a frenzied orgy of death! Mind falls into utter chaos and confusion, destabilized and clueless ("one-fourth"). ("One-fourth" is the inverse in meaning of "four," which is mental strength and stability. "One-fourth" is terrible mental instability.)

Much of mind must die within. Some mindareas will deactivate in violent, terrible conflict ("sword") with Soulmind or Spiritmind. Others will wither and perish due to spiritual starvation ("famine"). These disappear because there are not enough thoughts to "feed" them. Others will die by "death," which means "plague." (This symbolizes mental diseases that are lethal to certain thoughts.) These are "infected" with toxic or deadly content, such as fear, or "evil." Other thoughts are killed by lower ("animal") thoughts ("wild beasts"). These are those of rape, pillage, sheer power, violence, injustice, general ignorance, and related hellthoughts.

Verse 9. "And when he opened the fifth seal, I saw underneath the altar the souls of those who had been slaughtered through the Logos of God, and through the witness that they had."

COMM: Thoughts that support surrendermind ("altar") support lambmind as a haven from the cruel world.

The surrender-generating area ("under the altar") is in the Unconscious. It is the "inner space" where thoughts of yielding incubate before coalescing into clear ideas. Here are deactivated ("dead") thoughts. Here also are very deep thoughts ("Souls").

The deactivation ("slaughter") of some mindelements was part of the perfect expression ("Logos") of Lovemind. Their "death" was predestined by Soul, part of the Plan all along. They contribute their lifenergies to the higher life of the Logos, the deepest and truest expression of Love. This Logos is the Soul (see 19:13-15) It is also God (Jn. 1:1)

Now, the Soul Selftestifies ("witness").

Verse 10. "And they cried out with a great voice, saying, 'Until when, Master of the holy and true, are you holding back from judging and avenging our blood from those who inhabit the earth?'"

COMM: The psyche is a mess! It is whacked out, thrown off-balance! The "Lord" at the Center of Mind will evaluate ("judge") the mind's contents, revealing just how screwed-up it is! Cosmic Mind will make necessary adjustments ("avenge"). This affects hypersensual ("earth") mind. Balancing is the creation of parity between the active energies of life and those of death within the psyche ("avenging ... blood").

Literalization here has thrown commentators for a loop! For "avenge" is a loaded word! But it is *not* literal. *Like all other contents of Revelation,* it is symbolic. So, we are not discussing the tantrum-throwing behavior of a petulant, capricious Jehovah here. Instead, this is the Lord of purest Love, creating perfect harmony and balance.

"Killing off" thoughts requires energy, and so does maintaining living thoughts. These mindforces must be balanced, life against death. (This is "avenging...blood.") So, "avenging" is not "vengeance" as punishment for evil. It is compensation. When mental energy is used, it triggers an automatic response from the deep interior Lovemind. This often results in helpful thoughtdeath. For *when negative thoughts "die," it is a positive event!* It creates mental harmony. The meta-phoric meaning removes the negativity usually associated with this explosive verse!

Energy of deactivated (dead; "blood") thoughts is fed back into the system. As in any good system, nothing is wasted! Hypersensual mind ("earth") resists the will of the One. It generates antiagapic (counter-Love) ideas. When they "die," their "energy" is recycled back into mind.

Lovemind ("master") creates perfect balance between the thoughts headed for predestined death, and those of hypersensuality ("earth"), which is responsible for some murder. So it is against "earth" that the balance ("vengeance") is directed. How were thoughts killed by hyper-sensuality?

Sense dominated mind brings a strong sense of vulnerability and mortality. If you say, "I am just a body," then you admit to a thousand weaknesses and inevitable death. No other destiny is possible. This fear slays thousands of thoughts. This is enough, at any rate, to scare to death those thoughts which are already fearful. So the deactivation (death; "blood") of these thoughts must be the responsibility of hyper-sensual mind ("those inhabiting the earth").

Verse 11. "And to each of them was given a white robe, and they were told to rest a little, until their fellow slaves and brothers were ful-filled, the ones about to be killed, as they had been."

COMM: You are stark naked, vulnerable, without selfimage. A special subtype of selfimage ('garment') covers your nakedness--"robe." It is unstained and pristine ("white"). So, it is that of the pure Self, the deepest Self, Spirit. This is a miraculous transfiguration of identity. You say, "I am no longer just an animal, no longer an ego, no longer a mind or Soul; I am an incarnation of Lovemind." This min-drocking burst of Light flashes only after Spirit has revealed Itself. It has said, "I, Lovemind, am the deepest part of your Unconscious."

After this awakening, the mind is utterly pure Mind. It is one with the One. This is the source of Its intrinsic purity. For there are two types of purity, so intermingled that they are one: 1) intrinsic, due to oneness with Lovemind, and 2) bestowed by grace. For the sake of convenience, and purely symbolically, we could say that the "white outer garments" represent intrinsic stainlessness, and the "white robes" the stainless state bestowed by grace. That bestowed by grace has the same root as intrinsicity: It is the awakening of the mind to the fact that it is a part of the stainless One. So, it dove-tails, and merges, with intrinsicity.

Egomind is unenlightened. It is unawakened to the full operation of grace (being already "saved" or enlightened by Lovemind). So, it must be awakened. This is a tricky irony, and a bit paradoxical: Only when it fully learns of its purity can it be truly pure. (Otherwise, it dirt-ies the water with antiagapisms-- counter-Love stuff.) It is this awakening by the aware mind that is "purity by the bestowal of grace" ("white robe").

Back to the text, and the "dead" thoughts: These deactivated ("dead") thoughts, then, are not in the Unconscious. They are nowhere. They do not exist. They are just potentials, with potential energy. They are literally active nowhere in Mind. But when they are awakened, they will come to conscious attention: they will be formed in the aware mind. For that is the Mindarea unenlightened. And this is just because of its gross ignorance. The conscious mind is relatively unenlightened, but no mind is absolutely unenlightened. Its darkness is its own illusion. All unenlightenment is part of the world of *maya* or illusion.

All thoughts that array themselves in support of surrendermind ("fellow slaves and brothers") get behind enlightenment, all the way! They are also entheognostic (God-discovering) mind ("under the altar"). Some of these thoughts have been deactivated ("killed") by fearmind (satanmind). But they obviously come back to life and join Soulthoughts in service to Love. For, in Revelation, death is a survivable experience. Death is also not negative or frightening. In fact, the "death" of these thoughts would actually complete or satisfy ("fulfill") them!

Verse 12. "And I saw, when he opened the sixth seal, a great shaking occurred, and the sun became black as the sackcloth of hair, and the whole moon became as blood."

COMM: Your being is rocked by a massive earthquake! All your ideas are shaken loose from their foundations ("great shaking"). You start to remember that you are not a body, not an ego, but an invisible and eternal being-- a birthless, timeless, deathless Soul. Your mind is turned topsy-turvy. It swirls and spins in confusion.

It's time to be transformed! Your mind shifts into high gear! You are becoming spiritual Mind.

Instantly, a "darknight" of the Soul occurs. The great spiritual Light at the Center of being appears to be extinguished ("sun became black"). You know that It is within you. You have touched It before. But nowhere in your psyche can you now find Lovemind. You become hopelessly lost in the twilight zone of Mind. You panic. Then, you fall into despair. You then move through periods of mourning and repentance ("sackcloth"). You might feel with exquisite sensitivity your 'unworthiness.' This can bring catastrophic sadness.

But only when you are pushed beyond tolerable limits do you break through into Lovemind, once again. So, you are forced to recognize your human helplessness. No matter what you do, it seems, you can do nothing to 'save,' or even to help, yourself. But the magic moment of enlightenment does not come until you have fully given up. Since the "sun" has been blocked by this black mood like a "cloth," this mourning and repentance must occur in darkness (ignorance).

Egothought ("hair") blocks identity with Lovemind ("sun"). When you are busy thinking 'me-thoughts,' Lovethoughts have no place; the mind does not have 'space' for them.

Enlightenment occurs only when you drop the baggage of materialism. *You cannot be both enlightened and wealthy in a poor world such as ours.* You must also drop hypersensuality. *You cannot be both enlightened and greedily selfindulgent* (although enlightened mind enjoys sensual delights). Self, not cosmos, must change! This mystical mindchange is based upon your interpretations. It does not arise from any real change in the cosmos, or in the divine One.

Big parts of the Unconscious ("moon") appear to die ("blood"). Inaccessibility to the Unconscious by conscious mind is "death." The mind says, "Hello? Anybody home down there?" The silence is thunderous! During this painful crisis, even Lovemind is silently inaccessible. For It is putting mind to the test. The Unconscious is out of touch, out of contact, with the conscious mind. The mind can no longer contact Mind. It is as if the mind were a small boat on an infinite ocean, and, abruptly, the ocean dried up, leaving the person in the little boat to die of thirst, alone, all alone. So, the great Unconscious safety-net has not disappeared; it has, to shift analogies, just sailed out of sight. Still, this produces great agony, and much pain. This is the essence of the notorious "dark night of the soul".

But power is unlocked through pain. It turns Mindenergy into lifenergy. Pain is the tool of choice for the Soul. It uses pain to make abstract ideals practical. Pain forces the mind from an isolated and "safe" ivory tower. Even if your head is in the clouds, your feet must be in the soil. And the Soul will hold them to the fire! This practical energy supports and enhances life. This means that you change from the path of *talking* about Love, which can be just so much "blah, blah," to actually *living* in Love. It is unlocked by crisis. And no crisis is greater than the darknight.

Verse 13. "And the stars of heaven fell into the earth as a fig tree throws its unripe figs, when shaken by a great wind."

COMM: The subterranean caves and underwater caverns of mind desperately need spiritual Lovelight ("stars"). Like the star-peppered velvet of the glorious Milky Way, this mind is dark, but filled with potential and accessible Light! This Light originates in Lovemind ("heaven").

The mind reaches into the deep well of the Unconscious, and draws up 'buckets' of data, now made aware. Chunks of this data emerge ("fall into") hypersensual mind ("earth").

Bodymind is illuminated! This hypersensual mind must be explored! You take your first trepidatious steps into the inner psyche. You deal with early sexual issues. You are discovering that you are an invincible, invisible Soul! But you might still carry scars from the past. In time, you must grow to embrace sex as the exquisitely beautiful gift of Love (grace) given to you through nature. Still later, you must grow to celebrate sex as a splendid Lovexpression.

Action-potential ("tree"; compare 2:7) moves in! It is not enough simply to *understand;* you are challenged to act, to move, to change both attitudes and *actual behaviors.* All the mindmechanisms and processes that change thoughts into actions ("tree") become engaged!

Ideas not fully comprehended, but still in formation ("unripe figs") grow from the conscious mind's action-potential. The mind is making plans for action, but they are still vague, foggy, fuzzy, amorphous, and nebulous ("unripe").

These ideas serve as mind's nourishment. The mind receives illumination, becoming stronger from spiritual food. ("Figs," a common dietary staple in the Middle Eastern culture of the first century.)

The "wind" is Spirit Itself. (The Greek for "Spirit" and "wind" is the same word.) Spirit removes ("shakes") embryonic ("unripe") ideas, so that mind does not act ("tree") on them. For this would consume energy towards a dead-end! A plethora of ideas is produced during this crisis-period, some of them good, some bad, some ugly, and some just plain useless. It is the Spirit that prevents premature action, by putting a stop on impulsive behavior.

Verse 14. "And heaven was separated from [earth] like a little book being rolled up, and every mountain and island was moved from its place."

COMM: Love ("heaven") is starkly, dramatically polarized against hypersensual mind ("earth"). Hypersensual illusion is dark abyss, while Love is sunfilled brightness!

Many Lovebased ("heavenly") memories ("little book") are lost ("rolled up") to the mind. They live in the Unconscious, but are inaccessible to the conscious awareness.

Isolated and small hypersensual ideas ("islands") float up from the Unconscious ('sea', implied). These are violently shifted due to the "earthquake" that sends the mind reeling. More elevated hypersensual ideas (religious, philosophic "mountains") also leap up from their places. If faith can "move mountains," so can explosive spiritual crisis!

But what is the earth-shattering idea that rolls mountains and islands around like dustmotes? It is the most fantastic, breath-taking, exhilarating knowing (gnosis) possible: All mind is Lovemind! Only It is absolutely real. So, It is the "Absolute" or Reality. All that is real within cosmos is Mind, all that is real within Mind is goodness, all that is real within goodness is Love.

Verse 15. "And the kings of the earth, and the greatest men, and the chiliarchs, and the rich and the strong, slave and free man, hid themselves into the caves and into the rock-masses of the mountains."

COMM: Dominant, controlling thoughts ["kings", great men, military commanders ("chiliarchs"), rich, and strong] are matrix-thoughts, around which other thoughts crystallize or coalesce into patterns (concepts). These dominate ideas dictatorially. The thoughtgroups that result are often ideological concepts, doctrines, or dogma.

The mind is bewildered and scared out of its wits by the immensity of the stunning, startling, unexpected cosmic Mind within itself! These powerful matrix-thoughts are stunned into humility. They react to cosmic Mind out of terror! So do common, ordinary thoughts ("every slave and free man")!

They fled into the Unconscious, through suppression/repression ("hid themselves"). The ego was terrified by its inner mystical vision! Its thoughts retreat into the hidden subconscious ("caves"). They flee into stubborn, 'carved-in-stone' dogmas ("Rock-masses").

Although rooted in sense-dominated mind, religion spouts elevated concepts ("of the mountains"), which evolve into dogma. Trying to solve confusion by cognitive reasoning does not seem as "sexy" as being dogmatic. At least, that gives an *appearance*, however hypocritical, of certainty. But every student of psychology knows that *the louder a dogma is shouted, the more rabidly defended, the less certainty exists!*

Usually, these dogmatists just give up. The quest for real answers, they dismally cry, is an idealistic dream. Settling for a comfortable religion can be the end of viable spirituality. This is exacerbated if the religion claims to have all the answers, and that all its answers are "right" or final.

Verse 16. "And they are saying to the mountains, and to the rock-masses, 'Fall upon us, and hide us from the face of the One sitting upon the throne, and from the wrath of the lamb.'"

COMM: When a rock-mass falls upon you, you are squashed like a bug! You're history! So, dogmatic mind would rather be deactivated (killed) than truly, honestly to wrestle with the deep, complex answers to the great, mystical puzzles and mysteries of life.

It is amusing to picture a 'wrathful lamb'! But sheep, oddly, are the metaphoric objects of fear here! Displeasure ("wrath") is felt roaring within surrendermind ("lamb"). Why? Because so many thought-groups insist on willful, stubborn 'parting' from Lovemind. This is, of course, illusion, since *no thought* can ever separate from the One. No idea can ever exist without, or outside of, Lovemind! Because no mind can.

The mind freaks, and hides from its distorted vision ("face") of Lovemind. For It appears to be like mind, an ugly, chaotic thing. But this is merely a dark nightmare fantasy. It is a distortion of the Infinite. For mind believes that It is vengeful, petty, and punitive. For centuries it has been modeled upon the ancient template of Jehovah. But It is

Love. Cosmic Mind has not a microparticle of Jehovah's ghastly responses -- anger, vengeance, loss of control.

The mind approaches a shattering crisis. Thought is impotent to rescue it. At this depth, thought is of no value.

The mind is driven by terror, infected with virulent pneumophobia (fear of Spirit). So, it flees, evading Spirit, and wandering through the nooks and crannies, caverns and mountains, in the polychromatic landscape of the Unconscious. But it cannot hide from Lovemind. For Lovemind is its very Center!

The mind fears the displeasure of the thoughtgroups ("wrath") of surrendermind ("lamb"). Despite arrogance, mind is "chicken" at heart!

Verse 17. "'Because the great day of their[29] anger has come, and who is able to stand?'"

COMM: Disapproval and strong displeasure ("anger") are felt. But is this displeasure felt by the "kings" or by Lovemind and surrendermind? Although it could be either, it is probably Love/surrendermind, for the "kings" are the ones panicking, and fleeing! Of course, Lovemind cannot feel literal anger, for It is Omnipotent. (Anger rises from frustration, and you cannot frustrate omnipotence!)

The Unconscious is disturbingly displeased with the mind's cowardly responses. It feels enormous displeasure with its lack of Love! During the darknight crisis, all that mind wanted was to hide! It did not want to grow spiritually. It ignored becoming wiser and stronger. It turned tail and ran, instead of facing the crisis head-on. Instead of valiantly facing down its dragons and demons, it panicked. It became a pathetic tower of gelatin, in the awful face of terrifying fear, Love's (conceptual) opposite.

---

[29] The KJ deliberately mistranslates the Greek text here, and speaks of "his" wrath, but other renderings are more accurate, rendering it "their anger." This signifies both Lovemind and lambmind.

Chapter 7

Verse 1. "After this, I saw four angels, which had stood upon the four corners of the earth, holding fast the four winds of the earth, so that they would not blow upon the earth or the sea or the trees."

COMM: Stability creates strength ("four"; compare 4:6). "Four" is, in sacred geometry, the number of the "four-square." The geometric form of "four" is the sacred square. (In 21:16, New Jerusalem is laid out as a perfect three-D "square" or cube.) "Four" and "square" are both archetypes of earth. "Earth" is hypersensual mind. This is solidarity and stability. Spiritual forces ("angels") are also stable and solid ("four).

They repress ("holding back") other spiritforces ("winds"). They keep a cap on Lovenergies. But why would Love ever be suppressed? Love is an illimitable, immeasurable Power! Exposing the mind to It too soon, or too quickly, would blow it apart! Like fine crystal in the path of a hurricane, an unprepared mind could be blown and shattered into a billion pieces by the Power of naked Love! Enlightenment is no game! It is no picnic! It is not all fun and roses! It is not for spiritual toddlers or infants. It requires meditation, preparation, and education. Spiritual forces ("winds") can wreak tornadic havoc upon hypersensual, material, or sense-dominated mind ("earth"). This is what can happen in the darknight.

Spiritual forces can also affect the Unconscious ("sea"). They could also damage earthly thoughtgroups that produce action ("trees").

Verse 2. "And I saw another angel stepping up from the sunrise, having a seal of the living God, and he cried out in a great voice, to the four angels to whom [the task] was given to harm the earth and the sea."

COMM: Abruptly, stunningly, angelmindpower is given the task of deliberately creating mental damage ("harm")! Why? Because a little damage is unavoidable. It is important that mind be exposed to Spirit, and harmed. The "safe" alternative would lead mind down the 'comfortable' path to evil and insanity. Here, mind takes a big gamble and risk! For the risk-free path would prevent mind's being exposed. The healthy parent allows her child to play in the park, knowing that the little girl will be "harmed" by many hazards, such as thorns and rocks. She will scrape knees and elbows. The child could be kept much "safer" if locked in a closet filled with cotton! Like an overly protected child, mind would lose many vital skills if the Soul's only goal were to protect it! But the Soul wants mind to grow, to experience pain and loss.

Spiritual Light flashes up from the very beginning of the interior Journey ("sunrise"). The dawn of enlightenment has only just begun, as a nascent awakening.

The spiritual mind ("angel") holds a Mindmechanism ("seal"). Its use is to select, identify, and mark Lovethoughts. They are to emerge from the slime and brine of muddy, stinking sense-dominated mind ("earth").

Verse 3. "He said, 'Do not harm the earth, the sea, or the trees, until we seal the slaves of our God upon their foreheads.'"

COMM: The Spirit demands that stable Mindelements ("four angels") not dare to harm three areas: 1) hypersensual, sense-dominated mind ("earth"), 2) the Unconscious ("sea"), and 3) the mind-action potentials ("trees").

This lasts until Lovebased thoughts ("slaves of our God") have been identified and separated from the rest of mind ("sealed"). What clearly marks these good thoughts? They are marked by serving Love with the intellect ("foreheads"). This implies a clear distinction between Lovethoughts and others. Lovethoughts are separated from the rest. They are destined to emerge from the pit, the hideous darkness, of unregenerate and subconscious mind.

Verse 4. "And I heard the number of those sealed, a hundred forty-four thousand, having been sealed out of every tribe of the sons of Israel."

COMM: Apocalyptic numerology appears. 144,000= 12 x 12 x10 x 10 x10, or twelve squared times ten cubed. Twelve represents cosmic order, the principle of heavenly wholeness.

"Ten" is earthly (hypersensual) completion, closure, even enlightenment ("ten"= "gold"). So, 144,000 is the penultimate, the zenith, the apex. It is *all thoughts of Love* (already identified with Lovemind). The "144,000" are already spiritually complete, whole, or holy. This is the whole collection of the best of the best, the most spiritual thoughts within the entire psyche. These are the luminous minds and thoughts of Lovelight-- pristine, whole, uncontaminated.

The ignorant, Hebreogenic (Hebrew-originated) culture of the first century was similar to the so-called "Christian" culture today. Many discolorations and distortions appeared in their knowledge about God and his relationship to Jehovah, and about Israel and its relationship to the church. Already, some Christians had distanced themselves from the brilliant, spectacular universalism of Jesus. Already, many had fallen back into the pit of religious (and even racial or national) bigotry. (Christian historians call these regressive types "Judaizers." Their goal: Present Christianity as a variation of Judaism.) Compromising the Way of Love, they reverted to their long-standing prejudices. They saw "Israel" as symbolic of special obedience to law. The Judaizers of the early church were no feeble minority, but powerful and influential.

Those mindelements in harmony with the strict laws of religion ("Israel") were legalists, mechanists, and Scripturalists. But why, then, do the 144,000 overlap with this type?

Because *following the Law of Love includes following all good religious laws as well.* Following laws and religion does *not* increase spirituality, and so *will never* lead to enlightenment. But those who follow Love are as "obedient" to any reasonable compassionate law as any Biblicist or legalist. So, "Israel" has nothing to do with literal racial prejudice or religious superiorism. Also, then, this reference has nothing to do with Judaism as a faith. Generically, "Israel" represents a large collection of religious (some spiritual) thoughts.

Verse 5. "Out of the tribe of Judah, twelve thousand were sealed; out of Reuben, twelve thousand; out of Gad, twelve thousand..."

COMM: Celestial order ("twelve") joins earthly completion or enlightenment ("ten") in synergy ("twelve thousand"). The symbolic number is twelve times ten cubed. So, it is celestial order imposed upon hypersensual mind, bringing a sense of wholeness, completion, and sense-based enlightenment, ("three" or "cubed").

Judah ("praise") is those parts of mind that glorify Love. [In Richard of St. Victor, the mystic of the eleventh century, who allegorized the "sons of Israel" according to mystical understanding, Judah represented love of justice.] Reuben ("vision of the son") is those mindareas that see the Son of God as the deeper Self. [In Richard, fear of punishment.] Gad ("good fortune") is the entire collection of thoughtfeelings and ideas that recognize blessings. [In Richard, abstinence.]

Verse 6. "... out of Asher, twelve thousand; out of Naphtali, twelve thousand; out of Manasseh, twelve thousand..."

COMM: Asher ("blessedness") is all blessed thoughts. [In Richard, patience.] Naphtali ("intertwining") is the thoughts that bring awareness that the Soul is intertwined with Spirit, and Mind with world. [In Richard, images of spiritual things.] Manasseh ("forgotten") is all thoughts that create amnesia, or block the conscious mind from remembering what is in the Unconscious.

Verse 7. "... out of Simeon, twelve thousand; out of Levi, twelve thousand; out of Issachar, twelve thousand..."

COMM: Simeon ("hearing, obeying") is all thoughts that obey the will of Love. [In Richard, grief of penance.] Levi ("uniting") is all thoughts that lead to Union with Lovemind. [In Richard, hope of forgiveness.] Issachar ("reward, compensation") is all thoughts that reward you through a positive selfimage. [In Richard, joy of interior sweetness.]

Verse 8. "...out of Zebulun, twelve thousand; out of Joseph, twelve thousand; out of Benjamin, twelve thousand were sealed."

COMM: Zebulun ("dwelling, abiding") is all thoughts that recognize that the human mind is the dwellingplace of the Lord. [In Richard, hatred of vices.] Joseph ("increase") is all thoughtideas that bring true increase of spirituality. [In Richard, discretion.] Benjamin ("son of fortune") is all the thoughtideas that recognize the son/daughterhood of the mind (with God as "Father" or "Mother"). [In Richard, contemplative ecstasy.]

Verse 9. "After these, I saw, and look! There was a large crowd, which no one was able to number, out of every nation, tribe, people, and tongue. They stood in sight of the throne and in sight of the lamb.

They had white robes thrown about them, and carried palm [fronds] in their hands."

COMM: An ocean of thoughtfeelings ("crowd") interacts in infinite combinations. This innumerable gathering is all the rest of Mind (apart from that described). They arise from all areas of the psyche-- every thoughtcluster, thoughtgroup, and thoughtaggregate, from very large ("tongues") to smaller groupings ("tribes"). They can be seen (known, "in sight of") by Lovemind ("throne"), and by surrendermind ("lamb").

Divine Love amidst the desert of mind ("palms") is in their conscious control ("hands"). This desertmind appears during the darknight period. God seems to have vanished into thin air. But God is really just "out of mind." For God is hidden from the conscious mind, in the deepest Unconscious.

These thoughts are all as pure ("white") as clear crystal. This is purity bestowed by grace ("white robes"). For God sees the whole Mind as pure.

Verse 10. "And they are crying out with a great voice, saying, 'Salvation [belongs] to our God, sitting on the throne, and to the lamb.'"

COMM: We must "be saved" from the vicious carnivores of the lower nature and ignorance. But this is not due to "works." *Any fool or hypocrite can "go through the motions." It does not take a genius to be religious.* Any common fool, any hypocrite, can give sermons, attend meetings, sing songs, pray publicly, study the Bible, or raise money for the church. *None of this is spiritual.* True spirituality is Love, and that *does* require an odd kind of genius. This is the gift of disappearing into deepest Mind; and when you disappear, by definition *you take no credit.*

Salvation originates with none of these "busy" activities. It originates with only grace. *It comes, unbidden and unearned, from the Love of God* (Lovemind).

But it is still a dance between Lovemind and mind. For it also requires the mind to respond with surrender ("lamb"). However, even this "letting go and letting God" (excuse the worn cliché) is made possible by grace. *Grace creates regeneration (rebirth), and is not itself* created by "good works." *Grace and regeneration always come to-gether as an unbroken set.* Grace creates good works, *not* the other way 'round! In the Enlightenment Tradition, when the mind wants Unity with Lovemind, it is really Lovemind wanting to unify Itself, since all is Lovemind. So, when "you" want Love, *it is really Love yearning for Love!*

Verse 11. "And all the angels stood to circle the throne, the old people, and the four living creatures. And they fell in sight of the throne upon their faces, and worshipped God."

COMM: The magnificent spectacle of the whole spiritual Unconscious spreads like an infinite ocean before mind, in a perfect "circle" all around. It ("all the angels") gratefully, gracefully acknowledges that Its Source is the Center (Lovemind). Spirituality fulfilled and completed in closure emanates ("circle") from shared cosmic Mind.

The Mind lets go of the hell of pursuing personal control ("falls"). Selfconscious, restless concerns about how it looks to others ("face") die with ego. "What will she think of me if...?" is the fear/worry of fools! The Mind no longer is bound, affected, or influenced by what others think of It! It soars into utter freedom!

The whole Mind, in this mystical moment, turns over all activities to Love ("worship").

****

For every act of Love is worship!
****

Verse 12. "They said, 'Amen. Blessing, glory, wisdom, thanksgiving, honor, power, and strength to our God, into the ages of the ages.'"

COMM: Spiritual splendor ("glory") and intrinsic Power ("might") were ascribed to the divine Center earlier (1:6). As progress is made, more qualities are recognized. So, "glory, honor, and power" are in 4:11. And by 5:12, there is an entire list of seven (spirituality), but that list differs from this one. Here, the list is: blessing, glory, wisdom, thanksgiving, honor, power, and strength. In 5:12, the list is: power, riches, wisdom, strength, honor, glory, and blessing.

The two lists overlap. But the major difference is in their order, or priority. "Riches" from 5:12 is here replaced by "thanksgiving." So, the quest changes from one seeking mental abundance to a recognition that it already exists! An attitude of gratitude appears.

The two lists contain the same elements, but in different priorities. In 5:12, mental energy ("power") is first on the priority-list. So, gnosis, the direct knowing of inner Lovemind, is sought in the earlier record *as a source of energy.* Mental approval ("blessing") is the first priority in this list, and last on the list of 5:12. (Symbolically, "blessing" is the opposite of "anger.")

Recognition of inner splendor ("glory") is second here, and second to last, or sixth, in 5:12. So, in the later, more mature experience, "glory" comes right after the approval of deepest Mind, which is first. This means that splendor arises from grace. That is, exclusively positive selfimage is the gift of Love.

Mental discernment ("wisdom") is third on both lists.

Immediately following wisdom in the more experienced state is gratitude for it ("thanksgiving"). In 5:12, earlier, wisdom produced only determination/tenacity ("strength"). So, the mind is becoming more sensitive to the indwelling One, and its indebtedness to Lovemind.

Stainless selfimage ("honor") appears fifth on both lists. In the more mature, later phase, here, it is followed by mental energy ("power"). It comes after mental discernment ("wisdom"). This implies that selfesteem must be born from psychospiritual growth. That same growth increases Mindenergy.

In 5:12, the recognition of inner splendor ("glory"), does not come until a positive selfimage ("honor") has developed. In the lower phases of mystical illumination, inner splendor relies on selfimage instead of selfless grace. In reality, splendor ("glory") is the gift of grace. It is not earned by us. It does not depend upon accomplishment, selfimage, or other factors. Grace depends only on the Love of God.

Verse 13. "And one of the old people answered, saying to me 'These with white robes thrown about them-- who are they, and from where did they come?'"

COMM: Deeper Mind (the Unconscious) quizzes mind. It repeats this periodically.

Verse 14. "And I said to him, 'My Lord, you know.' And he said to me, 'These are the ones coming out of the great trial, and they washed their robes and whitened them in the blood of the lamb.'"

COMM: The mind (John) responds with admirable humility. He calls Lovemind "my Lord." This deepest Mind knows that a revelation is exploding within awareness. Lovemind deliberately reveals Itself, bit at a time. The mass of thoughts ("crowd") is those who have survived a traumatic, mindcrushing event ("great trial"). This is the darknight of the Soul, when the conscious mind believed God to be absent. (It could not feel Love, and thought itself hopeless.)

These thoughts have made brightly spotless the mind's selfimage ("washed their robes... whitened them"). This they did by killing mindparts, by stormy but voluntary egomindeath ("blood"). This accompanies surrendermind ("lamb").

But is it not surrendermind itself that dies ("blood of the lamb")? Here again, we arrive at the same paradox encountered earlier, with the "slaughter of the lamb" (5:6). The lamb itself is *a kind of death.* So, as a double negative is a positive, the "death of death" would be a kind of life. But that is not what is implied here. Surrendermind exists *completely due to what has "died."* So, in this context, many kinds of egothought and fearthought have died ("blood") to make possible "the lamb's" very existence. Surrendermind rises out of egodeath ("lamb" is born out of "blood").

Verse 15. "It is through this that they are in sight of the throne of God, and they serve him day and night in his divine habitation. And He Who sits upon the throne will tent upon them."

COMM: These thoughts serve Love consistently, continually ("day and night"). They envelop unconscious areas. Some of these produce vivid visions at night during sleep (dreams). They dwell within Lovemind (Center of Soul). (Compare "Chart of Mind.") This is the Love in which cosmic Mind exists ("divine habitation").

God is not found in any temple, sanctuary, church, cathedral, mosque, or synagogue on earth. For He/She lies subtle, silent, hidden very deeply within the psyche. That is why the Greek text says literally that God does not tent "with" these thoughts, but "upon" them. These redeeming, purified, positive Godthoughts are within the supreme Mind, and so, It is "upon" them. They are Its foundation and support.

Verse 16. "They will not still hunger. They will not still be thirsty. The sun will not fall upon them, no burning heat."

COMM: This is a portrait of Mind satisfied. It no longer longs ('hungers or thirsts') for Its true Object of fulfillment. For Mind has found It. In the cascade of waterfalls of Love, all selfish desires are washed away. Mind desires only Lovemind.

The blazing Lightsource (Lovemind; "sun") does not crush and shatter mind ("fall upon them"). For mind has prepared itself. Coming into Lovemind is discovering an overflowing, cool, refreshing oasis in the desert. It gently illuminates their world with beauty and loving warmth. It is never seething and incinerating ('hot'). It is moderate, temperate, gentle, and tender.

Agonies of 'hell' and 'purgatory' ("burning heat") have vanished in the refreshing coolness of affectionate Lovemind. At the touch of Lovemind, pain ends. All states of pain are terminated. Mind has been brought temporarily into the sweet Light of Love, through gnosis.

This is illumination, not enlightenment. What is the difference? At various stages of the inner journey, the seeker is given moments of Union as previews of the bliss to come. These temporary and brief moments are called "illumination," and together constitute the Illumi-native Way of the mystic. (This is midway between the two other great phases of mysticism, the Purgative Way, a time of testing, and the Unitive Way, when you are fulfilled forever.) Full enlightenment does not come until you begin the next phase in growth, (the Unitive Way). In Revelation, it does not happen until near the end.

Still, these minor "glimpses" of Lovemind are completely satisfying. They bring fullness and contentment. They take Mind temporarily out of the world of "burning," tormenting passions (egodesires).

Verse 17. "Because the lamb, the [one who is] up the middle of the throne, will shepherd them. He will guide them upon the fountains of the waters of life. And God will wipe out every tear of their eyes."

COMM: This illumination is stunningly beautiful, but temporary. It blossoms in the mind as a momentary glimpse of full enlightenment. (Compare 21:4.)

Surrendermind is "up the middle" of the "throne." This means that it is at the very Center of Lovemind. This can mean only that it has become Lovemind. This is the essence of the mystical experience.

****

Deep in the mind, mind is Soul; deep in the Soul, Soul is Spirit.

****

So, mind is Spirit. You are God-- not, of course, in totality, but in nature. (You are an incarnation of Lovemind.) Here, surrendermind ("lamb") is in the place of supreme Mind. For it has become one with the Center, Coremind. It is in the process of becoming, or merging with, the One. The One "sits upon the throne," and is the "throne." Surrendermind is at the very Center, implying that it is the Center. It guides the whole mind.

Mind is "upon" the "fountains." Like sunlight, Mind penetrates and merges with the crystal droplets of water (Unconscious). A human-engineered concept or idea ["fountain" contains contents from the Unconscious (water).]

Surrender brings the mind to the threshold of Lovemind. When the mind touches Lovemind, all sorrow ("tears") are "wiped" away by It.

Chapter 8

Verse 1. "And when he opened up the seventh seal, there was silence that occurred in heaven, as [if] for a half-hour."

COMM: Sweet stillness ("silence") encounters serene mind. This all occurs in Lovemind ("heaven"), the deepest Unconscious. Stillmind is not just absence of sound. It is a profoundly altered, bliss-filled, positive state of consciousness. It is a thoughtfree state, like the one recommended by Jesus.

For when recommending the perfect life, he told his disciples to live like flowers, birds, and nursing infants. These amazing, astonishing examples imply that our best living is done from a state of "acognition" (thoughtfreeness). Buddhist mystics call this state *sunyata*, or "void," because it is empty of conscious content. But the perfect mind is by no means an empty-headed "numbskull"! Mind is void-- of only conscious thought. It is "empty" of linear, logical intellect, but never of Lovemind.

Stillness arises from Lovemind ("heaven"). This tranquil stillmind is sparkling crystalmind; it makes the aware mind transparent to the inner Lovelight. This lets Lovemind shine through into the world without blockage, without shadows.

This quietude is deepest tranquility. It allows the conscious mind to "hear" the subtle voice of memory ("seal" opened). But this altered state is short-lived ("half-hour"). [Gregory, the "mystic of Light" (died 604) said that this half-hour signified the imperfection of all contemplative (mystical) silence in this life.]

Verse 2. "And I saw the seven angels who have stood in the sight of God, and seven trumpets were given to them."

COMM: These dazzling, bright beings ("seven stars" of 1:20) create enlightenment. In sharp, stunning contrast with the "silence," there is about to occur a mindblasting wake-up call ("trumpet") from the deeper Mind ("seven"). In ancient times, a "trumpet" often called to warfare. So a conflict is coming.

Verse 3. "And another angel came, and he stood upon the altar, having a golden censor, and many incenses were given to him. This was so that he would give to the prayers of the holy, all upon the golden altar in sight of the throne."

COMM: On the altars of ancient peoples, innocent lambs had their throats slit until the place was drenched in blood. This Mindforce ("angel") is surrendermind ("upon the altar"). It symbolically 'sacrifices' itself: A part of spiritual Mind is sacrificed. This spiritual Mindarea ("angel") is lost to the mind, when the mind becomes confused during the darknight. But because this section of spiritual Mind is 'sacrificed to God,' this Mindforce ("angel") simply slips into Lovemind. So, it is lost to the conscious awareness. It sinks below the waves, and becomes deeply unconscious. It "dies" into Lovemind, and thus sacrifices all.

The mind moves through a phase of confusion. It loses its grip on spiritual Reality, and cruel illusion strikes up a duel. It has let go of so much! It has found so much detachment! But now, it is in danger of letting go of even its valid spiritual guidance. So, only surrendermind ("altar") can come to the rescue!

Surrendermind immerses itself in sweet prayer ("Incenses"). Both prayerful mind ("censor") and surrendermind ("altar") accelerate earthly enlightenment ("gold").

Verse 4. "And smoke of the incenses moved up, out of the hand of the angel in the sight of God."

COMM: Infinite Mind links with mind. Superconscious Lovemind enwraps and enfolds mind in its gentle Love. Unification is subtle ("smoke"). The mystic Gilbert of Foyland (died 1172) used the "smoke of glory" as a symbol of Unity with Godmind. Thoughts also "float up" from the conscious mind, to the superconscious Lovemind ("smoke"). Also, as smoke is made of tiny particles of matter, so prayer also carries upward tiny millipsychons of the human or hypersensual biomind. These Communionthoughts 'ascend upward' to God. (They 'rise' to a 'higher' Mind.)

Voluntary action or implementation ("hand") causes ideas to become movement. This is the motive behind communal prayer. It is not a selfish end in itself. It is not to 'get what you can' from God. Nor is it a fleeing in panic from the harsh world. It is a metamorphosis of being: it transforms you into the reflection of Love!

Verse 5. "And the angel took the censor, and filled it out of the fire of the altar, and he threw it to the earth. And thunders, voices, lightnings, and earth-shakings occurred"

COMM: Spiritmindpower ("angel") fills the prayerful mind ("censor") with spiritual learning derived from pain ("fire"). The mind is burned in fire, which then is transformed into Light! This educational suffering has arisen from selfsacrifice ("of the altar"). But what is lost?

This agonized torture is loss of personal will. When mind says, "I want absolutely nothing," at first, it feels dead. It seems even to disappear, for so much of its old ego-identity *depended on* its vast, immense network of personal desire. The dropping of this *feels like hell*. But it is the opening of the gates of heaven! Personal desires have been exchanged for the will (desires) of Love.

When this surrender is exposed to hypersensual, sense-dominated mind ("thrown into the earth"), it feels like burning fire. It is searing agony, sizzling intensity. This is the fire that consumes the last vestiges of personality, transforming it into Light and energy. All mind is becoming Lovemind, consciously.

When purifying pain ("fire") encounters hypersensual mind ("earth"), the results are explosive. They are: 1) the awakening of intuitions of coming psychic storms ("thunder"); 2) communication among mindareas ("voices"); 3) awakening of free energy ("lightnings"), and 4) shifting of paradigms or worldviews ("earth-shakings").

Verse 6. "And the seven angels who had the seven trumpets prepared themselves to trumpet."

COMM. Spiritual ("seven") mind excites itself to blast awake ("trumpet") the lethargic mind.

Verse 7. "And the first trumpeted, and hail and fire occurred, mingled with blood. It was thrown into the earth. A third of the earth, and a third of the trees, were burned down. All greenish-yellow vegetation was burned down."

COMM: Frigid hail beats the world to death. Thoughts coalesce into rigid dogma ("hail"). Subconscious thoughts ('water') freeze into unyielding solidarity, creating nightmarish disaster. Dogma arises with purifying suffering ("fire") and mystical, interior death ("blood"). Emotionally cold, dogma resists Love!

It is agonizing! Here are the mystic phases of 1) the Purifying Way and 2) the Unitive Way. Before Union with Lovemind, the mystic must be pure! Only tormenting "purgatorial" (purifying) "fires" can do this. Soon, a*ll that is not God (Love) must be "burned up," leaving only Lovemind* in all the totality of the mystic's mind. She is gutted of personal desires. A big chunk of her mind perishes (dies; "blood"). In time, her whole mind will "die" into cosmic Mind. Surrendermind gives up the will voluntarily. But that is not the case here: Hail, fire, and psychic shock bring death ("blood"). These horrors do not shower down from "heaven" or from the "angel"(cosmic Mind). These three symbols just appear ("occur").

How do dogma ("hail"), purifying pain ("fire") and death ("blood") relate? Let's start with dogma ("hail"): Attempts to "freeze" Mind into dogma paralyze it. This creates pain ("fire"), inner torture. If studied, this pain can teach. If we learn enough, lower parts of mind die ("blood").

If we try to replace living, bright spirituality with the dead dogma of religion, we enter hell. Dogma is cold, for it is mechanical, formal, legalistic, and ritualistic. It loses the warm flame of Love.

Rigid dogma and purgative pain create destruction ("burned down"). This hits a symbolic "third" of hypersensual mind ("earth"). What does the fraction mean? The clue is "three" (wholeness). [This is seen, for example, in the three parts of human nature (body, mind, and Soul) or the three parts of the "triune" God.] So, "three" represents the zenith of wholeness. The best of wholeness is that in Love. By extension, then, three represents a mind suffused with total grace. One-third is the inverse of this: So, one-third represents all parts of mind that believe themselves to be "outside" of grace.

Its inversion ("one-third") is mind in a hideous condition: "fallen from grace." But, outside of grace, is it not damned, irredeemable? No. No mind is ever "outside" of grace! That state is sheer illusion. Grace is cosmic, allencompassing! If God (Lovemind) is doing it right, "outside" must be a sick delusion. He is, and it is! Every mind is enfolded and ensconced within perfect, redeeming grace. All are saved by only the inner action of Love. So, "one-third" is illusionmind. In mesmerizing delusion, this "one-third" mind believes itself to be "outside" of grace.

In its view, it is only a mechanism randomly tossed into infinity. [For sense-dominated, hypersensual mind ("earth"), intangible realities seem illusory.] This nightmarish, "graceless" illusion petrifies the fantastically beautiful Power of grace. The world is a desert of despair. The mind is only that of a monkey with car keys! In this desolation, nothing-- not even Love-- has any meaning. The graceless mind has been stripped naked of all beauty, wisdom, and truth. It is locked into a suffocating and frigid hell of nihilism/atheism. Here is a most important clue to the spiritual life:

****

When mind turns lifenergy (spontaneous mind) into dogma, it falls into the "one-third" state. The mind falls from natural grace, just as human nature did in the "Eden" allegory of Genesis.

****

The beauty of spirituality is that grace never really vanishes. It slips underground, into the Unconscious, and we lose sight of it, but always and still lives! In this tormented condition, Love is replaced by existential emptiness, which is ugly, shattering, cold, and chaotic. Or it is replaced, but never equaled, by mere religion. Scriptures and dogma attempt to replace tranquility and bliss. This empty "one-third" mind is destined to disappear ("burn up").

The combined positive, healing synergy of pain, inner death, and dogma teaches about futility! In time, it kills the hopeless, despairing, graceless mind.

When dogma ("hail") encounters growth-inducing suffering ("fire"), it melts. In other words, real suffering in the mind, body, or world serves to destructure comfortable dogmas, driving one higher, into true spirituality. Dogma is not enough to get you through life.

A subsystem of hypersensual bionature is action-potential ("trees"). All spiritual ideas that are stimulated into action work through the biophysical bodymind, sense-dominated mind ("earth") and all "trees" grow from it.) All which bought into the dangerous illusions of graceless mind ("third") were also destroyed ("burned up"). (Compare 2:7 and 7:1.)

Next, very primitive thoughts, stuck between intellect and Love ("all greenish-yellow vegetation") were destroyed. This does not mean that they disappeared forever. It means that purifying suffering turned this primitive energy into Lovethoughts, recycling them into higher thoughtforms. In this case, unlike the "earth" and "trees," it was not just a "third" that was dissolved, but "all." Why? Color-symbolism helps: In 6:8, the gruesome "horse" of symbolic interior "death" was also color-coded "greenish-yellow." Vegetation represents thoughts very low on the scale of spiritual evolution, primitive. These thoughts were sandwiched between the color of intellect (yellow) and that of Love (green). But the text does not say that they were "yellowish-green," but "greenish yellow." So, they were still "yellow." This vegetation, then, represents all primitive, undeveloped thoughts still stuck in the intellect, unable to support Love. That is why the text says that "all" of them died, not just "one-third." For these thoughts had already fallen from the state of the pure recognition of grace. They were all locked in illusion.

Verse 8. "And the second angel trumpeted, and [something] as a great mountain, [similar] to a fire burning itself, was thrown into the sea, and a third of it became blood."

COMM: A gigantic mass is hurled dramatically into the sea, creating immense tidal waves! This is not a mountain, but, in the text, "as a mountain." So, this is a thoughtcluster that only seems to be elevated hypersensual mind ("mountain"). It is an idea that seems even inspired. But it is not a true vision of "higher Mind." It is a fake, a phony, a lie! This "mountain-like mass is religion, in its low, mechanical, legalistic, ritualistic form. It appears to be spirituality, but is not.

Religion creates Soul-agonies! It leads away from the blissful and tranquil Center (Lovemind). A practical "hell" is "separation" from Love. And much in religion creates exactly this kind of hell. As Lovemind is pushed away, frenetic attempts are made, in futility, to replace Love with doctrines, dogma, hymns, Bible-study, and other phonies.

Oddly, this is a pain that purifies, purifying itself ("fire burning itself"). This implies that, when mental pain reaches a certain threshold, purifying pain is itself purified by purifying pain. How does pain purify pain? Pain increases compassion. This happens in two ways: 1) When we are in personal pain, we no longer callously dismiss the pain of others, but feel it. And 2) when we are suffering, this elicits natural compassion from others.

Pain becomes Love's servant. It teaches compassion. (This is a major variety of Love.) It can then be embraced as a teacher, rather than fiercely hated as an "enemy."

It becomes less intensive and painful as growth proceeds. Pain awakens realization: Pain is also a part of the One. The One is utter purity, ultimate Love. *Pain is also a variety of Love.* Without it, spiritual growth of some kinds is impossible! Thus, by pain is pain made pure.

This mountainous thoughtcluster, external religion, is thrown into the Unconscious ("sea"). Ideas of mere external religion sink down, through the subconscious, into deeper levels of the Unconscious (Soul). The Soul is weakened. The pain causes the Unconscious to lose much of its accessible energy. For all practical purposes, large portions of It are dead ("blood").

Of course, the whole Unconscious does not die. Death strikes only the mindpart that regards itself as outside of grace ("third").

Verse 9. "And a third of the creatures of those in the sea died, those having souls, and a third of the boats were corrupted."

COMM: Some thoughts, from the Soulevel ("souls"), become completely lost in still deeper Mindlevels, or in the Soulevel. They are deactivated ("died"). This "psychocide" occurs unconsciously ("sea").

Mindstructures ("boats") on, but not under, the unconscious (water) are enslaved to illusion ("corrupted"). These are conscious.

But again, only thoughts in graceless hell ("third") suffered.

Verse 10. "And the third angel trumpeted, and a great star fell out of heaven, burning itself as a lamp, and it fell upon one-third of the rivers, and upon the fountains of waters."

COMM: Spiritlight ("star") is Lovelight. It comes to a dark, ignorant, illusionbound mind (often subconscious). Enlightenment flares up only through purifying suffering ("burning"). The human mind must cooperate, creating inner structures of Light ("lamp").

Streams of thought ("rivers") flow into the Unconscious. Some of these are rather complex but deluded ideas that you are living outside of grace ("one-third").

This Lovelight ("star") is Lovemind, and also emerges straight from It ("heaven"). It also touches down upon human-engineered ideas ("fountains"; see 7:17). So, flowing from the Unconscious, Light modifies conscious concepts.

Touching Lovemind changes everything! It alters every view, every idea, every concept and preconception, about the self and the world, about Mind and matter.

What you do is lifted to new heights by enlightenment. But even more critically, your *motives and desires* are wrenched into brand-new configurations! So, Light changes not only *what you do,* but *why you do what you do!* Mechanically or forcefully changing behavior does not improve a person. The multiplication of laws does not make people more inclined to live well. *Only if the "law" comes from within does it change the person.* Only then is it reliable. It gets to the root of the behavior-problem, rather than merely trimming off the top leaves.

When you are improved inside, all your behavior improves. This is not mere mechanical change, nor is it mere pretension. (It is not shallow legalism, mechanism, or scripturalism, *none of which changes a being inside.*) Teach a starving person to use a fork, and she might make all the "correct" moves, but is still starving. Religion is the mechanical use of the "fork." Give her real food, and, even if she does not know how to use the fork, she is no longer starving! *It is much better to have spirituality without religion than mere religion without spirituality!* Technique means nothing, motive means everything. (Religion is the "fork," spirituality food.)

This is the most crucial lesson taught by the violent, ignorant Moslem fundamentalists, with their utter disregard for life and decency, but complete and precise obedience to religious law:

****

Religion without spirituality is a dangerous monstrosity!
****

So, religion can never be enough, as it is just form, without spirituality.

Verse 11. "And the name of the star was Absinthe, and a third of the waters became absinthe. And many men died out of the waters, because they were made bitter."

COMM: Commonly, commentators give a ghoulish meaning to this verse. For absinthe (wormwood) is quite bitter. But most enlightenment comes through bitterness, pain, illness, loss, or suffering. To embrace these as God, or the Love of God, is one of the most challenging aspects of the mystical Way of Love.

The "star" is ubiquitously enlightenment. (The Nativity story says that the wise astrologers were led to Christ by a star.) The Light of Love can be agonizing (compare "burning" from previous verse). "No pain, no gain" is also a spiritual principle.

Absinthe is a green alcoholic liquor containing wormwood and other strong aromatics, and is notorious for its bitterness. During the mystical Journey to the Center, you go through dry states ("desert"), in which you feel unproductive and barren. Even worse are those times when your anger (often at "God") flares up into sour and ferocious bitterness ("absinthe").

This spell floats up from the Unconscious. This is the scary "darknight." Some of its unconscious contents ("waters") believe themselves "outside" of grace ("third"). It is these in graceless hell that "become" absinthe. *The whole mind is not changed.* Only illusion-mind, locked into duality, is made so bitter. *This part of mind becomes toxic.* During the darknight, all sweetness appears to have disappeared. Life tastes very bitter indeed. Potentially helpful human thoughts ("many men") are deactivated ("died").

Verse 12. "And the fourth angel trumpeted. And a third of the sun was given a strike. And so was a third of the moon, and a third of the stars. This was so that a third of them might be darkened. And daylight was darkened for a third of it, and the same with the night."

COMM: That's the night that the lights went out! Love no longer appears to save and to light those thoughts in graceless hell ("third")! Both conscious ("day"; "sun") and Unconscious ("night"; "moon") do not realize the luminous wonder of grace. You lose not only awareness of grace, but the *feeling* of being 'grace-full'! Their light is taken from awareness ("removed"). The mind is baffled; it hasn't a clue.

The stars no longer shine for desolate mind. The mind plunges into temporary blindness. Mind and sky are alike filled with the blackness of void, a naked, icy vacuity that is a hell! Hopelessness and helplessness sweep over the mindscape, and the inner "sun" is eclipsed, leaving inky, smothering blackness. But not all is as bleak as it seems! For helplessness opens mind to a cosmos in which *dependence upon, trust in, Lovemind becomes absolute!* How? The mind realizes that *it can do nothing to save itself.* It cannot change the world. So, it must trust the Mystery that does have the Power to alter the cosmos! It is at the point of *complete giving up* that *complete faith* dawns! This is the genesis of faith! And it is the gate to the inner Way.

Verse 13. "And I saw, and heard, an eagle, flying in midheaven, saying in a great voice, 'Woe to those dwelling upon the earth, due to the trumpet voices still left, of the three angels about to trumpet.'"

COMM: Far-seeing wisdom ("eagle"; compare 4:7) flies between hypersensual mind ("earth") and Lovemind or "heaven" ("midheaven"). So, it is not bound to sense-dominated mind, but it has not yet fully reached higher Mind. "Eaglemind" already senses what is going to happen: excruciating, agonizing turmoil. So, it warns hypersensual mind ("those dwelling upon the earth"). More communications ("voices") of inignorable power ("trumpet") are heard in the echoes of inner space. What is destined still to come will mean tears ("woe").

Chapter 9

Verse 1. "And the fifth angel trumpeted. And I saw a star out of heaven, having fallen into the earth. And the key to the pit of the abyss was given to him."

COMM: This verse could not possibly be literal. For a literal star would be millions of times the volume of planet earth. This again illustrates the fact that Revelation is allegorical.

Illumination ("star") tumbles "into" hypersensual mind ("earth"). It emerges directly from Lovemind ("heaven"), the Source of all Light. Lovelight goes *deeply within* the sense-dominated mind. It does not just light "upon" it, superficially.

Spiritmind ("angel") is given wisdom ("key"). This allows mind consciously to look directly into the horrors, insanities, and awful secrets of the subconscious ("pit-abyss"). It is a nest of serpents and scorpions, unbelievably hideous suppressed and repressed memories. Psychotherapeutic selfunderstanding can be the beginning of enlightenment.

Verse 2. "And he opened up the pit of the abyss, and smoke arose out of the pit, as smoke of a great furnace, and the sun and the air were darkened from the smoke out of the pit."

COMM: Transcendental, ascending, spiritual thoughts ("smoke"; compare 8:4) strain towards deepest Mind (moving "upward" towards heaven). But they still contain hypersensual mind (particulate matter from "earth"). These are very good and helpful.

But too many of them envelop mind in a blanket of thick darkness, blinding the inner eyes of insight. They obscure the inner, deepest Unconscious, the Lovemind of sheer Light ("sun").

They also obliterate awareness of Spirit ("air"). If the symbolism of astropsychology is being used here, oblique reference is to the quality of intelligence. It is being blocked by the obscuring "smoke." (For "air" is the archetype of intelligence.) True, spirituality positively blocks overactivity of intellect. But this positive aspect might not be what is indicated here.

A "great furnace" creates purity through agony ("fire"). We all wish that there were some easier way, but the only Way to purification is through suffering.

Here the mind has entered a phase in which it is overly eager to enter Lovemind. This triggers hyperintellectual activity. Spirit and Cognition combine to create mental opacities ("smoke") which actually has the paradoxical effect of pushing Lovemind ("sun") and other unconscious factors ("moon") so deeply into the great Unconscious that mind can no longer "see" them. This is overthink: the mind is simply producing too many thoughts. Although they are spiritual (ascending) they are also sensual (made of particulate earth). There are so many intellectual thoughts in cognitively studying spirituality that they block actual spiritual experience.

Verse 3. "And out of the smoke came locusts into the earth, and authority was given to them, as the authority that the scorpions of the earth have."

COMM: Mind is "bugged" by the buzzing of countless bugs! Although these are heavenaspiring, they are ominous and eerie! They are pestilence! Serious primitive, destructive, tiny thoughts add up to form a swarm ("locusts"), a plethoric abundance of overwhelming proportions! This is the same "overthink" of the previous verse. Tiny, they are capable of great damage! They threaten to consume spiritual "food" (sustaining Mindelements of Love). They fly through "air"; they are spiritual airpollution.

They seem to be spiritual, for they come out of the "holy smoke" and they also have wings (transcendence) But they are insidiously and incredibly corrosive and destructive! This includes much in mechanical, legalistic, scripturalistic, technical religion. In religion, the lighting of candles, the singing of hymns, the study of the Bible, the recitation of rote-prayers-- all of this has no spiritual value. Indeed it can be damaging to the mind. Even the sharing of Communion (Eucharist), if done automatically, lacks all spiritual meaning, and so, is worthless.

Billions of spirit-aspiring thoughts ("smoke") draw their energy from hypersensuality (earth-produced thoughts) as it is purified ("fire"). But something goes terribly awry and the energy that should push thought toward Lovemind is suddenly abducted by the lower nature (fear). So, what emerges is an entire army of tiny, but ugly and destructive, thoughts.

So, all these higher-potential thoughts are hoodwinked and kidnapped in service to fearnature.

If astrosymbolism is an archetype here, these thoughts, influenced by libra ("air"), are given the power of scorpio ("scorpions"). Instead of acting with balance and indecisively, following libra, the mind is granted penetrating lucidity, tenacity and intensity. It is intensity, ferocity, and extremism! This "scorpion-locust" force is allowed by the higher Mind ("given") to influence the other mindareas ("authority").

Verse 4. "And they were told not to harm the earth-vegetation, any greenish-yellow thing, or any tree, but only those men who do not have the seal of God on their foreheads."

COMM: Back in 8:7, "all greenish-yellow vegetation" was "burned up." But here it still exists. So, the account is symbolic, not chronological.

Thoughts of a spiritually primitive, undeveloped nature ("vegetation") are here *separated* from the color "greenish-yellow." But in 8:7, "vegetation" was blended with the "greenish-yellow" symbolism. This formed the single symbol of "greenish-yellow vegetation." But here, "all vegetation" and "greenish-yellow thing" form two separate categories.

So, two entities that to be damaged ("harmed") during the coming spiritual war include: primitive, undeveloped thoughts of the hypersensual mind ("earth-vegetation"), and other thoughts that were stuck in intellect, that could not quite make it to Love ("greenish-yellow thing"). These latter had to be given sufficient time to grow and blossom into Love.

Greenish-yellow, from the chakral view, is the transition from intellect to Love. Here, unlike in 8:7, these thoughts are allowed to remain: They are not only not destroyed during this phase, but are protected. This is so that they can grow.

The mind-action factors ("trees") are also protected. The targets of the harmful little thoughts ("locusts") were quite specific: They were to attack only thoughts of the human Mindlevel; intellectual thoughts, ("men"). Why were they to attack intellectual thoughts? Because these dominated the whole mind and if they were not eradicated they would continue to block spirituality even as they are doing here.

These are intellectual ("foreheads"). These had not been selected ("sealed") by Love ("God"). So, the hideous, dirty, horrible little thoughts serve Love after all. For they attack only the antiagapic (counter-Love) intellect!

Verse 5. "And it was given to them, so that they should not kill them but so that they will be tormented five months. And their torment was as the torment of scorpions, whenever it hits man."

COMM: The little horrendous thoughts ("locusts") are not assigned ("given") to annihilate human thoughts ("man"). They can only attack them. They hideously, hellishly torment these intellectual thoughts.

The human mind ("five") participates in the creation of these hellstates. What are these hells? They are the attempt to reduce all spirituality, and all the cosmos, to intellectual descriptions. They are the lie that *intellect contains all the answers.* For Love is transintellectual, above the reach of mere intellect. So, some of the blame is laid squarely on the door of human intellect. Historically, and in psychology, the intellect has indeed led to hellstates in the forms of existential emptiness, nihilism, atheism, and other excruciatingly empty forms of reasoning.

The intellect creates these monstrosities because it is trapped in time ("months"). So, it cannot see the larger, cosmic, timeless perspective. It falls into the delusion that only what it knows can exist. This myopia leads to total spiritual blindness, and that exacerbates the inner hells. This is mind attacking itself: spiritual questions that have no intellectual answers proliferate and torment the mind.

In fact, one of the most damaging thoughtpatterns is the inability to release time. We are called to the mystical path. This is "timeless," the Way of the "eternal now." This precludes time. *Time does not really exist within the mind of enlightenment.* It is a part of the dreamworld of illusion, or *maya.*

This is hell, trapped in and circumscribed by time. We forget that time is a mindcreation. We then become victims of countless extremely primitive (insectoid) thoughts. These are denizens of the subconscious. They are viciously vindictive, and nightmarishly obliterating.

But Lovemind exists above time, in the timeless condition. It is *always in the eternal "now."* The "torment" consists largely of clinging to time and events. This is the hell of unforgiveness. It is a series of primitive, harmful, toxic thoughts ("scorpions"). Truest "hell" is refusal to forgive the self and/or others. This is hell's definition: Separation from Love, always illusion.

Verse 6. "And in those days, those men will seek death, and surely not find it. And they will desire to die, and death is fleeing from them."

COMM: Human ("men") thoughts create hells. The human mind falls into despair. Human thoughts, breaking away from Love, seek selfdeactivation ("death"). But this psychosuicide will not come.

Verse 7. "And the likenesses of the locusts were like horses having been prepared for war. And upon their heads were crowns as of gold. And theirs were as faces of men."

COMM: This juxtaposition of symbols is complex. "Horses," as in 6:1, are bionature in human service. These come from the subconscious ("pit").

They are prepped for inner conflict. Their authority ("crowns") only gives the illusion that it directs towards earthly enlightenment ("as of gold"). But this is not the real thing, genuine gold. These thoughts only appear to control other thoughts. But, like the phony selfdelusions which they are, they do not have the right to do so.

They express something similar to the human mind, about midway between the "animal" and "Spirit" ("as faces of men"). As intellect and cognitive reason, these tiny thoughts are incapable of spirituality (Love).

"Face" is how these subconscious elements appear to the mind. It believes that they can be controlled by intellect. It is in store for a jolting shock!

Verse 8. "And they had hair as the hair of women, and their teeth were as those of lions."

COMM: A collection of still smaller thoughts ("hair") concerns itself with inner conflict. The gentler, more nourishing, supportive side of mind, the yin side of the inside ("hair of women") is the attractively soft and nurturing side of human nature. It is the more tender, kind, compassionate side, the sum of redeeming qualities that mark attractive females. (Here, of course, it refers to qualities within asexual mind.) This more excellent, tender side of human nature has managed to insinuate itself even among these antiagapic thoughts. So they are not completely "evil".

But a darker side exists. Vicious interior hunger ("lion's teeth"; compare 4:7) pushes the "insectmind" (very primitive subconscious) to assimilate thoughts even by interior violence against other thoughts! Nevertheless, this animal force is also one of potential nobility ("lion"). This savagery and brutality make these thoughts dangerous. These locustlionthoughts roar and rage in conflict!

The tiny, subconscious, insectoid armies tell the mind, "Resistance is futile; you will be assimilated," like the Borg of "Star Trek." Their goal is to force more thoughtenergy "underground," to force it into the subconscious. This vicious repression/suppression flares fiercely against enlightenment. For Light elevates more thoughts from the dark dungeons of the subconscious into the bright light of awareness!

Verse 9. "And they had breastplates as of iron, and the sound of their wings was as the sound of chariots, of many horses running into war."

COMM: "Preschooler's mind," "kindergarten mind," or "toddlermind," as in 2:27 ("iron") defends the heart of Love. How? Obviously, this is a clumsy, stumbling mind, just beginning the Journey. But its intentions are good, as it does want to support and protect the Lovenature ("breastplates").

"Iron" covers the heart. This means that Love is eclipsed by the ignorance of toddlermind. (The "girdles of gold" covered the "breast" in 1:13. This symbolized the heart enlightened.) The "heart" (Lovenature) is covered with black iron. This signifies that the Lovemind, at this preliminary stage, is locked in, obscured by, darkness and ignorance. In fact, It is not known, by the conscious mind, even to exist as Lovemind!

A signal is given to the mind ("sound of their wings"). It implies subtly the certainty that these thoughts will later metamorphose into transcendental forms ("wings"). However, this is not the sound of communication, or spiritual blossoming, but of conflict ("chariots"). The mind rushes to divide its forces into two conflicting armies ("running into war")! The mind "hears" the rumbling! But it has no cognitive idea what is occurring. A strong presentiment of conflict appears.

Verse 10. "They have tails like scorpions, and stingers. And it is in their tails that they have authority to harm the men for five months."

COMM: Pain is tied in with human ("five") time ("months"). So, what factor is obviously painful, human-linked, and time-linked. The parameters all fit with unforgiveness. So, here, the mind is being tormented by its lack (or complete absence) of forgiveness. This creates a terrible, nightmarish hell. The human ("men") mind is harmed.

The ability ("authority") to harm comes from the dreaded, dreary subconscious ("tails"). But even this must have the tacit approval of Lovemind. It is part of the spiritual destiny that will drive all mind into enlightenment.

This pain lasts for some significant but unspecified time ("months"). For the mind does not get over its childish nature, the tendency to hold grudges and to hate, overnight.

Verse 11. "They have upon them a king, the angel of the abyss. He is named in Hebrew Abaddon, and in Greek he has the name Apollyon."

COMM: Commentators err when they declare him demonic. For the text says that he is angelic. His name means "destroyer," in Hebrew, and the Greek is the even more forceful "complete annihilator." It is easy to see how he has been interpreted to be satanic.

But destruction, and even annihilation, are not always destructive processes in Revelation. If what is destroyed is bad, then destruction is good. Yes, the powerful thought is the ruling matrix-thought ("king") of the subanimal subconscious annoying thoughts ("locusts"). But even this does not prove that he is an infernal symbol. For even they, at the end of the day, are servants of Lovemind.

He dwells in the subconscious. He is a destroyer. So it is logical that his purpose is completely to obliterate subconscious thoughts. He explodes and demolishes all the Light-blocking data and memory of the subconscious. But he waits until they have served their valid purpose. For these thoughts of hatred, revenge, violence, sexual careless-ness, greed, and general stupidity serve Lovemind. How?

These serve as necessary obstacles to enlightenment. The Mind de-signs and assigns thoughts to resist spiritual development just to test the sincerity and power of the mind. These thoughts show the futility of taking the paths. The positive angelic thoughtgroup called "Abad-don" draws its power and force from the subconscious. In fact, it gets strength from fighting the thoughts of this lower nature. It aids the mind to become wiser and stronger.

Verse 12. "The one trouble is over. Look! Two more troubles are coming afterward."

COMM: A paingrowthcycle ends. In Revelation this entire horde of locust and all its horrific accoutrements simply vanish. So, this is a problem that appears to "solve itself". Two more paingrowthcycles are destined.

Verse 13. "And the sixth angel trumpeted. And I heard one voice out of the horns of the golden altar in the sight of God."

COMM: An alert is sounded! The mind hears "one" communica-tion ("voice"), instead of simply "a voice." The signal is: There is Unity of Mind beneath apparent diversity/multiplicity ("one").

The message, uniform and consistent, cries from animalmind ("horns"). But the Source is not ordinary animalmind; it is that which is embedded within surrendermind ("altar"). For practical purposes, then, it is the "lamb" who is speaking. Animalmind supports its own earthly enlightenment, or that which comes through the senses ("golden").

It does this by using the senses to educate mind. It demonstrates in-ternally that: 1) it *can prove that nothing in the "outer" world has in-dependent existence.* This leads to: 2) Of all things and events, *only mind can be known to be real.* This shoots like an arrow towards: 3) God, or the Absolute, *must exist in the mind.* And that evolves into: 4) the cosmos must be a dream of ultimate Mind.

Here, animalmind ("horns") supports surrendermind ("altar"). This paradox parallels the intro to the lambsymbol (5:6), where the same was true. Animalmind ("lamb"), in this case, *was a form* of surrender-mind.

Verse 14. [The voice] said to the sixth angel, who had the trumpet, 'Loose the four angels who have been bound upon the great river Euphrates.'"

COMM: The two symbols, ("tree" and "Euphrates") converge in "fruitfulness"-- a meaning of "Euphrates" is an unconscious thoughtstream that can produce Love. It is a motivating force. It can force mind to act in Love.

Spiritual powers ("angels") are paralyzed ("bound") during a darknight. These Mindforces ("four angels"; compare 7:1) are stability and balance. The mind has just passed through a terrible period of imbalance and cataclysmic change. Now, order is restored. Now, their forces are about to be released, to support spiritual flowering.

What "binds" the "angels"? It is overproductivity in other areas of mind, outside of the immediately spiritual. Mind has become distracted. It is far too busy! It just doesn't have "enough time" for Spirit. It is glutted with other pursuits, interests, studies, hobbies. It is very "fruitful" artistically, perhaps emotionally, creatively, and psychologically. It might be economically productive. But spiritually, it is restrained, restricted, and shackled. This builds up gargantuan frustration in the Unconscious. *For spirituality is all that the Unconscious mind wants or needs.*

It requires immense energy, force, and pressure to hold down thoughtfeelings in the subconscious. To paralyze them drains energy from every other part of Mind. Now that enormous energy is about to explode!

Verse 15. "And the four angels were loosed, those who had been prepared, into the hour, and day, and month, and year, so that they can kill a third of the men."

COMM: This "release" had been very carefully planned (timed) by the Unconscious ("hour, day," etc.). No random, helter-skelter occurrence was this. It did not just fall out of the blue sky, or pop up randomly from the Unconscious in a spontaneous dreamimage. This precise planning was formulated and calculated at either the deep Soulevel or deeper Spiritlevel. (See "Chart of Mind.") Their mission: Deactivate ("kill") all human ("men") thoughts in graceless hell ("third").

The graceless hell had already been established in the subconscious ("waters") when they were corrupted into absinthe (8:11). Then, human thoughts ("many men") died. For human thoughts (intellect) are fully dependent on unconscious thoughts. Here, also, graceless hellthoughts grow more deeply into the subconscious.

Similarly, in 9:4, the locusts were instructed to kill "only those men who do not have the seal of God on their foreheads." These were intellectual ("men") thoughts that had not been selected and/or marked by Love as Love's own. The ultimate goal: Leave unharmed *only Lovesupporting thoughts!*

Verse 16. "And the number of the army of the horsemen was two myriads of myriads, for I heard their number."

COMM: The mind sees another army. These are animalforces whose intent is to serve human will ("horses"). But they are strictly guarded, watched, and regulated by intellect ("horsemen").

They serve destructive duality. This ghastly illusion is taken to an almost absurd extreme! For it is here represented by the number two hundred million-- which reduces to two. (This numeral always signifies duality. Duality is splitting the cosmos between absolute good and an "absolute evil" that is just as real as the good. This was, in Genesis, the "original sin." Its most basic form is division of the cosmos into "god" and "not God," when it is all God.) Still, in the end, all serves Love.

Verse 17. "And thus did I see the horses in the vision, and those sitting upon them. They had breastplates that were fiery, and like hyacinth, and like sulfur. And the horses' heads were as the heads of lions. And out of their mouths was going fire, sulfur, and smoke."

COMM: The heart of Love is ignited, often by passions. This results in a purer heart, but only after suffering ("fiery"). It is protected ("breastplates"). This metamorphosis beautifully transforms mind when thoughtfeeling is redirected from passions of greed and hypersexuality to higher Love. In time, this strong guidance brings the mind to enlightenment!

Chakrally, red ("fiery") is sheer animal force. It is, at its worst, greed and survivalism. But it need not be so dismal, "red in tooth and claw." For bio-energy can come into the service of Love. Here, it offers itself to Lovemind, is at Its service. It might be altered and elevated by intellect (yellow) for fire contains both red and yellow. It protects the heart. It remains, still, a fairly low form of energy.

Higher thoughts ("sulfur") are also stimulated. These are linear, logical thoughts (third chakra; in chakras, yellow represents intellect.) But by thinking, by using only linear thoughts, mind keeps itself in "hell" ("sulfur" supports "fire.") Why?

Because it does not open itself up to higher, spiritual (Lovebased) feelings and thinking. Also, in alchemical symbolism, sulfur is thoughtfeelings that support and fuel growth through suffering ("fire").

Blue ("hyacinth") is even higher. It is a blue that borders on indigo, darker than cobalt. This is the energy of inner vision, or in-sight. So, in the chakrasystem, it symbolizes the "inner eye."

So, the Lovemind, Love-nature, or "heart," is protected by the synergy of bio-energy, intellect, and insight ("fire, sulfur, and hyacinth").

In 9:8, the army of primitive insectoid thoughts ("locusts") threatened to assimilate violently other thoughts ('lions' teeth'). This army presents intellectual danger ("lions heads"). The serviceable, usually friendly, docile, animalmind ("horse") has mutated monstrously into perilous, threatening blood-lusting things. These thoughts are way off-course! They are buying, big-time, into the perilous illusion of separation or dualism. This makes them dangerous! Everything that they think, after deciding to follow this illusion, will be contaminated. Crippled by this worldview, they create a plethora of distorted thoughts. Symbolically, there are "two hundred million" of them ("two myriads of myriads"; see previous verse). This engenders suffering ("fire").

This illusionmind is supported by expressions ("mouths"). The mind cannot help itself. It cannot but express its deepest assumptions about reality. So, in everything that it thinks, says, or does, with few exceptions, it will be saturated with dualism. Expressions of ignorance support pain.

But not all thought-expressions are illusions. The Mind can, in all the cacophonies of confusion, create thoughts of exalted and noble aims ("smoke"). Still, most of these thoughts are eclipsed by the agonies of suffering and the distractions of intellect.

Verse 18. "From the three plagues, a third of the men were killed: Fire, smoke, and sulfur, coming out of their mouths."

COMM: The three mental dysfunctions or disorientations ("plagues") are: 1) fire, or purification (thus, growth) caused by suffering, 2) smoke, material thoughts that aspire to a higher state, and 3) sulfur, intellectual factors of distortion that support, with intellect, both illusion and suffering.

Pain is also purification. It is a condition horribly lethal to the egomind. But why would aspiring spiritual thoughts ("smoke") be a dysfunction ("plague")?

Lovemind does not so regard them, does not interpret any of these factors as undesirable ("plague"). But Revelation is recorded by the conscious mind (John). And far from being omniscient, it more closely approximates "omnignorance"! When enlightenment begins, the whole mind is turned inside-out. It is wildly confused, massively disoriented. This, although temporary, creates purification through pain, confusion, dysfunction ("plague").

But Lovemind knows that even dysfunctions serve Love. In stunning contrast, the lower mind thrives on fear, Love's opposite. The conscious mind, and its illusion-darling, egomind, fear almost everything, all the time. So, they can interpret every phobocidic (fear-killing) impulse as scary, deadly!

Love is lethal to fear! For when Spirit (Love) clashes with fear-based ego, ego is destined to die. And ego knows it!

These mental disorientations affect only graceless hellthoughts ("third").

The source of the plagues is submissive animalmind ("horses"). They come from the expression ("mouth") of animalmind. So, at least some of these plagues result from hyperindulgence in the lower nature, i.e., giving in to sexual and other appetites. *When you let anything but Lovemind become your "master," you create a disorientation of confusion, or mental disfunction, ("plague").* So, these plagues, like all selftormenting hells, are selfcreated. They are selfgenerated by the decisions of the conscious mind.

Verse 19. "For the authority of the horses is in their mouths, and in their tails. For their tails are like serpents, with heads. In them, they are creating harm."

COMM: These animalforces regulated by intellect ("horses") control ("authority"), other thoughts. This control arises from the thoughts' expressions ("mouths"). That is, by interactions that express these thoughtfactors-- by thought, speech, and action-- they bend other thoughts to their wills.

They also give commands and directives. Some of these expressions ("mouths") might occur only in the privacy of the self.

Power derived from the subconscious ("tails"; compare 9:10) supports them. (The "locusts" had "tails like scorpions." These are "as serpents.")

The serpent, in the Genesis allegory, contrary to popular myth, is never equated with the devil. The basic archetypal meaning of "serpent" is free will, "broken away" from the will of the One. It is mind locked into dualism. So, these strange mindcreatures express the Unconscious ("tails") through the use of free will ("serpents"). This understanding originates with very early Christians who were the "symbol specialists" of the first two centuries, the gnostics. (When it does not begin with a cap G, the word "gnostic" is a generic equivalent to "mystic." Most early Christians were "small g" gnostics.)

This gnostic! So, these "tails" represent the subconscious regulated by intellect. The subconscious interpretation is reinforced by the fact that the serpents have "heads," or intellects. Tails have heads is the mental garbage-bin. Here, in a sector of the personal Unconscious, are suppressed and repressed materials. It is full of dark, putrid, stinking, and dangerous thoughtideas. (In Revelation, it is both the "pit" and the "abyss.")

The serpent (free will) leads into the darkness of duality. In this painful hell of illusion, you come to see yourself as "separate" from cosmos and Mind. But the serpent symbolized also enlightenment. For that is where free will leads us after we give it up.

****

The only intended use for the creation of free will was so that it could be freely given up or surrendered.

****

So, this symbol, too, is about surrender of the personal will to the will of Love. Free will must give itself up by its own voluntary action.

So, the serpent is a symbol of both light and darkness. It leads us into the darkness of dualism only to show us the Light of the monistic cosmos. (In this "monism," all is Godmind or Lovemind.) This is symbolized by a serpent swallowing its own tail, and hence, "devouring" itself! This meant that the human will was assimilating itself. Free will says, "I give up free will." It then becomes one with Lovemind. By its own free decision, free will was "swallowing" free will, neutralizing it, taking it out of existence. The ancient mystical symbol for this process, among gnostics, was the oroboros. This symbol formed a perfect ring and so symbolized eternal Mind This is what appears after "free will" "swallows" itself.

Verse 20. "And the men left over, who were not killed in the plagues, did not repent out of the works of their hands, so as not to worship the demons and idols, made of gold, silver, copper, stone, and wood. They are able neither to look, to hear, nor to walk about."

COMM: Some thoughts survive mental disorientation ("plagues"). They are the stronger parts of mind ("ones left over"). The voluntary transformation of thoughts into activities ("work of their hands") causes people to embrace materialism. Why?

Because they are impressed with their own minds. Their minds have expressed themselves in "matter" rather than spirituality. They have created wonderful technologies and toys, sports, money, and games. But they are spiritually arrested and starved amidst all their material "abundance." In time, this can be twisted into a demonic autoadoration, or selfworship. This is an evil mindforce ("demons"). It is a fake, a phony, artificial, illusory God-replacement (Love-replacement; "idols").

The material things created by Mind correspond with various levels of Mind. Even the very highest product of Mind (your own earthly enlightenment or "gold") is never to be worshiped. It is wrong to worship any earthly creature, any creation of Mind, no matter how beautiful, powerful, or noble. It is also idolatry to worship any deeply unconscious part of Mind ("silver, copper") or the less-advanced states of mind ("iron, stone, wood"). [Other common idols include people, such as gurus, ministers, rabbis, imams, or priests. But even if they are enlightened on earth ("gold"), this false worship is demonic.] The only valid worship is that given to bottomless Mind (Spirit, Coremind, or Lovemind).

Even "goldmind" (enlightened earthmind or hypersensual mind) can take no valid credit for enlightenment. When it dawns, egomind fades.

Other Mindexpressions are of much less value than the "gold" of earthly enlightenment. Starting from the highest, we move downward to silvermind, coppermind, woodmind, and stonemind. (Woodmind is related to tree-symbolism.)

There are five levels. Five is the numeric symbol of human nature; this factor translates thought into activity.

1) Gold symbolizes enlightenment within a human context.

2) "Silvermind" is the Mind in continual contact with the Unconscious. It is understanding that floats up from deeper levels, including the personal Unconscious and the Soulevel. (See "Chart of Mind.")

3) "Coppermind" is the periodic and imperfect reflection of Love, including sexual Love. It is often intellectual, and can even vaguely resemble Lovemind at times. It is truly moving in the right direction, towards full identity with Lovemind, but is not quite there yet.

4) "Woodmind" was mind in fullest activity, when it was alive as a "tree." But under the influence of humanmind (intelligence), formed by it, this woodmind has become less active. It is mind reduced to the service of intellect.

5) "Stonemind" is even lower. It is mind in paralysis, rigidity, immobility, petrification, or a dead (inactive) condition, analogous to "clay" in the classification-system of 2:27. This type or condition of mind can be marked by inflexible dogma. Still, its higher potentials can be seen in the high gloss to which stone can be polished.

These five inner "idols," created by the five human senses, are impotent. They cannot create or discover real spirituality. Their incapacity and helplessness are represented as inabilities to perform sensory functions ("able neither to look, to hear, nor to walk about").

Verse 21. "And they did not repent from their murders, or their drugs, or their fornication, or their stealing."

COMM: The mind has gone bonkers in several ways:

1) killing divine Love-thoughts and/or Love-feelings ("murder).

2) the destructive creation of altered states through practices of sorcery, occultism, or actual drug-use ("drugs").

3) the betrayal of Love. (It is often replaced with a counterfeit "love.") Many religious people are guilty of this ("fornication").

4) the attempt to find a shortcut to Lovemind, taking thoughtfeelings that should be used to support spirituality, and using them for sensual indulgence, materialism, greed, intellect, etc. ("stealing"). The discovery of Lovelight is attempted without doing the work or enduring the pains of genuine growth.

At this point in development, there are still thoughts that try to justify these behaviors. So, they do not express sorrow or regret ("repent"). They become defensive and even "righteously indignant" and haughty, betraying arrogance.

Chapter 10

Verse 1. "And I saw another strong angel stepping down out of heaven, with a cloud thrown about him, and a rainbow upon his head. His face was as the sun, and his feet as pillars of fire."

COMM: Another powerful spiritual energymind is revealed in humanoid form. It steps right out of Lovemind ("heaven").

To the mind, he appears to be covered with an obscure, dark, foggy, or unclear understanding ("cloud"). His intellect ("head") is surrounded by a Light (Love).

But it is not in its purest (white) form. The blinding, dazzling white-light energy of the One is broken up. It expresses as a prismatic spectrum ("rainbow"). This is the one Light manifesting as the physical cosmos, which is all beautiful and all good, because it is all Lovemind, as Creatormind (Dreamer). Manifested (dreamed) cosmos ("rainbow") is pure, bright, and lovely when seen with Love-eyes.

This "rainbow" has a secondary meaning as well: In the system of the chakras, each color represents an activity of Mind. (Since *everything is Mind*, this is relevant.) So, although in its larger sense, the rainbow symbolizes the entire cosmos, in terms of metaphysical psychology, it represents the following Mindfunctions:

1) red-- survival, bio-energy; 2) orange-- sexuality; 3) yellow-- intellect;

4) green-- Love; 5) blue-- communication; 6) dark blue-- spiritual insight; and 7) violet-- enlightenment.

How this part of Mind appears, to itself and to others ("face"; compare 4:7; 6:16; and 9:7) is as a nuclear Source of Light ("sun"). And it truly is. The sun, the center of the local solar system, represents the Lightfilled Center of Mind, or Lovemind. So, this being is a mirroreflection of Lovemind. If so, it is Logos; and if Logos, it is Soul (compare 19:13).

The "feet" represent spiritual progress. (Compare 1:13) Progress has supported ("pillars") the Mind all through Its journey inward But progress has also been a source of purifying suffering ("fire"). How does progress in the Way produce suffering?

For one, it creates an inward struggle of titanic proportions between Love and fear, Spirit and ego. Ego, and its egofear, will do anything to survive; it resists Love, often violently, at every turn. Fearing its own demise, ego joins fearmind in vicious inner battles against Spirit, some of which are described here in Revelation. The gigantic stresses between higher (spiritual) and lower (hypersensual) natures create sparks and set some large fires raging all over the mind. So, the pain of spiritual "fire" would be unknown without spiritual progress. Also, pain can be actually produced by progress.

Verse 2. "And he had in his hand a little booklet that had been opened up. And he put his right foot upon the sea, and the left upon the earth."

COMM: Mind opens up an unknown, and scary, small area ("little") of unconscious memory ("booklet"). The mind recognizes detailed micromemories. It is evenly supported by two factors: 1) the Unconscious ("sea") and 2) the hypersensual mind ("earth").

Progress ("foot") occurs through conscious direction ("right").

Unconscious ("left") progress ("foot") also is learned through the senses ("earth").

So, the Soulmind maximizes its marshalling of all its wide array of both conscious and unconscious forces.

Verse 3. "And he called out with a great voice, as a lion roaring. And when he cried out, the seven thunders spoke, with their own voices."

COMM: The Unconscious thunders, not without danger ("lion"). For spiritual ("seven") intuition tells of coming crashing, crushing interior thunderstorms ("thunder"; compare 6:1 and 8:5). This warning parallels the realization that suffering ("fire") accompanies progress ("feet"). (See previous verse.)

Verse 4. "And when the seven thunders spoke, I was about to write. And I heard a voice out of heaven, saying, 'Seal what the seven thunders spoke, and do not write them.'"

COMM: This message emerges directly from Lovemind ("heaven"). The mind forgets, tucks away ('seals') the revelation.

"Seal" has two meanings: 1) a barrier in Mind that prevents data from being viewed by the conscious mind, and 2) a mechanism/method of selecting and 'marking' thoughts (often, that serve Love). Since "writing" is memory, the first definition fits more closely. The conscious mind is instructed by deeper Mind to suppress certain memories.

It is to forget, neglect, its own strong intuitions about coming interior storms. Why? Perhaps because it would be so fearful that it might not continue the spiritual journey to the Center of the Soul. Perhaps this is for its own peace. If it remembered the primal terror of intuitions ("thunders"), it might try to avoid the overwhelming, fearsome Way altogether.

Verse 5. "And the angel whom I saw standing upon the sea and upon the earth lifted up his right hand to heaven."

COMM: Voluntary, deliberate action ("right hand") engages conscious will. The coming attraction, or action, is in harmony with Lovemind ("to heaven").

Verse 6. "And he swore into the One living into the ages of the ages, who created heaven and the things in heaven, and earth, and the things in it, and the sea, and the things in it: 'There is no time [to wait].'"

COMM: This angel vows "into" the One, shares Mind with the One. Omnipresence ("ages of the ages") marks the One (Center; compare 1:6).

The Soul says, in 1:18, that he also shares omnipresence (lives "into the ages of the ages"). What does this mean?

God is the Center of the Soul. He/She is everywhere. Why? *"Place" and "mind," like salt and pepper, or two bookends, must arise as an unbroken set.* Without mind, there can be no "place." It is the same with matter. Without Mind, the material cosmos, Its dream, would disappear.

This conflicts with old traditional notions of materialism, especially the antique Newtonian varieties. But the most modern quantum physics strongly suggests this mystical principle. If all minds in the cosmos were suddenly snuffed out, the cosmos would also disappear, cease to be.

****

Wherever "place" or matter is, Mind must be.

****

For "place" and matter are created by Mind. A place or "material" thing does not exist until it is sensed by Mind.

It follows that Godmind must be *everywhere.* *"Wherever" you are, place is; and wherever place is, God is! Wherever God dreams a place into being, there God is. God is filling your "space," both inner and "outer," at this very minute!*

The deeper Self, (Soul, of chapter one) presented here, is part of the cosmic Mind. With so many precise parallels, chances are good that the present Being being described is also the Soul. Both have an appearance ("face") like Lightmind ("shining sun"). (1:16).

Soul is, in its ultimate identity, Lovemind. For this Soul is in the place of the Omnipotent ["sitting upon the throne" (4:9, 10)]. This is the same One Who, in 4:11 "created all things...by your will."

Lovemind is also Creator of Lovemind ("heaven")! It is Selfcreated. This is God acting as Creator/dreamermind. This Creator is a subsector of God. It is so much so that the word "Creator," with a cap, in Western religions, is a synonym for "God."

Time for something explosive to occur.

Verse 7. "But in the days of the seventh angel's voice, when he was about to trumpet, the mystery of God was finished. This he declared as good news to his slaves, prophets."

COMM: "Mystery" is "good news." So, the evangelion (Greek, "good news") was the esoteric message of Jesus. This "secret," shared with only disciples, was the best news imaginable! It brought perfect liberty and Love, fulfillment and bliss! It was all about the intimate interactions (Love) between the One and the mind.

Mystos ("mystery") is gnosis (direct, immediate knowing of God as interior Lovemind).

Mind is known fully; knower merges with Known in a Mindmeld. The barriers vanish! The two become one Mind. This full identification between the deeper Self of the human nature and the cosmic Mind is the best news imaginable! This mystery is, in fact, the subject of the whole Revelation. The greatest secret in the universe is the best news

202

possible and it is this: You are God (in nature, not in totality), an incarnation of Love.

The Spirit, through the Soul, declares this message to his followers (the literal rendering is, the "slaves of himself"). He reveals them to be those parts of the psyche in alignment with his will ("prophets"). (The expanded meaning of "prophets" includes all messengers of Love, not just those who predict the future.)

This mystery is completed ("finished") with the final revelation of the deep oneness between divine and human nature.

Verse 8. "And the voice which I heard out of heaven, again speaking with me, said, 'Go under, and take the little book, which was opened up in the angel's hand who stood upon the sea and upon the earth.'"

COMM: Another vital message from Lovemind ("heaven"). Every easily accessible translation ignores the Greek text, which says, "Go under...." The mission of mind is to explore the "underworld" of the subconscious. The reason? To gain under-standing. This ghastly chamber of horrors (subconscious) houses demons and dragons, wild beasts and supernatural mental forces. The mind remembers ("take... little book").

The Mind of revelation (apocalypsyche) rests upon two foundations: 1) the Unconscious ("sea") and 2) hypersensual (sense-dominated) mind ("earth").

Verse 9. "And I went off toward the angel, telling him to give me the little booklet. And he said to me, 'Take it, and eat it down, and it will make your cavity bitter, but in your mouth it will be as sweet as honey.'"

COMM: Mind grabs the initiative ("went off toward the angel")! It demands ('tells') that the memories ("little booklet") be given to it. In Greek, the Mind ("angel") says, "Eat it down." This is usually ignored in English translations, as idiosyncratic. (It might well be. It might be analogous to our, "eat it up"! But it might also "wordveil" a deep truth.) This "eating down" might signify, through location-symbolism, that the images/information are processed by a "deeper" mind. (We know that ancient writers were conversant with "level-symbolism," of Mind, as so often in Revelation.)

The ideas here are assimilated ("eaten") by the Unconscious ("down").

A similar fate, in English, marks another word ("cavity"). It is assumed to mean nothing more than "stomach." (It might also have deliberately obscured meaning. Remember that Revelation was a "secret document." Its symbolism might have been deliberately made as obscure and subtle as possible.) For the Way is implemented best by the "empty" mind ("cavity"). This "empty" mind is not empty-headedness! It is the mind free of personal will. Lao Tzu says that "true usefulness" arises "from what is not there."[30]

Mystical consciousness begins with "cavitymind"-- a mind cleansed and empty of conscious content. A cavity is a hole, a hole has nothing in it, and so "cavitymind" is stillmind, crystalmind, empty of cognitive content.

The Way is "sweet" in expression and poetry ("mouth"). But inside the psyche ("cavity"), the Way is purchased at a very high price. It enfolds much suffering, loss, anxiety, and uncertainty ("bitter"). The gate to the Way is destabilizing and disorienting. It seems that, at times, you have sunk into an ocean of relentless pain ("bitterness"). The Way creates agonizing states of conflict upon first entering the unaccustomed unknown Mind. It brings suffering and sorrow. (Compare the pain accompanying enlightenment, described in 10:1, comm.) This is the darknight. These pain-reactions are due to habitual responses of the clinging mind.

Verse 10. "And I took the little booklet out of the hand of the angel, and I ate it down, and it was as sweet honey in my mouth, but when I ate it, my cavity was made bitter."

COMM: The mind is flooded with stunning memories ("little booklet")! They flow from the Unconscious. Spiritmind ("angel") voluntarily acts ("right hand"). It causes them to float up to awareness. These memories are sweet when expressed ("mouth"). The Enlightenment Tradition sounds like all roses on paper, or when described ecstatically in words. It seems to promise a never-ending kaleidoscope of rainbows and roses, sweet fragrance and delicious oceans of light,

---

[30] See my new rendition of the *Tao Te Ching*, "The Book of the Great Mind and Its Expression," in my *Luminous Jewels of Love and Light*, Volume 2, Part IV, *op.cit.*

contentment, sunshine, and satisfaction. These rewards are so real that they come with an airtight guarantee: They will never cease.

And this is true: As long as mind remains in the oceanic Mind of Love, basking in the rose-kissed sunlight of Love, these sweet ecstasies *will never end.* But mind has inertial power created by habits. And, shortly after the spiritual refreshment is touched, these "ugly" memories (from the "little book") reassert themselves, after you "come back down" from the bliss.

Mind soon begins even to doubt the reality of the bliss which it has touched. The concerns, anxieties, stresses, and worries of the "real" world start to crowd back again on the Lightfilled and Lovefilled, utterly pure mind. Ecstasy dims, and might soon go out totally. Voluntarily but ignorantly, mind moves a short distance from the rapturous Lightmind. Through inertia and ignorance, it soon drifts farther from Lovespirit. Before long, it finds itself once again locked into the sour state of "normal" mind-- to which it had hoped never to return! When the memories are processed ("ate it down"), they lead to the subconscious mind.

This requires a stripping naked of, and exposing, the subconscious garbage-dump of mind! Mental disturbance and spiritual conflict emerge into the spotlight of awareness. These are the subjects of most of the rest of Revelation.

Verse 11. "And they are saying to me, 'It is binding you again to prophesy upon peoples, and to nations, tongues, and many kings.'"

COMM: Mind has a mission: Tell in advance ("Prophesy") about spiritual evolution. Describe what the mind must endure, before it actually happens. Warn of the terrors, and delight with the tastes of bliss! This is to be shared with larger, organized thought-constellations ("nations," etc.).

Many controlling matrix-thoughts ("kings") are sucked into the disturbing whirlwind of revelations.

Chapter 11

Verse 1. "And a reed like a staff was given to me. And someone said, 'Rise up, and measure the divine habitation of God, and the altar, and those who worship in it.'"

COMM: Who commands? Some authoritative but mysterious Being. It is no doubt deeper Mind-- Soul, or Spirit. He/She orders some detailed measurements. ("Measure" shares wordroots with "matter.") So, mind struggles valiantly to evaluate gnosis with science and psychology. Psychometric attempts to understand Mind ("reed") aren't nearly enough! Ego (John) seeks to define and interpret infinite Mystery in merely human terms.

The mind is told to evaluate ("measure") the dwellingplace of the Infinite ("divine habitation"). To measure the immeasurable is, of course, a challenge in the impossible. Why is mind even given a task that is clearly incapable of achievement? To demonstrate its many limitations. The mind tends to arrogate to itself powers and abilities that it simply does not have. Here, the balloon of its pride, the bubble of its arrogance, is popped with the sharp pin of Reality.

It is also challenged to measure selfsurrender ("altar"). While it does not need to quantify its surrender-- nothing so crude as saying, "I'm seventy-four point three-eight percent surrendered"-- it is supposed to remain *mindful* or aware of just how much it has indeed surrendered. This is to protect it from everpresent selfdelusion.

Of course, when it knows that one hundred percent surrender is one hundred percent enlightenment, it *always longs to think of itself in the best terms.* So, far too early, and far, far too often, mind dares to regard itself as already *fully surrendered, fully enlightened.* But this is usually premature; and it is a real danger signal: It implies that the little tiny ego is still in charge.

Arrogance and pretension *disappear completely* with enlightenment. *The enlightened does not know or regard herself as enlightened;* for she does not compare herself with others. Every minute, she just does the best that she can. She never struts pea-cockishly, never dances in the spotlight, never laps up attention, as pathetically as an abused puppy! The enlightened *have no interest whatsoever* in impressing anyone. For praise, even notice, from other humans tends to strengthen the ego.

Jesus said, "If you receive a reward from men you will have no reward from your Father. (Mt 6:1) Considering how desperately self-styled "teachers" lap up attention these are scary words ! Only when ego is dead can a being be honored, noticed, and praised without being *severely injured* by it. If so-called "spiritual teachers" took this seriously each would race and rush to be most "invisible".

Even worship ("those" thoughts in the interior "temple") is also to be evaluated ("measured"). But all these are like trying to measure the distance between stars with a tape-measure! They are quite beyond accurate relative measurement by the mind. Nor can they be comprehended within material techniques amenable to science. Spirituality is as far above ordinary human intellect as advanced nuclear physics is beyond the infant mind! Still, measuring the self is an exercise in reality.

Verse 2. "And [regarding] the courtyard, outside the divine habitation, throw away [any attempt to measure]. And you should not measure it. For it was given to the nations. And they will trample upon the holy city for forty-two months."

COMM: Multiple and complex Mindlevels compose Mind. (See "Chart of Mind.") Those which closely orbit Lovemind, just "outside" of It ("courtyard") constitute the collective Unconscious. At this very deep Mindlevel, *all minds are telepathically connected.*

This level is not to be evaluated. The conscious mind is a dullard in these deep Mindlevels. It is lost and bewildered, in way over its head. There is nothing that it can possibly use to measure these deeper Mindlevels. It is a three-year-old trying to explain the neurochemistry and neurophysiology of the brain! It is simply too severely limited to understand the depth and brilliance of this shared Mindlevel. For the collective actually *brings into being* consensual "laws of science." (It turns out that these are *descriptions familiar to observers.*) The collective verbalizes all scientific laws and limitations, with their perfect mathematics and geometricities.

The collective does prespiritual work. But why is its work not truly spiritual? Because Spirit is immeasurably deeper. In fact, It is nuclear Mind, Coremind, Lovemind, cosmic Mind, or God. It's the indivisible Stainless Nucleus or Core of all Mind. *This does not belong to any person or culture, group or religion.* It is both collective and universal. (Compare "Chart of Mind.")

This collective Mindarea, consisting of thousands of layers just "above" Lovemind ("courtyard") belongs to only Lovemind! *All Mindlevels belong to Lovemind, for they are all a part of it!* But it was turned over ("given") to large mindsegments ("nations") within the *conscious* mind. So, Lovemind, its true Owner, allows the conscious mind to regulate parts of the Unconscious as though it were the Mastermind. In tragicomic delusion, the conscious mind comes to believe itself to be *the ruler of all Mind.* In fact, sinking ever more deeply into the quicksand of illusion, it comes to believe the stark irreality that *it is the only mind in existence!* (This is solipsism).

The "temple" is within the precincts of a larger Mindarea ("holy city"). This is a complex set of humanengineered and humaninfluenced ideas and concepts. It lives within Coremind (Lovemind). In fact, *Lovemind creates this "city."* So, although dreamed into being by Lovemind (Creatormind), it is dreamed up *through* the human mind.

The human intellect and conscious mind are allowed *without limits* to design and to select the contents of this "citymind." But if this is so, why is it sacred ("holy")? It is holy in the larger view, the holistic and inclusive sense. *All mind is Lovemind,* and so, all is holy. But this adjective might also imply a filtering process in which the mind sorts out, and allows, thoughts of *only* goodness, kindness, and compassion to enter the "city precincts." (Compare "New Jerusalem," later.)

Many people find the whole idea of an "inner God" incredible! It is blasphemy! For they are stuck in childish images of the "big daddy in the sky." Their "inner children" lure them into a fairy-tale kingdom in which God is their personal genie! Or, God is a childlike "Wizard of Oz."

****

They do not exist to serve God; God exists to serve them!
****

That there exists a deep level of Mind that contains oceans and galaxies of beauty, wisdom, and Love is fiercely resisted and rejected! Why?

Because primitive, sentimental, even sappy, godimages are much more comfortable than growing up!

It is a stunningly ugly and sad thing when even professionals use the word "impossible." But many professionals would so describe the collective Unconscious. Theirs is a "kindergarten" approach, but reflects the way that a primitive mind handles the unknown.

This is how the human mind abuses ("tramples") holy Mind. "Trample" is a strong word, implying the use of deliberate and overwhelming force. So, the mind does not simply benignly neglect the existence of a massive holy complex within the psyche. It denies it viciously, intensely, with bluster, explosions, fire, and heat! The most subtle blinding of inner mind occurs through static, dogmatic religions, which label the inner God "blasphemy" or "dangerous" heresy!

Why is a holymind denied with such excited brutality? Denying that large sections of mind constitute a "holymind" allows the mind to rationalize that it is just a biosystem, a brain. It is nothing more than a product of mindless bio-evolution. Or it is rationalized that people were created by an unstable, unkind god -- Jehovah. Using this argument, it can justify any behavior. After all, the tired old argument goes, people are just "animals." Monkeys with car keys are still monkeys!

As for stuck-in-the-mud traditional religionists, they want Someone-- the ultimate Extraterrestrial-- to come from outer space and solve all human problems. These sad types have completely given up all hope for themselves, or other human beings, to be able to solve human problems. With typical sexist language, they bemoan the interpretation that "man" cannot find solutions to "his" problems. Global problems have simply run so out of control, for so long, they whine, that reason and cooperation are not enough! The world requires divine intervention! They are bleak, hopeless pessimists. The only power that can bring even a hint of a smile to their dour, taciturn visages is their imaginations. They imagine their god swooping down out of the clouds, carrying a huge sword, and slaughtering his children by the billions, and then, laying the entire planet on a silver platter for true believers. These people are much too infantile to grow up and assume realistic, and adult, responsibility. They just want their "big daddy," Jehovah, to make all the "bad things" and "bad people" just "go 'way"! They are also hopelessly stuck in an archaic mindset from ancient cultures and Scriptures.

Although humanmodified, the holy thoughts of holymind ("city") are not humanfabricated. They are all created by Lovemind. In the relative world of spacetime ("months"), this holymind was abused for forty-two months.

But what is the Apocalyptic numerological meaning of "forty-two"? It is two times three times seven. Two is duality, three is wholeness, and seven is spirituality. So, "forty-two" is an esoteric way of summarizing three phases. The mind must pass through all three: duality, wholeness, and spirituality. (The same mindstates are iron-copper-gold.)

First comes duality-- splitting the self and cosmos into absolutely separate entities. In mystical tradition, this is the "Purgative Way," because you are undergoing purification ("purgation"), often by "fire." This is agonizing. This is the numeral "two."

Next come glimpses of wholeness. These come and go. This phase is the "Illuminative Way." Small tastes of the Lovemind make their wondrous, stunning, mindboggling appearance, but might not stay very long. This is the partial realization of absolute Good. In illumination, you know that Lovemind has no real opposite. You also know that you are not separate from It, but a part of It as Mind. Still, this knowing, like Its experience, comes and goes. It is not yet a permanent steady-state. This is the numeral "three."

Then comes spiritransformation. You gradually, subtly, incrementally exchange your merely human self for a deeper, more real, Self-- your Soul. "Your" mind was never yours. It is an incarnation of the One, for That is also Mind. You are an incarnation of Love. You are beautiful beyond imagining, good beyond measure, wise beyond comprehension. You are everlasting, timeless, and invincible. (You are not your body.) This is completion, "the Unitive Way." It is becoming Love. As this interior Love becomes a steady-state, instead of fading in and out, you start to enter the highest Mindphase. This is the numeral "seven."

But there is also an alternative numerological explanation: Forty-two months = three and a half years, which gives this number the meaning of three (wholeness) and a half (duality). This joined opposition is the perfect symbol for a very deep spiritual conflict. It occurs between the vision of cosmos as One, and seeing it, through the illusion of dualism (separation), as divided into many realities. The cosmos does not exist split between Love and non-Love. Antiagapic forces also are illusion. Only the One, the Mind, is absolutely real. Only It truly exists. (This is "monism".)

Lastly, "forty-two months" is also equivalent to "1260 days"-- all phases of spiritual evolution from animal into God. (See Commentary on following verse.)

Verse 3. "'And I will give to my two testifiers, and they will prophesy for 1260 days. They will have sackcloth thrown about them.'"

COMM: Dualism ("two"; illusion) sticks out its ugly head again. The mind, while still locked into delusion, catches prescient glimpses of its own destiny ("prophesy"). The delusional and dualist ("two") mind attempts to serve ("testifiers") Love. But it is still immersed in ignorance. It is still confused. Indeed, at times, this part of mind will serve the lower mind. Still, it serves as an instructor for the rest of mind.

A type of Mind is here symbolized, as well. We will call it "bimartyrian" mind. (Greek, bi, "two" + martyr, "testifier.") Since this is a real mouthful, it will be abbreviated to "bimind."

"Bimind"=all parts of Mind that have some direction from higher Mind, but obey the divine will imperfectly. This mind usually has good intentions, but is weak. Its spiritual education is imperfect. It knows a little about Love, but stumbles in drunken confusion, staggering, lost.

Bimind is told to try to figure out its future ("prophesy"). While locked in relentless strangle-hold, it is still deeper than the conscious mind. It bridges the Unconscious with the conscious mind, and sometimes can be either, or a blend. It is also larger, more powerful, than the conscious mind. That is why it is commissioned by Lovemind. It is consigned to do the will, be the marionette, of Love. For, in time, it will cooperate in the enlightenment of the whole Mind! Since bimind acts in ignorance, it is, in its own illusion, "outside" of Coremind. (Compare "Chart of Mind.")

1260, when factored to its primes (expressed in numerals that cannot be further evenly divided), is: 2 x 2 x 3 x 3 x 5 x 7. What is the "translation"? An elaboration of the story of spiritual evolution: Long periods ("days") are spent in the hells of dualism. That is why there are two twos. Then, wholeness is discovered, and the mind hangs onto it for quite a while; that is why there are two threes. Then, the human nature and limitations make a final appearance for testing (the "five"). Finally, the psyche ends up fully and completely "spirit," having been transformed into Love (the final "seven").

An alternate explanation is that 1260 days = three and a half years= forty-two months. So, these symbols are identical. The three and a half combines wholeness ("three") with duality ("half"). It means violent conflict at a deep level in the ocean of Mind. But for a short time, this leads to ultimate enlightenment. This very serious conflict threatens to divide even the Soulmind.

The bimind has recognized at least some of its imperfection. It is beginning to lose its grip on a relentless dualism. So, it is in repentance ("sackcloth";. Compare 6:12.) It feels genuine remorse for its many, many errors and screw-ups!

Verse 4. "These are the two olive trees and the two lampstands that stood in the sight of the lord of the earth."

COMM: Dualism ("two") infects all of bimind! Ignorance permeates it! Still, it manages to fabricate something that at least looks like peace ("olive"). But this comes only from activity ("trees"), not from the genuine Love-source. This is the counterfeit "peace" of exhaustion.

For absolute, permanent peace is not possible outside of enlightenment; and bimind is not enlightened.

This is the fake "peace" that infests workaholics, who refuse to give themselves any rest! There is no real tranquility in exhausting yourself through hyperactivity. Activity fills every day. But unless it helps others, it is a black hole that can never be filled! For *more work, or working harder, cannot itself bring peace! This "works" view teaches that you must work hard for even salvation, as a dog for its dinner.* It is unhealthy, and eats up the mind!

Thoughts become action ("trees") under the influence of hypersensual mind ("earth"). For trees grow from earth, and are dependent on it! So, thoughts-to-work effects are not always only positive. For *too many works can replace grace in the mind.* This is the sour attitude, "I really do not need the famous Love of God, for I am such a good and righteous person that He has no other choice but to save me!" This type of hypocrisy is not healthy self-confidence, but sick arrogance and sicker superiorism. It can make a person smug and snotty, so that people do not want even to be around her.

Instead of developing, it actually diminishes, Love! Far too many have fallen into this "sin," called "selfrighteousness." So many assume that *only their religion is right,* and, since they have been "smart enough" to have joined their church, God will save only them! In essence, they have lost Love; they say, in effect, "To hell with the rest of the world; I've got mine!" Tirelessly, they try to "convert" others, usually just making a major nuisance of themselves!

These people do *not* believe that salvation comes from the Love of God. *They believe that it is a "reward," a kind of bargain.* They are saved because they are better, or smarter, than average! Their "salvation" arises not from Spirit!

This is the illusion of "works," which conflict with grace. The "works" idea says that we are granted everlasting life and blissful salvation because of *what we do.* So, of course, some will be "saved," and others "damned." (This is the darling of many churches. It is dogmatic, ignorant, and closed-minded, but it does support the premise that *you need the church.* For you cannot find salvation without it!)

"Work offers no genuine serenity, *unless it helps others* (becomes Love). Another proof of the falsehood of bimind, and its fake "peace," is that it exists in "twoness." In its darkness, bimind stands not before Lovemind. It stands before only the ruling thoughts ("Lord") of hypersensual mind ("earth"): Bimind is being monitored by the sense-dominated, lower, mind.

Even its spiritual illuminations ("lampstands"), such as they are, are not real! They are also stuck in duality ("two"). Even the densest darkness can reflect traces of faint light, and the most grotesque lies are those which contain particles of truth. So, even though blinded by dualism, bimind does have a rudimentary grasp of truth (Reality).

Verse 5. "And if anyone wills to harm them, fire goes out of their mouths, and eats down their enemies. And if anyone wills harm to them, he is bound to be killed in this way."

COMM: Disharmonious thoughts ("enemies") are ruthlessly deactivated ("killed"). What neutralizes them? It is the expression ("mouths") of bimind. If bimind kills thoughts of falsehood, it logically must express some truth. So, these must be expressions of Love, although not of the highest variety (monism). These grow out of learning. They are thus experience. Bimind has been educated through suffering and purification ("fire").

Here's how: Bimind is educated by loss, agony, and other "purgatorial" and "hellish" states. When it is so educated, it begins to express itself spiritually, even mystically. The Way of Love, the Enlightenment Tradition, is lethal to anything disharmonious. Bimind starts to evolve into the mirror of Lovemind. So, as the wisely educated bimind begins to express itself, egothoughts are actively slaughtered. High ideals kill antiagapic thoughts.

The whole drama is about nightmarish conflict between two wills-- that of Love, and that of antiagapic "demons" or "dragons." (In Greek, the fire "eats down" the Love-hating demonic thoughts.) They are driven into the ghastly, ugly subconscious ("down").

The bimind communicates regularly with the conscious mind.

Inner "enemies" do not even have to actually harm bimind in order to be incinerated by the scorching conflagration of purifying suffering. No, they have only to *will* it harm. As mindelements, these harmful thoughts are actually made of will.

Verse 6. "These have authority to shut up heaven, so that rain may not moisten the days of their prophecy. And they have authority upon the waters, to turn them into blood and to strike the earth with every plague as often as they want."

COMM: Spirit-gifts (unconscious "water" or "rain" from "heaven") can be forced by bimind to remain in the subconscious. Bimind can slam shut the door between Spirit and mind. It can opacitize crystalmind. This means that it can cloud the natural transparency of Lovemind that marks the mystical condition. Lovemind is not permitted to "shine through" a dark mind, into the world.

Deeper Mind appears to close down. This happens during the time that the lower mind is predicting what it will undergo in its spacetime journey ("days of their prophecy").

When mind most desperately needs refreshment ("moisten") from Lovemind, bimind shuts down the connection between the two. This is so that the darknight time of challenge might be complete in its fullness of agony. The conscious mind is driven into the deepest inner hells so that it can know how pitiably weak and clumsy it is when trying to force-design its own life.

The unconscious Mind ("sea") is inaccessible during this period. This is so that the mind might seem to itself to be all alone in the cosmos. For all practical purposes, the Unconscious seems dead ("blood"). (This same phenomenon has occurred before, in 6:12. There, using a related symbolism, the entire "moon" became "as blood." In 8:8, a "third" of the "sea" became "blood.")

During this crisis of hair-pulling, pressure-cooker tension, the mind seems to lose touch with Lovemind. This time of emptiness and horror, of vacuity and hopeless despair, graphically spotlights the mind's total incompetence, ineptitude, and impotence in being able to save itself. This is the notorious, horrifying "darknight" through which every mystic must pass. *Bimind makes this test possible.* It acts *in service to mind by resisting it.* It hurts it in the shorterm to help it in the longterm!

Bimind also has the power to attack ("strike") hypersensual mind ("earth"). This produces disturbing, disorienting mental disorders or dysfunctions ("plagues"). Indeed, bimind is partly hypersensual (although it is not sense dominated mind or "earth"). Mental "diseases" leave both mind and body drained of energy, severely weakening both. (Full recovery might take weeks, months, or, in some cases, years.)

These pathologies are psychogenic (mind-caused; caused by bimind). In destructive dualism, the mind undergoes radical and chaotic confusion during this "darknight."

Verse 7. "And when they finish their testimony, the wild beast that steps up out of the abyss will make war with them. And it will conquer them. And it will kill them."

COMM: Thoughts suppressed and repressed in the subconscious ("abyss") are primitive and animal ("wild beast"). They are brutal, uncivilized, cruel, greedy. They are repressed rage, ferocity, fierceness, frustration, demonic anger, satanic fears, rampant sexuality, and other ghastly, nightmarish "animals."

The energy of Mind is soon to be divided between Lovemind and this "wildbeastmind" ("war").

This is the "animal nature" of the human mind. It is locked away, usually hidden like an old nutty uncle, in the "basement" of mind, the subconscious. The energies of all these thoughtfeelings coalesce and unite, and are personified as a single "beast." They have enormous power. They deactivate ("kill") bimind. That mind was already in a weakened state due to its ignorant dualism.

Still, it has fulfilled its purpose ("finished"). It has led other parts of mind into Lovemind ("testimony"). It has guided the conscious mind to the Christnature or Lovemind. Bimind has taught all that it could. It has taken the rest of mind as far as it can go during this phase. When the conscious mind has learned all that bimind has to teach, this teaching Mindarea is deactivated ("killed"). The subconscious ("beast") deactivates it.

Verse 8. "And their fallen [bodies will lie] upon the broad way of the great city spiritually called Sodom and Egypt, where their Lord was also crucified."

COMM: Bimind is not hypersensuality ("earth"), but it has a strong sensual component. The sensual, material part of mind ("bodies") of bimind lies deactivated ("dead").

The "bodies" are found in the datatransport pathways ("broad way") of the mind. Why? Because the nervous system and brain (datatransport mechanisms) usually are in full service to the material/sensual mind ("body").

But within that area of the shallower Unconscious called "bimind," biodrives are temporarily deactivated ("dead"). Why? During the darknight condition, energy is taken from the nerve-pathways ("broad way") that regulate biomechanisms. This energy must be transferred to *spiritual development.*

To do this, Mind removes needed energy from *biodrives.* Biodrives such as the need to sleep, eat, or engage in sex are disoriented and weakened during the crisis of the darknight. Appetites vacilate and shift.

Purification through suffering ("fire"; "Sodom" means "burning") tortures hypersensual mind. The biomind (not to be confused with "bimind") goes through hellstates during growth. Development does not occur without some suffering. Various states of pain and agony ("Sodom") seethe within mind. It passes through these hells when biology loses dominance over bimind ("bodies...dead").

This torment is obscured ("hidden," another meaning of "Sodom") from the mind. It is deeply tucked away in the subconscious. Even while we sleep, and dream, we are *actively engaged in growth.* These "sodomprocesses" include disappointment, anger, sadness, depression, frustration, anxiety, and stresses.

States of limitation ("Egypt") create frustration. These also curb the lower-nature mind. Egomind is filled with fears and natural boundaries. Lovemind, by contrast, is illimitable. So, it is a combination of suffering ("Sodom") and constraint ("Egypt") that leads to the death of hypersensual mind as master ("Lord of the earth")! (Compare 11:4, where this "lord" is identified.)

The sensual, "material" part of mind ("bodies") dies only as master. Temptations arise through bodymind (sensuality). When the sensual bodymind, as a "lord," is "killed," the Soul is finally free! The senses no longer dominate! So, it is easier for mind to know that it is a nonphysical reality.

Verse 9. "And they-- from among the peoples, tribes, tongues, and nations-- will look at their fallen body for three and a half days. And they do not let their bodies go off to be put into a memorial grave."

COMM: Bimind knows (gnosis) a beautiful moment of spiritual unity with Lovemind (one "body"). But, of course, bimind is not at all aware of this, for it is a big-time believer in dualism! So, shortly after their deactivation ("death") as master, they manifest as two (dualism; "bodies"). (Bimind includes all parts of Mind that receive aid from Lovemind.) Bimind blends sensual ("body") and Lovemind. So, a biomind nests deeply within it. This biomind within bimind fuels appetites both hypersexual and hypersensual. So, bimind is related to hypersensual mind, and often, even dominated by it. Given half a chance, this biomind would take over all of bimind, and balloon from there into mastery of the whole Mind. But bimind's bionature, its domination by bodymind, goes deep into the subconscious ("dies"). And this happens before it can take over with a *coup d'etat.* This disturbing crisis occurs during the darknight of the Soul.

That is also when the rest of Mind grasps, for only an instant, the truth of nonseparation. This is when other mindfactors ("people") see the sensual and spiritual aspects of bimind as one ("body").

Wholeness ("three") stood immovably against dualism ("half"). It had the stunning effect of the immovable object being struck by the irresistible force! Deep philosophic conflict ("three and a half") explodes within mind! This is the perennial raging conflict at the bottom of the Mystery: Which is real-- the single Mind or the polymorphic (many-formed) cosmos?

So, after bimind has been deactivated ("killed"), the rest of the mind falls into a darknight crisis.

The rest of mind has no respect for bimind. This is because bimind acted and believed in ignorance (dualism). So, bimind is granted no longstanding or fond memory ("memorial" tomb). The rest of mind just wants to forget all about it, that it ever even existed! Its lessons are not remembered or respected!

Verse 10. "Those dwelling upon earth are rejoicing on them and making themselves well-minded. And they will send gifts to one another, because these two prophets tormented those dwelling upon the earth."

COMM: The hypersensual mind ("earth") celebrates the deactivation ("death") of bimind! But since bimind was often ruled by sensuality, why is the rest of mind glad? Although part human, bimind was also part Spirit (Love). Even in its ignorance and delusion, there was a point of Light within it. So, it refused to support earthmind, or its interpretation of reality. It refused the naked materialism of reducing reality (truth) to a product of the senses. Bimind, although it could not articulate the truth, sensed that there was more!

Earthmind rejoices "on" the "dead" bimind. This means that hypersensuality draws some of its Mindenergy from bimind. Hypersensuality builds its worldview on the foundation of dualism, illusion supported by the larger bimind. When bimind "dies," its energy becomes available as free mindforce, up for grabs! Hypersensual mind is there to suck it in, absorbing it!

Hypersensual mind is *not* bimind, even though bimind contains some bionature, with accompanying sexual and sensual urges. When bimind is deactivated, in fact, hypersensual mind becomes more "well-minded" (the word used in the ancient text). This means more than simply having a good time. This "well-mindedness" represents a true mental healing.

Hypersensual mind exchanges positive thoughtfeelings ("gifts") within itself. One part of the mind instructs and shares with another.

The Hypersensual mind is so happy because bimind predicted ("prophesied") the coming difficulties and challenges (Revelation's theme). This severely terrified ("tormented") hypersensual mind ("earth"). It's happy to be free of such dire and grim predictions! It believes that, now that the messenger is dead, the message itself has evaporated.

Verse 11. "And after the three and a half days, the spirit of life, out of God, entered into them, and they stood upon their feet. And great fear fell upon those beholding them."

COMM: Astonishingly, Lovespirit resurrects bimind! A crucial mission of bimind is to describe the coming spiritual catastrophes. Its assignment is not yet completed. There is something still hidden! The rest of mind does not rejoice at the prospect of having a peek into this mysterious "prophetic" knowing. It responds with only fear-- terror of the unknown ("agnophobia").

Resurrection happens after mind overcomes dualism ("after the three and a half days"). Conflict is resolved. The two vicious combatants are monism ("God is all") and dualism ("cosmos is separate from

God; "one-half"). When bimind comes to life, the rest of the mind is awe-struck ("fear"). It is stunned to see how much of its beautiful spiritual nature survived, buried and locked away in the Unconscious (dead).

Verse 12. "And they heard a great voice out of heaven, saying to them, 'Step up here.' And they stepped up to heaven in a cloud. And their enemies beheld them."

COMM: Bimind integrates with Lovemind ("step up" into "heaven"). This is the flowering of bimind's enlightenment. Unified "monomind" blossoms. But bimind enters the process without clarity about its final destination ("in a cloud"). [Christ (1:7) is coming "with the clouds."]

Bimind is enfogged by its limitations. The rest of mind is even more lost. (It has fought bimind as an enemy ("enemies"). Still, the whole Mind sees with stunning clarity ("behold") bimind's astonishing ascent to ultimate Mind ("stepped up to heaven"). But mind hasn't a clue what is happening, confused by the abrupt shift in mental energy, and its direction. It knows nothing about future implications.

Verse 13. "And in that hour, a great shaking occurred. And one-tenth of the city fell. And in the shaking were killed seven thousand names of men. And the ones left over became fearful; and they gave glory to the God of heaven."

COMM: Immediately after bimind's enlightenment (having solved the question of duality), the entire Mind shifts radically ("great shaking").

"The intellectual complex ("city") lost power ("fell"). But it "fell" in a special way ("one-tenth"). "Ten" is earthly (hypersensual) enlightenment. This is a dim light based on the senses. But it is still genuine.

One-tenth is its inverse: A state of incompleteness, imperfection, inner darkness, ignorance ("tenth") results. Why? Hypersensual thoughtpatterns collapsed, lost integrity and cohesion ("fell"). The senses began to serve painful darkness, and fell into hell. They fell into lower mind-- to an even lower state than bionature. In fact, they could have fallen all the way down into beastmind. The senses, totally distorted and twisted into ugliness, served the "satan" of fear.

Antiagapic forces mushroom against the simultaneous awakening of Love! The mind is rocked by the irresistible force of the infinite Unconscious as It begins to emerge. Antiagapic ("one-tenth") concepts of human intellect ("city") are destroyed! The mind begins spouting gibberish in defense of its obscenities. Its carefully crafted justifications dissolve. The mind finds its own arguments laughable and absurd!

Lovemind is touched at the end of the darknight period. A blaze of Love dissipates all darkness, and shadows flee in the brightness.

If antiagapic thoughts are lower than bionature, then what is lower? Beastnature! It is not deeper. In fact, it is part of the shallowest mind, the conscious mind. [Its origin is the subconscious (garbage bin), tucked into the personal Unconscious (see "Chart of Mind.")]

Spiritual ("seven") thoughts were deactivated ("killed"). These originated with the One, intensely magnified ("thousand"). Alternatively (as a multiple of ten), these were of hypersensual ("earthly") enlightenment ("thousand"). The senses, which could have led to a realization of Lovemind, were simply scattered. They were wasted on indulgent hypersensuality. So, an immense, massive part of mind falls into the inaccessible Unconscious ("dies") during this Mindtransformation.

Fascinatingly, only exclusively human identities ("names of men") were lost to the deep Unconscious ("killed"). Note: The text does not say that intellect ("men") was killed, but only the *names* of men. So, it was false *identities* that died during this agonizing transition.

But why would mind have more than one "human identity"? Why is it "names," plural, and not simply "name"? This implies more than one human identity. It is a peripheral reference to the "game of life" played by the Soul through the centuries! It indicates polybiography. (Gnostic Christians, and others in the ancient Christian faith, were believers in reincarnation.)

But each merely "human" identity is false. *You are your Soul. You are Spirit. The human identities ("names") are just roles or masks of your deeper Self, the Soul. (The Soul is a role of deepest Self, Spirit.)* So if, in a previous life, your name was Jim Jones, and if, in a life before that, your name was Mary Smith and if, in five hundred other lives you had five hundred other names, these "names" (identities) all died. The egomind believes itself to be only the mindbrain of the current body.

Ego thinks that it is a body. It believes that *all mind is egomind.* This lie about "who I really am" sprouted from intellectual ideas ("men") with spiritual potential ("seven"). Going through the "games" of these false identities leads to the enlightenment of the whole Mind. For, at its deepest level, hypersensual mind is already enlightened ("thousand"). ("Thousand" = ten cubed). *It is the Lovemind.*

In schools of Buddhism, it is said, "You are already the Buddha." Early Christians had a precisely parallel one: "You are already the Christ." [31]

In dualism, egomind has separated, within illusionmind, from the Supreme. It feels alone, isolated, empty, in black infinity, adrift in immeasurable space. Abandoned and rejected, it feels dejected. It feels vulnerable and scared. It falls victim to the relentless enemy of Love ("fear"). (In other contexts, "fear" is awe, but here it is the pathological antiagapic force.) It then finds itself quite "outside" of Reality altogether. This is sickeningly terrifying, psychotogenic (crazy-making)!

The hungry need for Love is still there. Mind honors It ("gave glory to... God"). God (Lovemind; "heaven") is acknowledged, but this response does not emanate out of Love. This was only a mechanical response to Love's opposite, fear. So, these parts of mind were just afraid, not enlightened.

Verse 14. "The second trouble was over. Look! The third trouble is coming quickly."

Verse 15. "And the seventh angel trumpeted. And great voices occurred in heaven, saying, 'The kingdom of the world became [that] of our Lord, and of his Christ. And he will reign into the ages of the ages.'"

COMM: Superconscious Mind (Coremind, Lovemind) cries an inignorable message ("great voices... in heaven") to the conscious mind. Hypersensual mind (bodymind; "kingdom of the world") is

---

[31] For this and other forgotten sayings and teachings of Jesus and early Christians, see my *The Mystic Gospels of Jesus the Christ* , op cit.

turned to gold by the Midas touch of Lovemind ("...became the kingdom of our lord..."). This is earthly enlightenment.

This area of mind ("kingdom") was formerly ruled by hypersensuality, the sense-dominated mind, the bodymind or bionature. It becomes the "kingdom" of Lovemind. Love takes over the whole mind.

Lovemind rules in every nook and cranny of Mind ("ages of the ages").

Delightful, celebratory, ecstatic integration sweeps mind into Mind! Then, mind is staggered by the realization that lower mind is really just a distorted mirrorimage of the only Mind in existence! *The egomind is just a "mask" of Soulmind!* Even human personality, with its incomprehensible quirks, is also this Mind!

All people are fragments of the one Mind! So, they are already enlightened! This is like grace: All sentient beings already have it; they differ only in their *realization.* But their realization, or lack of it, *does not alter the fact that all sentient beings are in one hundred percent grace.*

In the same way, everyone is already one hundred percent Lovemind. This Supermind is just "playing roles" when It pretends to be ignorant, unenlightened, or even evil. At the beginning of human history, It willed Itself to forget that It was the One, the only Mind. Those parts of Itself (people) who have not yet remembered are, for all practical purposes, "separate" from the One. But they are still intrinsically, by nature, and in Reality, one with It, extensions of It.

Grace blossoms from the perfect Mind, the Love of God, so how could it be anything less than perfect, complete, one hundred percent!

Enlightenment follows the same pattern. At the Core of your mind, *you are already enlightened,* with a full and clear understanding of the whole cosmos and all Mind. But it does you no practical good *until you awaken to the fact.* It is this awakening to the pre-existent condition of Lovemind that we call "enlightenment." All Mind, including your own, is the property or "kingdom" of God.

Verse 16. "And the twenty-four old people in sight of God, sitting on their thrones, fell upon their faces, and worshiped God."

COMM: Experience ("old people") joins the rest of Mind in Love! Love is the truest meaning of "worship."

Verse 17. "[They were] saying, 'We are giving thanks to you, Lord, God, the Almighty, the One being and the One Who was, because you have taken your great Power and reigned.'"

COMM: Older mind shows an attitude of gratitude ("giving thanks")! Lovemind controls the whole Mind ("reigned"). It exudes mental energy ("power")! Love rules!

Verse 18. "'And the nations were made angry, and your anger came. And [came] the assigned time for the dead to be judged, and to give the reward to your slaves-- prophets, holy, and those fearing your name-- the small and the great, and to corrupt those who corrupt the earth.'"

COMM: Immediate displeasure ("anger") stirs the mind to white-hot intensity! Giant chunks of hypersensual mind ("nations") scream their fierce disapproval ("anger")! Lovemind screams right back!

What has them both so upset? They are frenetic over deactivated ("dead") but still explosively controversial thoughts.

The dispute is about evaluation ("judged"). Are these thoughts worthless, as hypersensual mind might argue, since they give no sensual feedback about the world? Or can they provide valuable Mindenergy if resurrected by Lovemind? Perfect standards of Love have the answer.

After divine Mind shines, It pries open the subconscious. This is a time for therapeutic scouring of all antiagapic thoughts!

Lovemind also strengthens ("rewards") positive thoughtstructures. These include prescience about the future spiritual path ("prophets"). These also include thoughts of obedience and service ("slaves"). Finally, they include all healing thoughts of Love ("holy"). These rewards express as feelings of contentment, satisfaction, and joy.

Reverential awe ("fear") is expressed by some positive thoughtgroups ("fearing your name"). The identity ("name") of Lovemind is recognized by them as supreme over the whole cosmos. The divine identity ("I am God in nature") supercedes and overrides the human identity ("I am Mary Smith"). At this point, the Mind realizes that It, to use Paul's words, "has the Mind of Christ." (1Co: 2:16) It is merged in mystical Union with that deepest Mind.

Here is a great mystical secret: Even those thoughts which abuse ("corrupt") hypersensual mind ("earth") are the One! For it is the One who alone can guarantee that karma boomerangs back on those who scatter energy, wasting it in hypersensual indulgence ("corrupt those who corrupt the earth"). The One has no real opposite. For all that oppose It are dreamillusions.

Through the cosmic law of perfect symmetry (reflectivity) or karma, this omniscient Mind sees to it that actions return to the actor just as they were sent forth into the world.

Verse 19. "And the divine habitation of God, in heaven, was opened up, and the ark of his covenant was seen, in his divine habitation. And lightnings, voices, thunders, and quakings, and a great hail occurred."

COMM: Lovemind ("divine habitation") is opened to cognitive view. Historically, the "ark" was a box that contained the recorded words of Jehovah, whom ancient Jews mistook for the God of illimitable Love. So, the collection of lawbased thoughts that misinterpret and misunderstand the true nature of God ("ark") present God as a cultural or religious exclusive possession. This "arkmind" sees God as a phenomenon of history, as bound by human behaviors and weaknesses (anger, jealousy), as all male. It buys, in a word, into the Jehovah-myth. This produces a disastrous national preference. Since this is thinly disguised bigotry, it has no place in Coremind (Lovemind).

Arkmind does not belong in the temple (God). It is an intrusion, out of place, an antique set of misunderstandings. It is created by mind, and then, artificially forced or superimposed upon the pure Love-nature, as mechanical religion. Lovemind is spiritual; *it is not religious.*

Arkmind has been illegitimately pushed into templemind. When it is seen, and contrasted with true Lovemind, the Mind rocks! It gazes at inner Infinity, the inner Beloved, [32] the "inner other," the true templemind. This blows the whole mind! It gazes dumbly at the Illimitable and the Immeasurable! A hurricane of rapid transformations occurs. Radical shifts ("shakings") transform hypersensual mind.

---

[32] For more information on this dazzling, radiant experience and its effect on life, see my *Falling In Love With Yourself: Love and the Inner Beloved*, op. cit.

Terrific shifts of energy ("lightnings") flash through mind! Messages ("voices") fly from one Mindarea to another! Intuitions of coming Mindstorms ("thunders") rock the interior world!

The godimage of Jehovah begins to fade. In time, it will be replaced entirely by the more enlightened view of the kind Lord of boundless Light and Love. Unlike Jehovah, this true God possesses illimitable forgiveness, and immeasurable compassion. (Compare 8:7.)

Dogma, cold and unloving ("hail"), includes religious mechanism, legalism, scripturalism, and Jehovism. It creates severe mindamage! It throws the psyche off-balance! It engenders dangerous extremes and catastrophic misunderstandings! [*This is to replace spirituality (Love) with mere religion.*]

Mind sees how decimating are the unloving dogmas ("hail") of the ancient wargod. And how wrong are they!

Chapter 12

Verse 1. "And a great sign was seen in heaven: A woman with the sun thrown about her, and the moon beneath her feet. Upon her head she had a crown of twelve stars. And she was pregnant."

COMM: This occurs in Lovemind ("heaven")! A few insufferably arrogant, tremblingly insecure, female "teachers" have claimed to be this "woman"! Literalism has thrown them into confused delusion! But the structure of the scene makes literalism impossible: stars, sun and moon are in impossible literal relationship.

In reality, this is the most ancient and powerful archetype in history. It is at once mother and goddess. (In anthropology, it is often called the "mothergoddess.")

She symbolizes the feminine aspects of cosmic Mind. In ancient cultures, she was Asherah, in Hebrew terms, *Shekinah*, in Egypt, Isis, in Babylon, Ishtar, in Greece, Persephone, in Rome, Venus, in Christianity, the Virgin Mary or Sophia, in Buddhism *Tara* or *Kwan Yin,* in Hinduism, *Parvati.* She is the right hemispheric functions of creativity-- dream-capacity, emotional, and much spiritual, thinking and feeling. As the wellspring of nature, mental fertility, and inner nourishment, she is a form of perfect Love. (Early Christians worshipped the goddess as "Sophia," a Greek name meaning "wisdom.")

Goddessmind is a part of Godmind. She is in the Center of, enveloped by ("thrown about her") the Lightmind ("sun"; Lovemind). She glows and shimmers with Lovelight. She is a major archetype of Lightsource, or divine enlightenment. "God is Light," said John (1 Jn. 1:5)

She is the Totality of Lovelight in the psyche. Fully enlightened, this breathtakingly beautiful collection of Mindareas makes progress ("feet") through the Unconscious ("moon"). The Unconscious gets behind, supports, her enlightenment ("beneath"). The moon's reflection of sunlight is the Unconscious coming into the light of conscious awareness, and also, illumination. It is this same moon that, in 6:12, dies to awareness ("turns to blood"), when the conscious mind loses access to It.

So, Light cannot be discovered without the cooperation of the positive Unconscious. (This is not the same as the subconscious-- the "garbage-bin" within the "personal Unconscious." See "Chart of Mind.")

Using her intellect ("head"), she exercises control ("crown"). She "rules" over positive areas of the Mind, both conscious and Unconscious. This is celestial, Lightfilled Mind ("stars"). It is cosmic order, arrangement, and wholeness ("twelve"; compare 7:4).

In their first appearance (1:16), "stars" are spiritual ("seven"). In 1:20, they are "angels." In 2:28, the beginning of Illumination is the "morning star." In 6:13, stars fall "into the earth." (So, they bring Light to hypersensual mind.)

So, the beautiful woman is immersed in oceans of Light, galaxies of Light. She is also ready to create a brand-new Mind-aspect ("pregnant").

Verse 2. "And she is crying out, being in birth-pains, and being tormented to give birth."

COMM: Psychic birth is no picnic! It puts you through arduous tortures ("pains" and "torment")! The mind knows that something is going on, for it can hear the cries of the Goddess (nature) within. But it has not a clue about what is happening. For her calls are inchoate. They convey no message except, "Pain!" The agony can drive this part of Mind to the verge of madness! When the mind hears the cries of the Unconscious, it is severely disturbed!

Verse 3. "And another sign was seen in heaven: Look! A great dragon, fiery red, with seven heads and ten horns. And upon its heads rested seven diadems."

COMM: Lazily to 'follow the leader,' in understanding this verse, goes nowhere fast. Many commentators, for two thousand years, have dogmatized! They follow each other like sheep. This powerful animalmind ("dragon"), says dogma, is irredeemably, irretrievably evil. It is irreversible devil and satan! And "he," all theologians agree, is the opposite of God, the immoral, evil, bestial, obscene Lord of darkness.

It was because the principle of evil was so personified that orthodox Christians became so paranoid about "devil-worship." Anyone, they contended, gripped by horrors of the diabolical, who did not worship *their* God (far too often the violent Jehovah) must be actively involved in the nightmare of satanic devilry! In the late Middle Ages, this led to the horrors of the truly diabolical "witch-trials," in which the only "demons" were the "Christian" inquisitors. They used and abused helpless girls and women to indulge their most despicable, lascivious, and perverted lusts. This led to tortures so horrific that the reader will be spared them, since even *their description* or contemplation might well be seen as an insane activity, so utterly and unutterably horrific were they!

So, instead of following earlier "Christians," who might well have been insane, it is better to let the symbolism speak for itself. It enfolds some real shockers!

"Dragonmind," at any rate, later is identified with fearmind ("devil"). But since it is synonymous with fearmind (satanmind), are we not force to conclude that it is indeed in violent, irreversible, hostile rebellion against Lovemind?

Yes, if we follow tradition, we are forced into that corner: God has lost control, goes the line, of at least a part of His/Her cosmos. This is usually seen as earth, ruled by Satan, a particularly creepy, filthy, and freaky being who is the Lord of evil. By far, he/it is the most wicked critter ever to exist! But if we dare to step outside of the old "tradition and orthodox" box, another perspective, that of monism, strikes a resonant if heretical chord! For all the internal evidence speaks against the facile assumption that the "dragon" is absolutely evil:

First, he appears "in heaven." What the hell is he doing in heaven? Our studies have shown beyond reasonable doubt that "heaven" is consistently the perfect deepest Unconscious-- Lovemind, Spirit, or God. (Compare 3.12; 4:1, 2; 5:3; 6:13; 8:1, 10, 13; 9:1; 10:1, 4-6, 8; 11:6, 12, 15; and 12:1.) This is pristine, stainless, flawless Coremind. What could be a more horrific heresy than that *the "devil" lives within God? Yet the text of the Bible itself* places dragonmind in "heaven." But Lovemind is the noblest, deepest Mindarea of all Mind! Traditionalist explanations are feeble at best. It is terrifying and frightening to contemplate the Lord of evil *inside* or somehow within the Lord of Love! And it is a scary step to turn away from centuries of orthodoxy in search of better answers. Still, if we are willing to be thrilled, even scared a little, in our inward journey, another explanation offers itself:

This dragonmind is, sorely, at its best, a servant of Lovemind! There! The awful, terrible, dangerous heterodoxy has been verbalized! This idea scandalizes and terrifies the average believer! And even if she does not run screaming bloody murder from the impact of this idea, it still knocks her socks off!

But, with a little patient and reasonable consideration, it will become apparent that the philosophy of monism allows for no other explanation. This flatly contradicts and denies the harsh, unyielding dualism of the later Orthodox Church. (It is the "monistic" cosmos, in which only the One exists. Early gnostic Christians embraced this philosophy.)

If true, this threatening mind ("dragon") must work not only with permission, but as expression, of Lovemind! In its tiniest, immediate incarnation, this horrible mind, dragonmind, is "satan" ("devil"). It is fearmind. Keep in mind that fear acts out of ignorance, not always out of evil. But in a larger overview, a cosmic perspective, it must exist within the One. This is far from obvious to the cursory glance. Even indepth research often misses it.

Please be patient. We know how terribly antichristian this sounds. So, let it be known here that the author is a Christian, although not an orthodox, historical, organized one! This monistic perspective seems to fly in the face of all that is reasonable! It seems to threaten the very fabric of compassion and logic. In fact, all that is sane and holy seems to butt heads with it!

But is it really that horrible? In past centuries, women were raped and butchered by ecclesiastics for this heresy, and men were tortured and finally beheaded. To the dualistic fanatics, the truly horrific implication was, "You might as well worship Satan as God, for all is God anyway." This was hideous ammunition used by heresiologists (specialists in heresy) to burn people alive! These people, who were so sickeningly barbarous, were traditionalists and orthodox. When we know that, it makes it easier to consider some unorthodox views!

So, when we look at monism objectively, stripped of religious terrors and bigotries, what do we find?

Well, to begin with, it is *certainly not* the same thing to worship Satan as to worship God. Rape is not the same as Love. Murder is not equivalent to mercy. Monism does not wash away or neutralize all eth ics and morality. (This is a common lie, told by its ignorant enemies.)

Historically, monists included mystics, and mystics included saints! So, monism is not a demonic, demoralizing, diabolical philosophy designed to dominate weak and unstable minds. (It is just another lie that this is its effect or appeal.)

Monism holds simply that God (Love) has never lost control of the universe. It also teaches that *the world makes sense.* It explains, as does no other philosophy, that *there is a reason for evil.* It carefully distinguishes between God's *active* will, which is always Love and joy for all, and God's *permissive* will, which permits Souls to experience "bad" things, so that they might perfect their own interior Love.

Many monists embrace reincarnation. For its fullest effect, and greatest explanatory power, monism *must be combined with reincarnation.*

This philosophy, embraced by innumerable spiritual Jews, Christians, and Moslems through the centuries, gives meaning to life. *The majority of the world's population has always believed in reincarnation.* In the twenty-first century, we are beginning to discover that an incredibly high percentage of Christians, Moslems, and Jews are closet reincarnationists! This philosophy sees the earth as a school. When people "fail a test" in this school, they have to take it again, until they pass.

After decades of the most careful research, in which every philosophy and spiritual tradition has been studied, this is the conclusion of the author: *No explanation of evil is as efficacious and allembracing as reincarnation.* Those who suffer now do so at times because they have brought suffering upon others. But not all are guilty of this. At times, the Soul chooses a particular painful limitation or imperfect body, family, or environment in order to teach the mind a particular lesson.

This makes for a balanced and just world. It also makes a great learning agenda possible. The very poor of this life, for example, might have been the very rich of the past, who mocked and brutalized the poor. Very weak people were once so strong that they took advantage of, and abused, the weak.

But the Soul can also choose to take lessons that are not this kind of reflective karma. Many saints, for example, suffered from various biomedical conditions. This implies that their Souls chose these conditions before birth in order to polish or perfect certain characteristics, such as compassion, humility, sympathy, empathy, understanding, softness, gentleness, generosity, tenderness, or Love. This implies that the Soul has knowledge of, and the ability to manipulate, the genome.[33]

The possibility that, despite all appearances, Love continues to rule, can become evident only when personal will agrees with divine will. When it does not, which is often, dragonmind symbolizes the parts of mind turned away from God, obedient to fear. And fear is the conceptual opposite of God or Love. Dragonmind can be satanmind. (Fearmind is satanmind.) But that in no way makes dragonmind voluntarily evil and irredeemable. For it to be absolutely evil would mean that evil is just as real as absolute Good or God. But all in the Enlightenment Tradition agree that *God is the most real Reality in the cosmos.* It is partly because God is more real than you and me that we owe Him/Her worship.

The root-falsehood of "dualism" is the essence of all illusion. Dualism starts with the premise that *anything can exist apart from Mind or Lovemind.* While this sounds harmless on paper, it leads to countless indescribable hells. Monism, by contrast, holds that the cosmos is the dream of Lovemind, and, being Its dream, nothing could possibly exist without, or "outside" of, It.

How does this "dragon" fit in with the will of Love? The will is for us to grow. We must often do that through suffering, which is "fire." The "dragon" is "fiery-red." (Compare 6:4 and 9:17.) Pain pushes the bio-energy of the first chakra (red) into higherspectrum energies. This bio-energy is converted to mental, and later, to spiritual, Mindenergies.

---

[33] For a fictional account of how this might really happen, see my novel *Luminous Ecstasies and Passions: Journeys Into Afterlife* (Liberty Township, Ohio; Love Ministries, Inc., 2000)

(Other symbols use the colors yellow and green as markers of this growth.)

In time, mind, with its polychromatic forces, actually becomes Lovenergy or Lovemind (supreme Mind). So, the existence of the inner dragon is *permitted* by cosmic Mind; but it is also *created* by that Mind. For there is, and has always been, only one Creator. That is why positive spirituality ("seven") marks the intellectual part ("heads") of this mindarea ("dragon"). For Love's sake, cosmic Mind continually and repeatedly exposes us to every form of agony and nightmare. This is not because the cosmos contains no Mind, or is merciless. It is, in fact, preparing us to receive God's greatest gift-- Him/Herself, as Lovemind!

Even fear, Love's opposite, is precisely this type of growthinducing hell. Fear is used by cosmic Mind as a tool to force agonizing growth. Fear often pries the mind out of deep ignorance. Even when we are unwilling to progress, fear often drives us forward! Even if we do not know that we must progress, fear is often the instrument of choice. Cosmic Mind uses it to create the fertile soil of luxurious growth, so that the bloom of Love might blossom.

Fear is the servant of Love. It is also a fine aid in our everyday spiritual growth. Demons and ghastly nightmares literally "scare the hell out of us," as hell is suffering in Loveless darkness. It is but a tiny baby-step in philosophy to hook up fear with fearmind, and then, to connect the dots, so that fearmind is seen to be serpentmind, a term used later. This, when serving fear, is dragonmind, and this, at least in some contexts, is satanmind. Exposure to fear is, in fact, how we become wiser, stronger, more patient and loving. So, saying that the "devil" secretly serves God is just a way of implying that Love, being supremely wise, uses fear for Its own intentions, will, or purpose. It is smart, and sharp, enough to do this! *Only in monism* has God (Love) *never* lost control of the whole cosmos. For even the "enemies" of God are "working for" God, to force Souls into Love-development!

But is it not sheerest, most obvious, madness to claim that the evil serve Love? It does indeed seem quite nuts to the human mind. But in the most spiritual collection of ideas, which represents the supreme best of the best from all religions, cultures, and centuries, there is a secondary teaching: The cosmos is the "dream of God," dreamed up through you and through me. If this has any merit, then monism (One Mind is the only Reality) must follow. For *nothing can exist outside of God's dream, which is the whole of creation (reality, cosmos).*

This idea has not historically appealed to fools, neophytes, or gullible followers. For in this intercultural, interreligious, and timeless Way (called the Enlightenment Tradition) have appeared some of the greatest spiritual luminaries-- including Jesus, Solomon, Al Hallaj, the Buddha, Patanjali, Lao Tzu, St. Theresa, St. Catherine, and many other diamonds of history. Here, we find men and women who made it *their job to figure out the cosmos!* They took this task very seriously, and *invested all their time in it.* They refused to settle for easy or quick answers. They paid for their wisdom with the currency of timenergy, and also with real blood, sweat, and tears! They were, in short, history's most serious students of Reality. And they embraced monism!

The big clue that dragonmind is a potentially positive force comes from its spiritual ("seven") intellect ("heads"). So, dragonmind uses intellect which, when in harmony with the divine will, strengthens us in Love. It teaches and elicits Love by resisting It!

How does the lower intellect resist Love? It creates a bundle of ideas and a packet of philosophies that seem to make perfectly reasonable sense, but that leave out Love. It can make even religions that do this. These "dragonreligions" are antiagapic in the extreme, and include many silly cults. (Cults are defined not by size, but by mindcontrol, and by following egos.) *Just because something seems logical is no reason to make it the foundation of our eternal Soul-journey!* For this Journey, in the final analysis, is not about only "brains," but is all about Love!

It is clear that, when dragonmind serves fear, it is "satanmind."

Each "head" has a "diadem." (a type of "crown"). Like the One upon the throne, like the old people, dragonmind is also given authority, influence, or control ("diadems").

It is appointed by God. How can we know this? Because, by very definition, *God is ultimately in control of everything.* (Even dualists usually believe this.) Also, when the diadems on the heads are mentioned, the writer goes out of his way to mention the "seven" again. In this context, a positive (spiritual) influence is implied. (The Greek uses the word "diadem," which technically differs from a crown, for it is a kind of soft turban worn by rulers in Middle Eastern cultures. But the symbolism is the same.)

Dragonmind also has animal-nature ("horns"). It can be deadly, wild, and vicious. Fear can terrify, destroy, or cripple. It can move into your life like a chain-saw through butter, mangling the mind and torturing the heart. But, still, the positive mind also draws strength from bio-energy ("fiery red"). The brain itself is a biostructure. It is the organic (biological) interface with the nonphysical Mind or Soul. Brain, unlike supernatural Mind, is nature. Although some humans seem to lack functional brains, it is a structure shared in common with a wide spectrum of creatures, especially sentient mammals. It grows from bionature.

In fact, this is doubly emphasized in symbolism. For the dragon has "ten" horns. "Ten" is hypersensual (earthly) enlightenment, which is not full enlightenment. Still, this indicates that dragonmind is intimately woven into this state of joy and wisdom.

Verse 4. "And its tail is dragging a third of the stars of heaven, and it threw them into the earth. And the dragon has stood in sight of the woman who was about to give birth, so that, when she does give birth, it might eat down her child."

COMM: The subconscious ("tail") does dragon's nefarious work. (Compare 9:10, 19). The subconscious is the stinking, acrid, ugly, antiagapic garbage-dump of Mind. It is filled with filth and putrescence, things rotten and repulsive. It perceives no grace. Its most illuminated elements ("stars") are not very bright. It lies, and tells you that you are outside of grace ("third"; compare 8:7-12 and 9:15, 18.) Thus does it sabotage the realizations of grace.

The spiritual Light of Lovemind ("stars") must be later forcibly pushed ("thrown") into hypersensual mind ("earth"), which is beginning to see the Light. And this is all thanks to dragonmind. This is the right use of free will! ("Dragonmind", later called "serpentmind," is defined as, among other mental operations, free will. See later.)

The tender, nurturing, maternal, fertile components of Mind, the "feminine" ones ("goddessmind") can perceive ("see") dragonmind.

She is about to create ("give birth to") a new and very complex thoughtstructure. It can be fairly inferred that she, as Goddess, will give birth to a divine entity. "Goddessmind," then, is about to produce a magnificent Love-producing and -supporting Mind. She is going to birth a god! She reorganizes Lovemind, and this coalesces as new realization. From mind's view, this realization is just now coming into being ("born"). But it has always existed, within the mothergoddess.

The inner rebirth ('coming baby') is psychospiritual. By contrast, the red color of the dragon proves that it is of the bodymind, sense-dominated, or earthly nature. ("Red" is bio-energy.) Dragonmind wants to bring down and assimilate ("eat down") the rebirth-energy ('baby'). It wants to drag its spiritual energy down to the bionatural and hypersensual level. It wants to turn potential Lovenergy into fearenergy. For dragonmind knows how to work only through body-identification, even body-obsession. Dragonmind wants to appropriate neopsychicmind (the 'baby'). But the infant is destined to fulfill a higher purpose.

Does the dragon represent cruelty? Not necessarily. Like everything else in Revelation, "eating" and 'baby' are symbolic. So, as repulsive as the literal act is, it is not representative of great horror when seen symbolically. "Eating" represents the assimilation and use of Mindenergy. This process is not "evil." (Compare 2:7 and 10:10.) It is a very disturbing, unforgettable, graphic, absorbing symbol of mental energytransfer.

Verse 5. "And she gave birth to a son, a male, who is about to be shepherding all the nations in a staff made of iron. And her child was snatched toward God and toward his throne."

COMM: In 2:27, it is the Soul that must "shepherd the nations in a staff made of iron." Here, then, is the Soul in its 'baby' phase. It has just emerged from the union of nature (mother) and Spirit (father).

This scene takes us back in time to the original "birth" of the Soul ('baby') from primal Spiritmind. It is retrospective. Before this act of spiritual creation, Mind was all alone in the void. Then, It projected itself as a "baby," letting the feminine side of Its own mind ("woman") nurture the new being, as well as the process. For the first time, Spirit, as Soul ('baby'), came into an entirely new sensation-- vulnerability.

For, in addition to playing the "woman," to keep things exciting, another part of the primal Mind was playing "dragon." It was threatening to "attack" the new and vulnerable Soul.

Why was the Soul so weak? It was a sector of divine Mind that the divine One had willed into a state of amnesia, to keep existence fascinating and spicy (read "compelling," with Mind-gripping action!) The moment that the Soul forgot its full identity with Spirit, it then became limited, according to the rules of the game. Seeing this illusion of separation as reality, it inevitably fell into delusion, forgetting also that the rest of the cosmos was also perfect Mind. That was the steep deep downside to the "rollercoaster" of earthly life, from which it is just now beginning to recover (within some human minds).

The Soul is a crucial, indispensable "player" in the drama. It is at present unenlightened, still suffering from Love-induced amnesia. This is just only now starting to wear off.

But in the beginning it felt very vulnerable. Even after a sense of fallibility and openness to harm had set in, however, the Soul longed for even ever greater adventure. The Soul fears nothing, for the same reason that horror-movies do not really scare grown-up people: They know that movies are not real, and that, after the movie, they can just get up, walk out, and return to normal, nonthreatening life! This is exactly how the Soul feels about the "virtual reality" (dream) of this life.

The Soul takes nothing that happens with absolute seriousness-- except Love! It knows that nothing in this life, except Love, is real. It is all *maya*, illusion, or dream. So, nothing can really scare you at a Soulevel!

The most dynamic way to make life more exciting, It decided, was to imitate Its Master, Spirit. So, Soul, taking a cue, willed Itself to forget. It forgot that it was Mind-- nonphysical, timeless, eternal. It plunged unabashedly into the dream, and allowed the dream of "material, physical, external reality" to swallow It. It tumbled into full identification with hypersensual mind, sense-domination; then, it fell even further down, into animalmind. Like a man dreaming that he is a dog, Soul dreamed that it was a lower form of life, a human being. It slept, and dreamed Its dreams. Early Christian gnostic texts portray the Soul as both "asleep" and "in Hades".

One of those dreams is your current life. In fact, it is what you are doing at this precise moment. Your Soul is dreaming that it is you, and you are dreaming that you are reading these words. This explains the great mystery of why "enlightenment" has always been synonymous with "awakening"!

At the last breath-taking moment, the vulnerable Soul ('baby') is 'saved' by divine Power ("snatched towards God")! In Its infancy, it has only just emerged from Godmind (when Godmind was playing the role of Goddessmind). Just when it was on the threshold of being swallowed by animalmind ("dragon"), Love came to its rescue, drawing it into the Light of invulnerable Lovemind ("God" and "throne"). So, the Soul's energy was allowed to be cycled into fearmind. It was preserved to be invested in Lovemind.

Here, at this point in Revelation, Soul has emerged from the "womb" of Lovemind. It has not moved far away from Its Source. But within a very short time, It is already in danger and peril! It needs actively to be shoved closer to Sourcemind (Lovemind) again. This proximity to Lovemind is Its natural condition. It must be protected from dragonmind (free will in the grip of fear).

This retroanalytic psychochronology takes us back eons, to the moment when Soul first mentally "parted" from Spirit. Actually, Spirit/Soul *never separated! This division was only conceptual.* They shared the common *dream* that the Soul was separating from Spirit. Stated variantly, Spirit began to "play the game," or don the mask, of the Soul. It began to play the role of the Soul upon the stage of the "material" cosmos. That was when the allpowerful, omnipotent Spirit willed Itself to forget.

But Spiritmind has also willed that, at the end, It will remember, and rule the entire hypersensual mind ("all the nations"). This is the Soul's destiny. But its final, ultimate, supreme destiny is to remember that It is, has always been, Spirit.

Still, Its first growthphases are marked by primitive mental states ("iron"). These are collectively toddlermind.

Verse 6. "And the woman fled into the desolation. For she has there a place prepared from God, so that they can nourish her there 1260 days."

COMM: Goddessmind withdraws after she has performed her miraculous work of rebirth as ("giving birth" to) neopsychicmind. She retires not to die, but to be nourished. She still lives, integrated with Lovemind, after this powerful psychotropic event.

This withdrawal from activity occurs in a place prepared "from God." This mental space ("desolation") originates within the cosmic Unconscious. The place, like the Goddess, is actually a part of Lovemind. Monism: (*all things originate from Lovemind*). But this is a dry, unproductive Mindarea ("desolation"). This desolate Mindspace is traversed by Goddessmind during the darknight. Mystics are always saying that one must go through the "desert" or "wilderness" to find God. When you go through hell to get to heaven, both have their being in the one Mind.

Goddessmind is nurtured for 1260 days. Numerologically, this is precisely the same symbolism that we already encountered in 11:3. There, the bimind was to "prophesy" for this same time. 1260 is a recapitulation of the entire spiritual journey. Just to make it simple, broken down into its primes, in order, it is: 2 x 2 x 3 x3 x 5 x 7. Here is a quick recap: You spend much time in dualism (ignorance-- the "two twos"); then, you spend as much time in wholeness ("two threes"); then, human nature tests you ("five"); and finally, you become an incarnation of Love ("seven"). The part of your mind called "Goddessmind" consciously becomes Lovemind.

This 1260 is also the "three and a half years." So, it is the conflict between wholeness ("three") and dualism ("half"). This is a battle that *you personally must fight and win. It is that between monism and dualism.* If you opt for dualism, you arrest your own development, decelerating spiritual blossoming.

The most tender, nourishing aspect of Lovemind (Goddess) goes through a period of conflict. This is mercifully limited in and by time ("days"). This is the dreadful wilderness experience (darknight) of the mystic. (Although filled with pain, Mind is actually being nourished during this agony.) In fact, it is being "nourished" by the pain, for pain is teacher.

Verse 7. "And a war occurred in heaven. Michael and his angels warred with the dragon and its angels."

COMM: Conflict ("war") abruptly breaks out in Lovemind ("heaven"). Lovemind is transcendent of any true conflict. It knows that this "war" is ultimately illusion. But this conflict will not alter mind unless Lovemind "plays along". Spiritmind is all the "players" in the "play." God is both "sides" of the conflict. This reminds us that *everything, pleasant or otherwise, occurs in Lovemind.* Yes, the dragon is illusion; so, then, is the "war." Still, the entire "virtual reality" occurs in deepest Mind, Godmind, and is seen (known) by the conscious mind (John). This, yet again, is monism: The sensory, "material, external" universe is not all there is to God. But God pervades and indwells all as its Dreamer. We return to the mystic formula: All is Mind, and Mind is God.

Dragonmind (fearmind) is very deeply pervasive. It exists as potential, imagined or experienced, within many levels of Mind. Fearmind, working secretly for Lovemind, is permitted for a time even within the unstained, flawless Lovemind (Coremind, Essence, Spirit, God, Absolute).

The presence of the bestial and repulsive fearmind (dragonmind, satanmind) as a psychoholographic[34] illusion within Lovemind generates a natural, powerful counter-response: Lovemind produces Michaelmind.

But Michaelmind is not enlightened, despite its valiant defense of the good. For it still beholds a cosmos divided between "good" and "evil." That dualistic illusion of separation is, in fact, the source of "war."

There are "two" mindfactions. Traditionally, Michael (pronounced "Me'-kah-el," not "My'-kul") means, "who is like God." So this is obviously a positive thoughtgroup. It is produced by, and reflects with a fair degree of accuracy, the Love of Lovemind. In fact, although willed into darkness and duality, it is a subset of Lovemind. Since Michael is

---

[34] A "psychohologram" is a dream-illusion image that appears to exist independently in the "outer" world, but is really an image within the mind. I coined this word in 1986 in *The Way of Universal Love* now rewritten and republished as Part I of *Luminous Jewels of Love and Light* Volume 1 (Liberty Township, Ohio; Love Ministries, Inc.,2003)

an archangel, a lord of angels, "Michaelmind" is the ultrapowerful aspect of Mind that regulates much goodness.

Yet the dragonmind is also aided, not by "demons," but by "angels." This is yet another important clue that it is secretly working for Lovemind. So, both sides are positive, in the big picture. "War" is as symbolic as everything else in Revelation. In the ultimate analysis, the "war" is not real. It is a kind of pretend-war, a war occurring in only illusion, or being dreamed up. For both Michaelmind and dragonmind "work for" the same "boss," Lovemind. It is, even more startlingly, the One Who plays both roles. "War," then, is not only conflict, but a division of energies (see 9:7; 11:7). This is essentially, but secretly, a friendly division of gigapsychons of Mindenergy.

For the divine Mind does not, cannot, exist divided from Itself. It cannot be at war with Itself. A secret but healthy agreement exists between both parties-- Michaelmind and dragonmind. But this is known only in the deepest Unconscious. Revelation is the view of the conscious mind. Here, "war" is an apparent disagreement regarding the best, healthiest, most positive use of the Mind's spiritual energy.

Verse 8. "And it [the dragon] did not prove strong. But no place of them was found in heaven."

COMM: A test of strength, like a gymnastic competition, is this apparent "war." Evil, ignorant animalmind was not anywhere nearly as strong as the Mind of goodness (archangel "Michael"). So, its regular hang-out in Lovemind ("place") was lost to it ("not found"). Vicious animalmind dragonmind and its "angels" ("them") was booted out of Lovemind, as illusion-contaminant, disgusting and repulsive. Lovemind ("heaven") then returned to a state of sweet pristinity. So, boosting the drama to a crescendo, the plot thickens as "conflict" heats up!

Verse 9. "And the great dragon was thrown into the earth, and his angels were thrown with him. He is the archaic serpent, who is called 'devil' and 'satan,' who is causing to err the entire inhabited [area]."

COMM: Free will in the strangle-hold of fear ("satan") *gains strength. At its peak of power, it actually becomes* an embodiment of fearmind. Regular, consistent Love turns you into God, so consistent fear turns you into "satan"-- a *mindset that is harmful and destructive.*

For it swallows you into the nightmarish disease of anagaposis (a love-less state) or even antiagaposis (the mental illness of resisting Love). *(A good, practical definition of "hell" is any condition "outside" of Love. No real state could be external to Lovemind, so all hells must be illusion.)*

"Satan" *is* not a "person," but is symmetric with God: God is Love, satan fear. Satan is not a "fallen angel," But even this archaic myth, when seen as symbolism, has its own truth to tell: Satan's original name was "Lucifer," which means "Light-bringer." The original satan was created by God (Love) as one of the most powerful and wisest aspects of spiritual Minds ("angels"). *It was clearly God's will that even "satan" serve the good.* Was God's will truly frustrated?

God is omnipotent, which means simply that *God's will can never be frustrated.* God is also omnipresent, which means that God is *within you at this moment-- and present everywhere else in the cosmos.* So, Lovemind must be the real core even of the artificial fearmind. God is also within me, and everybody else-- including satan! (If this were not so, God could not be truly omnipresent.) And there is no such condition as "semi-omnipresent"! So, the will of God can be side-tracked. It can be postponed. It can be *partially* deactivated, neutralized, or cancelled. But the will of God is absolutely irresistible. *It cannot be totally eradicated.*

It was, and is, God's will that satan serve the good. Monism suggests that satan does serve the larger good by resisting the shorterm good. Satan is like the weights that resist you in training, strengthening your muscles. The weights are genuine resistance. But they are the only vehicles that can increase your strength. The mental cosmos is analogous: *Without resistance, you could never grow.* Satan provides exactly this type of "dynamogenic" (strength-creating) resistance. So, behind the scenes, *even fear works to create, strengthen, and increase Love.*

Here, though, it is banished from highest Mind. Dragonmind (fear-control) is forcefully pushed down ("thrown") "into" hypersensual mind ("earth"). Fear enters the nervousystem via the brain, and so, comes "into" mind through the senses. That is how it is moved into the sense-dominated mind.

Why? Because the entire sense-dominated mind must be *"tested"* *by exposure to fear* in its most naked essence. This is terrifying, and it is not unusual for a highly developed spiritual being to take *her most important spiritual tests* through her senses! This occurs, in turn, through the body, as in the "test" of sexual indulgence, or appetites for food!

Hypersensual mind can become even *her most important teacher.*

Endogenous fear (fear from within, not caused by the world) amplifies fear. It is deeper and more mysterious than "exogenous" fear (caused by an "external" stimulus). A fear that is based, for example, on a neurotransmitter imbalance can seem to come from nowhere, and to be caused by nothing. It can be so severe as to cause the victim to *doubt her very sanity.*

Fear is designed to drive you to surrender! But you must not surrender to the fear. You must simply "give up" any idea of being able to "save" or "repair" yourself. As this helplessness sinks in, you finally get it: You must yield to a larger Mind, deep within your own mind-- the Lovemind. You will have lost control of even your own mind! *Forced into surrender, you are forced onto the path of ultimate enlightenment.*

The aim of "biofear" (fear based on physiology), the secret servant of Lovemind, is to drive the victim totally into *personal hopelessness.* Only when she has been forced to *give up entirely* on her personal resources is she then ready, and able, to surrender to Lovemind. Stubborn human nature, being what it is, must lose all other available, and personal, alternatives before it takes the great step of surrender.

But what about the titles "devil" and "satan"? Do they not prove dragonmind to be evil-- indeed, the ultimate evil? It would be very easy, at a glance, to believe so. Almost every commentator has indeed stated it this way and it would be very easy to play "follow the leader". In fact, this has been done many times. But let's look a little more carefully, trying to strip off the accumulations of acculturation: The first identification was as "the archaic serpent."

To early Christians, "serpent" was a symbol of free will. Their most famous serpent-symbol was that of a perfect circle or ring, formed by the serpent swallowing its own tail. (As noted earlier, the circle is a symbol of infinity.) This serpent was at once a representation of darkness and of light. But how could it have been both? This complex symbolism included two factors: 1) the darkness of following free will, and 2) the light when free will freely, voluntarily gives itself up. The mystical Christians (gnostics) knew that free will created all kinds of horrors, as karma. But they also recognized it as a "Savior," or Way out of the mess! The grabber is that dragonmind is irredeemably evil, absolutely evil, according to the official dogma of the dualistic Church.

Dragonmind does have a very dark side. It can serve fearmind. It can be cloaked in ignorance. It is when these conditions prevail that dragonmind is satanmind. But what if dragonmind is *not always* satanmind?

Could it be that the mystically illuminated conscious mind (John) knows something that is not common knowledge? After dramatic revelation, including many secrets, could 'he' not suspect a "behind the scenes" synergy between dragonmind and the Lovemind expelling it? Could the two not be moving synergistically in a carefully, choreographed dance?

Monistics (mystics) do not believe that God lost control of earth. But official Church-dogma says that this is exactly what happened in Genesis. Does God control the mind of the "devil"? This is a very profound, and usually forbidden, question, almost never examined. For the average Christian, Jew, or Muslim, the entire inquiry is a dangerous absurdity. It is unworthy of attention. She believes that the monstrosity called "satan" is completely unregulated by God. But this independent "devil" is living and actual proof that God can lose control of part of the cosmos! So, as omnipresence is denied by dualism, here, omnipotence is also crashed!

God has already lost control on earth, says the dangerous dualistic myth. Having involuntarily lost the war against "evil" on earth, he is not all-knowing. He cannot be. Nor is He all powerful. Some loonier literalists go so far as to believe that God was outwitted and duped by a reptilian brain about the size of a small marble-- that of a snake! Since this silly literalism flatly denies all three cosmic powers ('omni's': omniscience, omnipotence, and omnipresence) of God, mystics reject it. The whole premise that God could ever lose control is flawed. But the only alternative explanation usually lamely offered is that God granted permission for real evil to exist. This he "had to do" says the lame absurdity, in order to "prove" that his power was greater than satan's. This reminds us of the strutting alcoholic who, in a drunken stupor, boasts that he is more powerful than any insect.! This, however, is an operational denial of the goodness of God. So, which are we to reject-- God's power or God's goodness?

But there is a third alternative: What if omniscient Mind knew that dragonmind, even though apparently working at cross-purposes against Love, was indeed serving to make minds and hearts stronger? Could satanmind be a valuable part of human spiritual education? (Dragonmind is free will under the control of fear.) Could it not be working in a secret conspiracy with Love, as the testing component of Mind?

Perhaps all the potential, undeveloped, or undiscovered spirituality (Love) of dragonmind has been obliterated, historically, by an insistence on ultimate, absolute dualism. Besides that, the devil makes a wonderfully convenient scape-goat. This stark sinister splitting of God from devil has created a human cosmos that apparently belongs to the latter! This belief is held solidly, immovable and immutable. But it creates horrific anxiety, and an ocean of fears. It also makes for some really sticky and deep questions about what the hell is really going on! Yet dualism has always marked the underlying philosophy and theology of the official, orthodox Christian church. Maybe the horrors and nightmare of its history can be explained by the fact that it has fallen into illusion, which it insists is the absolute "truth." Is it perhaps a higher wisdom to recognize that temptation and even suffering are a part of God's *permissive* will (although not His *active* will)? This perspective contradicts much in traditional Jewish, Christian, and Islamic orthodoxy. But, in the account of the ancient Hebrews, their godform Jehovah lost it in Eden! Control was wrested from his tight grip, and he was no match for the snake! The rebellion of their "devil" succeeded brilliantly! From the looks of things, he is still having a pretty sound victory on earth.

But what if, as mystics believe, the devil were not a person, but simply fear? This replaces the medieval view of the "lord of darkness" as the world's worst fiend. There is no "devil" as a horned person in a skin-tight, red suit carrying a pitch-fork. Could not fear be Love's negative polarity, Its complete absence? Fear is the root of moral error. Cruelty rises from fear. Often, fear can act even subconsciously. So, fear better fits the description of dragonmind given here. For it is creating mistakes in ("causing to err") the whole thought-filled ("inhabited") mind. Instead of being *deliberately and voluntarily evil*, dragonmind is creating error or making mistakes! John does not present dragonmind as a ghastly evil in fully conscious and aware rebellion against Love. No, instead, he presents it as in error or ignorance. This is much closer to a psychological explanation of the "devil." It rejects much that is totally superstitious, foolish, absurd, or illogical.

If the "devil" is the mental illness of fear, this does not dilute the serious nature of deliberate, intentional evil. It remains horrendous, ghastly, and nightmarish, even if much of it can be explained as fear. And deliberate evil does still create hells of unimaginable suffering!

Verse 10. "And I heard a great voice in heaven saying, 'Right now became the salvation and the Power and the kingdom of our God, and the authority of his Christ. For the blamer of our brothers was thrown, who blames them in the sight of our God day and night.'"

COMM: Dragonmind self-judges, or "blames." It censures and convicts. That is why it is called the "blamer". Many other translations call it "accuser," giving dragonmind the most negative spin. (Traditional translators all seem to be convinced that the dragonmind is the ghoulish megademon from hell.) When it points out responsibility ("blames") of the parts of mind that serve Love ("our brothers"), this observer need not be "bad" or evil. It might, in fact, act as the conscience, pointing out where/when mind acts against Love.

Does fear ever work for Love? Paradoxically, yes. For fear creates inner hells which demonstrate just how agonizing is the Love-starved life. Fear drives us away from fear; it also drives us away from false solutions. It drives us, in time, away from the "material" world. It drives us into the arms of Love. There, we can find no answers.

Fear serves our best interests by proving that materialism and hypersensuality are dead ends. For they create only fear, never Love.

Fear gives the same indirect protection as does poison ivy: It makes you feel so miserable that you want to avoid it like the proverbial plague. And simply avoiding fear can be the first step towards turning to its opposite, Love.

There were four instant responses when dragonmind was forced ("thrown") into hypersensual mind ('earth'; see verse 9): 1) salvation, 2) Power, 3) kingdom, and 4) authority given to the "Christ." Salvation implies grace: All beings are completely forgiven for all sins. They are absolved by an infinite Love that is greater than any conceivable sin.

Here, traditional dogmatists also encounter a sticky wicket: Which is greater-- the power of sin, or God's power to forgive? If a sin exists that is greater than God's ability to forgive, then God is limited, and weak. But the convenient cop-out here is that God *does not want* to forgive all sins. So, God could forgive all sin if He wanted to, but He does not want to. In Second Peter 3:9, it flatly contradicts this stupid argument: "The Lord ... does not want any to be destroyed, but wants all to attain to repentance." So, if the dogma of the Church is, as it claims, based upon the holy ancient texts of the Bible, this text contradicts the Church.

This text also, viewed objectively, implies a shattering "heresy" so malevolent to the status quo that it is regarded as the most demonic and satanic in the world: It implies that *everyone will someday be saved!* In John 12:32, Jesus said, "If I be lifted up, I shall draw all men to myself." Romans 5:18 shows a parallel between Adam's bringing death to "all men," so Christ brought to "all men" salvation. It says, "Through one act of justification, the consequence to all men is the declaration that they are righteous, for life." First Timothy 2:4 also says of the will of God, "... whose will is that all men should be saved..." Christ is identified in First Timothy 4:10 as the "Savior of all men." In Titus 2:11, "the grace of God, which brings salvation to all men, has been manifested."

Universal salvation has been anathema to the organized, official Church since about the year 200, but it exists in these document-texts of Christian founders. For, if taken literally, these texts *put the Church out of business*! The historical Church has practiced exclusivity, the opposite of the tolerant inclusivity of the first Christian message. The basis for universalism is a major theme of the Christian Greek Scriptures, and that is the teaching of grace. Grace teaches the astonishing truth that people are not saved because they are "good," or because they are Christian. In fact, they are surely not saved just because they are a certain *denomination* of Christianity. They are saved because it is the decision of cosmic Mind that they be saved. Salvation is not earned; it is a gift. All salvation originates with Lovemind. God's forgiveness is unlimited and illimitable. No sin is ever greater than Love.

Jesus said that God gave the sunshine and the rain to both good and bad people. This is an example of how God's Love is so great that it overwhelms and even neutralizes the effects of human stupidity and ignorance (sins). But the official Church fears that if people believe this, they will discover the terrible fact that the organized Church is unnecessary. Then, the institutional Church could begin to unravel, crumble, and collapse. The dogma is that the Church is part of the "chain" of salvation, with humanity on one side, and God on the other, linked by "holy mother Church." But the Scriptures clearly teach that only Jesus Christ stands between human and divine natures.

Does this mean that a person can just live any way in which she chooses, violating all the sexual taboos and other restraints imposed by the Law Of God? This is what worries whining organizationalists. Can she live carelessly, stupidly, ignorantly, and harmfully-- and just get away with it? Does this teaching of universalism mean that bad or careless behavior does not matter?

Not at all. This is a twisted misunderstanding. All creatures are in one hundred percent grace. But the *awareness* of grace can span the spectrum from zero to one hundred percent. So, you cannot have the realization (full awareness) of (being in) grace until you have experienced spiritual rebirth. Realization of grace is always accompanied by regeneration. Realization of Grace and regeneration are like salt and pepper, or matching bookends; they always come as an unbroken set. All live in grace. But it does not affect the heartmind until a diamond-solid surrender to Love occurs.

But because it is God who saves the cosmos, salvation is unaffected by your number of mistakes. Divine forgiveness is infinite. So, there is not even any reason to keep track of mistakes! No one is counting!

Jesus implied this shocker with his startling declaration that prostitutes and other sinners would "go ahead" of righteous, religious people into the "kingdom" of God. (Mt. 21:31)

After "salvation," the second manifestation of Lovemind is Mindforce ("power"). Power is unvacillating and stable mental energy.

After 1) "salvation" and 2) "power," the third manifestation of Spirit was all Mind ruled by Love ("kingdom"). The "kingdom" was a major theme of the ministry of Jesus. The word means "king's domain." The domain of God (Love) is not geographic; God does not rule New Jersey, for example. It is all in the heartmind. Jesus said that the "kingdom" is "within you." (Lk. 17:21). Since God rules as Love, this "kingdom" is the cleansed and purified human heart, filled to the brim with Love.

So, three forms of Love are coming into being: Love as perfect forgiveness ("salvation"), Love as renewed Mindenergy ("power"), and Love as the transformed heartmind ("kingdom").

The potential positivity of dragonmind is also supported by another fact. Like the four living creatures, the twenty-four old people, and other positive elements, he is close to Lovemind ("in the sight of our God"). Cosmic Mind is aware of his activity. Indeed, It is watching him. So, paradoxically, while ousted and banished to hypersensual mind ('earth'), he is still in higher Mind as potential ("heaven").

Does dragonmind aid the whole Mind towards goodness by pointing out Its imperfections? Is it possible that dragonmind, when not in service to fearmind (satanmind) serves Lovemind?

Verse 11. "And they conquered him through the blood of the lamb, and through the Logos of their observer. And they did not love their Soul until death."

COMM: Dragonmind is overcome through death ("blood") of surrendermind ("lamb"). Parts of surrendermind must "die" temporarily, or else, the "wars" of Revelation would come to an abrupt end, as surrendermind won the final victory. If the fearmind gave in too quickly to Lovemind, there would be no growth, education, or development possible to mind or Soulmind. So, surrendermind cannot, at this point, be at one hundred percent engagement, or full power.

Dragonmind is vanquished later. But this is possible only because certain parts of surrendermind have been deactivated (died; "blood"). If surrendermind were total, dragonmind would be immediately absorbed into Lovemind, and all the stages and phases of continuing development in the rest of Revelation could not occur. The story would end right here, right now!

Dragonmind-fearmind is partially neutralized ("conquered") by the perfect Expression of Love ("Logos"). This Logosmind also manifests as your Soul (19:13). An important aspect of the Logos is the "inner Observer," whose job is to study your behaviors, thoughts, and words, and to record them. It does this so that it might later create the perfect karmic balance. (To accomplish this, It must feed into the deepest Mind, the part called the "Creator/Dreamer;" see "Chart of Mind")

Creatormind dreams the world through Logos (enlightened Soul). Logos also observes the world through the personal mind. So, it is in Logosmind that divine and human minds meet. It is their plane of interface.

Several persons here share one Soul, "their Soul." This implies the unity of one Mind. "They" are all parts of one psyche.

Verse 12. "Through this, make yourselves well-minded, heavens and those tenting in them. Trouble [to] the earth and the sea, because the devil has stepped down toward you, having great anger, knowing that he has a little assigned time [left]."

COMM: Lovemind ("heaven") is thrilled by the exile of dragonmind!

In enlightenment, dragonmind (free will under animalcontrol) is booted out.

Dragonmind has nowhere else to go but to lower mind, including hypersensual, sense-dominated mind ("earth"). Hypersensual mind is threatened by dragonmind, for, as fearmind, it plans to take over. The Unconscious ("sea") is disturbed, because dragonmind reaches far into the mind! Fear goes down as far as the collective Unconscious. (See "Chart of Mind.") Hypersensual mind and the Unconscious have both been invaded by an understandable fear ("devil"). But this fear is destined to be short-lived.

Satanmind (fearmind) is thrown into chaos and confusion. This leads to frustration, and disapproval ("anger"). Fearmind disapproves of the whole unfolding scenario, for it realizes that it's lifespan ("assigned time") is limited. This idea brings predestination or predesign into the equation. Fearmind has always known, at a deep level, that it exists only to disappear, vanish, evanesce, or be completely neutralized. But it does not accept this philosophically when the time approaches. Being fearmind, it is filled with the utter agony of pure terror!

Verse 13. "And when the dragon saw that it was thrown into the earth, it persecuted the woman who gave birth to the male."

COMM: Dragonmind, which tests Souls, is exiled from Lovemind ("heaven"). It is forcibly injected ("thrown") into hypersensual mind ("earth"). Separated, in illusionmind, from Love, it is in hell! It attacks Goddessmind ("woman"), in mindless, unthinking panic. Free will, for the moment, serves fear, Love's opposite. It serves the "devil." (While it does so, dragonmind is "satanmind.")

Verse 14. "And the woman was given the two wings of the great eagle, so that she might fly into the desolation, to her place where she is being nourished, for three and a half times [years] , from the face of the serpent."

COMM: Far-seeing wisdom ("eagle" compare 4:7 and 8:13) lifts the feminine and divine side of Mind (Goddessmind). She is elevated from the ground of implicit earthmind (hypersensual mind). This is transcendence ("wings"). She ascends into higher Mind. But before she can get that high, Goddessmind must go through the darknight (desolationmind) to escape dragonmind.

This "desolationmind" is the psyche in withdrawn introspection, unproductive but nourished. This occurs during the mystical darknight, when inner nutrition is so deeply unconscious that even the mind does not recognize it. With an abundance of inner nutrition, it believes itself to be starving!

The *yin* (Goddess) Mind of Love is not fleeing in fear. The cosmic Mind is only distancing itself from free will locked in fear's service (dragonmind). Before the mind finds higher Mind, it must be driven there. Goddessmind is "driven" by "starvation" to find Lovemind. What drives it is the full realization that *egomind is desertmind.* The psychic darknight is not intrinsic to the beautiful and joyful Goddessmind, but is *created by egomind in response to Her,* due to its lack of understanding. Egomind is dry and barren when it tries to synthesize joy, Love, or tranquility. It makes only counterfeits-- about as satisfying as eating wax fruit. Desolationmind is transition. Mind is no longer only ego, but not yet Lovemind. It is stuck uncomfortably somewhere in between. It is stuck in Goddessmind (nature). It feels alone and abandoned. God (Love) has disappeared. A bleak and empty cosmos seems devoid of Love.

The contrary polarities of wholeness ("three") and division ("half") now lock swords. This serious cosmophilosophic conflict still haunts the psyche. Although commentators disagree, she is "nourished... from the face of the serpent." The serpent (free will) has turned away from its antiagapic distortions, at least, for the moment. It now nourishes Goddessmind. The same dragon tore the human mind from divine Mind. But now, it takes that mind amplified (as Goddess) back to its primal oneness.

Dragonmind, as free will ("serpent"), usually serves fears. It thrives on phobic responses, from insecurities to stark terror and phobic panics. But it can perform wonders of wellbeing, as well. Free will can also turn to the sunshine of Love. Even fear can turn the psyche back towards Goddessmind!

Your own fears test you. So, dragonmind (serpentmind; free will) can scare you into enlightenment. How? By threatening death. In the lives of some (but certainly not all) mystics, the biomedical condition has driven into the mind like nails the fact that *you cannot always help yourself.* In some psyches, this leads to the realization that *a greater Mind will come to your rescue* if you stop trying to direct the "show" yourself! But *this great Mind will not kick in until after you have surrendered!*

Verse 15. "And the serpent, behind the woman, threw out of its mouth water as a river, so that she might be borne by a river."

COMM: Serpentmind (free will) acts unconsciously ("behind"). This great serpent integrates with the Unconscious, has immense Power to direct enormous flows and floods of Mindforce ("river"). (Compare 8:10 and 9:14.)

All this gigantic Mindforce arises from the expression ("mouth") of free will ("serpent"): When Mind operates freely, without restrictions, and then expresses this freedom, it releases huge quantities of Mindforce.

The free will is not always conscious. So this is not a scenario of the conscious mind's performing magic to manipulate the Unconscious. It is just that free will also operates below the waves, deep in the Unconscious. This is the serpent under the ground or sea (the archetypal "sea-serpent"). Unexpectedly, his energy is supportive (Goddessmind is "borne by a river"). So, free will is beginning to serve divine will. Mind is using free will to decide to give up free will. The "serpent" is swallowing itself! That serpent becomes servant of Goddess.

Verse 16. "And the earth gave aid to the woman, and opened up the mouth of the earth, and drank down the river, which the dragon had drawn out of its mouth."

COMM: This is the "mouther" of all wars! The "mouth" of earth, and the "mouth" of the serpent are parallel, but in conflict. (The same Greek word is used for both.) Expression ("mouth, as in 1:16; 9:17-19; 10:9, and 11:5) conflicts: When hypersensual mind ("earth") expresses itself, it absorbs and assimilates ("drinks down") the expression of free will. This describes a phase, then, when free will becomes the temporary slave of sensuality.

If there is a conflict between free will and hypersensuality, guess which is the stronger! Free will might decide, "I'm never going to eat pastries again!" Then, hypersensuality comes along, and the best-laid plans... Or free will might say, "I'm never going to be interested in sex, ever again!" Then, hypersensuality shows up, and blows that idea out of the water! Biodrives, as expressions of sensuality, ("earth's mouth") almost always win over free will expression ("serpent's mouth"). Earthmind contains an entire spectrum of powerful biodrives, including survival. So, it is easy to see how it could overcome free will. By this action, by expressing the hypersensual primacy of survival, hypersensuality or bionature ("earth") saves Goddessmind.

Why? Free will usually, under normal conditions, expresses egomind. This is the false mask of an unreal and distorted self. Hypersensuality expresses something much deeper, more authentic-- "Edenmind." This can be very sexual or sensual. It is Mind in fullest harmony with nature (and God). So, "Edenmind" is also, "naturemind." Hypersensual mind almost always expresses Edenmind. By expressing ("mouth") Love through survival, sensuality, or sexuality, hypersensual mind ("earth") temporarily saves Love (Goddessmind) from being totally dominated by free will ("serpent").

Verse 17. "And the dragon was made angry upon the woman. And it went off to make war with those left over from her seed, of those observing the commandments of God, and having the testimony of Jesus."

COMM: Dragonmind is wrathfully displeased ("anger," as in 6:17 and 11:18). It does not want to cooperate peacefully with Lovemind. Love and tenderness (Goddessmind) displease free will. Why? Because Love *always implies standards of sexual honor.* Free will (serpentmind) prefers its animal nature (wildbeastmind), and unbridled lust! Serpentmind prefers pseudopower. Most crimes of sexual abuse are those of "power." (It is easy to mistake mere brutal dominance for power. But power is actually its opposite, growing from deep, strong security.)

Free will often supports ego, with its macho and obnoxious stubbornness! This serpentmind does not want to be controlled by the divine tendermind ("woman"). The very idea that it might so lose its 'freedom' horrifies it! Still, serpentmind draws energy from Goddessmind ("upon the woman"). But this energy has been hideously misappropriated and distorted! Fearmind, the master of dragonserpentmind, lusts to take over the whole mind!

Here, "war" has three possible shades of meaning: 1) Dragonserpentmind conflicts with thoughts of Goddessmind ("those left over from her seed"); 2) simple disagreement breaks out within the psyche (Compare 2:16; 6:4; 8:2; 9:7, 9; 11:7), or 3) a fairly peaceful disagreement about, and division of, Mindenergies, as in 12:7, occurs.

Free will begins terrible transformation. It rebels against surrendering to Love. It fears its own complete disappearance. This is terrifying. The conscious mind, exercising free will, disagrees continuously, and violently, with the deepest Mind (Lovemind). It creates conflict about just about everything.

The mind's highest thoughts are the teachings of Love ("testimony of Jesus"). Dragonmind does not know, or trust, Love. It is frightened and suspicious of giving itself away.

Verse 18.[35] "And it stood upon the sand of the sea."

COMM: Dragonmind climbs out of the Unconscious ("sea"). So, it ascends into conscious awareness. Instead of its using you, you begin consciously to use it. As fearmind, it is supported by the hypersensual (earth).

This special 'earth' ("sand") is silicone dioxide (crystal). But it is opaque, cloudy, unclear. It is formed from interaction between hypersensual 'earth' and Unconscious 'sea.' (It lies at the border.)

So, hypersensual thoughts, created unconsciously ("sand") will ultimately evolve into crystalmind, utter clarity. This will form Unity with cosmic Mind! But precrystalmind ("sand") is in an earlier stage of evolution. It is not yet transparent. This earthmind encourages, in fact, unhealthy adherence to materialism or hypersensuality. So it supports ("stands upon") the "beast" of fearmind.

---

[35] Some Greek texts do not contain any verse 18 in chapter 12. In some translations, 12:18 is in the beginning of the next chapter, and so, it is 13:1

Chapter 13

Verse 1. "And I saw, out of the sea, a wild beast stepping up, having ten horns and seven heads, and upon its horns ten crowns, and upon its heads were names of blasphemy."

COMM: The hideous dragonmind (12:3) has frightening similarities. This might even be an "incarnation" of dragonmind. It also enjoyed some spiritual ("seven") intellect ("heads"). This beast also has the potential for earthly closure/enlightenment ("ten"; compare 2:10). It too is of the animalnature ("horns"), like dragonmind. It has authority or influence over other mindareas ("crowns"). (Compare 7:4 and 11:13.)

This "beast" is "animalmind." It is all that is lazy, sloppy, undisciplined, careless, and indifferent. It is not always intentionally "evil." But it does promote the false gods of hypersexuality, materialism, and other bio-appetites. They want to grasp control of Mind, and to dominate. So this animalmind ("beast") uses and abuses hypersensual mind (earth) as its slave. It is lower in spirituality than "earthmind," however. For it is clearly animalmind ("horns"; compare 5:6 and 9:13.) It is lower. Here's a quick review of the "hierarchy" of Mind:

"Heaven" (Lovemind; at the top)
Goddessmind
Hypersensual mind ("earth")
Unconscious ("sea")
Animalmind (subconscious; "dragonmind"; "beast")

This beastmind convinces mind that mind is worthless, a piece of scum, useless mud. It hypnotizes mind to believe in horrible, destructive, antiagapic ("blasphemy") identities ("names").

God is truth (Reality). So, anything "outside" of Lovemind must be sheer illusion. So, beastmind is a nightmare -- all smoke and mirrors. Also, that which is illusion must exist "outside" of purest Lovemind's rule. So, beastmind buys big-time into, completely falls for, identity-illusion.

But beastmind does not have to fight against Love to become a sucker for illusion. Just saying, "I am Mary Smith," or, "I am John Jones" is enough to lure the mind into darkness. It slides into dangerous dualism, and from this one noxious weed grow all other hurtful ideas.

But intellect ("heads") inevitably serves higher Mind ("seven"). Transformation begins with an intellectual desire to learn, with books and ideas.

But like dragonmind, wildbeastmind is in terrible, hellish rebellion against Love.

Verse 2. "And the wild beast which I saw was like a leopard, and its feet as a bear['s]. And its mouth was as of a lion. And the dragon gave it his own power, and its own throne, and great authority."

COMM: More vicious than lions are leopards. As carnivores, they represent greater danger. (Wildbeastmind=leopardmind=animalmind.) Leopardmind also lacks the regal or noble nature of the lion. So, it is a much clearer symbol of naked danger.

Its spiritual progress ("feet"; compare 1:13, 15 and 10:1) is slow, inefficient, lumbering, and uncertain ("bear"). Still, even this dangerous, animalistic mind is able to pretend: It can cloak itself with disguises of nobility [express itself ("mouth") as a "lion"]. Many careless and destructive sexual activities, for example, come from wildbeastmind. Yet they have been disguised as "sophisticated" or "liberated," both of which are lies. This is just naked, bestial leopardmind (animalmind) trying to dress itself up as something more elegant and elevated.

Dragonmind ("satanmind") turns over to wildbeastmind its considerable influence over Mindenergy ("power"). So here the lower nature, designed to turn its will over to Lovemind goes exactly the opposite way and turns its will over to wildbeastmind. So wildbeastmind gains in power. Since satanmind is fearmind, the wildbeastmind survives and thrives upon fear. All that was within the inner kingdom ("throne") of fear is now commanded by animalmind. The gigantic influence ("authority") of fear is now loosed into the service of overindulgence. This is often giving in to dangerous and hurtful lust, and personal desire.

The perilous, filthy animalmind has free will as its slave. It seems to control life. You give in to gluttony, sexual obsessions, greed, etc. But happily, this stage is only temporary.

Verse 3. "And one of its heads was as if slaughtered, but the blow of its death was cured. The whole earth was made to wander behind the wild beast."

COMM: Overindulgence is immensely powerful! It bulldozes over intellect, and all attempts to control through reason. Intensely, its intellect ("heads") is partly ("one... head") deactivated ("slaughtered"). It violently shakes off control by logic. In wild urges, all reason is dropped, often with clothing. In passions or rages, all reason flees! Wildbeastmind is subconscious, so the mind cannot rein in its wild and crazy spurts. Passion and animal energies scream from the subconscious, demanding satisfaction! The conscious mind is dominated by fearmind (satanmind), which has already given its energy to wildbeastmind.

Here is a "house divided." (Wildbeastmind is a section of fearmind.) So, it outrageously steals for its own uses the whole hypersensual mind ("earth... wanders behind" it).

Summary: Dragonmind="serpentmind"=free will. When controlled by fear, dragonmind=fearmind=satanmind. Wildbeastmind=section of fearmind=leopardmind.

Verse 4. "And they gave worship to the dragon, because it gave authority to the wild beast, and they worshipped the wild beast, saying, 'Who is like the wild beast? And who is able to war with it?'"

COMM: Adoration ("worship") of wildbeastmind is that of dragonmind! For both dragonmind and wildbeastmind draw their being from fearmind.

Thoughts of hypersensual mind ("they" of "earth") fall into illusion. They divide their sacred honor ("worship"). It is split between the free will dominated by fear ("dragon") and animalmind ("wild beast"). So, hypersensual mind has zero energy left for the valid worship of Lovemind. It is led astray.

Also, mind opposes Michaelmind (spiritual Lightmind of goodness). For "Michael" means, "Who is like God." This is countered with symmetric mockery: "Who is like the wild beast?"

This dark karmic period of illusion might be short or long. During this period, the whole bodymind shamelessly follows its lust, its indulgence, and its greed.

Verse 5. "And there was given to it a mouth speaking great things, and blasphemies. And authority was given to it, to act for forty-two months."

COMM: Wildbeastmind expresses itself ("mouth") impressively (says "great things"). This it does as the flashy, stylish, seductive over-indulgence mind. Illusion, especially if very sensual, is often more attractive, prettier, or more impressive, to the conscious mind, than is truth. As Lao Tzu says, "Words of truth are not always beautiful. Beautiful words might not be true."[36]

Deeper Mind has given wildbeastmind the ability to express itself ("mouth"). But this is ignorance and destructivity. For it is alienated from Love by fear, and this has created an ugly, antiagapic ("blasphemies") mind. Truly impressive in justification of its behaviors, it rationalizes them intellectually, socially, and psychologically. This is a major lesson learned historically from those losers and users, the nazis, and from the crazy witch-hunters: The mind can justify any behavior, no matter how absurd or atrocious. It defends with fluidity and articulate patterns its errors. But it goes beyond justification of its indulgences. It acts deliberately to serve fear. It becomes voluntarily anti-agapic. It influences other thoughts and Mindareas ("authority"). But this is permitted for only a limited time ("forty-two months").

"Forty-two months," in various forms, is a most significant number symbol. [It appears elsewhere as 1260 (days), and three and a half (years).]

This number can be transposed with the three and a half years. When it is, it implies that the wildbeastmind is split at very deep levels. It struggles with the monistic cosmos (where only the one Mind is

---

[36] For a complete new rendition of Lao Tzu's mystical classic see my *Luminous Jewels of Love and Light*, Volume 2, Part IV, "The Book of the Great Mind and Its Expression," Chapter 81, *op. cit.*

Reality). This opposes the dualistic view (where an absolute evil exists as the real opposite of the absolute Good). (Compare 11:9.) [This is the conflict between wholeness ("three") and dualism ("half")]

This is the same as 1260 days (11:3). Summary: symbolically, "Three and a half"= 1260 = forty-two.

All three refer to the deep philosophic conflict between the "One" and the "many." Still, they have different shades of meaning. Forty-two can be factored as two times three times seven. This is mind moving through the nightmare torture-chambers of duality (two), then, into gentle harmony (three), and finally, into fullest spirituality, merging with cosmic Mind (seven). (Compare also 11:9, 11 and 12:14.) "1260" also factors as 2x2x3x3x5x7. This tells the same story as "forty-two" but inserts and acknowledges the human element.

Verse 6. "And it opened up its mouth into blasphemies toward God, to blaspheme his name and his tent-- those tenting in heaven."

COMM: Lustful, indulgent nature ("wild beast") spouts anti-agapicities ("blasphemies")! It criticizes the One. This proves how far "gone" it really is, sunk deeply in the stinking mire of dualism. In fact, it can damn as nonsense the idea of cosmos as the reflection/manifestation of one Mind. For it is not just God that is blasphemed, but his "tent," or dwelling.

This is the crux of the whole conflict. It is so tormentingly disturbing to wildbeastmind: If God lives within the Mind, then the hopes of wildbeastmind are all shattered. For it is a subset of illusionmind, and Godmind is Reality ("truth"). When God is discovered, the annihilation of all illusionmind cannot be far behind. The explosive vaporization of wildbeastmind would be like the confluence of matter and antimatter!

So, wildbeastmind denies that God lives in the deepest Unconscious as Coremind (Lovemind; "tents"). It would much prefer that the dwelling ("tent") of God be seen as the sky, outer space, or some temple-- anywhere but the Mind!

Verse 7. "And it was given to make war with the holy, and to conquer them. And it was given authority upon every tribe, people, tongue, and nation."

COMM: Wildbeastmind receives ("given") the power to influence or control thoughts ("authority"). Who is giving? The only One: It receives from Lovemind (Coremind). Wildbeastmind receives again ("given") an assignment. It is to create conflict, and to share mindenergies ("make war") with the agapic Mindareas ("holy").

Temporarily-- although this seems tragic to the mind-- wildbeastmind does win the battle. It dominates ("conquers") the victimized mind. For a hellish time, wildbeastmind dominates the psyche. This affects large Mind-constellations ("every tribe, people, tongue, and nation").

Verse 8. "And all those dwelling upon the earth will worship him, if their names have not been written in the little book of the lamb's life. This is the One Who has been slaughtered ever since the world was thrown down."

COMM: Wildbeastmind is so powerful! This antiagapic mind is admired and served ("worshipped") by many thoughts of hypersensual mind ("those dwelling upon the earth"). Especially through overindulgence in sensuality and sexuality, this is easy! It can even be fun! Hypersensual mind is, by definition, dominated by biodrives (wildbeastmind). So, what could be more natural?

These hapless victims are those thoughts whose identities ("names") are not recognized by surrendermind ("lambs"). For they are not recorded ("written") in the memory ("little book") of surrendermind ("lamb"). The mindsectors taken over ruthlessly by wildbeastmind are subconscious. Since they are hypersensual, they include body-regulating mindmechanisms. In terms of anatomy this includes the whole "limbic" brain.

The Mindarea that remembers all that really matters is surrendermind. It has surrendered personal will (desires), deep within the psyche. Ever since the cosmos ("world") of matter was created ("thrown down" from higher Mind), it has been destined to be so. The whole being has always belonged to Love.

So, mind does not literally surrender so much as realize that it is already surrendered. Human and lower minds are already a part of divine Mind. Even wildbeastmind is secretly a disguise, or horrible distortion, of the one perfect Mind. These Mindsectors need simply to awaken to this fact.

Verse 9. "If anyone has an ear, let him hear."

Verse 10. "If anyone is [destined for] captivity, she is going under into captivity. If anyone will kill in a sword, it is binding for him to be killed in a sword. Here is the endurance and faith of the holy."

COMM: Some thoughtfeelings drop down from the vast high Unconscious. They fall into the prison of the little, shallow subconscious ("go under"). This is to lose the freedom of selfdetermination ("go into captivity"). These thoughtfeelings wear the brand of wildbeastmind, and it rigidly restricts them, as the tyrant that it is. Any so degraded becomes the slave of illusionmind. It serves wildbeastmind as a minion of its perversities. It finds only agony and misery.

All thoughts that have violently deactivated ("killed") others will be themselves deactivated ("killed") through direct internal conflict ("in a sword"). Jesus said, "He who lives by the sword will die by the sword." Lao Tzu said, "A violent man will die a violent death." The same principles apply to violent thoughts. Holy thought-aggregates must be of strong constitution ("endurance"). They must believe that a higher Power will swoop down and save them ("faith") if they are to survive the cruel, merciless assaults of wildbeastmind.

Verse 11. "And I saw another wild beast, stepping up out of the earth. It had two horns, like a lamb, and it was speaking as a dragon."

COMM: This "hypocrite-mind" comes from hypersensual mind ("earth"). It manifests animalmind ("horns"). It still believes in the lie/illusion of duality ("two"). It chooses the many over the One.

Although a "beast" like wildbeastmind, hypocrite-mind has the appearance of surrendermind ("lamb"). It can disguise itself, feigning or faking giving in to the will of Love. Because of this, it is much more sly and subtle than the dragonmind of 12:3. It is all but invisible amidst all the other flurries of Mindsegments and Mindareas. But it has a powerful will of its own, often in serious clash or violent disagreement with the One. It still expresses itself ("mouth") as a servant of ignorance or even fear ("dragon"). Specifically, it serves free will dominated by fear (dragonmind). When free will gives in completely to this fear, it becomes a form of fearmind (satanmind). (So perfect is its symmetry with fearmind that dragonmind actually becomes satan-mind.) So, hypocrite-mind appears to serve Love, but is still locked in ignorance (dualism) and fear (satan). It is a massive, pathological, and dangerous liar!

Verse 12. "And it is doing all that the authority of the first wild beast allows. And it is in sight of it. And it is making the earth and those who dwell on it worship the first wild beast, the one that was cured of its death-blow."

COMM: The terrible, horrible object of hypersensualmind worship is animalmind (wildbeastmind; "leopardmind"). So, hypocrite-mind is a servant of the cruel wildbeastmind. But, in this phase, hypocrisy and pretension take the place of lazy indulgence. Still, it spouts the same garbage. Like wildbeastmind, hypocritemind abuses the mind through sickening hypersensual/hypersexual obsessions.

Hypersensual mind ("earth") was already a captive and sick slave of hyperindulgencemind ("wild beast"). It had been captured through oversexuality. But now, hypersensual mind's cooperation with these sick patterns of wildbeast is not enough. Hypocritemind demands a hell of a lot more! It wants hypersensual mind to honor and respect ("worship") wildbeastmind. The dark, evil conspiracy between wild-beastmind and hypocritemind is as obvious as the sun at mid-day. It starts its nightmare take-over by forcing mind into antiagapic blas-phemies.

Verse 13. "And it is doing great signs, so that it might make fire step down out of heaven into the earth, in sight of the men."

COMM: Cleansing agonies flash from deepest Mind ("fire" falls from "heaven"). But the origin of this suffering is not Lovemind, but the abuses of Lovepower by hypocritemind! But spiritual development is not the reason for this pain. This agony results from the stresses of hypocritemind's resistance to Lovemind. Unknown to it, this very re-sistance greatly empowers the Spirit of Love!

Hypocritemind convinces conscious, intellectual segments ("men") that it has access to Power ("signs"). At this point, the conscious mind makes a nightmarish error: It believes that hypocritemind is Lovemind! For hypocritemind is very impressive to the incompetent and stupid conscious mind.

From the view of the conscious mind, hypocritemind is mindboggling in power and knowledge! For it is subconscious, and hence, Unconscious. (The mind lacks discernment to tell the difference.)

Hypocritemind has a much greater Powerlevel than the mere conscious mind, which uses only intellect. Intellect, being unspiritual, is rather feeble, and easily fooled. So, at this phase, the mind puts faith in deeper Mind, but not in the deepest. It puts faith in the subconscious rather than the whole Unconscious. This deflects and distracts it from Lovemind.

This hypocritemind trust is represented by metaphysical schools which believe that the *mere conscious mind* controls everything. These are the "name it and claim it" schools. They claim that, by "correct thinking" you can have and do anything. This, of course, neglects the deeper Unconscious. Thus it deletes Creatormind (Dreamermind) altogether. This desperate, shallow fearconcept leaves out everything that really matters. It tries to reduce the Mind to the aware mind. This is a bit like mistaking the peanut for the elephant! For *all the stuff that really counts* is unconscious!

The true aims of hypocritemind are exclusively antiagapic! It fiercely, ferociously, viciously hates the Lovespirit! But, even while acting directly against Love, it is unconsciously forced to serve Love. For Lovemind is its Source. And all of its plenitude of dastardly deeds is already a part of the Lovemind's plan for ultimate enlightenment.

Suffering electrifies the mind! This response comes from the stimulation of hypersensual mind ("earth"). This agony finally attains the notice of the intellect ("men").

The Unconscious is an expert at getting conscious attention, even if it has to create hells to do it!

Verse 14. "And it is making to err those dwelling upon the earth, through the signs which were given to it, to do in the sight of the wild beast. [It is] telling those dwelling upon the earth to make an image to the wild beast who had the sword-blow and lived."

COMM: Hypocritemind screws up ("makes to err") hypersensual mind ("earth")! This is a *stubborn theme in Revelation:* Even the greatest "evils" are so often dismissed as error ("makes to err"). As noted, this implies that sin, not being deliberate and fully conscious, is easily, readily forgiven by Lovemind. Hypocritemind wants hypersensual mind to adore overindulgence-mind ("make an image of the wild beast"). This is not damned. It is recognized as error. Error, and karma, elicit pain responses ("fire").

Unusual mental abilities ("signs") are received ("given"). But by whom are these granted? When Revelation uses the word "given," the Giver is cosmic Mind. So, the lower Unconscious taps into true Power. It does not go deeply enough, however, to be truly spiritual (loving). It stops at the level of the mildly psychic.

Still, this is enough to blow away the hypersensual mind! It is amazed, and, as noted, easily fooled, tricked, and impressed. This means that there is a good chance that hypocritemind can get hypersensual mind to serve and adore ("worship") overindulgence mind.

But this worship is not direct. It occurs via an "image." Before the overindulgence "wildbeastmind" can be worshipped by hypersensual mind, that mind must form an interior idea of what it is ("image"). This can be accurate or way off base.

"Demonic powers" manifest in hypocritemind.

Wildbeastmind knows about them ("in sight of" it). In other words, animalmind is aware of what hypocritemind is doing.

And what, exactly, is hypocritemind doing? Besides its pseudo-powers, it uses, misuses, and abuses hypersensual mind. It feed hypersensualmind false data about animalmind so that this mind appears ("image") better than it really is. So, animalmind starts to seem like a good thing. It highlights hypersexuality and hypersensuality to paint a portrait of mind, to create a convincing, but phony and attractive lie ("make an image"). In this crisis, it believes that animalmind contains many good things. It has swallowed, hook, line, and sinker, the lie of hypocrite mind.

Verse 15. "And it was given to her to give spirit to the image of the wild beast, so that the image should speak. And it arranged things so that those who did not give worship to the image of the wild beast should be killed."

COMM: A mysterious she ("her") suddenly appears! Who is she? The only she is Goddessmind (chapter twelve). A deep secret is subtly implied: A hidden conspiracy has been contracted between Lovemind and fearmind (Goddessmind and hypocritemind). (For there is only one real Mind in all the universes-- perfect cosmic Lovemind.) This cosmic Mind has never fallen victim to chaos. It has *never* utterly lost control of any microparticle of the cosmos. All other minds, including fearmind (satanmind) must work for this Mind. For they all must be a part of It.

Goddessmind gives "spirit" or life to the internal image or understanding of animalmind. Why does she try to bring this Frankenstein to life? Because this is a dark, stinking, fiery tunnel through which mind must pass. Why?

In order to rise above its awful dementia. It must be shaken awake from its overindulgent tendencies that it is just an animal. It must see animalmind as it actually is not just as it would like to see it ("image"). This illusion is a paradoxical but vital part of seeing through illusions. We encounter hideous illusions to teach us to *see all the way through all illusions*. Before an art-expert can recognize *real* masterpieces, part of her training is to learn to spot phonies. Before we can wake up in lucid dreams, we must first recognize that all the "real" stuff around us is unreal or "mindstuff."

Life grants a similar training. And that is a part of vital wisdom.

This ability to magically, miraculously make this false ideal of animalmind appear real, and even spiritual ("give Spirit to" it) was bestowed upon ("given to") Goddessmind. It was the gift of cosmic Mind. It is the will of Lovemind that Its opposite, fearmind, exist, but for only a limited time. Then, in a flash of Light, fearmind is forever to vaporize into yesterday!

This chapter is about the ultimate loss of this false image that animalmind is good and pleasing.

The interior version of animalmind expresses itself ("speaks") by providing some of the future foundations for genuine joy. This it does through its acquired "spirit".

Verse 16. "And it is making all-- the small and the great, rich and poor, free and slaves--receive an engraving upon their right hand, or upon their forehead."

COMM: Hypocrite-mind has power! It can force ("make") other Mindfactors give loyalty to wildbeastmind. These Mindfactors include insignificant ("small") ones and very influential ("great") ones. They include imaginative and creative Mindfactors ("rich") and those that rarely if ever produce anything ("poor"). They include thoughts and thought-constellations not in service to or support of any idea ("free") and those which are bound up in service to particular concepts ("slaves").

The Mind is commanded to serve wildbeastmind, even to adore ("worship") it. Many resort, in ignorant desperation, to worship of their own egos, since they believe themselves, in absurd hyperegotism, to be the most important cosmic realities! In their brutal cosmos, there is no God or Love, and it is every person for herself! Only the toughest, strongest, smartest, or richest "animal" will survive! They have already come literally to worship animalmind. So, it is a mere hop, skip, and a jump to worshipping wildbeastmind, since they are already involved in worshipping themselves as similar "beasts." The practices of wildbeastmind-- hypersensuality and hypersexuality-- become their ultimate concerns.

This initiates consciously directed, deliberate action ("right hand"). Mind is also expected to serve and adore with its intellect ("forehead"). Wildbeastmind exercises complete ownership ("engravings") of thoughtfeelings and thoughtideas. Although the servants are many, reference is made to a single "hand" and a single "forehead." This implies hidden mental unity.

Verse 17. "No one will be able to buy or to sell except those having the engraving. [Or else he must have] the name of the wild beast, or the number of its name."

COMM: Transference of thoughtenergy ("buy/sell") is strictly regulated by the forces of darkness.

What is "transference of thoughtenergy"? Every thoughtgroup or feeling must be supported by thoughts, or thoughtenergy. When thoughtenergy is taken or drained from an idea or feeling, it becomes weaker. Conversely, when thoughts or thoughtenergies are used to *support* an idea or concept, it becomes stronger. Thus, the "economy of the mind" uses "thoughtenergy" as its currency("buy" or "sell"). Ideas favored by the constellations in charge (here the negative) are rewarded or "paid" by granting them energy, and making them stronger. But where does this energy come from? It must be stolen from disapproved thoughts. All Lovethoughts are disapproved by wildbeastmind and hypocritemind. So, during this harrowing period, thoughts are shifted from the support of Love to that of fear.

Here, thoughtenergy cannot be transferred from one part of the mind to another unless it is in synch with illusion. Why? Because the majority of the mind has already fallen into the nightmare-illusion of service to overindulgence (wildbeastmind). Those parts of mind that hold on to illumination, then, are outside the hallucination gripping the rest of mind. For practical purposes, they become paralyzed, for the whole rest of mind rejects them.

If a thought is devoted to a cause, it cannot "serve two masters." Since most thoughts are already committed to wildbeastmind, at this point, in this phase, this alienates thoughts harmonious with Lovemind. Thoughts are the only currency of Mind.

So, thoughts must be "budgeted." And it is also thoughts that transfer Mindforces around from one idea to another, shifting limited psychic energy. To "buy and sell," then, means to arrange and order thoughts, removing them from support of one idea, and integrating them into another. This is how "thoughtenergy" is moved, shuffled or shuttled within the psyche.

Spiritual psychosis is threatened. In that spiritual schizophrenia, only concepts that serve wildbeastmind will be able to rearrange and appropriate thoughts ("buy, sell"). These thoughts will buy into a false portrayal of animalmind (the "image" of "wild beast"). They think it is good. These thoughts are the lowest. Many thoughts will refuse "wild beast". They will also refuse its temptation to think in strictly linear thought ("number"),which can never lead to Love (God). The "number" of the "beast" (primarily six) is transition. Mind is paralyzed between the biohuman sensory nature ("five") and full spirituality ("seven").

Verse 18. "Here is the wisdom. Let the one having a mind calculate the number of the wild beast. For it is a number of man, and its number is six hundred sixty-six."

COMM: This number is 2 x 3 x 111. So, it talks about moving through duality and illusion ("two"), passing through various states of wholeness ("three), and finally arriving at "oneness," amplified like 666, by a tridigital repetition (three of the same numeral in sequence: "111").

This is both the "number" of the "wild beast" and of "a man." "Man" usually represents intellect. The number of man, or intellect, is usually five, not six. So, despite being the number of a "beast," or lower (animal) nature, it is also that nature *in the process of growth or selftranscendence.*

****

"Six" is mind, drawing energy from its human nature ("five") as it approaches its true spiritual nature ("seven").

****

For six is a higher level of consciousness than five.

It unites the two poles of the human and the superhuman.

Wildbeastmind is still stuck in duality, or two; human beings find some levels of completeness, three. 666 represents both qualities, since it is 2x3x111. And the divine is the One, 111, deeply ensconced or hidden in the symbolism.

Chapter 14

Verse 1. "And I saw, and look! The lamb, having stood upon the mountain Zion, and with it, a hundred forty-four thousand, having his name and that of his father written on their foreheads."

COMM: 144,000 is twelve squared times ten cubed. Twelve is celestial, cosmic order, and ten, earthly completeness (enlightenment).

So, 144,000 represents the totality of all enlightened thoughts-- all Godthoughts (Lovethoughts) in "heaven" (Lovemind) and on "earth" (hypersensualmind).

They have as foundation ("stand upon") an elevated philosophy rooted in hypersensuality ("mountain").

It is called Zion, which means, "a dry or parched place." So, despite their utter perfection, they arise from imperfect origins. These are two: 1) hypersensuality ("earth"). This proves that God (Love) is not found *outside or above* the senses, but *within* them; and 2) the darknight (the dry, parched wilderness period of pain and crisis). This dry condition is thirst for Unity with the Beloved, the One. (For "water" is the Unconscious, the only door to Love.) The Christ through Jesus said "I am the water of Life." (Jn. 4:10, 14) Christ spoke also of an inner wellspring "bubbling up" to impart timeless life (everlasting). Even when Lovemind seems to be absent, in this psychic desert, Love is still completely and immediately present.

This means that God is not a strange alien or something detached from, transcendent of, everyday, ordinary life. Instead, *God pervades ordinary life as Love.* The Buddhists say it like this: *nirvana* (ultimate bliss, enlightenment) is *samsara* (the everyday, ordinary world of the senses). So, God is not to be found in dark caves, cloisters, and restrictions of the senses. He is not found in religion, ancient texts, ritual, dogma, doctrine, or ceremony. God is not in administrations, churchbuildings, property holdings, halls, schools, and other structures. Ultimate Mind, Lovemind, is to be found *at the very Center of the sensory, sensual world.* All sensual needs are satisfied by surrendermind ("lamb").

The very best thoughts in all of Mind (144,000) support surrendermind ("lamb"). God is found in laughter, making love, playing, talking, writing, learning, and a million other life areas. They are, in fact, a part of It. They have a memory ("written"). It contains the identity ("name") of fullest human interface with Lovemind ("Christ").

This Unity with deepest Mind ("his name") is also recognized intellectually ("forehead"). Traditionally, almost all Jewish and Christian mystics have spoken of profound love-relationship with God. But they have usually stopped short of complete *identification* with God. This has been due to cultural and religious influences. But oneness is the major core-teaching of mysticism. This great thought-constellation of Godthoughts has realized its identity with the cosmic Lovemind (the name "of his father").

Verse 2. "And I heard a voice out of heaven, as the voice of many waters, and as [a] voice of great thunder. And the voice which I heard was as of harpists playing in their harps."

COMM: Communication ("voice") is the embryo of revelation. It comes from Lovemind ("heaven"). It unites mind with the oceanic Unconscious ("waters"). This intermingling of mindlevels is liquidic, as their boundaries disappear into a state of interfluidity.

The mind roars with stunning warning of coming mindstorms ("thunder"). It anticipates inner blazes of incandescent lightning. It will explode and demolish the old, to make room for the new. Sweet, tender harmony with Love ("harps") brings a message of happy wisdom.

Verse 3. "And they are singing as [if] a new song, in sight of the throne and in sight of the four living creatures, and of the old people. And no one was able to learn the song but the one hundred forty-four thousand, bought from the earth."

COMM: Unutterable, immeasurable joy from undiscovered sources ("new song") hides in the depths of the ocean of Mind. Blissmind is within Lovemind ("heaven"), Godthoughts within Mind ("in sight"). Ultimate Mind *is, in fact, this sum of Lovethoughts.* As mind approaches Lovemind, ecstasy explodes into consciousness.

Old symbols (chapter four) suddenly reappear. Perhaps the original author was interrupted by another visionary. Or perhaps the story just picks up here where he/she left off.

Among the old symbols: 1) throne, Center of Mindpower, cosmic Mind, deepest directing Unconscious; 2) four living creatures, or stable strong Godthoughts; 3) the "old people," the more experienced and wiser parts of Mind, mostly unconscious.

Only the spiritual ("happy, holy") Godthoughts can master joy ("learn the song"). These redeemed thoughts have been derived from hypersensual mind ("earth") reborn. Mind has learned to support these Lovethoughts, through the "school" of "hard knocks," in the sensory world of illusion.

Verse 4. "These are those who with women were not polluted. For they are virgins. These follow the lamb, where he likely will go under. These were bought from men. [They are] first fruits to God and to the lamb."

COMM: Sex seems damned here. For centuries, churches have so interpreted these words. But Revelation is written in symbols. Sexual "pollution" is a perfect metaphor for attempting forcefully, unnaturally to combine Love with antiagapic confusions, illusions, and general screw-ups. It is the bright purity of Love abused and misinterpreted.

So, while not exactly synonymous with the betrayal of Love ("fornication"), contaminating Love with antiagapic ideas (sexual "pollution") is still a serious sin. Some religions and cults have done this historically. They have condoned, indeed, taught, violence and cruelty in the name of the Lord of Love. When modern groups do this, such as in the equally monstrous teachings of hellfire and Armageddon, both of which make God out to be a fool and a monster, they are "polluting" themselves. So, "pollution with women" is a metaphoric way of referring to the contamination of tender, nourishing, supportive Lovethoughts.

Also, Love does not blend with condemnation and exclusivity. These are also major pollutants of Love. Yet fairly early in the Christian tradition, people claiming to follow the Way of Love were cutting each other's throats, raping, torturing, and murdering other "Christians." This atrocity was all in the name of "purity." "Correctness of dogma" became more important than kindness, mercy, or Love. All for the sake of a "clean" congregation, "uncontaminated" by heresy, people abused, betrayed, abandoned each other. This is all Love-pollution. What they failed to see was that this brutality, atrocity, and violence were themselves a gigantic "pollution." These hideous behaviors were *the worst "heresies" conceivable!* No "false teaching" could ever have been equivalent of this nightmare of incredible sexual, verbal, emotional, and physical abuse!

Love and fear do not mix. Like oil and water, they are by nature forever divided. Love-pollution is the attempt forcefully to ram together the antipodal opposites of fear and Love. It is the historical and philosophic absurdity of violence in the name of God, war in the name of the holy and just. It is injustice practiced voluntarily and deliberately.

An outstanding example of Love-pollution is the whole idea of a *jihad,* for *no war can ever be "holy."* Evil, no matter how you dress it up, can never become good, and fear can never become Love, or ugliness beauty.

In the "real," or everyday, ordinary world of spacetime, these are forever mutually exclusive, by the very nature of the relative cosmos. In this world, hatred/fear is always ugly, always false, always an illusion without true existence. It only just *seems* to exist "outside" of Mind.

Lovethoughts are loyal to Love. Love is pervasive, and affects all thoughts, words, and deeds. Mental purity ('virginity') is a must-have. This state always arises from good intent, careful to harm no living creature deliberately/unnecessarily.

These thoughts are of stainless pristinity. They surrender their personal wills to Lovemind. They desire nothing but Union with It. They accompany ("follow") surrendermind ("lamb"). Even in the spiritual journey, when lambmind visits animalmind, through hellstates, to lower states ("going under"), they follow, to learn. These thoughts are redeemed ("bought") by Lovemind from human, intellectual mindlevels ("men").

These thoughts are the best among the fruits of Mind ("first fruits"). This thoughtgroup, in other words, represents the very best of human productive thoughts. They are the finest, as in ancient sacrificial rites the very best among fruits was given sacrificially to the god. They produced the "fruits" of the Spirit, including Love, joy, and peace. (Compare "Euphrates," above; see also Ga 5:22.) These ideas were the first to grow and "ripen" spiritually. They blossomed into action.

Verse 5. "And in their mouth was found no lie. They are unblemished. And no falsehood was found in their mouths. They are stainless."

COMM: A secret unity is enfolded within these mysterious words: The use of "mouth" (singular) with "their" indicates that they all arise from, belong to, a single Mind, supremely pure.

This thought-constellation shines with the glowing stars of Light. Lovelight glows through ethics elevated. They are free of dishonesty ("no lie...no falsehood"). The deeper meaning is that these concepts are *not bound by illusion.* They are highlighted as pristine ("unblemished"). They are not overly 'soiled' or 'sullied' with too much earth (hypersensuality). They are islands of purity ("stainless"). These thoughts are free from dualism, violence, destructive anger, ignorance, and other animalmind limits. They are as pure as the driven snow.

Verse 6. "And I saw another angel, flying in midheaven, with timeless good news to declare as glad news, upon those sitting upon the earth. [It was declared to] every nation, tribe, tongue, and people."

COMM: This spiritual Mindfactor ("angel") is not in deepest Mind ("heaven"). Although positive and spiritual, its Mindarea ("midheaven") is not fully enlightened. It is not yet one with Lovemind.

Neither is it stuck completely in hypersensual mind (earth). It is midway between sense-dominated mind and fully spiritual mind. It communicates with mindareas still lower. It informs lethargic, lazy parts of mind ("sitting"). These are still locked into the gridlock of hypersensuality and bionature ("earth"). So, this spiritual messenger of Mind has not completed the inner Journey to the Center of the Soul.

Still, this spiritual messengermind is by no means static. It is on its way ("flying") to dizzying heights of spiritual Lovelight.

Its "timeless good news" was about: 1) timeless life, and 2) the discovery of joy. How can we know this? Because "good news" was a specific or technical term in early Christianity. It was not just the "generic" brand of good news, as in, "It's a girl?" or, "My car is finally running!" or, "The test results were negative." These can all be good news.

But in the first century, the Greek word *evaggelion* had a very special meaning: the Way of Love (mysticism) in all Its glory. The good news was: 1) You, as Mind, will never die, and 2) your truest, deepest Self is unending bliss and immeasurable Love. This will blossom once you have discovered your deepest Nature or Mind.

The revelation is received by: 1) large thought-constellations ("nations"); 2) interwoven, primitive thought-clusters ("tribe"); 3) large groups of intercommunicating thought-aggregates ("tongue"), and 4) huge generic thought-groups ("people").

Verse 7. "He was saying in a great voice, 'Fear God and give him glory, because his hour of judgment came. And you gave worship to the One Who made heaven, earth, sea, and fountains of water.'"

COMM: Approach Lovemind! This is Coremind, Creator, or "God." Come before Him/Her with reverential awe ("fear"). Touching Lovemind is the essence of ecstasy! It blows every circuit of the mind! It is the greatest rush, the most exquisite high! Throw yourself into It with blazing enthusiasm, passion, and a heart on fire, ablaze, with Love!

This message is powerful ("great voice")! Cosmic Mind must be acknowledged as the Source of all good, of the entire cosmos ("give God the glory"). This is a basic tenet of the Enlightenment Tradition. It gives birth to a second universal tradition of the Way: We must avoid assiduously any claims to personal merit. That builds only an immense ego! And no matter how enormous the fantasy, exaggeration does not make it one photon more real! Big egos are as phony as smaller ones! In fact, just as the least is the greatest, so greater egos are less real, for they drive us more deeply into illusion! (Godmind is Reality-- all that is real!)

Hyperinflated ego is also spiritually dangerous! It forces us away from Lovemind. It erects illusion-barriers between us and the Mind of the One. So, it drives us closer to fearmind (satanmind).

The illusion-opposite of Love is fear. The opposite of joy is dreary agony, often prolonged. Let's try to avoid inner hells by never taking credit, by never grubbing for attention, by never degrading ourselves by fishing for complements or recognition. The genuinely enlightened person is never loud or boisterous. She does not seek recognition by the crowd. She does not "dance in the spotlight" to impress an audience. She does not talk very much about herself. These are all techniques of spiritual losers. These are patterns of those who so hate, or mistrust, themselves that they need human validation to say, "Yes, I do have value."

But really spiritual people are gentle, nonintrusive, quiet (except when teaching), and introspective. When deepest Mind evaluates us, It sees us as perfectly good. The genuine master needs to know no more than this: She is produced by perfect Lovemind, and so, is exactly what she is supposed to be. *For her particular niche*, her place in life, she is perfect. (For God is allgood. It follows that a cosmos created from perfect Mind, and nothing else, must also be "allgood.")

When God evaluates ("judges") you, She/He will say nothing but that you are, as a dream of perfect Mind, "very good", as God said in Genesis Chapter 1. Adoration with joy ("worship") is the only fulfilling response to this sweet, allforgiving Spiritmind. He/She is deepest Mindarea and Lovemind ("heaven").

But this is also the Creatormind ("One Who made heaven"). This can mean only one thing: Ultimate Mind, cosmic Mind, Lovemind is *selfcreated.* As even the most ancient and traditional theologies teach, divine Mind is "autogenic," or selfgenerating.

She/He, at the Mindlevel called the "Creator" or "Dreamer," also makes *all other minds.* (See "Chart of Mind.") He/She is Creator of hypersensual mind *(*"earth"). He/She also creates the Unconscious ("sea"). Finally, She/He creates, through human mental engineering, ideas based on the Unconscious ("fountains of water").

Verse 8. "And another, second, angel followed, saying, 'She fell, she fell! Babylon the great, who has made all the nations to drink out of the anger of the wine of her fornication.'"

COMM: A gigantic mindcomplex of immense power ("Babylon the great") makes its entrance! It has forced vast mindareas ("nations") into disorientation ("wine"). This has been caused by the betrayal of Love ("fornication"). This has triggered disapproval ("anger") of deeper Mind.

The betrayal of Love can take many forms, but careless, promiscuous sex is the most common, popular, and dangerous. This is mere biosex, separated from Love.

So, "Babylon the great" is the biosexdrive without Love. When, after long trial and many tribulations, that mindless urge ceases to control the Mind, "Babylon" falls. Still, even after it does fall, it apparently is revived, for the announcement of Babylon's "fall" is repeated, much later in the narrative, in 18:4.

Verse 9. "And another angel, a third, followed them, saying in a great voice, 'If anyone worships the wild beast and its image, and receives an engraving upon his forehead or upon his hand,'" **Verse 10**. "'he will drink from the wine of God's anger, unmixed in the cup of his wrath. And he will be tormented with fire and sulfur in the sight of holy angels, and in sight of the lamb.'"

COMM: The fierce and fearsome disapproval ("anger") of Lovemind is triggered. This makes the mind stumble, in utter confusion ("wine"). It also amplifies the disorientation that already exists due to biosex without Love ("babylon").

Disorientation ("wine") is shared by both God and Babylon. This is a hint that, from the cosmic view, Babylon is secretly cooperating with cosmic Mind. Still, Babylon is a temporary servant of fearmind (satanmind).

Any thought that fell into the deluded selfimage, "I am an animal" ("image" of the "beast") will find only agony and ghastly suffering. Why? Because that idea or concept has removed itself from *all sources of joy* and Love. It ends up in Loveless hell!

Animalsex promised abundant joy, and seemed thrilling. But it was a desert for Soulmind, a deadend that led nowhere. The *whole* person cannot find lasting joy or fulfillment in a merely biological activity!

Disapproval is not diluted by other Mindfactors ("unmingled"). The relative, shorterm negative evaluation is clear and powerful. When the Soul feels the disapproval of Lovemind (Spirit), and is thrown into confusion, the result is restless discomfort, even suffering ("torment").

It touches suffering that leads to purity ("fire"). This "fire," and "torment," are supported by intellectual Mindfactors that fuel purifying suffering ("sulfur").

Yellow is Mind as intellect. So, pain is supported, probably exacerbated, by over-analysis or "overthink." This is a signal that it is time to stop thinking, to enrich the feelings.

Holy Mindaspects ("angels") know what is happening ("in sight of"). Surrendermind ("lamb') also knows.

Verse 11. "And the smoke of their torment is stepping up into the ages of the ages. And they are not having a resting up day or night. [These are] the ones worshipping the wild beast and its image, and receiving the engraving of its name."

COMM: She who allows wildbeastmind to control her thoughts and actions comes to see herself as nothing but an animal. So, she acts like a beast-- territorially, greedily, hypersexually, shoving Love aside, outside of her life. She adopts the identity ("name") of a wild, monstrous beast.

She defends this through evolution, presenting herself as an ape. She denies the special uniqueness of the human. This is another way of supporting the terrible "worship" of the "image" of bestiality. Her selfimage is corrupted, ruined.

But a joyful, redeeming promise follows: Lower mind, in innumerable and proliferating plethoras of thoughtfeeling, transcends ("smoke")! These thoughts are, with Lovemind's help, ascending to higher Mind ("stepping up")! They are pervasive, filling every mental nook and cranny ("ages of the ages"). They are finding Union with the timeless Spirit.

A highly active period ensues ("not...resting up"). The Mind never stops its frenetic pace ("day and night"). This exhausts lower mind, but relentlessly drives the whole Mind towards revelation. Amazingly, this includes even thoughtideas misled into animal identification ("engraved" with the ownership-seal of wildbeastmind). For, so illimitable and immeasurable is the saving Love of God, even beastmind will be redeemed!

Verse 12. "Here is the endurance of the holy, those observing the commandments of God and the faith of Jesus."

COMM: Transformation is as slow as molasses flowing uphill in January. While toxins (from wildbeastmind) are being outpaced, patience ripens ("endurance"). Simultaneously, Lovedevelopments do good works; Love is expressed, not just felt ("observe the commandments"). But this positive activity is not enough. This can be done by any fool or hypocrite. For it can be merely mechanical or legalistic. This is a religious, unhappy, bitter state.

To be really spiritual, these thoughts must also enjoy and embrace the belief, from gnosis, that God (Lovemind) is taking care of every micro-event in the cosmos. In these mindareas, *perfect faith becomes perfect relaxation.* This is the mystical mindset, as emphasized most fully in Taoism ("faith of Jesus").

Verse 13. "And I heard a voice out of heaven, saying, 'Write, "happy are the dead in the Lord, dying from right now. Yes, the Spirit is saying, so that they will be rested up from their labors, for their works follow them."

COMM: The dead resting? What is that about? Lovemind startles mind awake to memories ("write")! These deactivated thoughts ("dead") are not dead at all! For they are joyful ("happy")! Temporarily deactivated, and even deleted, from the mind, they continue, alive and well, in the Unconscious. But this secret life in the deep waters applies to only those thoughts that have become fused, melded, with Lovemind ("in the Lord"). This is *the totality of Lovethoughts.*

They are sinking down into the Unconscious ("dying"). Why? Because the conscious study and awareness of Love pushes It into the Unconscious. Every act of Love reinforces this. So, *Lovethoughts originate from the Unconscious, and then, sink back "down" into It. (For Lovemind Itself is deeply unconscious.) Love creates a conscious-Unconscious synergy of harmony.* Even while the infinite Unconscious continuously radiates Love, the conscious mind continues to choose Love, to create and implement new acts of Love, and to feed them into the Unconscious.

This occurs continuously; it is not a vague plan. It is not something from the past, or the future. It occurs only in the eternal now ("right now").

These are thoughtfeelings taken from egomind, and absorbed into Lovemind. "Inner death" is the final destiny of the whole egomind. That is, egomind is fated to "die into" Lovemind. These thoughts, then, are forerunners to that ultimate goal. Mystics call this the "personal egocrucifixion." Ego is dying voluntarily. It knows that it supports a false and shallow mind-- the conscious mind. Unless that mind dies, there can be no healthy rebirth. It is this rebirth that leads to a deeper identity: You start the growth-sequence with, "I am a body," then move to, "I am a mind," progress to, "I am a Soul," and cap it with the supreme, "I am Spirit." Then, You are God, or an incarnation of Lovemind.

Your conscious mind dies into Lovemind. This "death" is a form of inner vacation from stress ("resting up"). For it is reversible.

The results of former actions ("works") catch up with the mind-- a thumbnail summary of karma ("follow them").

Verse 14. "And I saw, and look! A white cloud, and upon the cloud, one was sitting like a son of man. He had on his head a golden crown. In his hand [he had] a sharp sickle."

COMM: Purity ("white") flashes forth. This, however, is a mystery; it is wrapped in obscurity and enigma ("cloud").

Alternatively, Spirit ("air") dances with the Unconscious ("water"). This conjunction creates synergy ("cloud").

This is hidden: The work is all.

The human mind ("son of man") infused and shining with the bright luminosity of Lovemind is the deeper Self (Soul, as in chapter one). It is not the deepest Self (Spirit). It is the temporary Ruler of mind ("crown"). Full rulership arrives, however, only after earthly enlightenment ("golden").

The Soul feeds on hypersensual mind. For It carries a sharp, dangerous blade ("sickle"). This implies an earthly (hypersensual) harvest. Grain can't be far off!

Mindfunctions which gather stray "foodthoughts" ("sickle") are guided by Soulmind. It gathers and prepares thoughts useful to Soulmind and Spiritmind. (Soulmind turns these thoughts into Love; the Essence of Spirit!) (Compare "vegetation" in Glossary)

These thoughts are: 1) undeveloped, 2) primitive, 3) small, and 4) earthly. We know this because these thoughts are represented by grapes (see verse 18). The sicklemind turns run-of-the-mill thoughts into nourishing forms. Mind thrives on "forms" called ideas. Thoughts have limited use unless they join hands and cooperatively form cohesive concepts. Sicklemind forms thoughts into crystalclear ideas. Sicklemind is the mind's natural ordering and processing mechanisms. They work to transform sensual, bionatural thoughts into spiritual "food."

Verse 15. "And another angel went forth out of the divine habitation, crying out in a great voice, to him who sat upon the cloud, 'Send your sickle, and harvest. For the harvest-time has come, for the harvest of the earth is ripe.'"

COMM: Soul is guided by luminous Mind ("angel"). They will energize and strengthen mind. The Soulmind begins gathering ("harvest") of abundant, nourishing, delicious hypersensual ("earthly") thoughts. They are ready to be assimilated ("ripe").

These bodymind (bionatural) thoughts are ready to provide spiritual nourishment.

Mind is ready to apply the sensual nature, including sexuality, to real Love.

Idea-processing abilities (part of sicklemind) enable mind to assimilate spiritual food.

Verse 16. "And the one sitting upon the cloud threw his sickle upon the earth, and the earth was harvested."

COMM: Sensuality and sexuality ("earth") are sweet emeralds to Spirit. For they nourish It. But before their energies are any good for the Spirit, the thoughts of "earth" must pass through collection and processing ("harvesting") by sicklemind in the Soul. Sex, for example, is just a biodrive in the bodymind; in Soulmind, it can become a Lovexpression!

Verse 17. "And another angel went forth out of the divine habitation in heaven. [He] also had a sharp sickle."

COMM: Another part of spiritmind ("angel") now joins forces with the Soul. This sacred Mindforce comes directly from Lovemind ("divine habitation"). It too has the capacity to process sensuality into spiritual nourishment ("sickle"). Soul and Spirit ("angel") cooperate to redeem from hypersensual mind those thoughtfeelings that support spiritual growth.

Verse 18. "And another angel went forth out of the altar, having authority upon the fire. And he spoke with a great voice to the one having the sharp sickle, saying, 'Send in your sharp sickle and gather in the clusters of the vine of the earth, because its grapes are ripe.'"

COMM: Surrendermind ("altar") is in charge. This "angel" is another face of surrendermind. It can modify, influence, or control ("authority") purifying suffering ("fire"). In other words, this "angel of the altar" is the part of the psyche that creates detachment in the midst of crisis or disaster. This part of Mind also uses pain to make sense of the cosmos; it derives meaning and lessons from the pain of suffering ("fire").

The power of detachment[37] is derived from body-detachment. Detachment is a lesson specifically of the earth-form; it is learned by discovering detachment from full control by the senses ("earth"). Those lessons of detachment and strength form a megacomplex of wisdom. This occurs through united cooperation. Smaller lessons ("grapes") come together, and are processed by sicklemind as a meaningful whole. This creates the state of Union or Communion with Spirit (wine, implied). This is the secret to suffering: It is all reinterpreted. Everything-- jewelry, money, occupation, house, car, career, reputation, heartmind, timenergy, pleasure, comfort-- is sacrificed to know God with fantastic gnosis! Sacrifice is a blast! It is a pleasure and a joy! Those who practice voluntary renunciation say that they pity those who have not followed this sweet path!

The Soul predesigned certain cases of suffering before birth. Knowing this lets you embrace some pain with deep tranquility. You are granted the "philosophic attitude." This strength arises from an altered state. It is the mystical state called "detachment."

"Clusters" are thought-clusters-- groups of related small thoughts. They grow from the Lovemind ("vine"). The ultimate Source of all

---

[37] For an indepth analysis of practical and spiritual detachment and how it can improve your life, see my *Teflonmind: Sex, Money, Life and Detachment, op. cit.*

thoughts is Coremind, Christmind, Lovemind, which said through Jesus, "I am the vine." (John 15:1)

Since grapes are purple, they represent both spiritual thoughts and the potential for Communion ("wine") with divine nature. These thoughts are just right to nourish spirituality ("ripe").

Verse 19. "And the angel threw his sickle into the earth, and gathered in the vine of the earth. And he threw [it] into the great press of the anger of God."

COMM: Lovemind is hypersensual mind ("vine of the earth").

Spiritual thoughts ("grapes") support fierce disapproval ("anger"). They will later create Love. They originate with hypersensual mind ("earth").

But before Love can blossom, the pressure-cooker tension ("press") of this disapproval must be released. The Spirit disapproves the careless hypersensuality of ego ("anger"). It intends to destroy, then restructure, the entire Mind. Fundamental explosive changes are on the near horizon.

The hypersensual expression of Lovemind ("vine") is first to go into the mindset of Communion ("press"). [The "press" is all processes that transform spiritual thoughts into actual Communion. Thus, secondarily, it represents egodeath (see next verse).] So, Communion, the perfect Union of cosmic Mind with human mind, begins with hypersensual mind ("earth"). This means that the most spiritual mind begins with the sensual and "ordinary," everyday, normal, average mind. Spiritual genius has its roots in the humdrum situations of the average life. The most ordinary events can be "spiritual" *if we are learning from them.* "Heaven" has its roots in "earth."

The spiritual thoughts ("grapes") from Lovemind ("vine") grow into dynamic and full Union ("wine"). During this state there is also considerable disorientation -- another, and secondary, meaning of "wine".

Verse 20. "And the wine-press was [used for] trampling, outside the city, and blood came out, out of the wine-press. It reached [as high as] the horses' bridles for one thousand six hundred stadia."

COMM: "Blood," a horrifying symbol, represents death. But this is not death of the whole Mind, but of egomind. Ego is a false identity that must die before we can awaken to the glorious Identity with Spirit. Only this death permits Union with Lovemind.

"Wine" and "blood" are here interwoven, interchangeable symbols. Both represent egodeath-- "blood" emphasizes the ego that must die, and "wine" emphasizes the Spirit of Communion, in which ego is lost through Mindfusion or Mindmelding. That these symbols are equivalent is highlighted by the fact that "blood" not "wine" comes out of the wine press.

Spirit's intention is to kill human nature. This process has already begun.

But why is it "outside the city"? A "city" represents a collection of Mindstructures, engineered and designed, mostly, by the human mind. Its alternative is nature. Egodeath begins "outside" the human frameworks of logic, linearity, and intellect. It is an emotional and unconscious process, so "outside" of intellect ("city").

It begins deeply within Mind. But the process, being natural, does not start with intellect. Instead, it begins with nature. Nature is outside the "city" of human mindsystems. The process of egodeath starts in the Unconscious.

It starts with the natural structure of deeper Mindlevels. It is supported by thoughtenergy from hypersensual mind ("earth"). Enlightenment is natural. All of nature, all of the human brain and nervous system, is designed to support it, to cooperate with it. Why? Because it is the irresistible destiny of mind. *Enlightenment is why mind exists. So, it is supremely natural.* All of nature was designed to culminate not only in *sentient,* but *spiritual* mind.

But, paradoxically, enlightenment can happen only with an influx of Lovemind, and so, is also supernatural. Its roots are in nature. But its ultimate flower is the supernatural state of unconditional universal Love.

Egodeath ("blood") accompanies communion ("winepress"). This mental "death" affects first the animal nature ("horses"). Human control ("bridles") of the rash, dangerous animal nature must yield placidly to egodeath. For although the micromind of ego is *never really in control,* it believes that it is. Before the lower nature can die, however, the human must regulate the animal. Egodeath ("blood") begins with the human regulation of the animal ("as high as the horse' bridles").

The number 1600 reduces to seven, revealing the ultimate goal as spiritual enlightenment.

Chapter 15

Verse 1. "And I saw another sign in heaven. [It was] great and wonderful. Seven angels had seven plagues. [These are] the final ones, because in them is finished the anger of God."

COMM: Lovemind ("heaven") shines with breath-taking beauty ("great and wonderful"). But mental dysfunctions that lead to purification by pain ("plagues") are nearby! A horror-response is normal! What insanity is this?

So, mental disfunctions/confusions, ("plagues") are good! They are gigantic challenges, nightmare puzzles that force mind into growth. They are "good" because their solutions will result in eternal bliss and tranquility. But as "good" as they are, they are ghastly, nightmarish, and horrible to the mind. Because they are "good" they originate in "heaven" (Lovemind). They arise from the deepest Love for the Soul! They are provided out of Love to give the Soul the greatest gift of all-- enlightenment, freedom, or salvation. Blissmind results, but this takes much time. That even the "horrible" has spiritual goals is indicated by the appearance of the sacred "seven," not once, but twice! This is a promise of endless beauty, stunning tranquility, and enormous compassion still to come!

The fierce disapproval of Lovemind ("anger of God") is completed. Later, disapproval turns to approval, and sadness to delight.

Verse 2. "And I saw [something] like a glassy sea, mixed with fire. And those who were conquering out of the wild beast, and out of its image, and out of the number of its name stood upon the glassy sea, having harps of God."

COMM: The Unconscious ("sea") is made absolutely transparent ("glassy"), so that Lovemind, in its Center, can shine through It unimpeded. This is the state of stillness so absolutely pure and quiet that not a single thought interferes with the Love of cosmic Mind. The Lovelight within shines, and nothing casts any shadows in Its pristine radiance! This is the altered state that mystics call "stillmind" or "crystalmind". It is lucidly transparent.

But this clearing the Mind of cognitive, conscious thought-content is anything but easy. Mystics call it "overthink" or "mind-clutter". It was to discover this inner state of quiescence, crystalmind, that all forms of meditation were developed.

Purifying suffering ("fire") helps. It is mingled with the still "sea" of the Unconscious. For it is suffering that drives the mind to understand that it is not in control of your life. It was never given this assignment. So, it was never given the power to regulate everything in your life. That awakening, in time, leads to surrender. That, with still more time, leads to stillmind, crystalmind.

You must acquire discipline over the unruly and chaotic mind. Then, you must push forward, to the depths of Mind, and touch crystalmind. This state supports all the healing and spiritual thoughts within the psyche. All the thoughts and ideas that overcame ("conquering") wildbeastmind are supported by this "sea."

Since according to the original text, they conquer "out of" the wild beast, this very beast is the source of some of the spiritual conquest. Energy must be tapped from the animalnature (wildbeastmind) to "conquer" that same animalnature. It is most efficient inner conflict, in which the energy of the adversary is turned against the opponent (animalmind) in a psychic *jiu-jitsu*.

These positive spiritual thoughts deny the interior idea ("image") that beastmind is good by nature. They draw energy from animalmind. But they refuse domination by it. They turn away from the tendency to identify their "selves" on the basis of linear, logical, mathematical thinking ("number"). This kind of naive, linear selfanalysis marks wildbeastmind.

This is the reduction of the "human" by merely scientific means. For the human being is far more than twenty dollars' worth of chemicals. Indeed, she is *far more than can be measured.* What you see is not all that you get. The greatest and most wonderful part of the human being-- the mind-- is invisible, and only partly amenable to science ("number"). That is, it is beyond mere chemical or material science.

The higher thoughts adamantly refused the identity ("name") of the wild beast as their own. This massive, awakening behemoth of the Unconscious ("sea") is rushing towards full harmony ("harps") with Lovemind ("God").

Verse 3. "And they are singing the song of Moses, the slave of God, and the song of the lamb, saying, 'Great and wonderful are your works, Lord God, the Almighty. Righteous and true are your ways, King of the ages.'"

COMM: The Mind has not yet found true Unity. Some dualities still thrive within It, blocking It through illusion.

One strong and confusing dichotomy historically reflected this illusion. It was that between religion and spirituality. Religion teaches that one is granted approval by obedience to mechanical law, while spirituality teaches that *we are all saved by the Love (grace) of God alone.* In ancient Jewish and Christian writings, the words "Moses" and "law" (religious) were synonymous. Instead of saying, "The Jewish law commands..." it was a kind of shorthand to say, "Moses commands..."

So, Moses makes a most natural symbol of religion. Religionmind is full of dogmatism, legalism, Biblicism, mechanism, external practices, and attempts to impress others. It is rigid and judgmental. It is childish and naive, and might well be spiritually dead. It emphasizes a false "selfcontrol," which is really nothing but fear as guilt. (Fear is Love's opposite.) But it can, in some situations, lead to a real state of genuine joy ("song of Moses"). Religionmind controls through a number of fearfactors, including spiritual "police" (elders, priests, rabbi, imams, ministers), scripturalism and legalism, the threat of Armageddon, or that of hellfire. Spiritual Mind is never like this, and has none of these hang-ups.

But at this point in discovery, there is still confusion. Mind (John) is confused. For although Revelation is a sterling mystical document, it is not infallible. That is, it was not written by God directly. In other words, *as with all sacred texts,* God (Lovemind) used a human being as His/Her instrument.

The absence of certain knowledge in the ordinary mind (John) would, then, necessarily confuse the issue. So, the Revelation itself is a bit clouded, opaque, or unclear here. At the time of this writing, Christianity was *just beginning to differentiate itself from Judaism.* Many Christians, then as now, might have been confused over this issue.

Even a mystic such as "John" could have been influenced by the language and assumptions of his culture.

Although "John" was a Christian, and so, not a Jew, we cannot simply dismiss the fact that many Christians of the time fell into the snare of regarding Christianity as a natural cultural outgrowth of Judaism. (It was not. It was an entirely new revelation of a very different religion, with a very different God.) Contemporary Christians, with nineteen hundred years of history under their belt, still make this catastrophic error.

The problem was exacerbated by attempts, even unconscious ones, to please the Jews, and even to make them supporters of the Christian Way. (Of course, this never worked with the majority.) Still, it appears that "John" had a difficult time separating Moses from God-- the cosmic Mind, everlasting Lovemind.

It is only with the benefit of retrospective history and detachment that we can get a better overview than was available to "John." It is absolutely crystal clear to us that Judaism and Christianity are different, sometimes opposed, religions. The former made a hurricane within the latter; Christianity was no peaceful, brotherly evolution within Judaism. So, when writing the Apocalypse, "John" was a little confused over this distinction. The problem is complexified and made more opaque when you consider the possibility that, according to internal evidence, "John" was *actually more than one person.*

This confusion is not allpervasive. Lucidity shines through, for example, in the clear distinction between the celebration ("song") of legalistic practices ("Moses"), and that of real surrender ("lamb"). Each had its own *separate and individual song.* Each had its own appropriate place in the history of spiritual evolution. So, there was some awareness that these represented different paths. But they are conjoined here in a kind of synergy which does not always mark traditional religion and the inner Way.

By this time, "John" must have known that Christianity, or the Way, did *not always get along well with Judaism.* Perhaps this was more hidden than conscious knowledge, but it is revealed in the presentation of symbols. The two paths celebrated ("song") the Love of God and the goodness of the cosmos in *different* ways. This was an implicit declaration of an explosively controversial truth: The life-pattern of a good, loyal Jew was not precisely the same as that of an enlightened person. In fact, Christians saw their "Way of Love" as distinctly superior to the legalism and scripturalism of Judaism.

This is not to say that all religion is bad or "evil." It can truly guide you in the right direction, when you feel that you need it. It is *just not enough*. Sometimes religion, which is all about the outer, *does not lead to real spirituality, which is all about the inner*. Sometimes it does. Even religious mechanism ("Moses") can be a real servant of Lovemind ("slave of God"). You can be *both religious and spiritual*. But this does not imply that religion is synonymous with spirituality. Religion promotes a false "righteousness" that is completely outside of real goodness. Spirituality supports a deeper, and true correct alignment with the will of Love (real "righteousness") that is a galaxy away.

But Mosesmind (religionmind) will never take the mind to enlightenment. In fact, apart from its production and support of external morality, Mosesmind is not a part of enlightenment at all. It is a product of the conscious mind, not of Coremind or Lovemind. For religion is merely what one does on the outside, but spirituality is all done within. Religion is a human and cultural artifice, but spirituality is intrinsic to Mind.

Religion usually supports the false teaching of "salvation by works," and denies God's grace as the *only* Way of salvation. Even religions that claim to accept grace say that you must believe the "right" things; and *belief is a form of "works."* So, even this more subtle lie is not true "salvation by grace."

It dismisses the unlimited Power of Love.

The activities ("works") of Love (God) are alone of true importance and awesome ("great and wonderful"). So, grace produces works; works never produce grace. Only the "ways" of Lovemind are the perfect alignment with the Law of Love, and Reality ("righteous and true"). Legalistic practices can make a person technically, falsely "righteous," but they cannot make her good. Also, since they are based on the illusion of duality, mechanistic religions cannot be "true." Indeed, they actively deny the core-truth of the mystical (enlightened) cosmos-- that *all is God manifest.*

Lovemind is the absolute, utter Ruler ("King") of all states of mind ("ages"). It is the Ruler of all levels of Mind-- the conscious, preconscious, Soul, collective, and Spirit. (See "Chart of Mind.")

Verse 4. "'Who will surely not fear, Lord, and glorify your name? For [you] alone[are] loyal. All the nations will come, and worship in your sight, for your righteous [ways] were made manifest.'"

COMM: Reverential awe ("fear") again illuminates the mind. The identity ("name") of God is more important, and more real, than your human ego-identity. It is to be regarded as sacred ("glorified"). This is the fulfillment in everyday life of the prayer, "Hallowed be thy name." This is making the identity of God central to our lives-- more central than our personal selves. For It is deepest Mind.

Lovemind is exclusively ("alone") to be recognized as immutable ("loyal"). Loyalty, even in its smaller, literal sense, flowers from Love. And *nothing in the world but Love is reliable.*

All the larger Mindsectors ("nations") will know the holiness of Lovemind. They will admire and serve ("worship") It. The perfectly aligned ("righteous") state of Lovemind is selfevident ("manifest").

Verse 5. "And after these, I saw, and the divine habitation of the tent was opened up of the heavenly testifier, and the seven angels came out of the divine habitation, those having the seven plagues."

COMM: Lovemind is "opened up" to the view of the mind. This is the beginning of a mystical experience.

The Lovemind ("temple") is also a more ordinary, everyday home ("tent"). This allegorical symbol demonstrates that the appropriate place for God (Love) is not in formal ritual, or special places, but every moment of every day. Love should permeate the minutes of our humble, ordinary, average, everyday lives ("tent"). Love is worship, and worship should *never* be limited to a formal church, or church-service or to any synagogue, temple or mosque. God *most fully*, in fact, lives outside the formalities ("temple"), and *most actively* lives in everyday life. A secondary meaning might be that Love, like a tent, is portable: You take it with you wherever you go.

This is also called the "tent of the Testifier" ("Observer"). This Mindsector records and evaluates all your most stupid and sublime intentions. This record guarantees that they return to you later as karma.

Verse 6. "They were clothed in clean, bright linen, and wore golden girdles about the breasts."

COMM: Selfimage ("linen"), through Love, becomes the more authentic Selfimage. It is pure and Lightfilled ("clean and bright"). This is when mind begins to identify its Self as Soul. (In 1:13, the Soul is decked in precisely the same "golden girdle".) The mind ceases to tell itself the lie, "I am my socially-defined self; I am this ego."

Then, it just begins to suspect that it is something more than "Mary Smith" or "John Jones." Slowly, gradually, it begins to dawn, "I am a nonphysical mind." Still later, this gradually grows into the realization, "I am a Soul," and much later reaches the zenith: "I am Spirit," or, "I am [an incarnation of] Love." The Mind has at last touched pristine Lovemind.

After centuries are spent in Love for this cosmic Mind, the mind is driven upward a thousand octaves. For it can no longer stand the separation that apparently holds it apart from the beloved Mind. Even as Love means that you do not want to be away from the Beloved, then mind wants *always and uninterruptedly* to be in the Presence of its Beloved (Lovemind). And even if imitation is a sincere form of Love, as of flattery, mere imitation is not enough: The mind is relentlessly driven to *partake* of its Beloved. And finally, if sexual union is Love (and it can be), then the *Union of minds* is the equivalent of sexual integration multiplied infinitely. This mystical touch has made the whole mind stainless, overflowing with Light, Love, and ecstasy!

Love is the treasure of the fourth chakra, located right over the heart ("breast"). (The *chakras* are energy-centers that regulate thought-feelings.) The heartmind has discovered enlightenment in its earthly environment ("golden"). This is protective ("girdle") of interior Mind.

Verse 7. "And one of the four living creatures gave to the seven angels seven golden bowls full of the anger of God who lives into the ages of the ages."

COMM: Godthoughts ("living creatures") give to spiritual Mind ("angels") a beautiful gift. It is bright, joyful Love. But this is tough love; it is expressed as displeasure ("anger"). But this mental disappointment leads finally to earthly enlightenment ("golden").

Angelmind and Godmind are both Lovemind ("seven"). Angelmind is Lovemind expressed as interaction. It thrives on Godmind, which is Lovemind as intrinsic feeling. Good things come in small packages, and this gift from Godmind is within a small Mindsector ("bowl"; spiritual nutrition is implied).

What is in this small Mindsector? It is not a very significant Mindvolume. So, it is not extremely important. It contains the disapproval ("anger") of Lovemind ("God"). This, despite appearances, is a spiritually positive ("seven") process. We are again reminded that the Mind is omnipresent ("ages of the ages").

Verse 8. "And the divine habitation was filled with smoke. [This came] out of the Power and glory of God. And no one was able to enter into the divine habitation until the seven plagues of the seven angels were finished."

COMM: Lovemind ("divine habitation") is filled with earthly transcendental thoughts ("smoke"). They are moving towards enlightenment in Love. These come "out of" Lovemind (God's "Power and glory"). God is the source of this "smoke." In other words, earth+Love+fire=smoke. This translates as: Hypersensual mind is tested and improved through purifying suffering and, when exposed to Love, turns into transcendence.

This growing enlightenment is totally unconscious. Not a single thought from the conscious mind can access ("come in" to) the Unconscious during the process ("No one was able to enter"). The conscious mind will not be allowed back into gnosis during this "darknight." It will not enjoy audience with Lovemind again until the spiritualization through mental confusions/disfunctions ("seven plagues") is completed.

Chapter 16

Verse 1. "And I heard a great voice out of the divine habitation, saying to the seven angels, 'Go under, and pour out the seven bowls of God's anger into the earth.'"

COMM: An inignorable communication ("great voice") roars out, earth-shakingly, from Lovemind ("divine habitation"). It commands spiritual Mind ("angels"). It tells them to work in the subconscious ("go under," in Greek).

They are to clear ("empty") small mindcompartments ("bowls"). They must clear ("pour out") Mind of Lovemind's disapproval ("God's anger"). But that disapproval does not just fade away, evanescing into nothingness. Instead, the energy of this disapproval is shuffled.

These disapproval-energies are transferred to hypersensual mind ("into the earth").

Verse 2. "And the first went off, and poured out his bowl into the earth. And a bad and wicked ulcer came to be upon the men, those who had the engraving of the wild beast, who worshipped its image."

COMM: Psychopathology appears from disapproval. This is a chronic mental condition ("ulcer"); it does not disappear overnight. It creates inner agony, continuous pain. It is exacerbated by stress (disapproval). Using these clues, we can hazard a guess that the "ulcer" is anxiety/depression. It is created partly by the suppression of valid disgust or disapproval. It is serious and agonizing ("bad and wicked"). Deliberate indulgence in evil contributes to its searing pain. It is also exacerbated, by resistance to Lovemind. But it does not corrupt the whole Mind. For only certain thoughts are infected.

Only those that voluntarily placed themselves in acquiescent service to wildbeastmind are struck. This "ulcer" strikes selectively only thoughts that supported the interior idea that wildbeastmind was good ("image"). This mental dysfunction and purifying pain ("plague") affects only intellect ("men"). Giving into inappropriate lusts, greed, and unclean sex (wildbeastmind) is just pouring salt into the ulcer.

Verse 3. "And the second poured out his bowl, into the sea. And it became blood, as of the dead. And every Soul of life in the sea died."

COMM: The Unconscious ("sea") dies ("blood") But it is not wholly paralyzed, and does not disappear irretrievably. It simply becomes inaccessible to the conscious mind. (Revelation is narrated from this perspective.) The Unconscious is, by definition, not within conscious awareness. But the mind is able to dip into it from time to time. Here, though, It plunges so deeply into the oceanic depths of Mind as to be irretrievable. Large areas of Mind, including the filthy, disgusting subconscious, disappear from conscious awareness. So, much psychic garbage vanishes.

But mind also loses touch with the *positive* Unconscious, heralding the black mind of darknight. It feels to the mind as if it were alone in the cosmos, isolated, deserted, abandoned. This feels like betrayal, and is the scariest phase of spiritual growth. The mind loses its former warm communications with even the Soul. Losing touch with the Soulevel ("every Soul of life") is agonizing.

But this state is a fluid and survivable condition. Of course, the Soulevel of Mind cannot be literally dead, for it is immortal until Spiritmind is reached. Only then does the Soul "die into" the Spirit, in final Union with It (See The Hebrew Scriptures, Ezekiel 18:4). In this darknight, Soul again enters spiritual crisis.

But even this is a gift from Lovemind. Keeping this in mind can help us to weather the storms. For Lovemind loves us enough to test us, to develop and cultivate maximum independence within us. Still, we do not have to like it, and we don't!

Verse 4. "And the third poured out his bowl into the rivers and fountains of waters. And they became blood."

COMM: Thoughtstreams ("rivers") feed into the Unconscious. They can be conscious. Often, the human conscious mind ("fountains") directs unconscious drives, especially the subconscious. These include biosex and hunger, for example.

When the depression of the darknight hits hard enough, even these conscious directives die ("blood"). As previously, the mind loses all contact with these organizing Mindstructures. The conscious mind completely loses touch with unconscious thought streams ("rivers..became blood"). This leaves the person gritting her teeth, pulling out her hair, feeling sorrowfully empty and hollow.

Verse 5. "And I heard from the angel of the waters. He said, 'Righteous are you, the One being, and the One who was. [You are] the loyal One, for you judged these....'"

COMM: The Unconscious manager ("angel of the waters"), speaking to Lovemind, declares It to be in right alignment ("righteous") harmonizing beautifully, It is the only Absolute. This is cosmic Law-- Love!

This is the only One Who has absolute Reality ("One being") and immutability ("loyalty"; compare 15:4). This One is Reality Itself. For within the "material and external" cosmos, this Mind permeates all things. It is the Reality indwelling all things, for It emanates all, and is immanent within all. In fact, *only this Mind is real.* It is the Mind that dreams the cosmos into being (monism). This Mind also has experience from the past ("was").

When the Absolute judges the absolute cosmos, It sees Its mirrore-flection everywhere. The cosmos is evaluated ("judged") to be all-good.

Verse 6. "'... because the blood of the holy and prophets they poured out. And you have given them blood to drink. They deserve it.'"

COMM: Vicious antiagapic forces array themselves against proagapic energies ("holy and prophets"). These positive thoughts were deactivated ("blood... poured out") by antiagapic monstrosities. So, in karmic balance, the brutal mindmonsters have had to survive vampirically on the death of other mindelements ("drink... blood"). They are scavengers living off death. From the thoughtenergy of abandoned (dead) ideas, they use the resulting free energy to rebuild and remold concepts of hatred, violence, and other forms of fear.

Verse 7. "And I heard [a voice] of the altar say, 'Yes, Lord, God, the Almighty. True and righteous are your judgments.'"

COMM: Surrendermind ("altar") speaks ("voice"). It confirms that Lovemind is Reality ("true"). It also declares It to be in harmony or alignment with cosmic law ("righteous").

Verse 8. "And the fourth poured out his bowl upon the sun, and it was given to it to scorch the men in fire."

COMM: Lovemind ("sun") sizzles when it meets, head-on ("poured out"), disapproval-energy (anger from the "bowl"). The displeasure comes from Lovemind.

But, It is not changed into a hell-furnace by this, Its own, reaction. Instead, the pain does not arise from Lovemind at all, but from intellectual interpretation ("men"). Intellect has misinterpreted the meaning of pain.

It interprets its pain as "punishment" from a vengeful or crazy god. Worse, it might choose to interpret pain as *more powerful* than Love. It grapples with pain, which it declares to be real, but intellect dismisses Love as only a fantasy, a dream made of smoke and fog. It feels as if it is frying alive in a searing flame. This is a wounded conscience, creating the torments of hell! Conscience spurned or neglected is wont to do exactly this. For conscience is the "hadeogenic" (hell-creating) factor of mind. When you act voluntarily, with intention, against goodness, the Light of Spirit can be too intense for your human mind to bear. What should be sweet Light is felt as ghastly, seething heat.

You can be blinded, then melted, by the Light! It creates purifying suffering ("fire").

Lovewisdom can be quite intense, supernaturally bright, and the human psyche quite brittle. So, the human mind can feel that it has been plunged into ferocious, ghastly flame ("scorched").

Verse 9. "And the men were scorched [with] a great scorching, and they blasphemed the name of God, who had authority upon the plagues. And they did not repent, to give him glory."

COMM: Intellect ("men") is severely hurt ("scorched"). For it intentionally goes against Reality or Lovemind. It thinks it can "figure the universe out" answering all questions using only science and logic: God (Love) is disposable.

The first encounter with It can consume egomind. How? The *relationship* between ego and Lovemind predestines that ego will disappear into cosmic Mind. The candle-flame merges brightly with the great fire of Mind. The dewdrop slips silently into the shining sea.

Small mind (egomind) is destined to fuse or merge with "big Mind," or Lovemind.

Earlier, egomind learned that only Mind is real. The entire "physical, material, external" cosmos exists only in Mind. Upon discovering this 'bizarre' truth, the egopsyche is boggled. The realization of reality ("truth") can cause you to 'lose your mind.' But this subtly sneaks up on you, in a positive, healing Way.

Egomind learns that the Core of Mind is Love. It must re-form itself, must "die" a few times before deeper Mind (Soul) emerges. All this "dying" scares the human psyche to death! For it is highly fear-based and survivalistic. This is part of its dysfunction ("plague"). Only God (Love) has the Power ("authority") to cure this disease. This pain is pushed towards purification, forced to serve Love!

But instead of yielding immediately to Spiritpower, the human mind arrogantly rebels. In ignorance, it might deny that the Holy exists, and it might even speak against It ("blaspheme"). This phase can last for a long time -- a life time or longer. During that time, the mind does not turn from its wayward course ("repent"). Indeed, it is usual for the mind, on spiritual pilgrimage, to go through atheistic or antitheistic phases. But do not panic! This is all part of your positive education.

Verse 10. "And the fifth poured out his bowl upon the throne of the wild beast, and its kingdom became darkened. And they chewed their tongues from the pain."

COMM: Vicious, ferocious, animalistic is wildbeastmind. The mind goes into a tizzy of confusion, even dysfunction ("plague") in response to the intensity and immensity of Power! It suffers screamingly from the disapproval ("anger" in the "bowl") of Lovemind. Now this painful force is shifted to ("poured out upon") the influence and control ("throne") of animalmind ("wild beast"). Only mental peril and destruction ever came from its dominance. Its entire Mind-dominion ("kingdom")is cloaked with deep ignorance ("darkness"). This increases its already gigantic stupidity, and agony. Its thought-members express themselves ("tongues") in painful, distorted ways ("chewed").

Verse 11. "And they blasphemed the God of heaven, out of their pain, and out of their ulcers. And they did not repent from their works."

COMM: Beginning the Journey inward, mind is terrifyingly confused. But its expressions against Love ("blasphemies"), as hideous as they are, do not arise from evil. Pain gives birth to them. This is why they can later be more easily forgiven.

The human mind ("men"; intellect) is tortured mercilessly by three sources: 1) the "sun" of enlightenment; 2) the insecure wildbeastmind, whose "kingdom" feels threatened; and 3) the "ulcers" given by an earlier "plague."

So, both positive and negative sources create agony. Where is the mind to turn? Much confusion and torment disturb the mind.

Verse 12. "And the sixth poured out his bowl upon the great river, the Euphrates. And its water was dried up so that the way of the kings might be prepared. [These are] from the rising of the sun."

COMM: Productive Mindareas ("Euphrates") dry up! The darknight swoops in! It seems as if there is not a molecule of goodness within the Mind, or cosmos! During this strange, lost period, you might suspect even that goodness, joy, peace, and Love are spectacular fantasies! They are diaphanous, and seem like filmy tissues of illusion. The mocking satanmind (fearmind) tells you that you are right: You are all alone. The highest realities in the cosmos, it whispers, are only figments and hallucinations of a desperate mind.

The Flow of Mind is stopped in its tracks. Absolute Mind seems to have evaporated. The conscious mind loses Its trail. This is the dry period, the "desert" or "wilderness" through which everyone must pass on the Way. It is the return of nightmarish, notorious darknight. Egomind feels dull and dead, completely unproductive. Originality and inspiration vanish. Mental torpor or stupor sets in. Interests are lost. You might come even to feel that nothing matters. A gigantic crisis looms! But this all occurs simply to shake loose from the grasping, clinging, craving, controlling ego. To enter surrendermind, you must usually hit bottom. You must learn that, no matter how desperately that you might wish otherwise, the conscious mind does not control the world. Those shallow, shabby quasimetaphysical systems that tell you that the conscious mind is God fall apart at the seams. Egocontrol dissolves. In panic, you try to increase control, often by last-resorts to affirmation, or praying like mad! But it's no good; ego has fully realized that it controls *nothing of solid value,* and it's too late to go back. You will never be lulled to spiritual sleep again by ignorant pseudometaphysics that thrives on fear. Finally, you do give in, but it is only after having given up.

This stark honesty equips ("prepare[s]") you for the next jump in spirituality. This is the dawn of enlightenment. Controlling thoughts ("kings") support your just-discovered enlightenment ("rising of the sun").

Verse 13. "And I saw, out of the mouth of the dragon, and out of the mouth of the wild beast, and out of the mouth of the false prophet, three unclean spirits, as frogs."

COMM: Cooperation with Lovemind ("three") is hidden even in the depths of the monstrous dark trinity! These horrible, satanic Mind-sectors express ("mouth") disgusting ideas ("frogs"). Ancient Egyptians worshipped the frog as fertility. So, a double curse damned them when the Hebrew god Jehovah "plagued" them with frogs, according to the legend. Hebrew writers hated Egypt and frogs, and had no special fondness for these helpless little creatures, these cute amphibians. Unfairly, they still bring to some minds subconscious affiliations of repulsion. They brought similar repellant responses from original Revelation-readers. For some of them, "frog" meant "plague"! So, "frog"= "plague"=mental dysfunction.

Expressions of dragonmind, wildbeastmind, and falseprophetmind are psychospiritual dysfunctions. They are hurtful, dangerous, and ignorant.

But these have a pseudospiritual content ("spirits"). They express religion. This evil trinity represents the mindset of fundies and other fanatics. They are wellversed in Scripture. But they have not a particle of true spirituality in them. For they are devoid of Love, empty of kindness. We must all remember the lesson of nine-one-one:

****

Religion without spirituality is a dangerous monstrosity!
****

Verse 14. "For they are spirits of demons, doing signs [which are] going out upon the kings of the whole inhabited earth, to lead them together into the war of the great day of almighty God."

COMM: In classical Greek, any spirit, including a beneficent one, could be a *daimonos* or "demon" (similar to the Roman "genius.") But in Christianity, "demons" were horrific, malefic, malignant servants of fear. They terrorized the psyche. "Demons" are violence, stupidity, arrogance, dishonesty, harmfulness, pride, greed, negative lust, etc. They tear mercilessly through the mind like a chain-saw, leaving only blood and ruin in their wake.

Pretensions by the subconscious mind ("signs") are parts of demons. They pretend to be ambassadors of religion. They disguise themselves as carriers of compassion. In some cases, they might even convey the message that they have miraculous powers with which to endow the Mind. For example, metaphysical systems that promise magical powers serve the demons of greed.

A wide spectrum of metaphysical systems promise total control of the whole world. This is demonic, yet compellingly attractive. Its illusionpower is supposed to occur through the "proper use" of the mind. This is nothing but recycled, childish "magical thinking." Psychologists tell us that it is appropriate that this kind of undeveloped thinking to be outgrown by age five. And in most people, it is.

But some otherwise intelligent and educated people revert, in desperation, to childish wishful thinking. They want to "wish upon a star." They give in to fantasy. And what could be more fun than that? What could be more alluring, more seductive, more tempting? They then believe that magic will "make their dreams come true." It is a fascinating fantasy, and can actually hypnotize the more primitive parts of the psyche.

There is, within everyone, an "inner child." This part of the psyche is regressive and arrested. It wants what it wants when it wants it. And what it wants is "right" because it wants it! And it wants everything right now! But it is all nothing. Metaphysical systems that rely on fantasy are fakes and frauds.

Demons play these metaphysical games to mislead the ruling matrix-thoughts ("kings") of hypersensual mind ("earth"). Why? Because they realize that with hypersensual mind as an ally, conquering the whole Mind would be fairly easy. (Mind tends, when unguarded, almost automatically to follow hypersensuality.)

Their sinister goal: to lead almost all the most influential thoughts into a war with Lovemind.

Verse 15. "'Look! I am coming as [a] thief. Happy [is] the [one] staying awake, and keeping his outer garments, so that he does not walk about naked, and they look at his shame.'"

COMM: Abruptly, the story changes voice. This is that of Christnature. (Maybe this is a change of author.)

Christnature is subtle ("thief"). Far from being public, and surely not to be publicly displayed, It comes to the deep Unconscious. It does not prance around in front of tv cameras, and those who bear it best do not either. They reject special titles and extreme attention. They repel actively any efforts to worship or elevate them. For this is not only damnably ignorant idolatry, but hopeless egotism! The Christspirit (Buddhamind or Brahmanmind) arrives in a period of very still quiet.

The Mind is directed towards mindfulness or watchfulness ("awake"). For this Christmind is almost indetectable. When first encountered, It seems weak, invisible. At the beginning of the inward Journey, conscious linear thought seems quite overwhelming. Then, surrender is discovered. The mind yearns to die into higher Mind.

It turns thought, words, and actions over to Lovemind. Still later, this yielding becomes easier and more natural. Like a cup of water poured into a river, the little mind flows effortlessly into the great Stream of the Unconscious. Like a dewdrop slipping into the shining sea, the conscious mind gains luminous life when it merges with the oceanic Mind.

Selfimage ("outer garments") can remain intact (be "kept"). During the crises and convolutions of spiritual development, the rollercoasters of growth, you can remain firmly rooted in awareness that you are Mind. Or else, you can slip into the delusion that you are just your name, your ego, and be corrupted by illusions. These convince Mind of Its own impurity. Selfimage is dangerously vulnerable ("naked"). The advice is, remain aware ("stay awake") of Who You are.

Fearforms of personal insecurity ("shame") will be generated by satan and demons (fearmind). It is not nearly the same as reasonable modesty. Embarrassment, hiding, overselfconsciousness, guilt, and negative selfimage can enslave mind ("shame"). These mercilessly can grip the egomind and its partner, the conscious mind. But these phobic responses have no hold on the greater unconscious Soulmind, or on the Spiritmind.

Verse 16. "And it led them together to the place called in Hebrew 'Har-Magedon.'"

COMM: Here is the *sole and single reference* to that horrific, hideous, ghastly, nightmarish "Armageddon." It seems somehow anti-climactic to discover it tucked away in the middle of a rather ordinary narrative. The way that fundies elaborate, highlight, and scream about it, you would think that Revelation mentioned it a thousand times, and that Jesus himself talked about it all day long. The truth is, *Jesus never used the word.*

And in the whole of Apocalypse, this word is found *only one time.* Technically, the word "Armageddon" is not found a single time in all of Apocalypse. Instead this is a Latinized transliteration of the Hebrew phrase 'Har-Magedon' which means nothing more diabolical than a valley in Palestine. More startlingly, it is *not even* linked with the scare-phrase, "end of the world." That is just evil, dark fantasy dreamed up by grim commentators. This word has freaked out, and even driven mad, students. Still, it is astonishingly benign.

"Apocalypse" is *not* synonymous with "Armageddon." Fearmongers who love to discuss these matters, in hushed and frightened tones, often make this ignorant error. Instead, "apocalypse," as noted, means simply "revelation," and "Armageddon" is a certain phase of conflict that happens to be mentioned in *this* apocalypse. So, contrary to ignorant but popular usage, "Apocalypse" does *not* mean the end of civilization. Neither, for that matter, does "Armageddon"!

In its correct usage, "cap A" "Apocalypse" is a book. It is the final document of the Christian Bible.

It is filled with conflict, disagreement, stresses, and even wars War is no big deal when discussing mind, which is more often at war with itself than at peace. In fact, Armageddon has a very secondary status. In the context of the mind's unfoldment, it is not a central concern. It is only one in a series of inner conflicts. And it *is not even the final conflict* mentioned in this as interpretators always assume. But with its application, for example, in popular entertainment and fiction, to "end of the world" scenarios, its illegitimate usage in popular fiction is guaranteed.

But its relative unimportance is indicated by the fact that it is called, not the "*war* of Armageddon," but simply the "*battle* of Armageddon." For this situation is *only a part* of a larger and cosmic "war" of good versus evil, reality versus illusion, Love versus fear.

Who were the "them" led to Armageddon? Before the narrative was interrupted (perhaps by another writer), the "them" was defined in verse 14 as the controlling matrix-thoughts ("kings") of hypersensual mind ("earth").

But what was the "it" that led them together to Har-Magedon? It is the "dark trinity" of false prophet, dragon, and wild beast.

And what is the "place" called "Har-Magedon"? It is from this verse that we derive the nonbiblical and Latinized "Armageddon." This terrifying word, for most biases, represents the end of the material world and/or civilization as we know it.

That, however, betrays only ignorance. In fact, it is a "mother" of ignorance, called "literalization." It is a popular, but most naive, way of looking at the book of Revelation. "Har-Magedon" means, "Valley of Megiddo" (pronounced "Meg-gid-doe"). This was a very notorious battle-field where many were killed by the Hebrews, and where they, in their violence, lost many. It is a symbol, then, of a major conflict between Love and the antiagapic forces of the Mind. But, contrary to popular opinion, it is not the "last battle" described in Revelation. There are more still to come!

"Armageddon" is a crucial crisis-point. It is a nexus in Mind. It is a significant turning-point. It is a polarization of interior good against inner "evil." During this event, many antiagapic forces are either transformed or dissolved. But Armageddon is no different from the many other conflicts described in the Journey. Centuries of mad, rampant, ignorant superstition have mushroomed the name of a dull and dusty battleground into the nightmarish moment when the whole cosmos, including God and Jesus, plunges into utter chaos, madness, and ruin! It is nothing of the sort!

Verse 17. "And the seventh poured out his bowl upon the air. And a great voice came out of the divine habitation, from the throne, saying, 'It has occurred.'"

COMM: A little mindsector ("bowl") of disapproval ("anger") returns here. (Again, it is as if Revelation had several writers, or correctors, down through the centuries.) This feeble force is sent into ("poured") the spiritual Mind ("air"). Something apparently climactically crucial has been completed ("has occurred"). What?

Love-creating (agapogenic) and Love-resisting (antiagapic) Mindareas are still in conflict. In creating Love (agapogenesis), the positive reveals Reality ("truth"). But in antiagapic mind, only illusions are seen.

The Lovemind (agapopsyche) has completely outpowered the antiagapic forces. To the Absolute, it is as if the conflict has already taken place. For the victory of Lovemind is certain ("It has occurred").

Verse 18. "And lightnings, voices, and thunders occurred. And a great shaking occurred, of the kind that has not occurred since men came to be on earth. [It was] so big, so great."

COMM: Huge, unimaginable quantities of mental energy ("lightnings") gush and explode! So do communications ("voices"), and intuitions of a coming storm ("thunders"). All happen in this phase of growth, in preparation for the mind-rocking conflict about to burst forth within the mind!

The "great shaking" is an earthquake. So, the senses ("earthmind") are blasted out of complacency, ripped away from any hope of neutrality. They must become the tools of Love! The hypersensual mind (bionature; "earth") is shaken apart and restructured.

This is the greatest shake up in the history of Mind, since there have been intellect ("men") and dominance by senses ("earth").

Verse 19. "And the great city came [to be] in three parts. And the cities of the nations fell. And Babylon the great was remembered in sight of God, to give to her the cup of his anger."

COMM: Human mental structures ("cities") are shaken to pieces! A giant mental complex ("great city") undergoes harrowing nightmares, its very wholeness ("three") shattered! It is unable to manage to hold itself together!

It "falls" from grace (producing "thirds"). It falls into an illusion called "graceless hell." (Compare 8:7, paragraph 6 of the Commentary; also see 8:8-12; 9:15, 18; 12:4.) Of course, *the mind can never really lose its grace,* a free gift that relies on *God's Love only.* But the mind loses its *awareness of grace.* The human aspect of mind is terrified that it is worthless, hopeless, irredeemable. It is lost, and will never be found, damned and never can be saved. This, of course, is darkest delusion.

"Cities" of the "nations" are organized systems of human ideas, concepts, thoughts, assumptions, feelings, etc.

The "great city" might be Babylon (biosex drive). If it is, then the mind has awakened at last to the humiliation, agony, emptiness, and nightmarish frustration that sex without Love is a cold and harsh, empty shell. This mindsector has lost, for a moment, its grasp on Love-reality. It has temporarily sunk into illusion and delusion, from full grace-realization. It has fallen into sin-consciousness, that condition from which Jesus worked so hard to liberate people.

Human nature is conceptually (although not really) "outside" of divine nature. This is not because it is evil, but because it is rather dully limited to intellect. This cannot reach the glorious, splendid heights of Love.

Other complexes of merely human thoughts ("cities") in large Mindareas ("nations") collapsed ("fell") under spiritual pressure. Before you can get the mind of Light, you must sacrifice all that is darkness. So, to gain the Lovemind, structures of fearmind must collapse. This means that they do not durably support the mind's quest for spiritual growth. In fact, they harshly resist it, filled with the venom of anger and bitterness. Still, the mind is relentlessly driven, by Mind, towards inevitable evolution. It is pressure from this, and its accompanying revelations, that breaks the back of merely human conceptual aggregates ("cities"). They then unravel ("fall").

Into the cosmic Mind comes a renewed awareness of the biosexdrive without Love ("Babylon the great"), and the fact that she still had some karma coming to her. The cosmic Mind is about to confuse the mind ("wine") with Its disapproval ("anger"). When the Unconscious disapproves, the mind, in ignorance, often has not a clue. So, it is thrown into disorientation, at least, until it can learn how it is violating cosmic law. When the mind finally realizes that the deepest Mind disapproves of its thoughts, words, and actions, it is stunned!

Verse 20. "And every island fled, and mountains were not found."

COMM: Hypersensuality begins to shatter, split, and fragment. Those parts of it that exist within the Unconscious "sea" ("islands") leave awareness ("fled"). Those parts of it drawn to elevated philosophies ("mountains") also become inaccessible to mind ("not found").

They are of "earth," so not fully spiritual. Some *appear* to be. Dead, empty religions without Love ("mountains") might have high ideals. But they are thoroughly lower-nature, empty of Spirit. Forms of Christian, Islamic, and Jewish fundamentalism fit this description.

Both "islands" and "mountains" are gone, at this point in the Journey.

Verse 21. "And hail as great as the weight of a talent stepped down out of heaven upon the men. And the men blasphemed God from the plague of this hail, because it is exceedingly great."

COMM: Thoughts from the Unconscious (water) have become cold, dead, and rigid. They have hardened into unreasoning dogma ("hail"). These thoughts, like *all* thoughts, arise from Lovemind ("heaven").

But *they are not intrinsically loving.* Instead, the *response of the stubborn, granitic conscious mind* makes them inflexible and emotionally cold. In this kind of thinking, there is only hell. So, this is the "hell of hail." Stubborn dogma ("hail") crushes intellectual thought ("men"). This is "heavy" [each stone weighing a talent (about a hundred pounds)]. So, holding on to dogma is torment. Dogma creates hellish agonies, closing down reason and compassion, strangling Love. The pain of dogma disrespects and dismisses the truly holy ("blaspheme").

Chapter 17

Verse 1. "And one came from among the seven angels with the seven bowls, and spoke with me, saying, 'Here I will show you the judgment of the great prostitute sitting upon many waters...'"

COMM: The Lovestarved biosexdrive ("Babylon the great"; see 14:8; "prostitute") returns to the spotlight! It is lazy ("sitting") and arises from a plethora or spectrum of unconscious sources ("many waters"). The mind is about to see, prophetically her destiny.

Verse 2. "'...with whom the kings of the earth committed fornication. Those inhabiting the earth were made drunk out of the wine of her fornication."

COMM: Biosex betrays Love ("fornication"). It neglects and dismisses Love. It pretends to be a species of It! The Loveless biosexdrive is insidious with tooth and claw! It is nothing but bioprocess disguising itself as spirituality. Loveless biosex is Love's nightmare counterfeit. But it is so compelling! Why? Because it is natural! It is solidly built into neurochemical and biochemical pathways of nature. So it tends to draw the whole Mind into its hells.

It is a mental process, although it involves your body when it expresses sexually. But "fornication" is *not* literal, and includes *any type of Love-betrayal*, including literal fornication or adultery. This is analogous to "adultery in the heart." For the most crucial sex-organ is not between the legs, but between the ears. But "fornication" involves friendship-betrayal, relationship-abandonment, broken vows and promises, back-stabbing, gossip, and a whole spectrum of betrayal activities.

Even dominating matrix-thoughts ("kings") betrayed Love under the hypnotic, compelling influence of the biosexdrive. The biosexdrive disoriented and confused ("drunk... wine") the hypersensual mind ("earth").

Verse 3. "And he bore me off into [a] desolate [area] in Spirit. And I saw a woman sitting upon a scarlet wild beast full of names of blasphemy. It had seven heads and ten horns."

COMM: This vision occurs in the deepest part of Mind ("in Spirit"). The Unconscious was consciously known. The mind is carried to an abandoned ("desolate") part of Mind. This is the wasteland, the desert, of the subconscious. Through this, the biosexdrive operates. Many other dark and bleak things live here. But attention is immediately fixed on yet another animalmind ("wild beast"), and a feminine aspect of mind ("woman"), who seamlessly seems to be a carry-over or residue from the previous vision.

Dragonmind was introduced in 12:3. It was "fiery-red." This beast is scarlet. So, these animalminds are directly related/connected: Both derive energy from the first chakra or energy-center (basic bioforces and/or survival, or color is red). This beast also has the spiritual ("seven") potential within its intellect ("heads"), exactly as the one from 12:3. These factors irrefutably link it up as almost a twin of dragonmind. Dragonmind is the force behind wildbeastmind and hypocritemind. We will distinguish this fourth major beast, this supporter of Lovestarved biosexdrive, as "scarletmind." So, dragonmind, wildbeastmind, hypocritemind, and scarletmind all serve-- are parts of-- fearmind ("satanmind").

Scarletmind is all the pathological aspects of lower mind that support the Lovestarved biosexdrive ("woman" in this context). It draws upon its unredeemed animal-nature ("horns") to achieve earthly closure ("ten"). This gives a false sense of security that arises from satiating the biosexdrive. This gives no real satisfaction or fulfillment, but grants a *temporary feeling* of restless semicompletion. Serving fearmind, the scarletmind produces a number of false selfimages, selfconcepts, or identities ("names). Each is antiagapic ("blasphemy"). Among these names are: "I am just an animal," "I am just a mechanical structure," "I am created only for sex and reproduction," and "Sex is the most important thing in the world."

Verse 4. "And the woman had thrown about [her] a purple and scarlet [garment], gilded with gold, precious stones, and pearls. She had a golden cup in her hand, full of disgusting things, and uncleanness of her fornication."

COMM: The biosexdrive has a deep spiritual potential. It can be redeemed and used fully to support spiritual growth. Although its "mental energy" is abused to betray Love ("fornication"), its essence is Mind. Mind can be used either purely or impurely, but is not intrinsically impure. The Power of Love is so unfathomable that even the Loveless biosexdrive can be redeemed!

The first clue is the spirituality ("purple") found in her selfconcept ("garment"). But this selfimage also contains the most base and primitive of biopsychoforces ("scarlet"). Red is the lowest, most basic form of energy in Mind. Purple is the highest.

Between red and purple lie five other colors, each of which has an archetypal, symbolic meaning.

Purple is not the only sign that "she" can, and will, be redeemed as a servant of true spirituality. Her selfimage ("garment") implies at least the appearance of earthly enlightenment ("gilded to gold"). She holds a small Mindarea that is truly enlightened ("gold cup"; compare "bowl") reinforcing the earlier "gold" symbolism.

In time, Loveless biosex will lead to sensual burn-out. When it does, the Mind will actively search for Love, the real thing. Tragically, it will waste time looking for It in all the wrong places! But this is how even Loveless biosex serves Love.

Her selfimage ("garment") is also studded with a spectrum of positive, elevated, exalted, altered states of mind ("precious stones"). Final enlightenment, drawing from the subconscious ("pearl") is also part of her jewelry. The pearl is a moonsymbol, representing unconscious activities. Jesus extolled enlightenment as the "pearl of great price."

The small Mindarea ("cup") contains repulsive thoughts ("disgusting things"). But it is itself potentially pristine, even enlightened ("gold"). Its thought- and feeling-contents, however, have been made impure ("unclean") because Love has been betrayed ("fornication").

Verse 5. "And upon her forehead was written, MYSTERY BABYLON THE GREAT, MOTHER OF THE PROSTITUTES AND OF THE DISGUSTING THINGS OF THE EARTH."

COMM: "She" will be redeemed, her Mindforces used for good. For her intellect ("forehead") is marked by deep wisdom -- "mystery". This word, in technical spiritual usage, has always implied the Soul-Spirit Union, the Mindmeld, Mindmerge or Mindfusion between Soul and Lovemind. That is the utter peak of spiritual growth, the world's greatest Mystery. This is the goal of the mystic. This is the factor that will "save" the Mind from the relentless grip of Lovestarved biosex: Illumination to the divine Being within the heartmind

The Lovestarved biosexdrive is identified as the source of all other "disgusting" things. It is the origin ("mother") of Mindfactors that betray Love ("prostitutes"). When you have betrayed Love enough, and have fried in the resulting inner hells of agony and deep frustration, the "prostitutes" of your mind will drive you squarely into the arms of Love!

Verse 6. "And I saw the woman drunk from the blood of the holy, and from the blood of the testifiers of Jesus. And, having seen her, I wondered with great wonderment."

COMM: The Lovestarved biosexdrive is utterly disoriented ("drunk"). "She" is so lost, she hasn't a clue as to what is really going on in the mind. She doesn't even know that Godmind dwells deeply within.

Other parts of Mind are deactivated ("blood"). Vampirically, she drains their life-energies. She wants them all for sex! Specifically, she absorbs the Love that should be reserved for sacred things ("the holy"). She expends it on sex. Those thoughts that follow Love ("testifiers of Jesus") are also dead ("blood"). The relentless biosexdrive has driven them "underground," into the deeper recesses of the Unconscious. (See "Chart of Mind"). Their energies have been illegitimately appropriated to serve the hyperbiosexdrive. The endless lust for sex has driven this part of mind crazy! It is insatiable! When the conscious mind finally realizes what the sexdrive has stolen from it, it is astonished ("wondered").

Verse 7. "And the angel said to me, 'Why do you wonder? I will tell you the mystery of the woman and of the wild beast that carries her, having seven heads and ten horns.'"

COMM: The mind gets bewildered. The spiritual Mind ("angel") snaps it back to reality. This greater Mind promises to explain the "mystery" and "beast."

Verse 8. "'The wild beast which you saw was, but is not. Yet it is about to be stepping up out of the abyss, and into destruction it is going under. When they see how the wild beast was, but is not, and will be present, those inhabiting the earth will wonder. None of their name has been written in the little book of life, from the throwing down of the world.'"

COMM: When the mind is ready for enlightenment, wildbeast-mind is no more ("is not"). But it did exist at one time ("was").

Deeper Mind ("angel") informs mind about another wild beast: scarletmind is getting ready, like a monster long forgotten, to ascend out of the subconscious ("abyss"). The conscious mind (John) can see it for only the briefest moment. For as soon as it rises, it will sink out of sight of the conscious mind ("into destruction"). In this so-called "destruction," however, the Greek of the ancient text says that "it is going under." Although it appears vaporized into nothingness, then, it actually simply "goes under," more deeply into the subconscious. Originally, it began there, and ultimately returns there. These thoughts are hypersensual ("earth"). They are annihilated from memory ("written... little book"). (Compare 13:8) In the Greek text, the "name" is singular. All these thoughts share a common identity. For they exist in the same scarletmind. These thoughts of ignorance have been predestined to destruction. This has been so from the time that the "world" (totality of conscious knowing) was "thrown down," (created from "higher" Mind).

Verse 9. "Here [is] the mind [of] the one having wisdom: The seven heads are seven mountains, where the woman is sitting upon them."

COMM: Spiritual ("seven") intellect ("heads") is misused to elevate biosexdrive. It is antiagapic, Loveless. Hypersensual mind creates elevated spiritual ("seven") philosophies ("mountains"). These are abused to justify hypersexual activities, ranging from carelessly switching partners through random sex with strangers to full orgies. All kinds of "logical reasons" are drummed up by the hypersensual mind to support indulgence in the hypersexdrive. Some of these appear to be very lofty and elevated philosophies ("mountains"). It is argued, for example, that, because we are "animals," it would be "unnatural" and harmful to regulate biosexdrive. It's only natural! It is destined by nature that we indulge in hypersex. It is what we really want to do, because we are animals. To deny this, go the smooth lies, is to deny obvious reality. It is, even worse, the same lies argue, to pretend to be something that you are not, creating a form of arrogance disguised as "spirituality."

Intellect ("heads") is equated with these noble-sounding philosophies ("mountains") because their *only* origin is intellect. The heart refuses to play along, and is, in fact, actually hurt by these headgames. The heart is designed to love. The emotional nature is never quite fooled. But the intellect is so thoroughly misled that intellect equals *ideas* ("heads"= "mountains").

Still, deeper Mind knows better: The redirection of sexual energy is a part of true destiny. For instead of wasting gigapsychons of energy on bio-expression, that blazing, vivid Mindforce is transmuted to psychospiritual energy. Then, it is used to support Love and enlightenment.

The intellect does indeed create some very spiritual-sounding arguments to justify sexual carelessness or promiscuity, defending an unregulated biosexdrive. But these, as convincing and attractive as they might be to the biomind, are always harmful and antiagapic. Previously, the hyperbiosex drive ("woman") was purely subconscious ("sat on many waters"). It is only as the conscious mind becomes aware of loveless sex that it must now be defended by high-sounding lies ("mountains").

Verse 10. "And there are seven kings. Five fell. One is. The other has not yet come. When he does come, he will remain a short time."

COMM: This verse seems to come out of the blue. (Perhaps it was inserted by another, or later, writer.) Dominant, controlling matrix-thoughts ("kings") have screwed up before. In fact, they lined up against Lovemind, in betraying Love ("committing fornication") with Babylon. That these powerful thoughts are antiagapic shows just how degraded the mind has become. And mind did not get this corrupt, dark, and murky overnight. Only after many centuries of apparent "separation" from Lovemind did it degenerate!

"Five" represents not a number, but a certain *type* of ruling matrix-thought ("king"). "Five" is "human," or sensual. It represents domination by the intellect or senses. "Seven" implies a "king" dominated by spirituality. Six is transitional. So, the dominant tyranny of the intellect/senses ("five") is over ("fell"). The mind is in transition ("sixth" king), at this stage. It is headed for spiritual enlightenment ("seven").

But why would this seventh "remain a short time"? Is not spirituality forever? Yes, but the *human* person does not remain long after enlightenment. Even if a human person were enlightened at age three -- very unlikely, that state would last *in the human framework* for only a few decades. True, enlightenment comes to mind, not to body, and that does indeed last forever. But not so the human framework. And Revelation was written from the viewpoint of human nature.

Verse 11. "And the wild beast which was, and is not, is an eighth. He is out of the seven. And into destruction he is going under."

COMM: How vicious, ferocious, and hideous the nightmarish, ghastly wildbeastmind is! It is everything that is the worst within all mind. It is negative and destructive, and enormously powerful. But lest we lose heart for the battle, here is a reminder that even wildbeastmind originates with the one Mind. For it comes from spiritual Mind ("out of the seven").

The former, previous wildbeasts were, and are, secretly working for Lovemind. They have a task to do in the world. They have Lovemind's secret "permission" to do their hideous worst-- or best. Their mission is to demonstrate to the mind how nightmarish life can be, must be, without Lovemind! So, in creating pain, agony, and doubt, the lower nature serves the higher. A person who keeps you from food when you are hungry is the best guarantee that you will eat a hearty meal when food is available! So the "beasts" serve Love by object-lessons that amplify how horrendous is life without Love! They thus create and greatly enhance an "inner appetite" for true spiritual "food."

The One is the only one. Lovemind is the only Mind that exists, has ever existed. All comes from God and finds final destiny by re-enfoldment within God. (This is "monism.") So, all the horrors of wildbeastmind will also, in time, be resolved into Love. All evil will perish utterly into Love. Here, the number eight represents the doubly grounded and stable, reliable Mind. This kind of extreme stability is a mark of deep sanity, not of the apparent insanity of the wildbeastmind. This proves that, if you go deeply enough into the Mystery of Mind, you strike sanity. Scratch a beast, and find God! So, even wildbeast-mind is sane, rooted firmly, at base, in eternal Love! This is another indication of the Union of all minds in the only One.

Verse 12. "And the ten horns which you saw are ten kings, who [have] not yet received [a] kingdom. But they are receiving authority as kings for one hour, with the wild beast."

COMM: Earthly closure or enlightenment ("ten") is the aim of mind. Ruling thoughts ("kings") are animal in nature ("horns"). That is why they serve wildbeastmind: These are greed, obscenities, harmful lust, territoriality, dishonesty, selfishness, power-hunger, egocentricity, and a plethora of other Pandora's box "demons." Lovemind uses them to achieve earthly closure. What is "earthly closure"? It is the full accomplishment of one's earthly task, mission, or assignment. It can be seen as a form of earthly illumination, leading to enlightenment. When earthly closure is reached, a being is ready to enter the next cosmos as a spirit-being. She is ready for the afterlife. It is time for her to "die". But death is part of the illusion.

These controlling skanky, smarmy pornographic thoughts ("kings") have not yet had other thoughts coalesce around them ("have not yet received a kingdom"). They meander, loose and aimless, for a time. Then, they are gulped up by wildbeastmind. Although potentially powerful, they are dissolved in the overiding passions of blind, often cruel, animality. They have been viciously, tyrannically dominated by greed, territoriality, and biosexdrives. Since the reign of wildbeast-mind is short, they share control ("rule with him") a very short time ("one hour"). These sick thoughts are only vicious subrulers in wild-beastmind's kingdom of evil. Beastmind distorts all impulses to its degraded service!

Verse 13. "These are having one opinion. And they give their power and authority to the wild beast."

COMM: An uncertain idea ("opinion") is shaky and unreliable. It is even further enfeebled by doubt. This is a disaster! In a crisis-phase, *most thoughts agonize over* this chronic uncertainty. This uncertainty can reach the profoundest depths: Does anything have meaning? Does God exist? Is life even worth living? They are made still more tenuous; many matrix-thoughts ("kings") are pressed into the unwilling service of wildbeastmind. These dominant thoughts even give their mental energy for control ("power") to wildbeastmind. They all serve "evil". But the resulting "unity" of Mind is a sham and a fake. For it lacks certainty.

Personality vaporizes in dissolution, and is reconstructed, under demonic influence. This precipitates a severe crisis! The consensus of mind ("one opinion") of all ruling thoughts ("kings") is to flee from Love. The tragic choice is to submit, humiliated and degraded, to the horrible strength of the inner beast.

Verse 14. "These will war with the lamb. The lamb will conquer them, because he is Lord of lords and King of kings. And those with him are called, chosen, and faithful."

COMM: The growing, confused negative mind conflicts hellishly with surrendermind ("lamb"). A major explosion occurs in Mind. But no power in the whole universe is greater than full surrender. For this creates stillmind, thoughtfree. This state allows the Infinite, the Immeasurable, Illimitable to shine through unblocked. Its brightness is unimpeded, unclouded. It is permitted full manifestation through crystalmind. Thus is the least greatest. For the lambmind knows the secret: To tap into, to become, limitless Power is to disappear into it.

This beautifully harmonizes with Jesus' famous, "He who would be greatest must be least." This is extended and expanded to its logical conclusion: To become everything, you must first become nothing. Surrendermind becomes the most potent of all Powers ("King of kings"). When the mystic gives up all personal will, she becomes endless. The Power running through her is irresistible! The Power that shines through her is Love. It is indefeatable.

Those who follow surrendermind into the Mind of Love (Coremind, Godmind) are: 1) given a mission by the Unconscious ("called"); 2) carefully selected for their mission ("chosen"); and 3) believe that Lovemind is more real than they are ("faithful").

This means that they: 1) hear the inner voice of the Absolute calling them to Love;

2) they are unconsciously chosen by It, because they have chosen It, and 3) they remain loyal to It as Love. In transparency, they have also opened themselves to the inflooding of Light and Power.

Verse 15. "And he says to me, 'The waters which you saw, where the prostitute is sitting, are peoples, crowds, nations, and tongues.'"

COMM: The biosexdrive ("woman") was lazy ("sat"), supported by high-sounding rationalizations ("mountains"). (See verse 9.) Now, she is held up, once again, by the subconscious ("waters"). (Those mental illnesses used to justify hypersex crawl up out of the murky, filthy, stinking subconscious.)

Mindsectors come in various sizes, and all fall in line in support of biosexdrive. The smallest thought-clusters are "crowds," simply groups of related thoughts. Next in size are thought-aggregates called "peoples." These are groups of crowds, linked together by shared and common themes. But each group is identifiable. Next in increasing size are the great thought-collections called "nations," which contains several "peoples." But the very largest of all thought-constellations are "tongues," which could include several nations with a common tongue. These all communicate well with each other despite their diversity.

Verse 16. "And the ten horns which you saw, and the wild beast, will hate the prostitute, and they will make her desolated, and naked. And they will eat her flesh. And they will burn her down in fire."

COMM: Once a person is dead, you can't kill her! And if you have already killed her one way, you can't kill her again! The redundant paradox of overkill can happen only in allegory: Even the pornographic animalmind ("horns,") gets sick of biosex-dominance! Other sick mindelements (wildbeastmind) are crazy with their own nuttiness and cruelty! But they too get sick of biosexdrive without Love. She has worn out her welcome!

These animal subminds are needed for earthly illumination ("ten horns"). But they are every bit as vicious and evil as she! When they turn on her, it is not a pretty sight! This sexual burnout has required centuries to flower into this bloody rebellion.

They cause biosexdrive to feel isolated, abandoned, and empty ("desolate"). Her mind is a horror of vacuum, her life a hollow shell of emptiness. She has splurged, wasted, and scattered the forces of Love, and now is left with nothing but a pain in the pit of her stomach. After torturing her, they expose her secrets! They degrade her into shame ("naked")! Then, they tear at, and viciously gulp down, her thoughtenergy ("eat")! Animalmind ("flesh") has proved vicious and terrifying, by absorbing sex without Love. It has left the mind in hopeless and restless depression.

Animalmind seethes with hot anger, and burns the energies of Babylon in purifying suffering ("fire")! But this gaping pit of void promises purification. By the time that they are finished with their atrocities, no cohesive Loveless biosexdrive remains! (Only its incoherent energy remains in the subconscious.)

All energy formerly was expended on Lovestarved biosex. Now, it is turned towards Lovefilled, positive Lovexpression! Some of this is sexual. Now all sex is synonymous with genuine Love!

Verse 17. "For God gave it into their hearts to agree with his opinion, and to share one opinion. They gave their kingdom to the wild beast, until the words of God are finished."

COMM: Lovemind's self-willed limitation ("opinion") is the nucleus of the drama! In the "play" of the pretend-world, the illusionmind, God has left behind omniscience. Most translations render the Greek word here as "purpose," which is much more focused and, well, purposeful.

In the plan of Lovemind, It must be limited. For It is playing all the 'roles' ("monism"). Godmind always knows the truth, the whole truth, and nothing but, about everything. ("Truth" is Reality, Lovemind Itself.) So, this is a part of Godmind that is selflimiting.

God has a trillion trillion trillion faces, masks, disguises, and roles. In these, he/she abandons omniscience for the "play" of ignorance. Godmind puts it in the heart of ruling thoughts ("kings") to synergize with his will ("do his opinion"). Direct, immediate Mindtransfusion blows the mind! So, God formulates "opinion" through egomind. And of course, it turns out to be exactly right on target!

This shines as guidance. The ruling thoughts ("kings") now believe ("opinion") that following Love is the right path.

All directed by Lovemind, they suddenly do the shockingly unexpected: They turn their power over ("give their kingdom") to wildbeastmind! (Notice: Many "kings" share one "kingdom," implying shared mind.)

So, it is the will of the Illimitable that these mindsectors yield to wildbeastmind. But this state does not stretch out into years. It remains only until the expressions ("words") of Love are manifested ("finished"). The wildbeastmind will rule the whole Mind until God is finished communicating. Communication ceases with Communion!

Verse 18. "And the woman whom you saw is the great city that has a kingdom upon the kings of the earth."

COMM: Biosexdrive ("woman") is a complex arrangement of human-engineered ideas ("city"; Babylon). It is supported by a complicated intellectual and emotional structure.

The Lovestarved biosexdrive rules over a vast system of interconnected and interactive mind ("kingdom"). It is so immense that it includes many smaller mindkingdoms ("kingdom upon the kings"). The biosexdrive is so gigantic that its power is overwhelming. It sweeps aside, during certain phases of development, all other considerations. It creates frenzies that blow away all reason, even all Love! It becomes a false and dark master, a rigid and unyielding tyrant. It even threatens to destroy all that is good.

Chapter 18

Verse 1. "After these, I saw another angel stepping down out of heaven, having great authority. And the earth was lighted up out of his glory."

COMM: A breakthrough: Higher Mind ("angel... heaven") infuses Lovelight ("lighted up") into hypersensual mind ("earth")! Hypersensual mind at last has the Power to shatter the unremitting shackles of the merciless biosexdrive! For *the first time in its history,* it is free! It is illuminated!

Before, hypersensual mind had been strongly antiagapic! It had conjoined and conspired with wildbeastmind, hypocritemind, scarletmind and Babylon! This is the beginning of a real turnaround, a rebirth! Things are really looking up for the psyche!

Verse 2. "And he cried out in a strong voice, saying, 'She fell! Babylon the great fell. And she became the dwelling-place of demons, and the prison of every unclean spirit. [She became] the prison of every unclean and hated bird...'"

COMM: When Love-starved biosexdrive collapses, ignorance and weakness ("demons") must be faced! These include feelings of insignificance, inadequacy, insecurities, and a spectrum of other selfimage challenges ("every unclean spirit"). Biosex hides many demons. It conceals them, or it appropriates their Mindforces in the mad pursuit of Loveless sex. It so distracts the mind that it does not notice these familiar (comfortable?) demons. The psyche can be even unaware of them!

But, when biosex loses its tyranny, suddenly you see a lucid, more vivid Mindview! Demons such as hurtful anger, violence, ignorance, bigotry, laziness, and greed then are revealed. As long as all timenergy was being consumed by biosex, you simply did not have the clarity for lucid selfanalysis. Only when her shackles are shattered can you even see yourself with detachment.

The biosexdrive used to eclipse everything else. Lost in hyperactivity, you knew nothing of value about the self. Now, with its demise, you can see that this part of Mind was a restrictive and suffocating state ("prison") which promised ecstasy but delivered nothing. In this prison of the subconscious haunted and wandered unacknowledged mental pathologies ("unclean spirits"). Also, this mindarea was a restrictive bondage for thoughts that have spiritual potential ("birds").

But these had been diverted to the service of the biosexdrive. Because these thoughts became obsessed with sex, they ripped off the Love destined for Lovemind, turning Its energy into mindless and hurtful lust. This made those thoughts impure ("unclean"), and resented by the mind ("hated").

Verse 3. "'...because out of the wine of the anger of her fornication, all the nations have fallen. And the kings of the earth committed fornication with her, and [so did] the traveling merchants of the earth. Out of the power of her unreigned luxury, they became rich."

COMM: Confusion ("wine") grips the biosexdrive! You begin to doubt that sex can really fulfill all the needs of Love. Previously, it had stood in the place of God (Love). For all the years, perhaps centuries, of this phase, it has been the god of life on earth.

For you lost your spiritual identity in hypersensual mind.

Abruptly, you are shaken awake by unconscious disapproval ("anger"), traceable to the active betrayal of Love ("fornication"). Biosex seems to serve Love. It is often mistaken for Love, especially in a backwards culture such as our Western civilization: To have sex is to "make Love," although the latter *should ideally* be so much more than a primitive biological act! To discover suddenly that sex can be a betrayal of Love ("fornication") is a real shocker! It is stunning! Under the resulting enormous pressure, all the great segments of Mind ("nations") collapsed ("fell"). The mind snaps, and loses it!

For the biosexdrive had controlled all mental energies ("power") for so very long! Its departure, or redefinition, has created an immense void! Controlling matrix-thoughts ("kings") are thrown into terrible, confused frenzy. Thought-distribution mechanisms ("traveling merchants") are also blown away. Both joined the biosexdrive in betraying Love. They were made more complex ("rich") by uncontrolled ("unreigned") sensuality ("luxury") or the immense force of unhealthy, unregulated lust.

Verse 4. "And I heard another voice out of heaven, saying, 'Come out, My people, out of her, so that you do not share together in her sins, and so that you do not receive from her plagues...'"

COMM: Mind sorts and removes positive thoughts ("My people") from the biosexdrive. This communication ("voice") is from deepest Mind ("heaven"). The biosexdrive has led the Mind into disastrous crises and horrible mistakes ("sins"). This is why the Mind torments this part of Itself, producing dysfunctions ("plagues") that lead to purification. The deep conscience gives no rest to the ignorant! NOTE: The call of Lovemind is not to "get out" of Babylon, but to "come out," implying invitation to join Lovemind.

Verse 5. "'...for her sins were stuck together [all the way up to] heaven. And God called to Mind her unjust actions.'"

COMM: The errors ("sins") of the biosexdrive are sequentially linked. (The Mind recalls them in a certain order.) It recalls one weakness and failure leading to the next. Each is linked with the previous one ("stuck together"). This forms an inseparable chain of events.

This leads all the way to Lovemind ("heaven"). This is another clue. It is an indirect hint that even serious errors, in time, lead to full enlightenment.

As noted, this is because mistakes are not deliberately evil. They are honest errors or weaknesses. This is crucial: *Error is not voluntary rebellion against the good.* It is imperfection, the making of mistakes. *There is a galaxy of difference between error and deliberate evil.*

But can it be held consistently that *most human "sin" is error?* According to the Christian Scriptures, it can-- but only with great caution. For the very word for "sin" used in the ancient Greek text of the Scriptures refers to error! This might well be why it was so easy for Jesus to forgive "sinners." He seemed especially gentle and forgiving towards those "sins of the flesh," which the Church saw as more horrific than murder! The reason? Sex is obviously a distortion of Love -- perhaps a very serious one -- but it is not usually a result of direct evil intent. It is also easy for modern, honest, sincere Christians to admit that we are all sinners. Because *if sin is weakness rather than deliberate evil,* it is much easier to forgive. Is this the great "secret" that God knows about sin? It is indeed!

All "sins" are fully covered by forgiveness, or "grace."

Still, any evil that is intentional will bring hell within the mind. Hypersexuality, for example, puts the psyche in serious and terrible imbalance, and real jeopardy! It creates difficult karma ("unjust actions"). Through the "Observer," Lovemind takes note of karmogenic (karma-creating) actions. Perfect justice states that those who voluntarily, *with intention,* create suffering for others must encounter that *very same* suffering. The worldview of polybiography makes this feasible and reasonable.

Verse 6. "'Give back to her also as she gave back, and double those in which her actions were doubled. In the cup which she mingled, mingle back to her double.'"

COMM: Lovemind calls for perfect justice. This does exist, but not on earth. Justice gets you through karma; it helps you to see things and events in a cosmic view. No good deed ever goes unrewarded, and no one gets away with any bad voluntary (intentional) act. Whatever Mind does will return to it in the exact same measure that It measured out to others. (The only exception is when real selforgiveness occurs.)

But if this is equal and just karma, how can "Babylon" receive back "double" what she gave? Like everything else in Revelation, this is not literal. "Double" is the double-vision of duality. The source of all "sin," (ignorance) is error. And the basic error is duality. It is responsible for all antiagapic activities. (Wherever the numeral "2" or "double" is used, it's symbolic.)

Duality is this: The moment that I believe that "you" are separate from "me," I can hurt you with *no effect on myself.* But when we both awaken to the fact that we are minds, not bodies, then we know that *we do not end at our skins.* We actually share Mind at some pretty deep levels of the Unconscious. And the same perfect Illimitable is pretending to be both of us. (This is "monism.")

So, "double" is unenlightenment. The biosexdrive is still trapped in the illusion that the world is absolute reality. It is not. She thus believes that minds "other" than the One truly exist. This includes "her own." That is why what occurs in "her" mind is seen by her as "absolutely real." But, of course, it is not. *Every one* of her errors matters greatly to her. She does not forgive herself. This is the hell of negative egotism. ("I am so important that every one of my sins is the most significant thing in the world.") This makes selforgivenss all but impossible.

Forgetting that she is Love moving towards Love, she creates karma by her illusion-beliefs. The mind binds her because of the ways in which she chooses to use it. It becomes her harsh and heartless jailer.

These words concern only smaller mindareas ("cup").

Verse 7. "'As much as she glorified herself and lived in unreined luxury, so much give back to her. [This is] torment and mourning, for in her heart, she says, "I am sitting [as a] queen. I am no widow, and I shall certainly not see mourning."

COMM: What is her "sin"? Surprisingly it is: 1) she glorified herself, and 2) she lived in the dominance of hypersensuality ("unreined luxury").

These were high-impact "sins." For they were the mothers of all others. They gave her the illusion of being in control. A high-voltage "sin"? You bet! It leads to an entire worldview. That is dualism. It presents self as "separate" from Lovemind.

The proud ego thinks that it rules itself ("queen").

Why is the core-sin selfglorification? It is the central error in all of life: Identifying "self" as ego. All the Enlightenment Tradition, from every century and culture, agrees that this is wrong. Then, that self is adored ("glorified"). It takes the place of God (Love). This selfidentification ("I am this bodymind") leads to all of our sexual and other sins. This is utter, unmitigated darkness. It is the inner fountain of black water, of all lumicidal (Light-killing) horrors. She is locked in duality or dualism. She sees the "self" as permanently separated from Godmind. So, in this verse, we find a clue about the most important basic teaching in all of the whole Enlightenment Tradition: You are not your bodymind (bionature, "psychosoma, or hypersensual mind.") You are not "earthly," in Apocalyptic symbolism, but "heavenly." You must not mistake your ego (role, mask, name) for your true Self. To glorify your self, to adore your self, as independent of God, is a catastrophic error ("sin"). It is mega-idolatry.

The second sin is equally astonishing: It is overindulgence ("unreigned luxury"). Deeper sin is just below the surface. This is giving in to the desires of the lower mind, *even when it hurts someone.* This is just a "list" of greedy, materialistic, and hypersensual wants, thinly disguised as "needs." Before you know it, you become consumed by rapidly proliferating desires. Like an insidious and invisible virus, personal desires can create tortuous mind-body sickness. Even worse, they can make you ill at the deep unconscious Soulevel of mind. (See "Chart of Mind.")

Desire is a wildfire of passions, stirred by greed. These include hypersexuality. This state symbolizes the greedy, antiagapic absence of compassion. It is mindboggling that a "prostitute" should get harmful karma for these sins, instead of, for what seems more obvious -- rampant sexuality. For these errors are not related directly to sexuality. Her larger sin is selfpride. She believes very much in her human nature, as if it were invulnerably trustworthy. She develops faith in it. She gives it Love that is due the sacred, the Lovemind. She falls into the illusion that she is the egoruler of her own life, through her will. This illusory belief must be shot down before enlightenment is possible.

Verse 8. "'Through this, her plagues will come, in one day-- death, mourning, and famine. And in fire, she will be burned down, because the Lord God Who judged her is strong.'"

COMM: Her arrogance forms agonizing internal sufferings. The Observer (conscience) is blessed with a crystalclear sensitivity to right and wrong. It refuses to bend the rules. The mind is invaded, and sickened, by dysfunctions ("plagues"), whose pain will purify. They are three: 1) mourning (chronic and acute depressions); 2) agonizing "death" of egomind, of which she is a daughter, and which she still treasures; and 3) spiritual "famine," (She starves herself. She abandons Lovesupporting thoughtfeelings.).

These catastrophes cripple her in the world of time ("hour"). They suddenly, abruptly attack her ("one hour"). Exposed to purifying suffering ("fire"), the Lovestarved biosexdrive is at last vaporized ("burned down"). Again this demonstrates Revelations achronicity: she was "burned down" before!

Lovemind "judges" the entire cosmos as "good." But because the biosexdrive does not see itself as good, she ceases to exist in the Mind. So, she disappears in the real universe, the psychocosmos. Ultramind is "stronger" (more real) than the world.

Verse 9. "'And the kings of the earth will weep, and they will strike themselves upon her, those who committed fornication with her, and lived in unreined luxury, when they look at the smoke from her firing.'"

COMM: The matrix ruling thoughts ("kings") give in to hopeless depression ("weep"). For they have lost the Lovestarved biosexdrive to give them direction. For sex was their very reason for existing. It led them astray, but at least, it gave them a clear path-- even if it led to nowhere! Sex had been mastering the whole mind for a long time. It was a comfortable and familiar hell-- almost always preferred to an unknown heaven! Sex was Its everything, back when the Soul was young and primitive. In many cultures, the phallus, or penis, actually became an object of "external" worship. (This was true of Roman culture, and among the Hindus, the penis was worshipped as the *lingam*.)

The "kings" of mind furrow their collective brow in consternation, and wring their hands with worry. This part of mind is infested with panic. It wonders what its purpose is. Without biosex, it feels empty and hollow. It has served sex, betraying Love ("fornication") for so very long! Alas, it knows nothing else! Now, forced into a corner, this part of mind will be force by Mind to explore new inner caverns and lagoons, discovering the real thing-- Love!

It wounds ("strikes") itself because it relies on her ("upon her"). It reviews nostalgically the 'good ol' days.' Back then, sex was fun, in the primitive mind, which played carelessly with karmic fire. It acted as if there were no consequences, no karma, no justice. Sex was just "recreational" and "casual." Naively, the mind thought that it would get away with whatever it wanted to do. It was totally wrapped up in itself, and did not really care whom it hurt, or how many times. Playing with the dynamite of sex, it could not have cared less if it destroyed a hundred lives. *All that mattered was its own instant sensual gratification!* All the while, it was *wounding itself.* Life was all about "good" sex, and the more, the better! The ruling thoughts ("kings") selfinjured by creating, in the subconscious, an inner hell of regret and remorse. They denied compassion, and greedy hypersensuality was all that mattered ("lived in unreined luxury").

In all this gloom and doom, a positive note sounds. Earthly thoughts still keep ascending towards Love ("smoke"). Here is the promise of ultimate redemption. The real Love that lives behind the Lovestarved biosexdrive still survives its terrible distortion and abuse-- attempted reduction to mere sex! And it moves towards Lovemind! It is regenerated! At last, it is saved from ignorance!

Verse 10. "'[A] long [distance,] they stood, out of fear of her torment. They said, "Woe, woe, the great city, Babylon, the strong city, because in one hour came your judgment."

COMM: Dominant matrix-thoughts ("kings") run away as fast as possible from the Lovestarved biosexdrive. They don't want anything to do with her; fear outweighs compassion. While sad for her eventual vaporization ("burning"), they are more worried about their own skins. This part of mind wants to live! So, they "distance" themselves from her, in conscious or unconscious dissociation.

They desperately pretend that they were more than the stupid, blind marionettes of sex! They do not want to admit that they were the mindless playthings, the pawns, of sex! This is shameful.

But, to their utter shame, *all that they did was* support the betrayal of Love. A multiplex of human-engineered thoughtstructures ("city") evolved from all this support. It reached its tendrils into every part of mind. And the "city" Babylon, supported by so much of the Mind, was immensely powerful ("great and strong"). It ruthlessly dominated the whole mind, perhaps for centuries! As Loveless biosex, it felt as if it would last forever.

Verse 11. "'And the traveling merchants of the earth wept and mourned upon her, because no one is buying their full stock anymore.'"

COMM: Thought-distribution systems ("traveling merchants") also fall into despair and depression. "What is a thought-distribution system?" This is the sum of all mental mechanisms that direct thoughts or thought-energy to support a given idea. The cessation of the tyranny of biosex has thrown mind into chaos. The mind feels lost, as if it does not know what to do with itself.

There are too many thoughts ("full stock"). But they are no longer being distributed ("bought") evenly throughout the mind. A crazy blend of overload and paralysis strikes the mind during its great guilt. Without logic to guide systems and methods of thought-distribution ("merchants"), thoughts can no longer organize into cohesive ideas. The mind blows apart, and chaos ensues, pushing it to the brink of madness!

Verse 12. "'Full of gold, silver, precious stone, pearls, fine linen, purple, silk, scarlet, scented woods, vessels of ivory, precious woods, copper, iron, and marble...'"

COMM: An itemization of thoughtpatterns ("full stock") begins selfanalysis. The thought-organizing mechanisms ("merchants") work frenetically to arrange them. They include: 1) earthly enlightenment ("gold"); 2) unconscious thoughtmaterials ("silver"); 3) positive, elevated states of Mind ("precious stones"); 4) unconscious thoughts of beauty and enlightenment ("pearls"); 5) selfimage concepts (as of "garment," "fine linen"); 6) spiritual potentials ("purple"); 7) very fine selfimage ("silk");

8) baser thoughts ("scarlet"); 9) bionatural thoughts growing towards Love ("scented woods").

Besides all these, there is an entire family of thoughts which are "vessels." In this family, humanmind serves as a conduit or container for supercognitive factors. These come in the following varieties: 10) precious thoughts originating with animalnature, tending towards purity ("ivory"); 11) bionatural (sensual) thoughts aspiring towards Love ("precious wood"); 12) Love-supportive thoughts, midway between toddlermind and spiritual ("copper"); 13) base thoughts ("iron"); and 14) bionatural (sense-based) thoughts creatively formed ("marble").

Verse 13. "'... and cinnamon, exotic spices, incenses, perfumed oil, frankincense, wine, olive oil, fine flour, wheat, animals, sheep, horses, coaches, bodies, and the Souls of men.'"

COMM: The inventory continues with: 15) bio-thoughts of hypersensuality ("cinnamon"); 16) exotic sensual thoughts ("exotic spices"); 17) thoughts from bionature (hypersensual mind) that aspire towards

Love; prayers ("incenses"); 18) sweet experience of spiritual "anointing" ("perfumed oil"); 19) gifting of the Christmind ("frankincense"); 20) thoughts that lead through confusion, and to Communion ("wine"); 21) peaceful intimations of the inner "Christmind" ("olive oil"); 22) bionatural (hypersensual) microthoughts, in billions, used to discover inner "bread of heaven," the Christspirit ("fine flour"); 23) bionatural (hypersensual) thoughts that support Love as inner nutrition ("wheat"); 24) thoughtfeelings of the lowest animalmind ("animals"); 25) selfsacrifice and/or surrendermind ("sheep"); 26) strong animal nature brought under human control ("horses"); 27) transport Mindmechanisms that move thoughts from one ideational structure to another ("coaches"; related to "merchants"); 28) thoughts originating with the body ("bodies"); 29) thoughtideas originating with the very deep unconscious Soul ("Souls").

Verse 14. "'And your juice-filled fruit, the desire of the Soul, went off from you. And all the fatty and bright [things] destroyed themselves from you, and they will certainly not be found anymore.'"

COMM: Who is addressed, and who speaking? This is Mind addressing mind. The end of all personal desire ("juice-filled fruit") is promised. This is the most wonderful blessing imaginable! For-- and the whole of the Enlightenment Tradition agrees-- personal desire is a path to hell.

Avoiding dangerous, crazy-making extremes, the Way does not recommend the total *end to all desire.* For even the desire to Love, to know God (with gnosis) is a desire. The enlightened do not become mindless, "vegetables," zombies who care about nothing, want nothing.

But the Way does teach the total snuffing out of all *personal* desire. This grasping, clinging, craving, or attachment arises from the lie of duality: It dissembles, and says that you are a separate mind. Being a "separate ego," you have many things that you need. And, in the "zero sum" cosmos, what someone else gets, you cannot have.

This is the root of greed and ten thousand related fears and insecurities. *Dualism leads directly to fear.* And fear leads directly to greed. The teeth of the beast that swallows you are desire. They are the ropes which tie you, the chains that restrict you, the prisons that hold you.

In our society, we are taught the lie that *we can find joy and fulfillment by gathering, accumulating, or acquiring more. You are expected to whip cravings into allconsuming passions!* Yet we know that this is a lie, because, historically, there is *zero correlation* between material wealth and happiness. We also know that this is phony because many people have achieved abundant material success *without ever having found happiness or contentment.*

This is the great secret that all corporations and other economic institutions *never want you to discover:*

****

Material things are boring.

****

For this secret unmasks as chicanery and charlatanism all their claims that enough money will make you happy. *Desire for more can never make you happy.* Why not? The best of reasons: By definition, the state of desire is one of incompletion and lack; and how can a sense of lack lead to a sense of satisfaction, since they are opposites?

But when your mind melds and merges with the great inner Mind, *you have no lack.* As Mind, you have *very little need for any material thing.* Of course, you still need food, clothing, and shelter. But the enlightened seek to fill these needs *with minimal doses.* Their clothes are plain and simple, as are their diets, and their homes. Lao Tzu says, "The sage wears plain and simple clothing; but inside, she carries the great jewel." He also writes, "In dwelling, remain close to the land."[38]

Enlightened people do not live to impress others. Nor do they obsess about sensual pleasures. (The senses are good; domination by them is not.) For example, they eat to live, but never live to eat!

In the inner Journey, personal desire is excess baggage that slows you down. It prevents contentment, *for, by definition, a person in desire cannot be satisfied.*

****

The clear choice is between desire and satisfaction.

****

---

[38] See my *Luminous Jewels* Volume 2, Part IV *op. cit.*

Since satisfaction leads to tranquility, and peace to fuller Love and Light, the wise opt for satisfaction. A wise ancient mystic, Paul, wrote the words of wisdom, "We will be content with what we have." Desire is a harsh and cruel task-master. The mind whips it into a frenzy, and then, *it can never be satisfied.* It is selfrustrating. *Personal desire is spiritual pathology.* Its satisfaction is an illusion. Since the disease is incurable, the best strategy is to avoid catching it!

When mystics renounce personal desire, they find truest satisfaction, contentment, and fulfillment. Since the "material, external" world can *never* bring this bottomless sense of wellness and joy, they are delighted to drop the burden of personal desire. Then, they turn their lives over to the "desires of Love." (This is the famous "Will of God.").

With progress, mind allows personal desires to vanish. Appetites ("fatty foods") disappear. *All needs are satisfied by Love.* The enlightened are happy! Love is the *only important pursuit. Mind is Love, and Love, Mind. Mind is Reality, and Reality, Mind. So, Love is Reality!* The enlightened can afford to drop obsessions with "Love-substitutes." These are pathetic and petty tinkertoys of Reality. They are sad, hopeless rivals to Love. They include: religion, politics, business, money, house, car, clothing, jewelry, career, intellect, etc. All this is just crap, or excess fat. Sensual attractions ("bright things") also lose their dominance. They can be enjoyed, but *no longer control!*

This is *not* "anhedonia," a pathological inability to enjoy anything. In fact, the enlightened enjoy the senses *more than the average person.* Why? Because the senses are a gift of God through nature.

****

Let's emphasize: The senses and sensory world are not bad.

****

Only hypersensuality resists spirituality. For it becomes a false master, replacing Love. Desire captivates and mesmerizes the ego (shallow social self). Egodesire is killed along with ego. But the death of desire must affect more than the conscious mind. Desire exists at deeper levels of the Unconscious, all the way "down" to the Collective level. (See "Chart of Mind.")

This deep wanting ("desire of the Soul") creates and maintains the madly spinning, out-of-control wheel of karma. But when you enter grace knowing (enlightenment), your karma is dissolved. It is neutralized by Love (including selforgiveness).

Verse 15. "'The traveling merchants of these, those who became rich from her, stand [a] long [distance] through the fear of her torment, weeping and mourning...'"

COMM: The organizing, Mindmechanisms ("merchants") try, as did the "kings," to convince themselves that they never had very much to do with the sexdrive. They dissociate from it; they "distance" themselves. The whole Mind abandons the Lovestarved biosexdrive.

To see yourself as an animalmind is shameful. The Mind is starting to realize that It can be so much more. But this is not real transcendence. It is merely denial.

Verse 16. "...saying, "Woe, woe, the great city, having thrown about itself fine linen, and purple and scarlet, gilded in gold and precious stones, and pearls...""

COMM: Ruling thoughts ("kings") had a similar dirge. It also began with, "Woe, woe..." But they did nothing actually to aid the burning whore. So, were they sincere?

The biosexdrive was never a mindarea purely "evil" to the Core. For it, too, was Lovemind distorted ("purple, fine linen, gold, precious stones, pearls"). While it dominated the Mind, it powerfully distorted selfimage ("linen"). The mind saw itself as a sexual device, a slave of sex. But even in the midst of dark sexual thralldom, the mind saw also its nobler potentials ("fine").

Lovexpressions showed through the evil disguise. Spirituality ("purple") is Love-potential. Earthly enlightenment (obtained through senses; "gold") was also deep within the prostitute, a real part of her selfimage ("garment; "linen"). Higher states of Mind ("precious stones") came into conscious awareness from time to time. Even hidden wisdom ("pearls") was a factor in her deeper selfimage.

Verse 17. "...because in one hour was desolated so much wealth. And every steersman, and everyone sailing in that place, and nautical people, and as many as work [with] the sea, stood at [a] long [distance].'"

COMM: "Kings" and "merchants" distanced themselves from bio-sexdrive. Everybody wants to get away from her! And now, thoughts from the Unconscious ("sea-workers") rush to follow. Unconscious guiding thoughts ("steersmen") also abandon the Loveless biosexdrive. Sex, one of the greatest powers, dominating virtually the whole sub-conscious, is losing its grip as master.

For Love is replacing it. These thoughts are a link between the Un-conscious and the conscious areas of mind.. For they are above the wa-ter. Others are simply accommodating, going with the prevailing winds ("sailing") or Spirit.

After centuries, Mind is starting to deny the mastership of hyper-sensuality, hypersexuality, materialism, and other false masters. This happens at even a subconscious level ("sea"). Frustration and anger create rebellion. Biosex promised everything, but delivered nothing. So, it turned the mind into an explosive keg of dynamite!

Verse 18. "'And they cried out, looking at the smoke from her fir-ing, saying, "Who [was] like the great city?"

COMM: Nostalgia haunts the subconscious ("sea" people). The subconscious brings to conscious awareness all the timenergy that had been consumed by the Lovestarved biosexdrive. The mind smiles sadly, regretting, uncertainly, the death of biosex. What is mind to do now?

Should it eradicate all sensuality? Should it consign the whole sexdrive to oblivion? Must the spiritual life be totally asexual? Or could sex, the nightmarish master, make a tolerable or even useful ser-vant?

Mind misses the sensual pleasure of sexuality, deeply. But it is cer-tain that it does not want to go back, to return to the state of hopeless addiction and thralldom. At its freedom, it heaved a gigantic sigh of relief. But, in many areas (including "kings," "merchants," and "sea-workers"), it is feeling pain, bitterness, disappointment, uncertainty, and severe regret.

Verse 19. "'And they threw dust upon their heads, and they cried out, weeping and mourning, saying, "Woe, woe, the great city, in which all those having boats in the sea became rich, out of her pre-ciousness. For in one hour, she was desolated."

COMM: Hypersensuality ("dust") dominates intellect ("heads"). It threatens, through depression ("weeping and mourning") to re-obsess the mind. Mindfactors mourn and miss the nightmarish dominance of the biosexdrive. They are so disoriented that their state is like that of the drifting people of Iraq: Tyranny seems preferable to chaos and the unknown. In total confusion, they mourn with a dirge that begins with the familiar, "Woe, woe..." Distribution-mechanisms ("merchants") were enriched by the biosexdrive. You did not have to ask difficult questions about how to use and order your mind; it automatically went, all of the energy, into sex! The "sea-people" (unconscious thoughts; "sea") also gained power, although sometimes it was very dark. Sexual thoughts, though often misdirected, can bring an enormous sense of naked power! Simple conscious ideas ("boats") floated up from the Unconscious.

The Biosexdrive taught the Mind many lessons which It would learn in no other way. It is a structure of ignorance. It is Loveless, and so, is hell. Still, biosexdrive gives something to Mind that educates ("rich"). *The strongest battles with ignorance create the most powerful wisdom.*

Verse 20. "'Be well-minded upon her, heaven, the holy, the apostles, and the prophets. For God judged your judgment out of her.'"

COMM: Mind is more than simply glad because she has been destroyed ("well-minded"). Most translations infer only a state of happiness from the Greek "well-minded." But the word in the ancient text might also imply a form of joy that is actually actively healing.

It is a command for holymind ("heaven" etc) to regard her, in fullest devastation, with a less critical, more forgiving, eye.

Also, the latter part of this verse is universally regarded in translation as a statement of vengeance. It is as if it were saying, "I will judge her for what she has done to you." But according to the Greek text, God "judged the judgment of you out of her." The *whole mind* is affected by how Lovemind evaluates the sexdrive. The "judgment" of Babylon is related to the judgment of the whole spiritual mind ("holy"etc.). The destiny of the biosexdrive is symmetric with the destiny of the whole Mind. Or, what happens to "her" reverberates throughout, affecting, the whole Mind.

Verse 21. "And one strong angel lifted up [a] stone, like that of a great mill, and he threw [it] into the sea, saying, 'Thus, with a great rush will Babylon the great city [be thrown], and surely will not be found anymore.'"

COMM: Babylon is compared with a rigid, heavy mass of hypersensual mind ("great stone"). To make this symbol consistent with stone-symbolism in other areas of the Greek Christian Scriptures, we must compare it with other texts:

Matthew 21:42 mentions, as Christ, "the stone which the builders rejected." The name given to Simon, in Aramaic, Cephas, or in Greek, Peter-- both mean, "stone." In Acts 4:11, "the Stone rejected... the chief Cornerstone," is also the Christ. (Compare Eph. 2:20.) The "living Stone" of First Peter 2:4 also references the "stone" as symbolic of Spirit.

All of these are positive spiritual references to the "stone." It represents numinous or holy realities. It is hypersensual mind turned into the glowing, flowing Light of Love! This is also the meaning of "precious stones" (positive altered states) throughout Revelation. Is this an indication that even the Loveless biosexdrive can be, must be, redeemed by Love? Since it implies the "mill," it is associated with "bread," another Christsymbol.

It is hurled into the Unconscious ("sea"). Significantly, *it does not die, is not killed.* The Lovestarved biosexdrive becomes free energy in the subconscious, where it can be repaired, restructured, recycled, and healed, emerging later as *any kind* of thoughtenergy. When it re-emerges, it will be all Love (God).

Verse 22. "'And the voice of harpers, musicians, flautists, trumpeters, will surely not be heard in you anymore. And every artificer of every art will surely not be found in you any more. And the voice of the mill will surely not be heard in you anymore.'"

COMM: Only stillness and dead silence pervade the troubled area which used to be so kinetic and frenetic. Where once were the sounds of communication and joy ("voices" and "singers"), there is now stillness. This Loveless sexdrive, after her descent into the Unconscious leaves behind only stillness. This alone can allow Lovemind to act through the person. Has the energy that used to be the lovestarved biosexdrive ("Babylon") at last been touched by the deep, tranquil stillness of spiritual Mind?

Not right away. For the "voice" of resonance/harmony ("harpers") is also gone. It has been severely if temporarily disturbed and shaken by the abrupt destruction of the Lovestarved biosexdrive. *The whole mind is traumatized by this inner death.* So are all communications of joy ("musicians"). Gone is sweetness ("flautists"). Vanished are announcements, of even war ("trumpeters"). Within the area of Mind that used to be devoted to biosexdrive, artistic and deliberate productivity (artificer") is dead. So is the assimilation/processing of inner nutrition or spiritual food, including communication of the inner Christmind ("voice of ... mill").

Verse 23. "'And the light of the lamp will not shine in you anymore, and [a] voice of bridegroom and bride will not be heard in you anymore. For your traveling merchants were the greatest men of the earth. For by your druggery, all the nations were made to err.'"

COMM: Lovelight, processed by mind ("light of a lamp"), has vanished from this Mindarea. A universal motif of sweet mystical Union of Soul with Spirit appears. That's the joining of a bride and bridegroom. This reflects mystical interpretations of the Love and romance of the Hebrew text the "Song of Solomon." In Jewish tradition, Israel was God's "bride," but in Christianity, she was "the Church." Mystics escaped the battles and confusion by claiming that "God's bride" was the individual Soul. Sexual Union, emphasizing intimacy and oneness, is implied. They are "one," for they share a single expression ("voice").

Soul and Spirit are not, never have been, two, but always One. This delicious mystical insight is reflected in even literal marriage. But, this Union of Soul and Spirit, too, tragically disappears for a time. This occurs after the death of the biosexdrive dominance. This blessed Union between mind and perfect Love is not possible through the use by the Soul of only the Lovestarved biosexdrive.

The organizing and distribution-factors of Mind ("traveling merchants") were ideas that kept mind in order. They were the most significant Mindfactors ("greatest men"). But they were not the most elevated. They were simply the most powerful in hypersensual mind ("earth"). The most crucial fact was not thoughts, but how those thoughts were arranged, put together, organized, and distributed. For when thoughts supported *only* the biosexdrive, they acted antiagapically.

The Mind was misled by the traumatic shifts in consciousness ("druggery") of the biosexdrive. Sexual activity does produce a number of pharmacoid (druglike) compounds and hormones. These natural psychotropics can have devastating effects on the brain, and thus, the mind. But since this is symbolic, what is spoken of here is the state of disorientation through which Mind passes on Its Way to enlightenment. Great constellations of thought ("nations") are caused to make erroneous moves ("err"), due to the confusing power ("druggery") of the Lovestarved biosexdrive. The symbolism here is similar to that of "wine," but "druggery" is much more powerful.

Verse 24. "'And in her, the blood of prophets and [the] holy was found, and of all those slaughtered upon the earth.'"

COMM: Babylon greedily gulped up, with unabashed selfishness, all the life-energy of the better parts of Mind ("prophets....holy"). When she vampirically drained them of all their lifenergy, they died ("blood"). (That is, they sank into the deeper Unconscious.) All timenergy was petulantly demanded by a fanatically insistent biosexdrive. She 'starved' all other Mindareas. This usurpation of all lifenergy for the sexdrive is a "slaughter" of all other Mindcomponents. Biosexdrive steals all the forces and contents of hypersensual mind ("earth"). *The hypersensual became the hypersexual.*

After Biosexdrive's death, the enlightened mind can still choose sexual Union as a manifestation of Love. But it is just not a simple biomandate. Instead, sexual sharing becomes *a spiritual option.* Sex need not disappear from the life of Love; but it can no longer *act as a master!*

Chapter 19

Verse 1. "After these, I heard as [if] a great voice, [as if of] a large crowd, in heaven, of people saying, 'Allelujah. Salvation, glory, and power [are] of our God.'"

COMM: The mind hears the Psychopolyplex ("crowd"). It is doing something strangely mysterious. It is eerily similar to communication ("as a voice"). But although it was a single voice-like phenomenon, implying oneness of Mind, it sounded like many ("large crowd"). This is, in a nutshell, a summary of the "many from the One" nature of the cosmos. It is "Unity in multiplicity."

It does something like talking, from Lovemind ("heaven"). It gives a message. It can be simply summed up: The whole Mind realizes that Lovemind is the Source of: 1) the Power to enlighten, and thus, save from ignorance and illusion ("salvation"); 2) all splendor and light-filled, Lovefilled transformation ("glory"); and 3) all energy of Mind, feelings, thoughts, conscious or unconscious ("power"). (Compare "power" as used in 4:11; 5:12; 6:4; 7:12; 11:17; 12:10; 13:2; 15:8; 17:13; and 18:3.) These beautiful qualities belong to, emanate from, Lovemind.

Verse 2. "'True and righteous are his judgments. For he judged the great prostitute who corrupted the earth in her fornication, and he avenged the blood of his slaves, out of her hand.'"

COMM: Lovemind is Reality ("true"). It harmonizes with all laws that agree with goodness ("righteous"). "Vengeance" symbolizes perfect balance created by karmic law, which often seems harsh. Sometimes, if the karma is particularly intense, agonizing, or terrifying, it can surely appear to be cosmic "vengeance." But, of course, there is no "outer" god keeping records. As Paul wrote in his great classic on Love (First Corinthians 13), "Love does not keep records of injuries."

Lovemind tore Lovethoughts ("slaves") from the control and will-dominion ("hand") of the Loveless biosexdrive ("Babylon"). These, formerly pressed into the service of biosex, now return to that of pure Love. It is their only and authentic master.

Verse 3. "And [a] second [time] they said, 'Allelujah.' And the smoke of her is stepping up into the ages of the ages."

COMM: Some thoughts aspire to greatness. They want to move beyond their lower and human nature and ascend ("stepping up") to a "higher" plane, or "higher" consciousness ("smoke"), as if freed from oppressive gravity. They want to be "where" Lovemind is. They move towards the inner space called "heaven." Some of the advancing, growing thoughts ("smoke") already pervade all states of Mind ("ages of the ages").

Verse 4. "And the twenty-four old people fell, and the four living creatures. And they worshipped God sitting on the throne, saying, 'Amen. Allelujah.'"

COMM: All sweet, spiritual, enlightened Mind is in glorious integration with Lovemind ("heaven"). This beautiful and wise Mind is monochromatically in full agreement with the service ("worship") of Lovemind. All parts of Mind join in support. This is mystical integration, a fully healed (whole) condition. The whole Mind joins in joy and tranquility. It all feels secure, fulfilled, satisfied, and content.

Verse 5. "And a voice came out from the throne, saying, 'Praise our God, all his slaves, those fearing him, the small and the great.'"

COMM: The command to worship Love emanates from Control-mind or Lovemind ("Throne"). Love thrives on Love, needs It to survive. Urgently, Lovemind derives Love from all other parts of heavenly Mind, Which is all Lovemind. Monistically, heavenly Mind is ordered to worship Itself: The whole Mind is challenged to awaken to the stunning fact that *It is all Love. There is nothing but Love in the highest Mind* (heavenly Mind).

And "heavenmind" consists of these three subsystems: 1) "throne" (controlcenter), 2) "old people" (more experienced parts of Mind) and 3) the four living creatures (Godthoughts). Lovemind calls all facets of Mind to serve ("slaves") It. These thoughts are filled with reverential awe ("fearing him").

Verse 6. "And I heard [a sound] as the voice of a large crowd, as the voice of many waters, and as a voice of strong thunder, saying, 'Allelujah, because our Lord God reigned, the Almighty.'"

COMM: The whole Mind recognizes that Lovemind rules over It. It is the only One who has ever really existed, the only Ruler. It has ever and always been in charge. All other masterthoughts (kings) are roles being played by the Master Actor. They are the "masks" of the One. They ruled only *in illusion.* They controlled, by Mind's permission, only in the relative dreamworld, the relative spacetime world.

They *never* ruled in the *real* world, the world of Mind. Even biosexdrive no longer rules. This condition of utter freedom is great enlightenment! Mind sees through the illusions of hatred, fear, and their uneducated, unsophisticated relatives. At this moment of lucidity, separation (as "dualism") vanishes. The conscious mind deliciously feels its natural Unity with Lovemind. It had long ago forgotten this, and meandered through the material world, for millennia, in miserable amnesia. Now, those ultrasweet memories, and depths of Mind, are delightfully, healingly blossoming in full and spectacular splendor!

Verse 7. "'May we rejoice and may we exult. We shall give the glory to him, because the marriage of the lamb came, and his woman prepared herself.'"

COMM: Mind invites you to "bliss," with its related states of fun, enjoyment, fulfillment, rapture, and ecstasy ("rejoice" and "exult")! This explodes into its lightfilled, Lovefilled zenith at the moment that the Soul ("woman") finds sweetest Union ("marriage") with surrendermind ("lamb"). *The Soul has never been anything but pure surrendermind. This knowing is joyfilled euphoria!* Next step-- full Union with Lovemind!

Verse 8. "And it was given to her to be covered with fine linen, bright and clean. For the fine linen is the righteousness of the holy."

COMM: Lovemind is the ultimate Source ("given"). This new female, the Soul, is the reincarnation of Babylon, but in a brand-new form. The biosexdrive was sluttish and waspish, but the liberated Soul is joyful, sweet, gentle, tender. Still, she is identified with the biosexdrive through her selfimage (garment of "fine linen" This is *exactly* how Babylon was dressed.) This comes from Lovemind, for all goodness arises from the God of Love. (Remember "monism.") The Soul is aligned perfectly with Spirit ("righteous"). It is "bright," like deep interior Mind, and pure ("clean"), like that perfect Mind. (Compare the bright condition of "original Mind in Buddhism.)

Verse 9. "And he says to me: 'Write: "Happy are those called into the lamb's marriage-supper."' And he says to me, 'These are the true words of God.'"

COMM: The mind (John) commits to memory ("write") a glorious revelation: Some splendid thoughts hear a special "calling." It is their bright destiny to celebrate the Union ("marriage") of Soul and Lovemind. These are profoundly blissful ("happy"). This state of bliss is the only real joy-- an axis-teaching of mysticism. This celebratory attitude also provides inner spiritual nourishment ("supper"). This message is all about truth ("true"; Reality; Lovemind) Itself.

Verse 10. "And I fell in front of his feet to worship him. And he says to me, 'Are you not seeing? I am [just] your, and your brothers', fellow slave. [They are] those who have the testimony of Jesus. Worship God. For the testimony of Jesus is the Spirit of prophecy.'"

COMM: The mind (John) is dazzled. It wants to adore ("worship") deeper Mind. But all deeper Mindlevels, even spiritual ones ("angels") are not intrinsically superior to the mind. Why? Because the mind also contains the same Spirit, Absolute, or ultimate Mind, the Lovemind nuclear to all the cosmos. So, there can be no *real or absolute distinctions* between mind and Mind. Greater Mindareas such as "angels" *are not superior* inherently. They simply express more of Lovemind than the "human" mind usually does. *But both are made equal by the indwelling, in both, of the Immeasurable.* This is why higher Mindelements describe themselves as just equal with ("fellow slaves") the mind. And it doesn't matter how impressive, how mindboggling, these inner unconscious "angels" are! The mind fully rejects any autoadoration (selfworship), and knows that *only Lovemind is worthy of worship.*

Other gifted parts of Mind ("brothers") exist, and "angelmind" is also not superior to them. For they have the ability to discern the changes in Mind before they actually arise ("prophecy"). The mind is ordered to worship *only* God or Love.

Verse 11. "And I saw the heaven opened up, and look! A white horse, and he who sits upon it is called faithful and True. And in righteousness, he is judging and he is warring."

COMM: The Godmirroring Soul, first portrayed in chapter one, re-emerges. It comes out of the deepest Mind ("heaven"). For this is the Source of all Souls. Why? Because the Soulmind is a shallower level of the Unconscious than is the Spirit (Lovemind or "heaven"). And *deeper* Mindlevels *give rise to more shallow ones.* (See "Chart of Mind.") Just as the Soul, and the whole Unconscious, exist within the mind, so the Spirit is within the Soul. Spirit "gives birth" to Soul, and supports It. To switch, and repeat, metaphors, the Soul is playing the role of the ego, and the Spirit is playing the role of Soul.

But, paradoxically, It is also supported by ("sits upon") animalmind. But this lower mind is pure ("white") and regulated by the intellect, or humanmind ("horse").

The Soul responds loyally to Love's will ("Faithful"). This is enormously amplified when it has, as surrendermind, given up Its own competing will. It moves towards its golden goal-- desirelessness!

All Souls are part of Reality. Why? Because *Mind is the only "reality" in the cosmos.* Lovemind is the deepest Unconscious, but Soulmind is also in the same Unconscious. Every "material" and "external" object or person is a dream of this deepest Mind, also called the "Creatormind.*" (See "Chart of Mind.") This One is Reality Itself. *Nothing exists without It, or "outside" of It.*

When the enlightened Soul evaluates ("judges"), It sees all the cosmos according to cosmic law; it sees it all as in perfect alignment with Lovemind ("righteousness"). Indeed, *everything is the exteriorization or projection of Lovemind.* At this highest level of Union, Soul sees the cosmos through the eyes of Lovemind. So, It knows that everything, and everyone, exists only in Mind, and thus, in the service of Love. It first sees, then lives in, the "allgood" psychocosmos ("heaven").

This monistic "Good," which is God, has no real opposite. In a moment of spellbinding enlightenment, the Soul is allowed to see this.

Even when It engages in mind-searing conflict with other parts of Mind ("warring"), It also acts in harmony with cosmic law ("right-eous"). For it fights to defend and establish Love.

Verse 12. "But his eyes [were a] flame of fire, and upon his head were many diadems. [He] had a name which no one knows except him."

COMM: This clinches it: this is the Soul. For both this form and that of 1:14 manifest purifying ("flame") energy operating through the senses and through insight ("eyes"). So, at the end of Revelation, we find the same figure with which It all began! This is Soul metamor-phosed.

Soul "sees" the cosmos as topsy-turvy and inside-out. It is psyche-delic (Soul-manifesting) in this explosion of re-vision! What It used to value is now seen as garbage, and what it used to ignore is now pre-cious, priceless treasure. The Soul interprets everything newly. It uses intellect ("head") to regulate, and to know, Its world.

The Soul has authority and control ("diadem"). But why was this exotic word used rather than the usual "crown." [The only other loca-tion of the word is in the nightmare vision of dragonmind (12:3), where the "dragon" wears "diadems."] This implies hidden mysteries within the Soul: It is a faithful servant of God (Love). But It has a ca-pricious lower nature that sometimes serves dragonmind (free will in service to fear). The Soul is gloriously stupendous compared with the mind, but even It is not perfect.

It has a secret identity ("Name"). No one but "he" knows it. For he is the only being in the cosmos who can actually *experience* this amaz-ing Self. This identity is the Soul-- timeless, birthless, deathless. As the Soul, he is himself the secret identity of the human mind. (See "Chart of Mind.") But what is *his* hidden, profoundest identity? You might have guessed by now: It is Spirit (Lovemind).

So, again, by a circuitous, amazing maze, we have returned to a basic truth of the Enlightenment Tradition: "Soul" is "Spirit." *Every Soul is played on the stage of life (cosmos) by the One, the ultimate Actor, God. God has a quadrillion quadrillion faces.*

Remember how, earlier, we said that the ego was a "mask" (*per-sona*) worn by the Soul, a role being played on the stage of earth? In the same way, even more astonishingly, the Soul is merely a "role" or mask of the One. This role is played, not only on earth, but in the larger cosmos. This Soul is virtually immortal; certainly, death of the body does not touch It. It moves inexorably from life to life, growing in wisdom and strength. In the overall view of eternity, though, *even the Soul is not immortal;* for It must someday "die" into Spirit. But rather than a cessation of being, this death is really an amplification of identity and Mind. For when the Soul awakens to the fact that It is the one Mind, dreaming up the cosmos, it dies only as an *apparently separate* identity. This is why dualism (believing that you are separate from the One) is the *most fundamental error,* from which all other illusions spring.

This identity is in the memory ("written") of the deeper Unconscious.

Verse 13. "And [he has] thrown around him an outer garment sprinkled with blood. His name has been called the Logos of God."

COMM: Selfimage ("garment"), has mystically died ("blood"). This has radically, positively shifted Soul's definition of "self." The experiences have been only small and momentary ones ('sprinkles'), but Soul has seen God within. That this has been temporary, even fleeting, does not make the event of God-seeing any less real. The Soul is Unified with cosmic Mind. It is the perfect expression ("Logos") of Lovemind. *It is Itself the "Word" or Logos, which is God.* (Jn. 1:1) So, the Soul is an embodiment (incarnation) of the Logos ("Word") *exactly as Jesus was: The Soul is the Logos, and the Logos is God (Love).*

Here, we enter purest, heavy-duty mysticism. *Its theme and essence can be seen as only oneness.* This is the meaning of fullest enlightenment. This is partaking of, becoming absorbed into, Christnature (Lovemind). The Soul is the "lowest end" of Godmind and the "highest end" of the human mind where the "two" overlap.

Verse 14. "And the armies in heaven followed him upon white horses, clothed in fine, white, clean linen."

COMM: All Lovethoughts (of goodness, purity, healthy, wholesome divinity) array themselves ("army") behind the Soullogos. Supporting Soul, they all are supported by the purified ("white") animal nature harnessed by the human will ("horse"). Like the Soul ("bride of the lamb"), they partake of purified selfimage ("white linen").

Verse 15. "And out of his mouth goes a long, sharp sword, so that, in it, he should smite the nations. And he will shepherd them in a staff made of iron. And he is trampling on the [fruit of] the wine-press of the anger of God, the Almighty."

COMM: This grotesque image is the Soul (1:16). His Lovexpression ("mouth") is deadly, lethal to, conflicting with ("sword") egomind ("nations").

Logos is identical with Soul. This is the major core-teaching of mysticism: The "Logos" is one with the human Soul, on the earthly side of cosmic Logos. But on Its heavenly side, it is one with Lovemind or God. The Soul bridges God and human. At Its deepest, It is Lovemind. At a much shallower level, Soulmind is (playing the part of) the mere human mind.

Logos parallels/symmetrizes with Soul: The Soul, *exactly like this Logos,* is "shepherding in a staff of iron" back in 2:27. And it was the Soul, in 1:16, that had the exact same "sword" coming out of his "mouth." So, it must gain control over surrendermind (implied "sheep"). The symbolism is just too precise and symmetric to recognize this Logos as anyone but the Soul.

The Soulogos is destroying spiritual thoughts ("trampling"). This he does to the small individual thoughts ("grapes"; "fruit"). But destruction of positivity is not the goal. Instead, individual thoughtbarriers and thoughts are crushed so that they can come together to form ideas that result from their union or combination ("wine"; implied). They form a blend, a cohesive idea. When they, losing individuality, combine into harmonious oneness, the result is Communion ("wine"). (In 14:20, "blood" (thought-death) came out of the wine-press. Since egodeath must precede Communion, this is a variant of *the same story.*) The "wine-press," then, is all Mindprocesses that transform lower spiritual thoughts ("grapes"; implied) into Communion ("wine"; implied).

Strong unconscious disapproval ("anger") explodes. As in 14:20, "trampling" is overwhelming force, crushing opposition while making progress. The "anger" stems from hurtful, dangerous mistakes made by egomind.

Verse 16. "And he has upon his outer garment and upon his thigh a written name, 'King of kings, and Lord of lords.'"

COMM: This Soulogos is also surrendermind ("lamb"). We can say this with certainty, for it is surrendermind that shares this dramatic title with Soulogos (17:14). Surrendermind is "king of kings" and "lord of lords." The surrendered mind is *the most powerful psychospiritual force in creation!*

Selfimage ("garment") is tangled up with the complex power of the lower nature ("thigh"). Both are marked in memory ("written"). Selfimage blossoms from lower mind. You say, "I am only human, can, will, never be anything higher." This is because of an inner "sea" of memories.

But what is impressed on the deeper memory? It is the truest Soul-identity ("name"). "You" are not just a body, but a mind! (Beautiful women have been trying to convey this for decades.) You are Soul, not body. You are Logos, and you are surrendermind. At the end of the day, you are Lovemind Itself. (In early church-writings, both "Logos" and "lamb" were synonyms for "Christ." This means that *you are the Chris, one of his many incarnationist.*)

Soulogos is "Ruler" over all mental "rulers." In 1:5, this "Lord" is the "ruler over the kings." So, he dominates even very strong, dominant matrix-thoughts.

Soulogos *becomes* surrendermind when It has given up all personal desire, for the sake of Love alone. Ruling the whole Mind, by having given up any ideas of rulership, the Soulogos now rules everything! By becoming nothing, It has become everything! For It is the Mind Who, by dreaming, indwells everything! The Soul, in full enlightenment, is Lord of all. It has grown into full Unity or oneness with the Lord of all, with Lovemind. This is what Paul meant when he told people of the Enlightenment Tradition, "All things belong to you." (1Co 3:21) And it was he who also wrote the amazing words, *"Christ fills all things, and is all things."* (Col 3:11) Barriers and boundaries between Soul and Lovemind have perished and evaporated.

Verse 17. "And I saw one angel standing in the sun, and he cried out in a great voice, saying to all the birds flying in midheaven, 'Come together into the great supper of God...'"

COMM: The Lovelight of enlightenment ("sun") supports spiritual mindelements ("angels"). This "angel" is "in" the sun. It is *within* Lovemind. So, it is a part of the Lightmind or Lovemind.

"Birds" are small animal-thoughts capable of ascending to higher Lovethoughts. These "birdthoughts" are noble, elevated, and spiritual. Lovemind has invited these birdthoughts to fill themselves with spiritual nutrition ("supper"). The usual place of these birds is between the hypersensual mind and the Lightnature ("midheaven").

Verse 18. "'... so that you can eat the flesh of kings, and of chiliarchs, and of the strong, and of horses and those sitting upon them, and the flesh of all freemen and of slaves, of the great and the small.'"

COMM: The grotesquery of those who literalize this verse is sickening. The lower mindset or worldview ("flesh") is here assimilated by small animalthoughts. Its energy is going to be recycled into spirituality through these birdthoughts. The eight thought-families assimilated by these transition-thoughts are: 1) governing or dominating matrix-thoughts ("kings"); 2) militant attitudes ("chiliarchs"); 3) powerful motivating thoughts ("strong"); 4) animalmind thoughts subjected to human will ("horses"); 5) the human will ("those sitting upon them"); 6) free-roaming thoughts not used to support any idea ("freemen"); 7) thoughts subservient to larger ideas ("slaves"); 8) large and small thoughtstructures ("great and small"). All have their energies recycled. This occurs also so that the whole Mind might move towards ever-greater enlightenment. (In the original text, the word translated "flesh" is literally "fleshes," implying greater complexity.)

Verse 19. "And I saw the wild beast, and the kings of the earth, and their armies, gathered together to make war with the One sitting upon the horse, and with his army."

COMM: Interior conflict is not yet over. Like a literal war, it drags on and on until you are quite sick of it, and certain that it might never end! Even after its brushes with temporary enlightenment, Mind is still divided. So powerful is the illusion ("separation"; duality)! A crystal-clear polarization occurs between 1) the illusory mind, ego, under wildbeastmind, and 2) the real Mind influenced by the Soul. Soul is Logos (Mindmirror of Lovemind). So, the two, Logos and Lovemind, are again synonymous. (Soul—Logos—Lovemind—God.)

Verse 20. "And the wild beast was caught. With it, [so was] the false prophet who did signs in its sight, by which he made to err those who received the engraving of the wild beast, and worshipped its image. Living, the two were thrown into the lake of fire, burning in sulfur."

COMM: Literalism creates catastrophic, hitlerian or saddamic, bestial sadism. No one is being hurled into a literal lake of fire, created by a ghoulish Jehovah to roast and toast his own children forever, while he and other sick sadists watch in psychotic glee! The "false prophet" (from 16:13) is all Mindareas that claim to know of sacred things, but do not. This lying part of the psyche is bound ("caught") by positive Mind (Lovemind). It is cast into a "lake of fire."

But nowhere in the Christian Scriptures is this symbolic description directly associated with Hades. (This is the name for the "place of the dead" in the Christian Scriptures. It is this word that kj and later translations rendered as "hell.")

This "lake" (water-symbol) combines fire and water. It is a "lake," but is filled with fire. What does this mean in terms of the Apocalyptic archetypes? "Water" is the Unconscious; and "fire" is purifying suffering. So, the "lake of fire" represents all the unconscious purifying suffering of the Soul.

This can include various selfcreated inner hells. For example, it can include states of regret, anger, dismal dejection, depression, or fierce violence. But more often, it is simply the agony that arises from Soulreview of our past mistakes. It is often the torture of selfunforgiveness. We are unaware of most of this, but still, it purifies deeper Mind. The conscious mind is not nearly so important as we tend to believe.

It likes to strut in the spotlight. The conscious mind likes to suck vampirically at all our timenergy. For years, it was mistaken for, and equated with, the *whole Mind.* It likes this delusion, and hangs onto it for dear life. *For the end of this delusion is death to the ego.* And it wants to survive, as trickster, disguised as master of Mind. But much growth occurs without it, as when we dream at night.

So, God does not just make "grease-spots" out of the "wild beast," vicious as it is, or out of the "false prophet," with its ugly, lying mouth. *Amazingly, even these hideous villains are not killed!* (Why? Because Lovemind knows that they serve illusion/delusion/error, which is not deliberate evil. They are, after all, working for "Him"!) Instead, he installs and recycles their energy in the subconscious "lake," and makes them pure ("fire"). So, as evil as they undoubtedly are, they are not reported here as having been "killed," or as having just vaporized. For their mental energy can still be salvaged and redeemed to serve Love. That is why, still possessing energy ("still living"), they were thrown into the "lake of fire." Their lives were preserved. Their lifenergies remain intact, and they remain at least partially cohesive. For Mind is not yet finished with them.

Verse 21. "And those left over were killed off in the long sword of the One sitting upon the horse, the sword that came out of his mouth. And all the birds were satisfied out of their flesh."

COMM: The "army" of negativity is deactivated ("killed"; "sword") by the Lovexpression ("mouth") of the Soulogos. Lovemind killed Its enemies! They "died" in unabated, full resistance to the Soulogos ("the One sitting upon the horse")!

Lovexpression is lethal to fear! All servants of evil are slaves of fear. The consistent, relentless expression of real Love-- by word, thought, or action-- is enough to kill off the demonic "army" of harmful thoughts in the psyche.

All the transformative small animalthoughts ("birds") are satisfied. The entire positive Mind settles into contentment and fulfillment. For the thoughts with spiritual potential ("birds") perform their whole, complete function. They are satiated by having transformed the "flesh" (animal nature) into Lovethoughts or "Spirit." These became integrated within (one with) Lovemind.

Chapter 20

Verse 1. "And I saw an angel stepping down out of heaven with the key of the abyss, and a great chain upon his hand."

COMM: A Lovenergy ("angel") manifests ("steps down") from Lovemind ("heaven"). He has the wisdom ("key") to understand the subconscious ("abyss"). (The subconscious is the Mind's wastebasket, a small part of the larger personal Unconscious. (See "Chart of Mind.")

This angel also carries a restraining mental mechanism, selfrestraint, suppression, or repression ("chain"). It restricts direct action ("hand"). So, this Mindenergy will be restricted to performing only Its function. The angel now heads threateningly towards the dragon, to repress him.

Verse 2. "And he caught hold of the dragon, the archaic serpent, who is devil and satan, and bound him [for a] thousand years."

COMM: The third member of the "dark trinity" of evil, the horrific, nightmarish animalmind ("dragon"), is grabbed in a strangle-hold by the forces of Love. He is completely under the control of fear, at this time ("satan"; "devil"). But even fearmind (dragonmind) is not vaporized. The force of fear is only "bound." It is restrained and controlled by more powerful thought-constellations ("angel"), then jettisoned to the subconscious dungeon of Mind ("abyss").

"One thousand" is ten cubed. So, it partakes of both earthly completion (enlightenment; 'ten') and wholeness ('three').

This is the meaning of the numbersymbol. But it is combined with a symbol that represents time-- "years." So, satanmind (fearmind, dragonmind) is stored in the subconscious. But it is not allowed to remain there forever. It stays there, as negative, harmful potential, only until full enlightenment or wholeness is discovered. Then, it reemerges into conscious awareness to "test" the validity of enlightenment, as we shall see later.

Verse 3. "And he threw him into the abyss, and he shut and sealed [it] above him, so that he might not cause the nations to err, until the thousand years are ended. After these, he is bound [to be] loosed [for] a little time."

COMM: Spiritmind ("angel") throws fear-dominated free will ("dragon") into the subconscious mind ("abyss"). The conscious mind completely loses access to this part of the subconscious ("shut and sealed").

"Sin" is error ("cause to err"). That sin is error is supported by the Greek word for "sin." It is borrowed from archery, and means "to miss a target." When an archer misses a target, it is not deliberate, but a mistake, imperfection. She is really trying to hit the bull's eye.

Does this imply that all "sin" can be simply dismissed as "processing errors"? Is there no such thing as *deliberate,* voluntary sin? This is an unhealthy extreme. On this basis, a person could exercise the most horrendous cruelties-- on the magnitude of a hitler or saddam-- and then claim that he/she was "only sick," and not responsible. If responsibility is to have any meaning, if choice is to guide our lives, a person must be held *fully* responsible for any deliberate or premeditated act against another living creature. Happily, this is the Way that the cosmos, and the psyche, do work: Any *intentional* harm given to another will have to rebound to the person who causes it.

Still, on the other hand, when you consider the neurological complexities of the brain/nervoussystem, it might turn out that much sin is indeed due to structural neuroanatomy. If this were so, then, the conscious mind would not be fully responsible for these particular sins. This would be a perfect basis for universal forgiveness. But, twisted, it could also justify deliberate evil. Take warning: Errors are forgiven, but *there is no such thing as an "intentional" error!* By definition, if you intend to hurt someone, you will receive back exactly what you have given out! So, forgiveness *is not "license to sins".*

The mind, more often than not, cannot "forgive" itself. *This does not mean that it is not forgiven absolutely by Lovemind.* Love always forgives. It does not, as Paul reminds us, in the "Canticle of Love," "keep records of injuries." (1 Cor. 13)

So, you are responsible for your conscious choices and for *other factors under your control. But you are not responsible for processes outside your control.* The mind contains many dark areas set against the Lovelight at the Center. Satanmind (fear) is the worst of all the "mindevils" portrayed in Revelation. It leads into illusion ("causing to err") large segments of mind ("nations"). After the Mind has entered fullest enlightenment, satanmind will again be allowed to emerge from the subconscious.

Verse 4. "And I saw thrones, and they sat down upon them. And judgment was given to them. And the Souls of those executed with an ax through the testimony of Jesus, and through the Logos of God, who had worshipped neither the wild beast nor its image, nor received its engraving upon their forehead and hand, lived and reigned with the Christ a thousand years."

COMM: This is the famous "millennial reign of Christ." Literalists have always claimed that it was about to begin at "any minute." (See Author's Preface for details.) The absurdly desperate fad reached frenzies throughout history. One of these peaked, not surprisingly, in the year ten hundred. Many people were utterly convinced that the "thousand years" would begin that year. Worldender frenzy underwent various deaths and resurrections throughout the Middle Ages. The issue of the "end" and the start of "Christ's reign on earth" has been a powderkeg with a very short fuse, and has exploded periodically in spurts of fanaticism and bursts of religious hysteria. A notable false prophet of the thirteenth century was Joachim of Fiore, who calculated carefully, from Scripture, that the end would arrive in 1294. It was insane to deny it, since so many "prophecies" were being "fulfilled" on every side!

Worldender frenzy was resuscitated many times in the seventeenth, eighteenth, nineteenth, and twentieth centuries.

Even early in the twenty-first, many among literalist Christians are expecting the "thousand years" to break out, and end history, at any moment. Literalists like to scare themselves with "science-fiction theology." This seems to serve the same sophomoric need as ghost stories told 'round the ol' campfire, or horror-films, or badly written comic books. With wide and fearfilled eyes, these literalists teach a "comic book" terrorism: we are living in the "last days" or "end times." They speak in hushed undertones, with trembling around the edges, of the "end of the world." Their teachers and representatives scream the same message, booming in "hellfire and damnation" volume from loud-speakers in churches, and at assemblies, everywhere. Nothing has changed in this area since the time of their primitive, superstitious religious forebears.

Of course, the psycho-exigetic (allegorical interpretation of Scripture) understanding removes all this symbolism from the calendar. What this verse means in psychosymbolism is that thoughts uncontaminated with the sins of the wildbeast will rule the whole Mind. This will occur with its natural inner Ruler, the Christspirit. This tranquil Mind will continue during all the time of peace that will bring enlightenment, and that enlightenment will bring. [For, after all the troubles upon the spiritual journey, a time of earthly completion and enlightenment (ten) and wholeness (three) arrives.] During this phase of inner peace, Love rules. During this time, divine awareness dawns that the entire Self is only good and pure ("judgment").

Soulthoughts or Christ-thoughts, at a sad time in the past, "died" but did not perish with pain and horrible violence ("executed with the ax"). Fearthoughts relentlessly attacked them! But they did not vanish; they simply went "underground," into the oceanic Unconscious. But, resurrected, these will reappear among the redeemed "rulers" of Mind.

Verse 5. "Those left over among the dead did not live until after the thousand years had ended. This is the first resurrection."

COMM: Thoughts die (sink below the threshold of the conscious mind) and come back to life. Their energies are recycled. So, after the whole Mind comes to enlightenment ("one thousand years"), many thoughts imagined to be dead will be found alive and well. Many Lovethoughts were believed to have perished in "wars" between good and "evil." Discouragement and depression became such colossal mountains of despair that the mind gave up completely on ever seeing a "happy" or spiritual thought ever again! This was during the darknight. But now, they come back to life, since they had never been completely wiped out of existence. Now, they are awakened by the Love seen in enlightenment. Now, they return to conscious awareness. This is called the "first resurrection," implying that more than one "resurrection" period occurs in mental dynamics. In Apocalyptic symbolism, if these thoughts die, they will die the "second death." (This is mentioned later.)

Can thoughts ever arise again after undergoing the "second death"? This would require a "second resurrection," and the "first resurrection" implies this. So, thought-energy can be recycled more than once, and even intact thoughts can survive in the Unconscious. Then, at any time that Lovemind chooses, these intact thoughts can be brought once again into the cognition-field of the mind ('resurrected').

Verse 6. "Happy and holy [is] the one having part in the first resurrection. Over these, the second death has no authority. But they will be priests of God and Christ, and will reign with him the thousand years."

COMM: Here, once a thought has gone through the Unconscious-to-conscious cycle ("first resurrection"), it is here to stay. Were it to go back to the Unconscious, that would be called a "second death." *But that is simply not going to happen.*

Holiness brings happiness. Enlightenment brings bliss.

These thoughts will not be deactivated ("killed") once they are resurrected during the enlightenment-period ("thousand years").

Verse 7. "And when the thousand years are over, satan will be loosed out of his prison."

COMM: This is the final test or exam. Is the enlightenment in Love real? This question is too important for its answer to be left up to chance or guessing-games. The only way that the reality of the enlightenment can be accurately gauged is to expose the mind to fear-mind one last time. This might take the form of very powerful bio-forces, such as the "temptation" to sex, drugs, or food. So, after the mind discovers the ecstasy of enlightenment while still on earth, satanmind returns to grapple once more.

Verse 8. "And he will go out to make the nations err, in the four corners of the earth, Gog and Magog, to lead them into the war. Their number is as the sand of the sea."

COMM: Illumination stirs up some odd "critters" in the mind. It also awakens spiritual forces. It can drive you to the brink of going nuts, and then shock you into the threshold of Lovemind. "Gog" arises from a root meaning "roof" or "top of an altar." "Magog" arises from a root meaning "from the top," "overtopping," "covering." These are two very related, if not interchangeable, symbols of transcendence. So, whatever they are, gog and magog are in at least periodic touch with the deepest Mind (Lovemind). In those often silly traditional commentaries, they are names for a whole string of countries and/or rulers over the years of history. They are really, of course, mindforces. And their etymology (wordroots) implies that they are positive, helping in the long climb to higher consciousness (deeper Mind). If so, traditionalists are wrong again!

They might also be another, and collective, name for all the great thought-constellations ("nations"). If so, they are the servants of fear, but later, come under Lovemind's rulership.

But the context does not make clear exactly to what the odd and quirky names refer. Due to their possible roots, they might indicate that, in the longrun of eternity, even fearmind is healed by the irresistible force of cosmic Love and total forgiveness. Even satanmind will be redeemed, as it too is an expression of the One, although captive in its own darkness and hellish ignorance (fear). Is this blasphemy?

No, it is highest praise; for it absolutely proves that

****

no sin can ever be greater than the Love of God.

****

Again, even after earthly enlightenment, it is clear that fearmind still exists, lurking in the dark backwaters of the subconscious. Mindfactors begin yet another polarization in preparation for yet another "war." A gargantuan number of thoughts ("as the sand of the sea") are involved in this struggle to the death between Light and darkness, Love and fear.

Verse 9. "And they stepped up upon the breadth of the earth, and encircled the camp of the holy and loved city. Fire flashed down out of heaven, and ate them down."

COMM: Evil or darkness seems, in this latest crisis, to be all around. It might even duplicate the appearance of infinity, symbolized by the "circle" of "encircled." These are thoughts/ideas that seem to be emanated by Lovemind, but are only play-actors (the original meaning of "hypocrites").

The army of ignorance starts by "stepping up" out of the subconscious to hypersensual mind ("earth"). It is then detected by the senses.

A complex collection of human frames, ideas, and thoughtstructures ("city") is "loved." This contrasts strongly and vividly with the previous "city," Babylon, the Lovestarved biosexdrive. This new city is, by stunning contrast, like New Jerusalem: It is all human-engineered thoughts and ideas in harmony with Lovemind.

From higher (deeper) Mind, purifying suffering ("fire") comes from highest (deepest) Mind ("down out of heaven.") *All difficulties, all suffering, is a gift from God, a blessing of Lovemind.* For it is only by overcoming complex and strenuous challenges that we grow at all. And this spiritual growth is *the greatest and most wonderful gift conceivable.*

This suffering thoroughly consumes the armies of ignorance and fear. But the original text says that the fire "ate them down." This implies that, instead of being completely vaporized into nothingness, their energies might have simply cycled back "down" to the subconscious mind. For literal "eating" is not destruction, but assimilation. Food is not destroyed but transformed into tissue.

Verse 10. "And the devil, the one making them to err, was thrown into the lake of fire and sulfur, where also the wild beast and false prophet [were]. And they will be tormented day and night into the ages of the ages."

COMM: Again, the grotesque, scary fearmind "makes them err," rather than promoting deliberate, voluntary evil. *This is important,* for it is repeated over and over in Revelation. Just how insane is the torturer, the rapist, the murderer? For exactly how much is he/she responsible?

Fearmind is the part of the subconscious responsible. So, the subconscious must suffer; it goes to the "lake of fire." This water-fire blend is agonizing. *People do "go to hell", often in the proverbial "hand basket", for their deliberate sins.* True, it is a hell of mind, and does not last forever, but it is as painful as flesh frying! More relevantly, it leads back to a state of unconscious ("water") purification through suffering ("fire"). (This is subconscious.)

Even the "devil" (fearmind) is not obliterated. It is the source of a spectrum of hideous evils. It is simply forced to endure the karma ("torment") of its own actions

English translations erroneously translate the final phrase of this verse, "into the ages of the ages," as "forever." But the "lake of fire" does not exist forever. The translators of the King James translation of 1611 were notorious. At any rate, they did set the precedent here, for the translation of this phrase as "forever." (They made the same error in putting into Jesus' mouth the promise of "everlasting life," based on a *mistranslation of the same world.* Jesus knew that *everyone, by virtue of having a Soul, already possessed "everlasting life."* So, he did not promise this as a "reward" to those who followed him.) Modern translations play "follow the leader" with the 1611 KJ, falling into lockstep conformity. The phrase has even other possible translations, including, "a very, very long time," or, "For many ages," or, "for ages of ages," or, "in other states," or, "in a timeless condition." There is *no reason* to translate it "forever."

This phrase can also be translated "in all states," implying that this "torment" of fearmind occurs at all Mindlevels. [Since the Greek word for "age" (*aion*) also means "state," this verse can imply that the torment is recorded even in, and created by, unconscious Mindlevels.]

Verse 11. "And I saw a great white throne, and from the face of the One sitting upon it, the earth and heaven fled. And no place was found for them."

COMM: It is vast ("great") and pure ("white"). It has a position of leadership ("throne"). "It" must be Lovemind. It doesn't require a brainsurgeon to identify the symbolism here! But both the hypersensual mind ("earth") and highest Mindarea ("heaven") rushed away ("fled") from Lovemind. It was as if both mindpolarities could not wait to escape from before Lovemind's appearance ("face"). Why?

The entire Mind is undergoing shocking transformation. "Heaven" is not here synonymous with Lovemind, although It is elsewhere. It *could not* be Lovemind, for it flies from Lovemind.

Here, it is the inner space where Lovemind resides. It is the Core of Mind. It is the Mind's nucleus. It is a *mindarea.* (A "mindarea" is a part of mind doing a particular task. It focuses upon a particular theme.) This is psychotopography, and so, is itself symbolic.) "Psychocartography" (mind-mapping) has nothing to do with literal areas in space. It is not, for example, brainmapping.

It is simply the recognition that *different "areas" (functions) require timenergy and Lovenergy. Inner space symbolizes areas of focus (themes).*

This verse describes the utter, ecstatic filling of every nanopsychon (smallest unit of mindenergy) with Love and Its family of thoughtfeelings! When the whole Mind becomes Lovemind, there is no longer a need for a specialized "area" (mindtheme) for Lovemind. Lovemind does not occupy just *some* thoughts; It pervades *all* thoughts. So, when the whole Mind is filled with the pervasive Presence of God, hypersensual mind ("earth") vanishes as a "separate" part of Mind. So, simultaneously does the mindarea called "heaven". ("Heaven" exists only relative to "earth". This dichotomy disappears here). For when the whole Mind becomes Love, there is no longer any need for hypersensual mind. It has been transcended. It has been absorbed into the One and Only. So, by the way, has "heaven," which used to be set apart from the rest of Mind as the "home" of Lovemind. Now, Mind is One, integrated, ubiquitous, all in all. It no longer has "Lovemind" and "not Lovemind" divisions!

Verse 12. "And I saw the dead, the great and the small, standing in sight of the throne. And little books were opened up, and [an]other little book was opened up, which is of life. And the dead were judged out of the things written in the little books, according to their works."

COMM: Thoughts thought to be "dead" were only dormant. They were just playing. They were involved in a complex game. They were only latent in the subconscious! So, now these thoughts are examined by Lovemind ("in sight of the throne"). Memories ("little books") are consciously recovered. The mind opens ("opened up") to receive them.

From Soulevel springs memory about the whole life ("of life"), from eons in the past. The memories are separated: are they horrors, or moments of bliss? They are evaluated ("judged"). The mind sorts them, to see which memories that it wants to keep, and which are useless trash, or even toxic: Have they enriched development or blocked it? Do they give energy, or drain It? Those which are not part of the solution become the problem!

Verse 13. "And the sea gave up those dead within it, and death and Hades gave up the dead within them, and they were judged, each one according to her works."

COMM: Mind blossoms into selfknowledge. Two levels of the Unconscious are examined: 1) the preconscious and 2) the personal Unconscious ("sea"). (See "Chart of Mind.")

"Thoughtdeath" must occur with thoughtmemories in the subconscious. In this kind of "death," they are giving up all their energy. [This differs from deactivation or sinking below the horizon of awareness, the two other "deaths" already encountered. (See Definition 3 in the "Glossary").] These denizens of the subconscious must "die"! Why? Because their energies are needed by the conscious mind to support its exploration. Energy cannot be used twice-- both in maintaining the subconscious thoughtmemories and in conscious spiritual exploration. So, something has to give! When the thoughtmemories "die" in the subconscious, they give their Mindforce to the conscious mind. It then recycles this mindenergy into its mission-- exploring the Mind. The process of thoughtdeath ("death") gives up its cache of energy-drained thoughts ("dead").

Hades is where "dead" thoughtmemories are stored. These are "killed" by suppression or repression. (Hades is in the subconscious garbage-bin.) When it gives up its subconscious thoughts ("dead"), their energies are also recycled into new thoughts.

This might require deep, often traumatic, psychotherapy. Hades "gives up" these, old memories long buried in the subconscious. They include sexual torments, shocks, terrors, and other nightmarish and ghastly memories. They can then surface to conscious view.

For example, you might have a deep subconscious memory of a sexual imposition or atrocity done to you when you were very young. This thought is "dead" to your conscious mind. But it still lives actively in your subconscious. It still has energy. In fact, it can have so much energy that it can ruin your life. Since this is always a horror, the "place" (mindfocus) where it is stored is called hades-- the Greek word for "hell."

In psychotherapy, these old thoughtmemories are evaluated ("judged"). The examination of the Mind is quite meticulous. It can be a horrifying spectacle, for the Mind misses nothing!

Verse 14. "And death and Hades were thrown into the lake of fire. This lake of fire is the second death."

COMM: This is a hassle for literalists. For it makes absolutely no literal sense.

However, it makes perfect *allegorical* sense: Mental deactivation ("death") is no longer needed by the Mind. Neither is radical transfer of energy-- the alternative meaning of "thoughtdeath." Deactivation and energy-draining ("death") are now disposable. For the entire Mind has now awakened to the fact that it is Lovemind. And *everything within Lovemind is now recognized as flawless and stainless. Nothing needs killed; nothing in all of Mind needs to die.* It has always been so, but the mind is just only now awakening to the fact! Mind is perfect, through and through. So, "mindeath," as a useful process, itself dies! This is how "death" is cast into transformative suffering ("fire") in the subconscious ("lake").

A Mindspace ("Hades") for accommodating thought-death is also logically thrown away. No "mindarea" (focus) such as this is needed, or wanted! So, the troublesome Hades, itself a part of the subconscious garbage-dump, creates pain and suffering in the subconscious ("lake of fire"); but, in the longrun, this heals and enlightens the mind! So, when it has served this fine purpose, Hades vaporizes.

The energies of these old thoughts are released as free energy. This is then recycled. Their energies go back into Mind to emerge as the forces of Love.

This "second death" is visited upon the process of thoughtdeath itself. It is thoughtdeath that dies here.

But the "second death" also affects thoughtmemories. It is designated as "second" because these thoughtmemories had died once already. They were resurrected, and now must "die" again.

Verse 15. "And if anyone was not found written in the book of life, [this person] was thrown into the lake of fire."

COMM: Thoughts of ignorance, violence, stupidity, hatred, and fear-- all produced by the human (intellectual; "anyone") mind-- are purified through water-fire interactions (pain in the Unconscious). That which is thrown into fire supports the fire.

****

In fact, it *becomes* fire itself!

****

So, these thoughtfactors become one with the Lovenergy of purification. They become "light," just as wood, when consumed by a campfire, becomes lightenergy. At this time, the enemies of Love have all become pure energy. When stinking trash is burned, it is purified of its smell and uncleanness.

The same occurs here: The false prophet, wild beast, dragonmind, death, and Hades are now joined by a big, undefined bunch of miscellaneous thoughtfeelings. They all end up in intense educational pain ("fire"), being transformed by it. They all, altogether, are transformed into pure energy. It is that of Light, or Lovelight. Their naked force, having no permanent form as thoughts or memories, is now perfectly integrated with, and into, Lovemind. (They all become the fire). It is Power used to make more Love. So, again, Revelation presents a sophisticated view of the Mindsystem as a series of complex, sometimes reversible or interchangeable, mental interactions. It avoids the naive simplism of "black-and-white" thinking, dualizing the inner cosmos into "good" and "bad" in the absolute sense.

Chapter 21

Verse 1. "And I saw [a] new heaven and [a] new earth. For the first heaven and the first earth went off. And the sea is no more."

COMM: The whole Mind is totally renewed, reborn. The former dwelling-place of Lovemind ("heaven") was a limited Mindarea (theme or focus); it was ensconced and hidden deep in the Unconscious. That "first heaven" is now gone. It is replaced by a "new heaven," in which perfect Mind is *everywhere,* and everywhere accessible to the conscious mind. As in the previous verse, it is not limited to a *part* of Mind. Rather, Love or "heaven" *has become the whole mind.* It is now pervasive, not "separate" from any other segment of Mind. Like an ocean, it fills Mind to the brim, from one side to the other. What was formerly deeply hidden is now fully revealed and manifest to the conscious awareness. It is Love!

In hypersensual mind ("the first earth"), the senses were dominant. They were a cruel and harsh taskmaster, relentless and tormenting. In the "new earth," the senses are glorified and amplified in their joy. But now, they are used in the service of Lovemind. They are no longer "master." They serve no selfish purpose.

After enlightenment, the senses are even more delightful. They are more intense and enjoyable. But they are no longer the dominant controller of mind. Hypersensual mind is not killed, as some extremists ("ascetics") claim, by enlightenment. Instead, it is renewed and refitted for the service of compassion and goodness.

Also, the troublesome Unconscious has disappeared ("sea" is no more). In fact, not only the *sub*conscious, but the universal, cosmic *Un*conscious ("sea"), including Lovemind, *has now all become conscious, one with the aware mind.*

Verse 2. "And the city, the holy new Jerusalem, I saw descending out of the heavens from God, having been prepared as a bride adorned for her man."

COMM: This complex arrangement of human-fabricated and human-altered thoughtstructures ("city") is one of two major complexes.

(The other was Babylon, the Loveless biosexdrive.) When these thoughtelements (ideas, concepts, memories, etc.) were configured as the "great city Babylon," they were antiagapic, lost in fear (ignorance). Now this fallen "city" Babylon is replaced by the resplendent "new Jerusalem."

This gorgeous city is the mind's collection of thoughtstructures (ideas, feelings, memories, etc.) that are in total harmony with the will of Love. Love both forms and controls the contents of the renewed, reborn "Jerusalemind." In this new complex order of thoughts, Love is pervasive, saturating and immersing everything. Mind is now completely unified with God (Lovemind). So the "city" is "stepping down" out of God's new interior dwelling-place-- the whole Mind (It is all "heaven"). All the Mind flows and flowers with the bright, clear waters of Light. Every nanopsychon is jam-packed with only Love. Fearmind has vanished. This superhuman "city" springs directly from Lovemind. (It is a subsystem within It).

The mystical motif of "marriage," symbolizing completed Union between Soul and Lovemind (God) is repeated here as a bride joined to her "man." This "man" is the bridegroom, which is Christ (God). This, again, emphasizes another perennial mystical motif: God dwells in, works through, the human mind and being. That is why we *need each other*. When we need help, it is *to human beings* that we turn, not to some "God" in the sky. For we all know, at least unconsciously, that God works through people!

Verse 3. "And I heard a great voice out of the throne, saying, 'Look! The tent of God [is] with men, and He will tent with them. And they will be his peoples, and He will be God with them.'"

COMM: Lovemind dwells in a portable and mobile state. It is a more ordinary, and homelier, dwelling than the "temple", highlighting the informality and immediacy of God ("tent"). There is nothing set in concrete, nothing formal, about this God or His/Her dwelling: Wherever thoughts ("people") go, there God is. These are not ordinary, everyday thoughts. They are luminous Lovethoughts ("his peoples"). Human nature ("men") comes from God; God is "anthropopsychogenic." (He/She creates human thought.) Now, "human" mind is Love. All Mind is surrendered! Lovemind takes over, "possessing" you!

Verse 4. "And he will wipe every tear out of their eyes, and death will not exist anymore. Neither will there be mourning, nor crying out, nor pain anymore. The first things went away."

COMM: At enlightenment, bitterness, frustration, and sadness ("tears") vanish ("wiped" away). For mind has merged seamlessly with Lovemind. So, all thoughts become perfect Lovethoughts, and there is no need for deactivation or repression ("death"). Mind's every thought is agapogenic (Love-generating) and proagapic (Love-supporting). Inner discomforts ("mourning,...pain") are all gone. Sweet bliss fills Mind, all past pains forgotten. The slate of the mind has been wiped clean of sorrow and regret. These mental agonies were the results of hypersensuality locked in illusion ("first things" of the "first earth"). They were generated when the Soul was just beginning, as a neophyte, its spiritual journey.

Verse 5. "And the One sitting upon the throne said, ' Look! I am making all things new.' And he says, 'Write, because these words are faithful and true.'"

COMM: There is nothing but Lovemind anywhere in the galaxies, in the whole cosmos! So, everything is seen in a new way ("all things new"). Everything becomes numinous and luminous! (It has always been so, but enlightenment permits awakening to the fact.) Only Mind, this one Mind, is real. In fact, It is Reality Itself ("true"). All that appears to be "outside" the One is illusion, a mere chimera, a dream. The whole "material" world exists within this Mind, as Its dream.

All contains God. So, all is good.

When you dream at night of a little red wagon, *you are in that wagon, because it is in you.* When you dream of a blue ball*, you are "in" that too, for it is also your dream. You are the wagon and the ball but neither is you. In the same way God is every mystic but no mystic is the totality of God.* So, God, by dreaming up the cosmos, *dwells everywhere within it. God is within it all, and it all within Him/Her!* This is the meaning of "omnipresence". This is the "allgood cosmos" inhabited by the mystic. This is the source of her "allembracing mind." Her whole inner world is a "heaven," filled with only Love or God. There is no room for "non-Love," which is an illusion. There is no place for fear, which is also illusion, is pushed out, cast away. When the Mind changes, it changes everything ("all things"). The cosmos is "made new." For mutating the mind alters world-perception. And it is clearly seen, as in the beginning, that all is "very good " (Compare the parallel Genesis allegory.) This gnosis of the allgood universe is a perfect knowing of Reality ("true"). The mind (John) is commanded to remember ("write") this overiding truth.

Verse 6. "And he said to me, 'They have occurred. I, the alpha and the omega, beginning and end, shall give out of the fountain of the water of life, as a free gift.'"

COMM: Lovemind opens a clear channel of communication to the mind ("he said to me"): All the nightmarish and ecstatic mindstates prophesied in Revelation have come ("occurred") to the mind. The enlightenment-cycle is drawing to a close, at its apex!

The One rules ("on the throne") the whole Mind. It is the unenlightened mind ("alpha...beginning"). But, simultaneously, "he" is also the Endgoal, fully enlightened Mind ("omega...end"). Both are equally the One. Lovemind is your mental origin and destination. How can this be? Even in its greatest darkness, stupidity, and wretchedness, the mind never ceases to be the One, Lovemind. Even if it cuts off completely its knowledge of, and conscious connections with, Lovemind, *it is still Lovemind.* Nothing that mind does, no matter how ignorant, can change *its essential nature.* So, Lovemind, perfect Mind, is also the embryonic mind of illusion. (This, again, is "monism.")

So, both darkmind and lightmind are Mind, the only Mind, at different levels of development. Every mind is God at some level. Omegaminds are simply further along the path of spiritual evolution than alphaminds. (Between the two is an entire "alphabet," including betaminds, deltaminds, gammaminds, omicronminds, etc.)

To the seeker, "thirsting" for Love (Reality), divine Mind gives the Unconscious ("water") realization. This is awakening to your own truest nature, your deepest secret identity: You too are God wearing a mask, pretending to be a limited ego, playing egogames. This is a realization of real existence as a spiritual being (Soul; "life"). This knowing (gnosis) is a free gift of grace. This is not, cannot be, earned. It exists solely due to the will of God, the Love of cosmic Mind.

He/She distributes it to all. It is given freely, due to Love, and equally to everyone. Your behavior has zero effect on divine Love (grace). It is never changed in the least nanopsychon. In the final analysis, "sin" is irrelevant to final salvation. For saving grace originates with theogenic (God originated) Love alone. But the effect of sin (ignorance) is to fill one's life with complexities, agonies, hells, and frustrations. It also delays enlightenment, promoting needless suffering.

Verse 7. "'The one conquering will inherit these things, and I shall be God to him, and he will be son to Me.'"

COMM: "Conquer" ignorance and the lower nature. You will be blasted into a gnostic (mystical) awakening. You will be stunned to learn that God (Lovemind) is the All. (The gnostic Christians called this Mind "the Father of the All.")

****

For Lovemind is all minds everywhere, in everyone.

****

He/She will be the great obsession of your life ("your God"). You will realize that you are not exclusively human. You are only "part human." That which is not human is divine! The deepest part of your Mind is pure Love and pure wisdom. This is the great Mind that you have intrinsically, from Lovemind ("inherit").

Lovemind is your "Father/Mother." You deserve to inherit all that belongs to Him/Her. The greatest and most luminous of all divine treasures is Love, and Lovemind gives you this in oceans, waterfalls of illimitable, immeasurable abundance! You are swamped by the sheer Power of illimitable Love, immersed in It, saturated by It! It is most excellent beauty and bliss, but It is not exclusively "yours." You arise directly from this perfect, flawless Mind, as if from analogous genetic inheritance. But godship does not work through the genes. It works through the Mind. The "daughter" or "son" of God "inherits" all the things belonging to God. That is, of course, *the entire cosmos, bar nothing!* At enlightenment, the whole Lovemind passes as a "heritage" to the Soul, and all Its dreams. When Lovemind gives its most fantastic, exquisite best, It gives Itself!

Verse 8. "'But to cowards and to unbelievers, and to all who have been made disgusting, and to murderers, and to fornicators, and to druggers, and to idolaters, and to all liars-- their part is in the lake burning with fire and sulfur, which is the second death.'"

COMM: Thoughtforms and thoughtpatterns that are removed from the enlightened mind include: 1) phobic thoughts, including the spiritually pathological thoughts of: A) mystophobia ("fear of mystery), B) psychophobia (fear of the Mind or Soul), C) theophobia (fear of God), D) pneumophobia (fear of Spirit and spiritual things),

E) autophobia (fear of the Self), and F) agnophobia (fear of the unknown).

It is delightful that the mind should be catharsized or purged of fearthoughts, servants of "satan." These are all identified as "cowards."

2) those thoughts that support the common views of God and reality, turning away from the stunning mystical truths of the inner God, Lovemind (Coremind), the dreamworld, the Journey, oneness of all Mind, the primacy of Love, God in all, etc. All common, orthodox, mainstream ideas are called "unbelievers."

3) Thoughtpatterns that suffered from exposure to the difficult lessons of life, took the wrong path, and ended up in antiagapic pursuits. These are the ideas that create life-mismanagement. These draw you into alienation, isolation, mental illness, immorality, and even crime. These are collectively called "those made disgusting."

4) Powerful thoughtideas. It is possible, even likely, that you might get carried away by some intense interest in something other than God (Love). You might suffer from fixation (arrest) or even obsession. This could be your hobby, career, sports, gambling, drugs/alcohol, sex, money, reputation, cars, houses, jewelry, or any other Love-substitute. This false passion gets so strong that it "kills" rival thoughts! So, these mad pursuits are collectively called "murderers."

5) Thoughtconcepts that betray Love are especially deadly to the Soul. They can rip into your Soul like a chainsaw, but can be so subtle that you hardly notice them.

****

Any thought that seems more important than the service of Love betrays Love.

****

This could be religion, politics, finances, career. These thoughts are collectively called "fornicators."

6) Thoughts that lead to confusion, disorientation, and illusion are maddening. The etiology (cause) of all psychospiritual confusion is dualism. This is the belief that *any mind exists separate from the One.* So, anything that reinforces the sense of lonely, cut off, isolated existence would also fall into this category. So would the careless, superficial, nonspiritual use of literal psychotropic drugs. This family of thoughts is called collectively "druggers."

7) Parts of Mind give Love to objects and "material" things. There is a paradox here: The enlightened cultivates "universal Love," so that she can learn to accept, and ultimately, to love *everything and everyone.* This she does consistently because of her deep, true Love for God, the Creatormind or Dreamer of the cosmos. He/She is all.

****

To love the Dreamer, you must love everything within His/Her dream!

****

But although she wants to love all as Godexpression, she does not want to fall into the trap of "loving" material things *in themselves.* Love is the very greatest gift of the heart. It is the supreme gift. It is not to be cheapened by bestowing it upon mere "things" or "objects" as "material" realities. This leads to the disease of materialism, and to the hell of material masters, rather than the One as Master. So, giving Love to any thing is wrong. These errors are collectively called "Idolaters."

8) Thoughts sometimes originate with, and/or support, illusions and voluntary falsehoods. This includes all thoughts that are lies, fakes, phonies. It includes lying to yourself. It includes charlatanism and chicanery. It includes dissembling and misleading. This family of thoughts also includes all hypnotic illusions, seeing the "common world" through the lens of the "mesmeric trance" of everyday life. So,

368

it includes the whole of *maya,* the great expanse of pseudoreality that mistakes the surrounding dream for reality. Everything, "all around you", is a very sophisticated, internally generated "virtual reality". This very large family of thoughts is collectively called "liars."

This verse has been literalized by the ignorant and is used to support the psychotic and monstrous nightmare myth of an actual pool of fire ("hellfire") for "sinners." But the close of the verse itself proves that the "lake of fire" is symbolic, for it is identified as the "second death." At sometime in their history, these great thought-families were deactivated ("died") and reactivated. So, this time, when they die, it is their "second" and permanent annihilation. These thoughts are not frying and crying; they are dead. In the "fire" of purifying suffering, they are themselves turned into the very essence of fire-- pure energy, which is then available for supporting and creating Lovethoughts.

Verse 9. "And one of the seven angels came out from among those having the seven bowls, full of the seven final plagues, and he spoke with this saying: 'Here I will show you the bride, the lamb's woman.'"

COMM: The return to an earlier symbolic set implies that perhaps the section to come was penned by an earlier hand. Abruptly we are returned to the spiritual ("seven") inner positive Mindelements ("angels"). We are reminded that they carry limited and small thoughtareas ("bowls") and contain spiritual ("seven") challenges and dysfunctional responses ("plagues") to further growth.

Again, the oft-repeated theme of the bride-bridegroom appears as a motif of the Soul's ("woman") Union ("marriage") to surrendermind ("lamb"). This is an echo, and restatement, of the Soul's Union with Spirit, making the "two" one.

Verse 10. "And he bore me off in Spirit upon a great and high mountain, and showed to me the holy city Jerusalem, stepping down out of heaven from God..."

COMM: The mind ascends into the highest realms ("in Spirit"). It is taken to an elevated area created by the renewed hypersensual mind ("mountain").

This seems irrelevant to the previous verse. But it is not. For the last verse spoke of the mystical "marriage." And in 21:2, "new Jerusalem" is presented as "having been prepared as a bride adorned for her man." So, it is the "marriage" motif that creates the continuity between the "lamb" and "Jerusalem."

The "lamb," though, symbolizes the groom, while both the "woman" and "Jerusalem" are the "bride." We can see how absurdly silly is literalization at this point, for we have the spectacle of a sheep marrying a woman, and the even more ridiculous drama of a sheep marrying a whole city! (The symbol of new Jerusalem appears as early as 3:12, where she is "the one stepping down out of heaven from my God.")

Verse 11. "...having the glory of God, the illuminator of it, like a most precious stone, like jasper, being clear like crystal."

COMM: The Jerusalem thoughtcomplex is found deep within the unconscious Mind. For she is here compared to a "jewel." This is pleasant, positive, spiritual altered states. She is found, that is, in the midst of mystical gnosis. This is not a part of mind that you would just stumble across during the day, while taking a walk or going to the store. It is as subtle as a feather. But once you realize it, the Mindarea balloons into an entire city! Then, it is so enormously, immensely powerful that you live "within" it!

But this "stone" is "empty" of color and design. It is just as transparent, still, and colorless as the "empty" mind of gnosis. This is, in fact, with its clarity, exactly what it represents. So, this "Jerusalem" represents the Mind transformed into pure lucidity. It is pristine, empty "crystalmind." It does not impede, by its contents, the perfect Flow of Love. It is what in mysticism is called "stillmind," which I have, in another place, called "crystalmind."

It is the mind in transcendental tranquility, where all conscious thoughts have vanished, all cognitive functions been placed on hold. It is as still, empty, and bright as space. It is this very stillness that permits the still, small "voice of God (Love)" communication with the mind. This is deep meditation, and only in it do you see Jerusalemind.

Verse 12. "She had a wall great and high, with twelve gates, and upon the gates twelve angels. And names were inscribed, which are of the twelve tribes of sons of Israel."

COMM: Crystalmind is not easy to enter. Thoughts and other distractions block entry. It is the sound of a most subtle and quiet flute at the other end of a large auditorium. The "busy-ness" of the business of everyday life and competing thoughts are trumpets, drums, trombones, tubas, and other loud instruments.

We are kept out of crystalmind by barriers ("walls"). These walls are excess thought/analysis and religion without spirituality. The "noise" of the world is not easily silenced. Nor are the walls quickly scaled. For they are intimidating ("great and high").

It requires discipline, tenacity, and practice to reach the state of transparency. In this state, the inner Light of Lovemind can shine through without egoshadows.

Fortunately, the thought-walls are selectively permeable ("gates"). There are a few good ways to bypass all the noise. But only after thoughts have reached cosmic order ("twelve") can the "gates" open. Enlightenment is on its way! Glimpses into or tastes of Lovemind, states that permit entry into Lovemind ("gates") facilitate the inward Journey. But you do not stay there after having entered via a gate.

Those orderly Lovethoughts support spiritual mind ("angels"). These angels promise imminent and immanent enlightenment. Like the gates, they harmonize with celestial order ("twelve").

But also there is a feeling of being snobbishly "special" before God (external religion). Contaminated by superiorism, this is religion stripped of spirituality (Love). This barren wasteland religion is a major barrier between Love and the human mind. This is a valid feeling *only* if it includes everyone else. If it does not, it results in only religious snobbery. It is the awareness that you are a special "chosen one" ("sons of Israel"). Even at this late stage of progress, you must still beware the power of egocontamination. For your false identities from various "roles" ("names") are "inscribed" on the *outside* of the wall. But enlightenment is *inside*.

Verse 13. "From the sunrise, there were three gates, and from the north, three, and from south, three, and from sun setting, three."

COMM: These "gates" represent entry into enlightenment. They take you *inside* "Jerusalemind." The four directions imply the "cross" of infinity, in an equilateral form (all the "arms" being the same length). This is a symbol of the immeasurable and illimitable, of the bottomless cosmos itself. The point at which the arms intersect is

Mind. Cosmos spreads out from Mind, emanates from It, (in "all four directions"). The infinite cosmos reflects the infinite Mind. This Mind is symbolized by the circle of infinity, which, in sacred geometry, often encompasses the equilateral cross.

Like the gates, enlightenment begins with the inner "sunrise." This is a striking and bright symbol for the beginning of interior Lightwisdom as it "dawns" upon the heartmind. Later, the mind creates a circle or closure in inner space by turning to the other directions. This reflects the six-direction blessing of both native American and Hermetic ceremony. Then, the cycle ends with "sunsetting."

But sunset gives birth to sunrise. So, "sunset" can represent darknight phases on the eternal journey, deaths that lead to new births.

It is an infinite system. In it, apparent opposites are connected. In fact, they are causal. This means that a previous state causes another, more enlightened. If John had been simply describing geographic orientation, he would have logically said, "east, south, west, and north." But his description is symbolic. So, he posits "sunrise" as the start of the phase, and "sunset" as the end. Some modern translations do violence to the text, losing this altogether, rendering "sunrise" invalidly merely as "east," and "sunset" simply as "west." This is reductionism, and loses much of the intent. The message is that the enlightenment process must pass through temporal phases, in a logical sequence. What is emphasized is the symbolic "Light" of enlightenment ("sun"). ("Sun" is Lovemind). The psyche, in its everlasting journey through eternity, goes through very slow phases of rediscovering of inner Light, and temporarily losing sight of It.

The equilateral cross here represents the whole Mind. In ancient symbolism, it archetypally represented the whole cosmos, infinity. So, hidden in the symbolism is the equation "Mind=cosmos."

Verse 14. "And the wall of the city rested on twelve foundation stones, and upon them, twelve names of the twelve apostles of the lamb."

COMM: Enlightened Mind rests on cosmic arrangement ("twelve"). It trusts Lovemind to control the cosmos-- in both its "macro" and "micro" forms. So, enlightened mind is freed from the awful "mountain of iron" burden of feeling that it must *always control events*. In all ancient cultures, "twelve" referred to the twelve primal divisions of the heavens. It represents celestial order. This points again towards God or transcendental Mind.

Positive altered states of mind ("foundation stones") lead to the discovery of Unity between mind and Lovemind. The first mere "glimpse" of Lovemind is the foundation of all subsequent spiritual growth. If you don't "see" It, you're not likely to go for It, much less to devote your whole life to the arduous Journey to become absorbed into Its sweet ocean of Light.

That the twelve "apostles" are Jesus' apostles is not stated. Revelation, except for metaphoric examples from history, is a *purely spiritual book*. It is, in fact, a classic of intercultural mystical literature. This means that *it has little to nothing to do with literal history*. So, these ("twelve apostles") are the psychocosmic Mindforces that follow lambmind into complete surrender. They are the "cosmic apostles" that live within everyone. That they are "twelve" is a double symbol: 1) They are arranged according to celestial order or guidance, and 2) they promise ultimate Union with Lovemind.

While your identity as a separatist religious person ("names" of "sons of Israel") identified the barrier ("walls"), your identity as cosmic messenger ("apostles") is the *very foundation* of all spiritual growth.

Verse 15. "And the one speaking with me had a golden measuring reed, so that he could measure the city, its gates, and its wall."

COMM: The enlightened mind is curious about the dimension of cosmic Mind ("city" and "walls"). Human intellect is still active; enlightenment did not strip away thought. It increased consciousness. So, "lower" function (intellect) still survives, but *only as a servant of Lovemind*. While intellect used to be master, or at least, threaten to be, *now Love has become the sole, unquestioned Master of all Mind*. Hu man intellect has dived into the bottomless ocean of Mind, and naturally wants to know exactly what it has gotten into! Although "measuring" is not literal, it does imply some kind of analysis or evaluation.

The mind boosts earthly enlightenment ("golden"). This is the Mind's struggle, in retrospect, to make some sense out of the experience of enlightenment. It seeks to explain, at least to the self, what has happened to the mind and the self. How did they become deeper Mind and deeper Self? How did ego become mind, and mind Soul, and Soul Spirit? This is *the greatest mystery in the cosmos!*

This measurement is a positive process. For what is being measured is not just enlightenment (crystalmind; "city"). The obstacles ("walls") to that highest mystical state are also being analyzed. The Way into deeper Mind ("gates") is also being studied. Both the conscious and unconscious mind become fascinated.

In English, "measure" shares a root with "matter." This is a hint that the human, intellectual mind is involved.

Verse 16. "And the city was lying in the form of a square, its length equal to its breadth. And he measured the city with the reed, [and it was] twelve thousand stadia. Its length, breadth, and height were equal."

COMM: Order and celestial arrangement ("twelve") are everywhere in Jerusalemind. It is enlightened; it shuns chaos. Human engineered Mindproducts ("city") have evolved into active Love. ("Twelve" is used three times, connecting it with the "three" of wholeness or closure. So, order leads to inner healing.)

It can logically be assumed that the city is a cube. But the measurements would also be equal if it were pyramidal in shape, suggested by a few.

The "square" of the city is 144,000,000 units (an obvious amplification of the 144,000 mentioned in 7:4 and 14:1). The 144,000 is the zenith of the enlightened human mind, the totality of its redeemed aspects. It is *all the best within the human mind.* What, then, can this supernumber mean when it is amplified by a thousand?

"Thousand" is earthly wholeness. 144,000,000 ("Jerusalemind") amplifies enlightenment galaxies beyond the human Mind. It is the Lovemind supernaturally realized. The Mind has grown superhuman. It is a Mind as far beyond human comprehension as is the number that symbolizes It. At its zenith, jerusalemind is the Mind grown beyond all human limits, into a breath-taking Mind quite beyond imagination!

Twelve cubed equals 1728. Obviously, literalism, exactly like all other worldender nonsense, fails miserably to explain 1728 chronologically. It is not a date. The "end of the world" did not come then!

So, 1728 must have some other meaning. To discover hidden meanings in numbers, numerologists use the *most simple and basic process in the whole of numerology.* They add up the digits that constitute the whole number, to "reduce" it to a single digit. This is the most direct way of encoding any hidden message. It is also obviously the simplest to decode. If we do that, we add 1+ 7 + 2 + 8. That yields 18. Eighteen in itself has no special numerological significance, but if we do the same process, adding up the digits, with 666, we also arrive at eighteen. This shows a hidden connection or relationship with the "number of the beast" and "New Jerusalem." (This is precisely parallel to the strong numerological connection between 666 and 144,000, i.e., 666 x 6 x6 x6 + 144= 144,000.) It is the same lesson: Lovemind must be reached through lower mind. Lower mind is, in fact, supreme Mind in disguise.

Verse 17. "And he measured its wall [to be] one hundred forty-four cubits, the measure of man, which is of [an] angel."

COMM: Pervasive "twelveness" is all over the place in Jerusalemind: Twelve squared (144) appears yet again. Amazingly, this is the "measure" of "man." 666 was the "number of man" in 13:18. So, again, a dramatic, undeniable link (correlation) between twelve squared and 666 is hidden, embedded in the math.

Could this imply even more? Could it imply a deep but secret *identity* between 666 and 144? It could indeed. This can be verified by another quirky clue in apocalyptic numerology: If the numbers are "reduced" (their numerals added) they are equal! (Reduction is the very simplest and most obvious process in the whole universe of numerological processes.) So, this, although "hidden," is the easiest to "see" and understand.

Here is how it works: To reduce 144, you must add 1+4+4, which is nine. To reduce 666, you must add 6+6+6, which is 18. But since, for reduction to be complete, every number must be "reduced" to a single digit, you must further then add 1+8, which equals nine-- the same as 144! (This also works with 1728.)

Also, to see them as polarized (real opposites) is to slipslide into duality-- the most fundamental error! This is ignorance (illusion). For the deepest gnosis of the cosmos reveals "monism" (the One being the only Reality, without opposite.) The highest nature lies fully, but unknown, within the lowest. And human nature lies within divine nature. The human is within the divine, and the divine within the human!

Lovemind lies at the root of even beastmind. They exist "within" each other. This is the most esoteric and carefully guarded secret of all spiritual arcana and mysticism.

And the word "secret" is not used here simply to be mysterious or alluring, as the word is often misused by selfstyled "occultists." No, historically, mystics have kept this monistic view of Reality deliberately hidden. Why?

Because, in the wrong hands, it can be an explosively dangerous teaching. For it appears to teach the nightmarish fallacy that the "devil" is "God," and that therefore no distinctions between "good" and "evil" as polar opposites is valid. This can be twisted into the *perfect excuse* for every kind of most vile abuse, brutality, or atrocity. It is exactly comparable to our discussion, earlier, of *deliberate* evil and "error" or honest "mistake." Upon such horrific misunderstandings were the Carpocratian illusions based and they were hideously destructive. Without philosophic understanding and sophistication, it can be degenerated to turn all of morality and ethics into a kind of gray goo, where *nothing is right, and nothing wrong.* While it is true that, in monism, good is the *only* reality, and "evil" simply its absence, the worldview does not justify barbarity, murder, sexual promiscuity, theft, or dishonesty. Of course, monism does not teach, validate, or even support, this monstrous insanity.

For the necessary distinction between good and evil is valid in our world. In the spacetime continuum-- the everyday, practical world-- it is absolutely morally and ethically indispensable, even critical, to distinguish between good and evil. This principle is valid in all minds, in every thought, word, and action. It is then crucial to follow the good and expel and reject the evil.

But the abuse of the "secret" of monism would create the most abysmal havoc, evil, confusion, and corruption. *It is potentially the most dangerous teaching in the world!* Monism is the greatest secret in the history of mysticism. Historically, some cap G "Gnostic" and "neo-Gnostic" groups have used this monism to justify nightmarish and ghastly behaviors. In these, beastmind has totally taken over the mind, thoroughly ruining it, and infecting even the Soul. The gnosis of the "allgood" cosmos must never be used to justify indulgence, carelessness, cruelty, or evil.

Verse 18. "And the structure of the wall was jasper, and [of] the city, clean gold like clean glass."

COMM: This is crystalmind. This is "empty" Mind, free of all personal desire. It can be free of even personal thoughts. It is stillmind.

The "walls" that separate the mind from the Lightfilled Mind are but thoughts. (They include overanalysis and Loveless religion.) So, when mind turns away from incessant thinking, the "wall" itself becomes beautifully transparent. The mind "sees" the Light! This occurs when the mind touches stillness, and stops filling itself with barrier-thoughts.

And these are not necessarily evil. *All thoughts* can insulate mind from cosmic Mind. It is not evil, but busy-ness of "overthink," that keeps mind out of Mind. This is crucial: *The average mind is alienated from Lovemind not by voluntary evil, but because it just does not have the time!* Mind also lacks clarity ("jasper") and stillmind (a mind "clean" of distractions/obstacles). Only when so "cleaned" does the mind find enlightenment through the senses ("gold").

The barriers to Lovemind ("walls") are created by only mind. And so, they can be "de-created" by only mind.

So, the wall is not a real barrier at all. *It has no intrinsic, independent existence.* It is psychogenic (mind-created). These mental opacities ("walls") disappear, or become clear, at the moment that we stop actively creating them through "overthink." What creates this barrier is overactivity, continuous analysis, hypercogitation. *The mind was simply never created to work nonstop.*

The lucidity and transparency of the city within (Jerusalemind) is again emphasized: Its earthly enlightened purity ("clean gold") is compared to the purity of crystalmind ("clean glass"). Total transparency is total enlightenment! Only when mind is clear of its own content can Lovemind shine through unimpeded!

Verse 19. "The foundation stones of the city's wall were adorned, each one, with a precious stone. The first was jasper, the second sapphire, the third, chalcedony, the fourth, emerald..."

COMM: Positive altered states ("precious stones") are the "foundation" of all spiritual work. The "walls" are challenges, environmental or interior. They block the Way, as puzzles and/or nemeses that force us to cultivate tenacity. They teach us by preventing our immediate, swift, or easy ascendancy, or access, to higher states. Yet they, with all their hardships, also originate with deepest Mind.

What most stands out about the crystals and gems, besides their beauty and light-reflecting chatoiancy, is their vivid colors.

What system can be used to coordinate the meanings of colors with Mindstates? Fortunately, there is one ancient system readily available. It is the one to which reference has been made before in this study. It could well have been known in the first century by a Christian writer. (Since it originates with the Unconscious, and is archetypal, it is not necessary even to postulate that 'John' did know about it consciously.) This is the chromosystem of the "seven chakras." According to this Mindenergy system, each color represents a Mindfunction along the Way to enlightenment. So, let's "decode" the colors:

1) jasper. It is often a variety of chalcedony that is red, due to ferric content. ("Iron" is also a symbol of inexperienced mind.) So, the gem is bio-energy in interaction with, and supporting, higher Mindfunctions. The "One on the throne" was like jasper (4:3). In that verse, jasper, in its clear state (form), represented infinite Lovenergy. In the present context, it signifies the bio-energy of survival. At one time, early in our spiritual journey, we were all "ruled" by the jasperspectrum Mindforces.

2) Sapphire is a blue variety of corundum. Since it is often dark blue, indigo, midnight blue, or cobalt, its chakra association is with insight. It is the color of the *ajna*, sixth, or brow chakra. So, sapphire represents the awakening of inner vision, inner sight, or insight. In Hebrew writings, "sapphire" usually represents lapis, a mineral with similar coloration. (Chromatologically, lapis and sapphire both represent insight.)

3) Chalcedony-- agate, bloodstone, carnelian, chrysoprase, jasper, and onyx are all varieties of chalcedony. At its most basic definition, it is quartz. So, what these minerals all have in common is their quartz-content. Despite its varieties of manifestation, quartz is itself clear. So, chalcedony represents the ability of mind to cultivate lucidity, or transparency. This mineral also symbolizes the ability of mind, through clarity and bright lucidity, to realize that it is all Mind, playing all roles in the cosmos!

4) Emerald-- a green form of beryl. Emerald described the rainbow around the throne (4:3). It represents archetypally the awakening of Love (fourth chakra) during the enlightenment process.

Verse 20. "... the fifth, sardonyx; the sixth, sardius; the seventh, chrysolite; the eighth, beryl; the ninth, topaz; the tenth, chrysoprase; the eleventh, hyacinth; the twelfth, amethyst."

COMM: 5) Sardonyx is a red and white chalcedony. So, it represents the bionatural forces (red) exposed to the spiritual forces, driving them upward through purity (white).

6) Sardius is red, perhaps carnelian. So, it also represents the primal forces at the beginning of the journey, the transformation of "earth" (hypersensuality) into spiritual energy. The beginning of the journey is arguably the most important step. So, many forms of red mineral are included to imply very basic, indispensable bio-energies. Everything starts with life. You partake of the great Mystery of life through the red-spectrum Mindforces.

7) Chrysolite is yellow. It symbolizes logical, intellectual thinking. It is used to push the energy of Mind "upward" towards spirituality. It is intellect. (This might also have referred to topaz and/or citrine.) But this is not simply intellect. It is intellect under the power of operational transformation by Spirit. For the word originates with the Greek for "gold stone." Recall that "gold" is earthly enlightenment (that obtained through the senses).

8) Beryl is a silver-white metal that is rare. Its color links it irresistibly with the moon. So, it represents the effect of the moon (unconscious Mind). (Compare "pearl"; also compare 6:12; 8:12; 12:1; 21:23.) It also means advances in purity (white).

9) Topaz is, in its ancient common form, yellow-green. So, it symbolizes Mindenergy halfway between the intellectual phase and the awakening of Love. (Compare "greenish yellow".)

10) Chrysoprase is light green. So, it symbolizes Mindenergy at the nascent point, the embryo, of the entry into the Love of infinite Lovemind. This is the beginning of the spiritual path. It represents the spiritual beginner or neophyte, but firmly planted on the Way of Love. She is well on her way.

11) Jacinth or hyacinth is orange-yellow zircon. So, it symbolizes Mindenergy moving from a purely biological, sexual, or selfish nature into the intellect. It is animalmind under human intellectual influence. (Compare "horse.")

12) Amethyst is purple corundum. It symbolizes the mind's having discovered total liberation or full enlightenment.

Verse 21. "And the twelve gates [were] twelve pearls. Each gate was [made] out of one pearl. And the broad way of the city [was] gold, clean as glass, beamed through [by Light]."

COMM: The Way to enlightenment (jerusalemind) is through the Unconscious ("pearl"; compare 17:3; 18:12, 16; compare "moon"). What is emphasized here is the "oneness" between and among various Mindlevels. Each ("gate") was made of "one" pearl. The main path or Way of the jerusalemind is "gold," or earthly enlightenment. It is "clean as glass," symbolizing crystalmind or complete transparency to the unimpeded Lovemind. The Light of Love is allowed to shine from ("beam through") this clear Mind, into both Mind and world.

Verse 22. "And I saw no divine habitation in it, for the Lord God Almighty is its divine habitation, and the lamb."

COMM: There is no reason that there should be a special inner space or Mindarea for the Being of Lovemind to dwell. It is now pervasive, filling the whole Mind. It fills Mind in two ways: As universal Lovemind, and as surrendermind ("lamb"). The two are interwoven, since it is surrender that transforms the conscious mind into the perfect Mirror of Lovemind.

Verse 23. "And the city has no need for the sun, or the moon, so that they might be shining to it. For the glory of God lighted it up, and its lamp was the lamb."

COMM: Jerusalemind has no need for the sun for the same reason that it needs no temple. A world alight with the totality of God, represented in a limited, local way by the "sun," no longer needs that great but limited light. All light, and the Lightsource, is within it. You don't have to shine a bright light onto a bright light. The Mind glows with bright light, and needs no "sun" to give it light. Both the conscious mind ("sun") and Unconscious ("moon") are filled with either the direct or reflected "Lovelight" of Lovemind.

Verse 24. "And the nations will walk about through its light, and the kings of the earth will bear their glory into It."

COMM: After a stormy relationship with Lovemind, the great thought-constellations of hypersensual ("earthly") mind ("nations") are renewed. So are controlling matrix-thoughts ("kings"). These are not destroyed but welcomed into healing transformation. Now, they all serve Love, in peace and bliss. So, the Lovelight now guides the inner "nations," and the "kings" contribute to It the very best of their thoughts ("their glory"). Whatever is good in all these thoughts is ascribed to, and gladly given to, cosmic Lovemind.

Verse 25. "And its gates will surely not be shut up during day. For there is no night there."

COMM: All thoughts that want the Light are welcome, and barriers ("gates") are gone. The "dark" Unconscious (including the subconscious) has now emerged into the light or "day" of conscious awareness. The subconscious can no longer influence your thoughts, speech, or actions, for it has been swallowed up by consciousness (awareness). Habits disappear; so do phobias, and fears of all kinds.

All darkness of ignorance ("night") has also disappeared. The whole Mind is submerged or immersed in Light. It is Light-filled, Light-saturated. It glows, scintillates, shines, radiates; it is brightly dazzling!

Verse 26. "And they will bear the glory and honor of the nations into it."

COMM: At last, the whole Mind functions as One, all in service to Lovemind. All that the mind/Soul has learned, all the beauty and wisdom found in earthlife ("nations") is brought to Lovemind, integrated with It ("into It"). All-- every datum, every understanding, every les-son-- is gladly used to support Lovemind.

Verse 27. "And surely will not enter into It any unholy thing, or anyone doing disgusting things, or liars. Only the ones written in the little book of the life of the lamb [will be there]."

COMM: This enlightened Mind is no place for the "common," to use the Greek term. This is no place for football-scores or Dow-Jones stock market concerns. The focus of holy Mind is not money, business, career, ego, jewelry, sports, house, clothing, or other Love-substitutes. And it is obviously no place for uncleanness, ignorance, violence, or evil ("disgusting things"). Only those thoughts in the memory ("writ-ten" in the "little book") as having completely surrendered ("lamb") to the will of Love will be in jerusalemind (enlightened Mind). Only the good will be enlightened, and the enlightened mind will contain only good.

Chapter 22.

Verse 1. "And he showed to me [a] river of water of life, bright as crystal, going forth out of the throne of God [and] of the lamb."

COMM: The Unconscious thoughtstream ("river of water") is all pure, pristine, stainless. Like original Mind, it is Lightreflecting ("bright") and crystalloid ("as crystal"). Everywhere, it is filled with Lovelight, and shines, shimmers, and glows with compassion and tenderness. The dragons and demons that used to inhabit the subconscious within the Unconscious ("water") are no more. The murky, stinking stagnant pools of the subconscious are now gone, evaporated by Light, replaced by the clear, sparkling sustaining ("life") Mind. This is crystalmind, transparent Mind, stillmind-- the endgoal of the mystic. Love has fully taken over all Mind, and the inner universe is cleansed and pristine. The water of thought flows from the inner control center ("throne"), the rulership of Love. In fact, note: Lovemind and lambmind share one controlcenter ("throne"). Unless the lamb is sitting in God's lap, we must conclude that they are one and the same! For two solid objects cannot occupy the same space at the same time. So, when surrendered, Mind recognizes only one Ruler-- Lovemind. When it fully knows It (in gnosis), it Becomes that cosmic Mind. Its says to Lovemind, "To know You is to become You".

Verse 2. "In the midst of her broad way, and of the river and on both [its] sides, trees of life produce twelve fruits, according to each month. [They] give back their fruit, into the curing of the nations."

COMM: This makes no sense if taken literally. If so, the main street must be flooded, for the "river" and the "broad way" of gold share a common center. The Way ("broad way") is the Center (unconscious "water")! The real Center is, of course, the Center of the Soul, or Spirit. It is "nuclear" Mind, Coremind, (Lovemind.)

Action-potentials ("trees") are analogous to the "tree of life" in the parallel Genesis-allegory. In Revelation 2:7, in fact, "the tree of life" is itself directly mentioned. It is said to be "in the paradise of God." (Compare tree-symbolism of 6:13; 7:1, 3; 8:7; 9:4; 11:4.)

The "twelve fruits" are food or inner nourishment. They are also the results of thoughtpatterns-- thoughts turned into action! They: 1) create and reflect celestial order ("twelve"), and 2) move the mind towards increased enlightenment. (That is why they are "twelve"). They are the "fruit of the Spirit," including most delicious Love, joy, and peace. (Ga 5:22)

They exhaust the double symbolism of twelve: 1) the passage through heavy duality into wholeness (2 x 2 x 3), and 2) they are also the results of celestial order.

The "fruit" is produced by inner Mind. It blossoms to support continued spiritual growth (all thoughts in jerusalemind). That is why the large aggregates or constellations of thoughts ("nations") are healed ("cured") by this sustenance.

Of what are they "cured"? Of many and various disfunctions/disorientations ("plagues") received during the Journey. Of the basic destructive illusion of separation ("dualism"). This is the diseased belief that any mind can exist apart from the divine Mind instead of as a part of It.

They turn thought into action ("produce... fruit") regularly ("each month"). Here, the connection of the "twelve" with time is reminiscent of the principles of astropsychology. (In this arcane art, twelve represents the cosmos as it marches through time.)

Verse 3. "And everything cursed will be cursed no longer. And the throne of God and the lamb will be in her. And his slaves will give him holy service"

COMM: A couple of unreliable, "mod" translations-- actually, no more than paraphrases-- have taken unwarranted liberties with this text. They have implied that this "put down" (original Greek phrase for "curse") came from God. But the "cursed" condition was a selfcondemnation, a selfgenerated curse. Curses cannot originate with Lovemind. For Its job description is "love plus nothing." It is simply not within either the desire or capacity of Love to curse. That is precisely why, when Love or God fills all Mind, here, *all curses disappear!*

Jerusalemind knows that any "curse" was an illusion. Any "curse" is simply a misinterpretation. Mind contains no elements, no traces, no hint, of any curse. All Mind has been "good Mind" from the beginning. It has all, and always, been God!

The complete control ("throne") of Lovemind will be "in her." It is ensconced within "Jerusalemind," or deepest Mind. That it is a shared throne implies how unified are God and surrendermind: They are so fused, melded, merged, and interidentified that the distinction between them is arbitrary at best. It is wrong, at worst. Here, any division evanesces and vanishes! The whole Mind is energized to give its very best ("holy service") to Love.

Verse 4. "And they will see His face and His name upon their foreheads."

COMM: This is complete Unity with Lovemind. His outward appearance ("face") and his identity ("name") are both embraced finally by a reluctant and somewhat skeptical intellect ("foreheads.")

Verse 5. "And there will be no more night. And they have no need of [the] light of [a] lamp, or of the sun. For the Lord God will shed light upon them. And they will reign into the ages of the ages."

COMM: This restates the state of "intrinsic Light" already discussed. Lovemind, the Source of all inner Light, replaces any other lightsource. The thoughts of jerusalemind, Lightmind, now take over the whole mind. It pervades every part, area, aspect, and level ("ages"). Love rules!

Verse 6. "And he said to me, 'These words are faithful and true. And the Lord God of the spirits of prophets sent his angel to show his slaves what is bound to occur, and quickly...'"

COMM: Lovemind ("God") is not interested in the "external, material" world. He/She has no interest in illusions, in the Mindworld or dreamworld, unless they impact spiritually. For Lovemind's *only interest* is the welfare of the Soul and related spiritual matters ("of spirits"). That is why Mind is impelled to reveal what will happen to your mind in its future enlightenment Journey ("of prophets").

All of Revelation is "prophecy." Although we are accustomed to thinking of "prophecy" as referring to calendars and nations, it can equally apply to the prediction of states of Mind. John could not possibly have been writing about the twenty-first century. For he says here that these things will occur without hesitation ("quickly"). Indeed, on the very day that he received Revelation, he had a genuine enlightenment-experience of his own! (We know this, because he wrote about his own vision as Revelation.)

Verse 7. " 'And look! I am coming quickly! Happy is the one who observes the words of the prophecy of this little book.' "

COMM: Lovemind says that He/She is arriving ("coming"). Paradoxically, this occurs only when *you* "come" to Lovemind! But when you do, It reacts without pause ("coming quickly"). When God returns as the "second coming"-- more accurately, "second Presence"-- of Christ, He/She will come to some minds at one time, and others later. Each mind decides when it is ready for the "inner Presence" of God in Christ.

God comes to the heart. He/She does not come, like a superalien, from outer space. He/She emerges from the deepest inner Mind, His/Her temple. For that is where He/She has always lived.

Also, God does not literally have to "come," for He/She is *already and always within the deep Mind.* No, His/Her "second Presence" is just a symbolic way of saying that mind fully awakens to His/Her Presence. He/She declares that the reward is bliss ("Happy") for the aware. Anyone who is exposed to ("reads") and understands ("observes") is blessed. To get this blessing of blissing, the Mind must know the contents of Revelation-- the changes that the Mind can expect during its long inner voyage. (Again, this is described as "prophecy.") To do this, Mind will have to compare the information with that already in memory ("little book.")

Verse 8. "And I, John, [was] the one looking at and hearing these things. And when I heard and saw, I fell to worship before the feet of the angel. [He was] the one showing these things to me."

COMM: The mind (John) impulsively feels an urgent desire to worship the deeper parts of itself (probably, the Soul). 'John' has already been corrected once for "worship" of the "angel" of his deeper self. But he is overwhelmed by the dazzling power and wisdom. He gets the same response again:

Verse 9. "And he says to me, 'Don't you see? Don't do that! I am [just] a fellow slave, of you and of your brothers, of the prophets, and of those observing the Words of this little book. Give your worship to God.'"

COMM: This is exactly the same response that mind (John) received before when he was impressed by the deeper Self, to the point of adoration. It is a "sin," or disastrous error, to give adoration to any being, leader, teacher, minister, pastor, priest, elder, guru, extradimensional, extraterrestrial, channeler, or angel. It is equally wrong to worship your own mind! The only valid and allowable, acceptable worship is that reserved for Lovemind (Coremind, cosmic Unconscious) alone. If this is not carefully observed, we might fall into the catastrophic mistake of idolatry. So, the enlightened recognizes no human being as her leader. She acknowledges no human "Lord." She respects all, takes advice from all, even admires some. But she will never give worshipful attention or adoration to anyone. Even angels are presented as "slaves."

Verse 10. "And he says to me, 'You should not seal the words of the prophecy of this little book, for the chosen time is near.'"

COMM: This book, like the rest of the whole genre of all spiritual literature, is not to be locked and sealed away. Its message is not to be "sealed" in the unconscious Mind. The selected time for enlightenment ("chosen time") for any one individual might occur at any second. So, this is a practical message. It applies to everyone. Revelation's message ("prophecy") is to be shared on a conscious (including intellectual) level with all. So, please feel free to share this information, this book, with anyone and everyone! Order copies from the author, who will special-order them at his wholesale price, and give copies to members of congregations and/or classes, at that same price. *This book was not written for profit.* Send the book to everyone about whom you care! Please feel free to audiotape limited sections! As long as you give simple acknowledgment and do not try to practice the sin and crime of plagiarism, freely share these insights! Order from: rmfrancis@juno.com. This permission, if you play by the rules, overrides any formal copyright. Please feel free to share this outlook in letters, sermons, and conversation. (You may even photocopy up to five pages.)

Verse 11. "Let the one doing unrighteously continue to do unrighteously, and let the filthy one continue to do filth, let the righteous continue to do righteousness, and let the holy one continue to be made holy."

COMM: At the fullest apex of enlightenment, there is no real evil within the whole Mind, including the Unconscious. This means that conceptual "evil" has disappeared also from the cosmos. (Absolutely real "evil" never existed at all.) This is the full zenith of Revelation, when it is purest Lovemind that is revealed to be the whole cosmos.

The "angel" describes a false apparent dualism between the "righteous" and the "unrighteous." This "split" of duality exists only in the relative (spacetime) world and the lower mind. This is a basic clue: We have now left the absolute perfection of perfect Mindmeld or Mindfusion with Lovemind. The angel is now talking about the small mind, the conscious mind. So, he is returning to a discussion with John about the pre-enlightenment mind. (Revelation can be timeless, outside of sequentiality.)

To repeat: This duality does not exist at all in timeless Mind-- either in intrinsic God (Lovemind) or in the enlightened Soul, one with Lovemind. It is finally and fully resolved only in the One.

The angel has returned, then, to the present, and is talking about our present minds, usually unenlightened. It might be telling the mind, "Trust God. God will change every part of your mind at its proper and appointed time. Let ignorant parts of your Mind find the Way out of their ignorance. Let it be! This is the only way that you can grow truly wise, strong, and independent. Do not try to force parts of your Mind to change before their time. And their proper time will be only when your Soul decides. Don't try to force things. God is still in charge." Thus, the mind, when beholding evil, is to take a Taoist attitude of relaxed Flowing. It is to embrace a gnostic/mystic attitude. It is to deny the illusion of real or permanent evil. It is to deny evil absolute reality.

Verse 12. "'Look! I am coming quickly! And My reward, within myself, is to give back to each one according to his work.'"

COMM: The highest nature or Lovenature, is not going to drag on slowly. This is the third time in this chapter that speedy action has been promised! It is not going to simmer or incubate forever. When the mind is ready and right, enlightenment will explode into it! When the conscious mind is ready, Lovelight is going to spring forth into full awareness. When the time is right, it appears "quickly." The interior Mind-nature of all Revelation is hinted at in the wording of the ancient Greek text, where it says, "the reward of me with me..." This is all Mind dancing with mind, the Self with the self, the Actor with many masks, roles, and disguises. The Soul is certain, in the long run, to implement the law of karma, and with it, the joyful, blissful Law of Love/enlightenment!

Verse 13. " 'I [am] the alpha and the omega, the first and the last, the beginning and the end.'"

COMM: All arises from Lovemind. It was where every Soul originated, and to It every Soul must return. The cosmos itself originated in Lovemind and, at its final end, will all have become the lovemind. God, the Author of all, will at the time of the endgoal of the psyche, be "all in all."

Verse 14. " 'Happy [are] those washing their robes, so as to have authority upon the tree of life. To the gates, they might enter into the city.'"

COMM: The enlightened have found the Way back to the "garden of Pleasure" ("Eden") in the heart. They have taken of the "tree of life." This undoes all the damage of "original sin." "Original sin" turns out to be "original forgiveness." This was dualism, the "knowledge of good and evil." The enlightened know all things to be "very good." For God (Lovemind) makes them. This is how the enlightened return to the inner garden with command ("authority") over their actions ("tree"). They also enter the enlightened human condition ("city") of full enlightenment (jerusalemind).

Verse 15. "Outside are the dogs, druggers, fornicators, murderers, idolaters, and everyone liking and doing [a] lie."

COMM: "Outside" of jerusalemind are all thoughts of evil or ignorance: 1) subhuman thoughts ("dogs"); 2) severe distortions ("druggers"); 3) Love-betrayal ("fornicators"); 4) thought-killing thoughts and ideas ("murderers"); 5) thoughts that define God as images or beings other than cosmic Love ("idolaters"); and 6) those who love and cling to illusion ("liking and doing [a] lie").

In the sweet Unitive event, still future in this "retroverse," only Jerusalemind will exist. There will be only sad, regrettable, somewhat demented but deleted memories from animalmind. But the angel is again bringing the conscious mind to a jolting reality: Now is reality. We must deal with the world, and the mind, of now. And at this moment, all these corruptions and imperfections continually threaten purity of Mind. Despite the perfect glimpse of purest freedom and joy given in the previous verses, the "real world" of inner Mind still contains a plethora of imperfections. Of these, we must be both aware and mindful.

Verse 16. "'I, Jesus, sent My angel to testify to you about these things, upon the ekklesias. I am the root and offspring of David, the bright star that belongs to morning.'"

COMM: Spirit incarnated in humanform ("Jesus") is the Origin of spirituality ("sent My angel"). This message was designed specifically to reach all the most sacred aspects of Mind ("the ekklesias").

In Revelation, John represents the mind. His name, and "David," both mean "beloved." So, both "John" and "David" represent your conscious mind, so beloved by the cosmic Mind. "Jesus" identifies himself as the Origin ("root") of the mind. He exists for you because of your knowledge (gnosis) of him ("offspring").

This "Godmind in humanform" is also its "offspring." For the conscious mind must discover Spirit before It can exist. So, God as Mind is Source of all; God in flesh is the product of Mind.

Jesus, as Spirit-flesh blend, is the nascent light just beginning to dawn in the heart ("star of the morning"). For human beings are not very enlightened beings. A stint in the human form, indeed, is like a visit to preschool or kindergarten. But at the very beginning of the dawn of the Lovelight of the Mind, we awaken to the fact that Spirit-flesh is also our own truest nature. We "see Jesus" at the dawn. We are also, not animals, but Spirit-beings on a voyage through, a visit to, the earth.

Verse 17. "And the Spirit and the bride are saying, 'Come!' And anyone who hears, let him say, 'Come!' And let the one thirsting come, and let him who is willing take [the] water of life as a free gift."

COMM: Here is the recurring motif of the Spirit and the "bride." They are joined in the Way of Union as "husband and wife." They, as Spirit and Soul, both work together for the successful "second Presence" ("coming") of Christ. This occurs invisibly, in the personal heart, at the moment of enlightenment. (Or, more literally, the mind "comes" to the Christ.) But the effect is the same.

Those who read these words ("anyone who hears") are being called to awaken. They need to be aware that these words were written so that the mind could be knowledgeably open to the "second coming" of Christ.

The "coming" of Christ is actually the coming of the person to Christ. So, the text continues to invite those who long for Union ("the one thirsting") to know the Presence ("come"). Only she who wills what Love wills ("who is willing") can take life's waters. This is the surrendermind that has given up all personal will to serve Love. She has sacrificed, gladly, all personal desires. All grasping, clinging, and craving have disappeared into fully satisfied Mind.

Love's life-giving, lifenhancing joy is a result of cosmic Love ("free gift"). It is of grace, or divine Love, not earned.

Verse 18. "I give testimony to everyone who hears the words of this little book of prophecy. If anyone should ever add to them, God will add to him the plagues written in this little book."

COMM: Through mind (John) the things of God are revealed ("testified"). All parts of Mind are able to understand ("hear") the words of the message ("prophecy"). If anyone adds to the outline of the changes described in the "prophecy," she will earn the disapproval of deepest Mind. She will suffer from the disturbing, painful dysfunctions ("plagues") described in this book.

But are not these "plagues" a part of the growth-cycle? Are they not inevitable when the natural mind moves towards spiritual mind? Why, then, are the "plagues" described as if they were punishment?

A couple of answers are feasible: This part of the scroll could have been added by a later writer, who knew that the work was sacred. He, believing in a condemning God, and wanting to preserve His sacred Word, did not want any other scribe making alterations or emendations to the text. This practice, which strikes us as dishonest, even dishonorable, was taken for granted as a natural matter of course, by first-century Christians. They wrote, in fact, an entire genre or body of work called the "pseudepigrapha," because claims were made *in all the books of this body* to have been written by great spiritual teachers of the past!

Everyone knew that this was a lie! Those books were *not* written by famous teachers. But Christians thought nothing of this technical lie, if it could help others.

When an early Christian received a Gospel or Epistle, he (this distortion was almost always by men) no doubt had *exactly the same attitude*. Especially if it were a complex document, and he "knew" what the author "really meant," he would not hesitate to *add his own original thoughts* to the manuscript. He did *nothing* to indicate that he had made any alterations in the text, and the next person to get a hold of it assumed that it was all written by one author.

Despite these scary warnings, textual shifts indicate that something similar happened with even Revelation. Both content and style shift radically from time to time. It is obvious that, during the twenty centuries that this ancient text has been carelessly passed around, and edited more than once, the writings of several authors appear here. They all claim to be "John." This was exactly the scenario that so terrified one of these scribes. Paradoxically, he was doing precisely what he never wanted anyone else ever to do-- adding to the text! But, of course, that was okay, because he was "defending" it!

As the superstitious always do, he resorted to fear-- almost the equivalent of a curse. Indeed, an amazing number of people who have studied Revelation as a chronodocument or "prophecy" about the literal earth, have gone off the deep end.

Another possibility is that the genuine mystical writer wanted no one to add to anything that he had written. (It appears that others did so anyway.) But this explanation is less likely. For if the book of Revelation was written by an enlightened mystic, he would have been fully aware that God does not use curses or threats, or indeed even punishment, to create obedience. He/She motivates only through Love.

Verse 19. "And if anyone should ever take off from the words of the little book of this prophecy, God will take off his part from the tree of life and from the holy city, from the things having been written in this little book."

COMM· This is a continuation of the same mysterious threat, based on the prescient fear that this book would be misinterpreted-- which it has been, hundreds of times.

Verse 20. "The one giving testimony of these things is saying, 'Yes, I am coming quickly.' Amen. Come, Lord Jesus!"

COMM: Again, for the fourth time in this chapter, the Christ ("Jesus") promises not to move slowly ("come quickly"). The conscious mind, eager, can hardly wait, and invites the Christ into the heart.

Verse 21. "The grace of the Lord Jesus Christ [be] with the holy."

COMM: Revelation ends with the brightest note imaginable, reminding us that the cosmos, and all goodness within it, originate with Love, or "grace." So do salvation, happiness, and enlightenment. In fact, the Enlightenment Tradition teaches that *all in the cosmos, all the cosmos, is none other than God!* The egomind cannot validly take credit for anything. For all credit must go to the Christspirit, and thus, to Lovemind.

REVELATION: GLOSSARY

Abaddon-- a strong spiritual force whose function is to obliterate subconscious materials and memories. (See "Apollyon.")

absinthe--apparent bitterness ("wormwood") that leads to ultimate enlightenment. Also, the darknight of the Soul.

age-- level or area of Mind.

ages of the ages-- within every level or area of Mind; pervasive of Mind, penetrating and existing in all "places" and "spaces" in both the conscious and Unconscious aspects of Mind.

alive-- active, creating effects, in either the conscious or the Unconscious Mind.

Almighty-- one of the titles of the Infinite, Immeasurable, and Illimitable; Coremind; Lovemind; Spirit; God; emphasizes Power.

Alpha-- the beginning-state of the inward explorer; beginner's mind.

Altar--Mindareas and thoughtgroups that support surrendermind ("lamb"). Also, synonym for "surrendermind".

amen-- expression of agreement and mental resonance. It can express the perfect synergy or symmetry between divine Mind and Its expressions.

amethyst-- Full enlightenment.

angel-- a powerful, positive, coherent, communicative spiritual Unconscious Mindforce. In 1:20, it is symbolically equivalent to "star." (Compare that.) This is because an angel brings Lovelight into the conscious and subconscious.

Angel of the altar-- the part of mind that draws meaning, and learns lessons, from purifying suffering ("fire"), or from surrender.

angel of the waters-- the spiritual and Unconscious power in control of forming thoughtfeelings and thoughtideas in the Unconscious.

anger-- an evaluation of (possibly immediate or sudden) displeasure. Disapproval.

Antipas--the collection of thoughtideas that recognize that God is not a literal "father in the sky." These all deny that God is a cultural artifact, and so deny the validity or truth of the godimage of the ancients in the form of their local tribal deity, Jehovah, who was a wargod.

Apollyon-- a tremendous spiritual force whose mission is to destroy memories in the subconscious. This is a Greek name, but the Hebrew equivalent was Abaddon. (See that)

apostles--thought-complexes (ideas) created by Love (God), chosen to serve wisdom. They are sent forth into the world; they are teachings of Love, peace, wisdom, and holiness (wholeness, healing).

archaic serpent-- probably the serpent in the ancient Eden allegory, which represented, not the devil, but free will detached and broken away from the will of Lovemind. Symbolized in early Christianity by the *auroboros*, the serpent-ring, the "gate of Light," swallowing its own tail; only when free will uses itself to give itself away does it fulfill its final purpose.

ark of covenant-- misinterpretation of the nature of God, understanding God to be male, and/or an exclusive cultural or religious "possession."

Armageddon-- major interior conflict between the forces of Lovemind and anti-agapic elements, but *not* the final battle.

armies-- large groups of thoughts cooperating with each other to conflict with other thoughtgroups.

Artificer-- artistic inspiration. The art of consciously creating or molding thoughts. Also, talent or ability.

Asher-- all blessed thoughts, made so by Love.

Asia-- the art of living according to the great spiritual teachings and mystic masters of the East, who emphasized introspection and Selfknowing.

authority--the power to regulate, influence, and control thoughts and thoughtgroups, commanding them.

Avenge-- to compensate, to create balance or harmony among conflicting areas of Mind.

Awake-- conscious or cognitive. Also, alert or aware.

Babylon the great-- the biosexdrive devoid of Love.

Bad men-- undesirable, destructive, intellectual human thoughts in service of fear.

Baalim--the mind's collection of antiagapic (counter-Love) thoughts and thought-groups, victimized by superstition, hence, by illusion.

Baalim-Balak complex-- the totality of all thoughts, thoughtgroups, and Mindareas that live in illusion.

Balak-- the mind's collection of ideas that anything other than Love is supreme, or of ultimate value.

Bear-- slow, uncertain progress of the mind along a spiritual path.

"beating themselves"-- selfinjury, or pain, selfinflicted.

bed-- rest for the Mind; a rest period.

behind--in the language of archetypal spatiality, coming from the subconscious or Unconscious.

Benjamin--all thoughts and thoughtgroups that recognize the son/daughterhood of the human mind relative to Lovemind.

beryl-- those aspects or parts of the Unconscious (altered states) involved in purity.

bimartyrian (bimind)- all parts of Mind that receive some direction from Lovemind, but still are locked in the ignorance of dualism. It obeys the will of Love, at times, but imperfectly. At other times, it might serve lower mind. It is a bridge between the Unconscious and conscious. It is an educational part of Mind, an instructor.

Bimind-- see "bimartyrian mind."

birds-- animalthoughts with amazing spiritual potential.

Bitter-- creating destabilization within, and temporary conflict.

black-- darkness, absence of spiritual Light; thus, ignorance. Also, the darknight of the Soul.

blamer-- one of the potentially positive roles of dragonmind, as a selfaware aspect of the correcting conscience.

blessing-- fullest approval of Self or selfimage.

blind-- lacking spiritual insight. Spiritually lost, unable to perceive spiritual Reality within the Mind.

blood-- death of a thought or thoughtgroup.

Boat-- consciously constructed Mindconstruct, supported by the Unconscious ("sea"; "water").

body-- bionatural mind. (Compare "earth.")

book-- section of memory, either conscious or Unconscious.

book, little-- memory of the conscious mind.

book of life-- timeless life drawn from cosmic memory or the cosmic Mind.

bound--restrained and/or controlled by a more powerful thought-constellation.

bow-- mindforce used against other mindfactors or thoughtgroups, polarized and opposed as "enemies." (Compare "war.")

bowl-- a small, limited section of Mind.

breast-- area of the heart, thus, Love from the heart; fourth *chakra*.

Bride-- the individual Soul, as it unites with Spirit.

Bridegroom-- Spirit or Lovemind, as it unites with Soul.

bridle-- human (intellectual) control of the animalnature or animalmind.

Bright things-- attractions of the senses.

broad way-- inner "information highway"; the complex of datatransportsystems of the Mind.

brother-- any thought or thoughtgroup that shares spiritual origin ("Father/Mother") with any other.

bull--strength and tenacity. Also, taurus.

burden-- too much mental input; overwhelming thought or analysis.

Burned down-- dissolved or destroyed.

Burning--purifying suffering that destroys a thought or thoughtgroup, recycling its energy into Mind.

Burning heat--selfcreated "hells," "purgatories" of suffering that purify the mind.

Buy-- to exchange or invest timenergy in order to assimilate a Mindcomponent.

buy and sell-- transference of thoughts or thought-energy in support of various mindstructures (feelings, ideas, etc.) Also, shifting thoughts from supporting one idea to supporting another.

captivity-- the state in which mind moves from deeper levels of the Unconscious into the more shallow and stifling subconscious.

cave-- deeply hidden parts of the Unconscious, including the subconscious.

Cavity-- the mind, empty of personal will.

Censor--the contemplative or still mind.

chain-- restrictive thoughtstructure; selfrestriction. Also suppression or repression.

chalcedony-- Lovemind, appearing in a wide variety or spectrum of roles, masks, and disguises.

children-- independent, but undeveloped, thoughts, thoughtgroups, or ideas.

chrysolite-- logical, intellectual thought, under spiritual Power.

Chrysoprase-- the awakening of nascent Love.

Church-- thoughtgroups dedicated and devoted to the service of Love or Lovemind. (See "ecclesia"; compare "lampstand.")

cinnamon-- pleasant thoughtfeelings generated by the senses.

circle-- The unlimited and illimitable cosmos; infinity; perfection; closure and completeness.

City-- complex collection of human (intellectually organized) thoughtstructures and thoughtconstructs, given design by conscious ordering and arrangement.

clay-- the very undeveloped state of mind that exists even before the spiritual journey inward begins. Lower, bionatural Mindphase, lower than "iron." (See that, "copper," and "gold.") (Compare "stone.")

cloud-- mindfactors that obscure inner vision; also, the conjoining of elemental air (intelligence, or Spirit) with water (Unconscious or intuition). Also, any mindfactors or mindprocesses that obscure the clarity of interior vision.

Cluster-- group of related thoughts; as grapes, tending towards spirituality or Communion.

Coaches-- interior thought-transport mechanisms, used to ferry thoughts from one idea to another. (Compare "broad way" and "traveling merchants.")

cold/hot--the ability of the mind to make crystalclear decisions and fully to support either the Reality of good or the illusion of "evil."

come-- the heartmind comes to Christ (Lovemind,) or Christ comes to the heartmind.

conquer-- to overcome or vanquish any part of the lower nature or darkness (ignorance).

copper-- Transitional state of Mind between spiritual "toddlermind" ("iron"; see that) and full earthly enlightenment ("gold"; see that). Also, erotic or sexual activity disguised as Love; this is counterfeit or incomplete "love."

Corruption-- enslavement to illusion (dualism).

countenance-- the way that Mindsegments appear or look to others.

courtyard-- a collective name for those layers of Mind just "above" or right outside of Coremind (Lovemind). Thus, the very deep collective Unconscious. (See "Chart of Mind".)

cowards-- phobias.

create-- the function of Mind in dreaming up anything, anyone, or any condition as reality.

creature-- animalthought; thoughtfeeling of lower bionature.

crowd-- the totality of Mind not included in other symbols.

Crown-- the power of control or influence over thoughts or thoughtgroups.

crown of life-- the power of control that results from the perfect surrender to being controlled by perfect Lovemind, and thus, the state of having found timeless life.

cup-- a very tiny area of Mind. (Compare "bowl.")

cured-- the final overcoming of illusion (dualism, separation). The complete conquest of mental disfunctions/disorientations ("plagues").

Curse-- selfcondemnation.

David-- the conscious mind; symbolic equivalent of "John" ("beloved").

day-- time-period, relatively short.

dead-- deactivated; Also "buried," latent, or dormant in the subconscious or Unconscious.

Dead in the Lord-- the totality of Lovethoughts in the Unconscious.

death-- deactivation of a thought or thoughtgroup, permanent or temporary. Also, below the threshold or horizon of conscious perception or access.

Demon-- negative subconscious or Unconscious force based in fear; "evil" Mindforce. Examples of common demons are unrestrained greed, lust, and pride.

Desolate-- dry, unproductive, but nourishing, condition of mind that occurs during the darknight.

destruction-- can mean merely the state of being sent to the subconscious mind. (Compare "death.")

devil-- fearmind; the mind in abject slavery to fear. (Compare "dragon," "fearmind," and "satanmind.")

diadem-- authority (see that) over thoughts or thoughtgroups.

discipline-- Mindcorrections made by deeper Mind.

disgusting--thoughts that pursue antiagapic aims and that harmed life.

distance-- psychological dissociation or inner "distancing."

divine habitation-- the Coremind, the deepest level of the Unconscious in which Lovemind dwells; Coremind or Lovemind Itself.

dogs-- unclean, subhuman thoughts or thoughtfeelings.

door-- the Soul as area between mind and Lovemind; inner passage to a new Mindarea. (Compare "gate.") Also, inner Christspirit.

double-- having to do with the basic illusion of dualism or separation from cosmic Mind.

dragon-- as "serpent" (see that) equivalent to free will. But in the service of fear, fearmind or satanmind. (See those.)

drug-- invalid, or even destructive, creation of an unhelpful or inappropriate altered state of consciousness, through sorcery, or with literal drugs.

druggers--thoughts that lead to confusion, disorientation, and illusion/delusion.

drunk-- confused; disoriented.

Dust-- lower nature.

eagle-- far-seeing wisdom.

ear-- the ability to absorb ideas mentally with understanding.

earth-- hypersensual mind; all parts of the psyche controlled, influenced, or dominated by the senses or biology; biomind or bionature; bodymind.

eat-- to assimilate into a thoughtgroup or Mindarea. In Greek texts, "eating down" means assimilating into a subconscious area of mind.

ecclesia (Greek, *ekklesia*)-- thoughtgroups dedicated and devoted to the service of Love or Lovemind. The most holy and sacred thought-collections or -aggregates, designed for worship of Love through acts of Love. (Compare "lampstand.")

Egypt-- a state of limitation, creating misery.

emerald-- state of perfect mental clarity, permitting the transmission of pure, unimpeded Love. Crystalline (clearmind, stillmind transmitter of Lovelight. Thus, Love transmitted from divine or cosmic Mind.)

endurance-- tenacity developed by the mind, allowing it not to waver when it comes to spiritual principles.

engraving-- behaviors or thoughts that show that the "wild beast" (see that) is their "owner," master, or controller.

Ephesus-- personal desire-structure which can block or eclipse Lovemind.

Euphrates-- ("fruitful") an Unconscious thoughtstream (leading to ideas or concepts) which makes practical and creative action possible. (Compare "river" and "tree".)

executed-- perished with pain and violence.

Exotic spices-- interesting, exotic thoughts

eye-- inner vision, or the understanding that accompanies it. In 4:6, eyes=spirits. (See "spirits.")

eye-salve-- thoughts or thoughtgroups that heal the mind's capacity for insight, producing, supporting, and enhancing wisdom.

face--the self as viewed or interpreted by others

faithful-- accurate; loyal and obedient to the direction of Love. Absolute trust in Lovemind.

Faithful, the-- collectively, all parts of mind that exercise simple, acognitive, trusting faith, imitating flowers, birds, and nursing infants.

"faith of Jesus"--through gnosis, awareness that God (Love) is taking care of every event in the cosmos. Here, perfect faith=perfect relaxation.

Fall (at the feet, or in sight, of)-- an attempt to worship or adore.

False prophet-- all parts of Mind (thoughts, ideas) that claim the wisdom of sacred things, but are fraudulent, fakes and phonies. (Compare "idols.")

Father-- Love in Its aspect of caring for the personal mind, and in maintaining nature and various inner natures. The *yang* component of the Infinite, emphasizing order and reason.

fatty foods-- appetites of ego.

fear-- reverential awe.

Fearmind-- the mind in total, abject slavery to fear; satanmind. (See that.)

feet-- progress or inner movement along a "path." (Compare "left foot" and "right foot.")

fiery-red-- suffering/pain that purifies through pushing up the Mindforce of the first *chakra*. (Compare "red.") So, this is bio-energy that is going to be transformed first into mental, then spiritual, energy or Lovenergy.

fig--ideas and understandings, with the potential to become actions, but only partly formed.

fine flour-- bionatural microthoughts, in large groupings, used to discover the Christnature within.

fire-- any experience of intense pain, suffering, or loss that produces/promotes interior growth/development.

first and last-- the state of the Coremind or Lovemind, which is present at the first hints of spirituality (deeper Mind, the call to Love), and also present and manifest as the final Union with perfect Mind.

firstborn-- thoughts that arise first in any sequence of progress.

first earth--condition/state in which the senses are cruelly dominant, and spirituality blocked.

first heaven-- Lovemind (the deepest Unconscious), not accessible to the conscious mind, and filling only parts of Mind.

Five-- human nature (five senses, fingers, toes, extensions from the trunk, etc.)

flame-- purifying but painful experience. If through the eyes, a painful, purifying sensual experience, of insight.

flesh-- the lower nature or mind; a lower, inaccurate worldview. Illusory interpretation of reality.

Flautists-- thoughts that create or support sweet states of mind.

foot-- see "feet."

forehead-- intellect.

fornication-- betrayal, usually voluntary, of Love.

fornicators-- thoughts that betray Love.

forty-two-- the story of the progress of Mind, through duality, then wholeness, then spirituality and completion (2x3x7), analogous to the states iron-copper-gold. (See that)

foundation-stones-- higher altered states in which Lovemind is discovered or touched.

four living creatures-- God expressed as world or cosmos; Lovemind in emanation, analogous to the four directions of the ancient cosmos (equilateral cross). Also, insight or understanding (compare "eyes") intrinsic to the divine nature or Mind.

Fountains of waters-- human-engineered thoughtstructures (ideas) meant to contain and influence Unconscious wisdom. (See "water.")

frankincense-- Mindgifts given to, and then by, the Christspirit.

free gift-- saved from ignorance and lower nature by Love, not by learning or works; grace.

free man-- a thought that does not serve a coherently organized idea. (Contrast with "slaves.")

frog-- harmful subconscious elements of animalmind. (Compare "demons" and "plagues.")

full stock-- total contents of the mind; also possible mental overload.

furnace-- intensely purifying Mindarea that learns and grows through pain and suffering. (Compare "fire.")

Gad--the Mind's collection of thoughtfeelings that recognize blessings.

garment-- selfimage or selfconcept, including selfpresentation. (Compare "robe")

garment, white-- intrinsic purity, reflected in selfimage.

gates-- mental conditions/states that permit glimpses or tastes of Union with Coremind (Lovemind). Also, those thoughts that bring you into Lovemind.

gift-- quantity of positive thoughtfeeling.

girdle--thoughtfeelings and thoughtideas that protect and bring light to the emotionature or "heart." Also, possibly, transformation of the poetic "heart" by earthbased enlightenment. (Compare "gold.")

"give God glory"-- to recognize and acknowledge cosmic Mind as the Source of all good, and, ultimately, of all.

Given-- bestowed by cosmic Mind (Lovemind).

glassy-- descriptive of the mind possessing mystical "transparency" as "crystalmind" (stillmind, emptymind, clearmind), in which egothoughts do not interfere with the bright inner Light of Lovemind.

Glorify-- recognize as sacred or holy.

glory-- recognition of inner splendor. The inner state of excellent splendor created by the inner presence of Lovemind; renewal in enlightenment. Holiness or sacredness.

gog and magog--the potential redeemability of even fearmind.

gold-- earthly enlightenment. Enlightenment triggered by the things, objects, persons, and events of earth. Enlightenment found by conquering bionature, or transforming it.

grace-- the state of being saved from ignorance/lower nature by Love, and not by morality, ethics, religion, or "works."

grapes-- spiritual thoughts. Also, thoughts tending towards Communion with the inner divine nature.

Great-- highly influential thoughts; same as "great men." (See that.)

great men--powerful thoughtideas with strong influence over other thoughts.

Great trial-- darknight of the Soul; a time of great testing.

Green-- Love, as the color of nature and of the fourth *chakra*.

greenish-yellow-- the condition of being temporarily paralyzed, or of existing, between the third *chakra* of intelligence and the fourth of Love. Thus, a condition of being "stuck" in intellect while reaching for the higher Love.

hades-- collective name for areas of the mind (subconscious) that are already "dead" or deactivated.

Hail--subconscious thoughtstructures that are cold and rigid; unloving dogma.

Hair -- individual, finer, tiny thoughts that add up to a part of identity-definition.

Half-hour--limited, short amount of time.

hand-- action, activity, or implementation, in a solid, practical way. (Compare "right hand.")

harp-- resonance, synergy, or harmony (with Lovemind).

head-- intellectual capacity; logical or linear thinking; reason.

Hear-- mentally to assimilate with understanding. (Compare "ear".)

Heart-- the name for the collective emotional centers of mind. Also, Love.

heaven-- deepest Mind; Coremind; Lovemind; also, divine habitation (See that), and the Mindarea (Mindfocus, thoughtgroups) in which perfect cosmic Mind exists.

"hell"-- see *"hades."*

holy-- a description of all thoughts and thoughtgroups of healing Love.

Honor-- high selfesteem.

horns-- animalmind or animalnature.

horse--Mindbioforce turned towards the service of human will.

Horsemen-- parts of mind, thoughts or thoughtgroups, in conflict with other aspects of the mind. This symbol combines the human (intellect) with the animal (instinct and energy).

Hour-- small time-period.

Hunger-- deep yearning for Union with Lovemind. (Compare "thirst.")

hyacinth-- inner vision or insight.

idol-- thought or thoughtgroup that pretends to be something spiritual, but is faking; a fake or phony pretension to reflect deep Mind. Common "idols" are materialism, hypersexuality, hyperintellectualism, hypereligiosity.

idolaters-- thoughts that love objects and "material" things more than they love Lovemind.

image-- selfimage or selfconcept, distorted by hypersensuality and hypersexuality.

incense--prayer (5:8); as "smoke," higher thoughts with ambitions for Lovemind. (Compare "heaven" and "smoke.")

incenses-- thoughts from bionature that aspire towards Lovemind.

inherit-- to be granted Lovemind through gnosis.

"in Spirit"-- consciously experiencing the deeper Mindlevels. Introspective, not focused on the world or the senses.

iron-- beginner's mind, the start of the inner (spiritual) journey to Lovemind. Toddlermind.

islands-- areas of sensual, bionatural ("earth") mind surrounded by, and isolated in, the Unconscious or subconscious ("sea"). These thoughtideas are only barely known to the conscious mind, but are really "mountains." (See that.)

Israel--to the ancients, an archetype of mindelements in service to God. So, Lovelements or Lovecomponents.

Issachar-- all thoughts and thoughtgroups that reward you through the creation of a better or good selfimage.

Ivory-- precious thoughts originating with animalnature.

jacinth --mindenergy moving from a purely selfish and sexual orientation into a more intellectual one.

jasper, clear-- the state of pure transparency to Love, in which Love can manifest unimpeded by egothoughts, egodesires, or egofeelings. Crystalmind. Stillmind.

jasper, red-- bioenergy, mindenergy applied to bionature or bioprocesses. (Compare "red.")

Jesus-- the divine-human (Godhuman) interface in deep Mind, where Lovemind blends seamlessly with the human psyche, bridged by Soul.

Jesus Christ-- the eternal Spirit of Love or Lovemind present within every human and sentient heart; the perfect incarnation of Love in human form.

Jews-- thoughts that seek to honor and worship God. But they are incomplete and imperfect. They are misled, corrupted with pride in the delusion that they consider themselves especially "chosen." They see God (Love) as being their *exclusive* possession. Also, the delusion that one has the "whole, exclusive truth" about all matters of Infinity and illimitable, immeasurable Mind.

Jezebel-- the mind's collection of thoughts and thoughtgroups that resist moral goodness; chaos and immorality.

John-- the conscious or aware mind. Like "David" means "beloved". (See that)

Joseph--thoughts and thoughtgroups that bring increase in spirituality.

Judah--the recognition of the relationship in which Coremind (Lovemind) is master, and conscious mind or egomind the servant.

judge (verb)--to see and evaluate according to the standards of cosmic Reality, i.e., all creation is "good."

Juice-filled fruit-- Desire. Also karma.

key-- mindstructures, including wisdom and understanding, used to penetrate the mysteries of the subconscious and Unconscious.

kidneys--internal Mindmechanisms for purifying the psyche.

king-- major, influential thought-matrix that rules or controls many other thoughts.

King of kings-- the most potent of all powers-- surrender ("lamb").

kingdom-- Mindarea controlled by a single powerful "king" or ruling, controlling matrix-thought, -idea, or -concept.

knocking-- signal of the Unconscious to the conscious mind, to alert it to the existence and activity of deeper Mind

lake of fire-- all Unconscious suffering in the Soul that leads to purification.

lamb-- the part of the Mind (later the whole Mind) which completely gives itself, in absolute surrender, to the great will of the cosmic Mind, abandoning the egowill (personal desires) altogether.

Lamp--human or consciously created thought-matrix containing or supporting Light.

lampstand-- the same as "church," or ecclesia (see those): thoughtgroups devoted and dedicated to the service of Love. Thoughtstructures that support Light, enlightenment, and Sourcemind (Lovemind, Spirit).

Laodicea-- the decision-making, justice-seeking aspects of Mind.

left foot--stable but unconscious movement along a spiritual growth-path.

leopard-- vicious and dangerous aspects of the mind.

Levi--all thoughts and thoughtgroups that support, and synergize with, the Union with inner Lovemind.

liars--thoughts that voluntarily support illusions and falsehoods.

Lie (noun)-- illusion.

lightning-- free, unbound mental energy or Mindforce that can support any idea or Mindstructure.

Linen-- selfimage.

Lion--courage, nobility, royalty. Also, possible danger. Originates with animalmind.

Locusts-- tiny, destructive, primitive mindcomponents, of which there are many, that threaten spiritual nutrition and general spiritual mind; mindpollution.

Logos-- Christmind; the plane of interface between the human and divine minds. Also, the perfect, stainless, flawless mirroreflection, perfect representation, lightfilled manifestation, Lovexpression of perfect Lovemind within the human heartmind.

Lord-- cosmic or universal Mind, Lovemind, Coremind. The Mind of illimitable and immeasurable Love, which regulates and controls all Mind everywhere.

lukewarm-- state of unpleasant indecision in which mind does not fully opt for the Reality of good over the illusion of evil.

Luxury-- hypersensuality.

man-- intellect; the sum of thoughts that serve logic and reason.

Manasseh--thoughts that create amnesia, including karmic amnesia at birth, or that prevent the conscious mind from remembering what is in the Unconscious.

manna-- inner spiritual nourishment, produced not by intellectual or affective mind-functions, but by the deepest Mind, Spirit, or Lovemind.

Marble-- strong bionatural thoughts amenable to human formation; it can be very beautiful when "polished" by Love.

Marriage-- Union between Soul and Spirit; Mindmeld, Mindmerge, Mindfusion between conscious mind and Lovemind. Supreme goal of the Way.

meat-- residual energy of deactivated ("dead") thoughts of animalnature, recycled into the Mindsystem to create new energy, to form new thoughts. (Compare "things sacrificed to idols.")

Michael--the ultrapowerful part of Mind that regulates goodness. It has authority, and serves the good, and leads in "war." Still, it exists in ignorance (duality or dualism).

might-- Mindenergy expressed as true strength. Mind is the only Source of power. Mental power to regulate thoughts. Power that arises from Spirit or Coremind (Lovemind).

Military men ("chiliarchs")-- warlike, belligerent, divisive thoughts that divide the psyche and keep it in confusion, pain, and selfconflict.

millstone-- having to do with two other symbols, "bread" and "stone," hence, a Christsymbol.

Month-- time-period greater than "day," but less than "year."

moon-- the Unconscious, especially that part which reflects the Light of Love, or is Itself enlightened.

morning star--the very beginning, the dawning, of Lovelight. (Compare "star.")

Moses-- legalistic, mechanical, scripturalistic religion.

mountains-- bionatural or sensual mind raised to elevated perspectives of higher Mind. (Compare "islands.") Also elevated philosophies supported by hypersensualmind.

mourning-- inner mental suffering or agony.

mouth-- expression; also, assimilation. (Compare "two-mouthed sword.")

murder--the invalid termination or deactivation of a thought or thoughtgroup, especially those that support Lovemind. (Compare "death.")

murderers-- powerful thoughts or thoughtgroups so strong that they deactivated rival thoughts.

musicians-- thoughts that support joy, happiness, and bliss.

"my people"-- thoughts that support Love and Lovemind.

myriad-- a number symbolizing stability and reliability of earthly completion or earthly closure.

mystery-- equated with "good news" in 10:7. The direct, immediate, inner knowing (gnosis) of Lovemind; the gnosis that Mind is One, unified as the only Reality, expressing itself within "your" mind, and within everything else in the cosmos.

naked--vulnerable (without inner spiritual protection). Also, exposed to shame.

name-- identity.

Naphtali--those thoughts and thoughtgroups that bring awareness that Soul is intertwined with Spirit.

Nation-- thoughtgroup above "tribe" (see that) and below "peoples." (See that.) Contains tens of thousands of thoughts.

New earth--the conscious mind largely made one with the Lovemind (see "new heaven"), and the senses become Its servants. Also, sensory mind metamorphosed as servant of Love.

new heaven-- the Lovemind made easily and instantly accessible to the conscious mind; the Lovemind made largely conscious. Lovemind filling the totality of Mind.

New Jerusalem--The mind's collection of thoughtstructures (ideas, concepts, memories, etc.) that are in full harmony with the will of Love or Lovemind. Also, the inner Origin or Fountain of Peace. Human mindstructures (compare "city") completely renovated by, ultimately absorbed into, Lovemind.

Nicolaitians-- those parts of Mind that justify the betrayal of Love. (Compare "fornication.")

noise-- indirect indication of psychological furor, implying conflict.

Number-- logical, linear, conscious thinking and categorization.

observer-- that part of the Mind that studies and watches the world through personal mind. Also, that part of Mind that studies the cosmos through the eyes of the enlightened Soul.

"observe the commandments..."-- perform good, helpful activities that arise from Love.

oil-- mental and spiritual nourishment, more assimilated.

Old person-- part of the Mind that is wise and experienced. Some are parts of the Soul.

olive-- inner peace or tranquility.

omega-- the highest state of spiritual development, when you are beginning to sense that you are One with the Lovemind. Perfection; completeness; end of the spiritual journey. Ultimate goal of life.

one-- the pristine state of undivided, undifferentiated consciousness as the One, the utter Absolute, Ultimate. The oneness of God (Lovemind) with all minds, and all things. As "ten" sense-based enlightenment (Compare "gold").

one-fourth-- instability or destabilization.

one hundred forty-four million--the Lovemind realized and fused, melded, or merged with a Mind now grown fully superhuman, beyond human comprehension.

One hundred forty-four thousand-- the penultimate, apex, zenith, highest representation of all that is spiritual in the Mind.

One-tenth-- incomplete earthly (bionatural) thoughtpatterns, in the sense that they do not support enlightenment.

One-third-- any part, area, function, or section of Mind that feels itself to be outside of universal Love-forgiveness ("grace").

One thousand years-- full earthly enlightenment, created by time.

outer garments-- selfimage, but especially as it might be perceived or interpreted by others.

"outside the city..."-- outside of human cognition or conscious awareness, as outside of logical, linear thoughtstructures.

palms--the promise of growing, living Love in the midst of desertmind-- the mind thirsting for Love. This desertmind appears during the Soul's darknight.

Patmos-- ("mortal") the human condition; the conscious mind.

peace-- inner balance and harmony.

Pearl-- enlightenment, drawing from the subconscious or Unconscious. (Compare "sea," "moon," "precious stone," etc.)

Pebble--a piece of the "Rock," or Christnature, that belongs to, and identifies, the individual Soul.

peoples--thoughtgroup above "nations" (see that) and below "tongues" (see that) in size. Contains hundreds of thousands of thoughts.

Perfumed oils-- sweet experience of spiritual "anointing" (becoming a Christ).

Pergamum-- matrix of reason; the Mind in its logical, linear thoughtpattern.

Philadelphia-- the Mind's collection of thoughts and thoughtgroups supporting brotherly Love.

pillar-- supporting thought or thoughtgroup.

plague-- mental disorientation, dysfunction, or confusion that leads to purification through pain. Also, gigantic mental and spiritual problem, often created for tests of endurance and education.

"polluted with women..."-- a betrayal of Love. Compare "fornication."

Poor--spiritually barren.

Poverty-- the state of mind stripped of intellectual, aesthetic, and spiritual riches, without enough even to sustain it. A state of spiritual barrenness and emptiness.

power-- mental or spiritual energy, or potential. (Compare "might".)

"power of judgment"-- the evaluation, from cosmic Mind, that all Mind, and all the cosmos, is good, and is Mind.

Precious stones-- spiritual "highs" and positive states of altered consciousness.

precious wood-- primitive bionatural thoughts aspiring towards Lovemind. (Compare "scented wood.")

Pregnant-- about to bring to conscious awareness the Christspirit, or the *neopsyche.*

press-- Mindprocesses that transform spiritual thoughts (grapes) into the "wine" of actual Communion. In this Union with Lovemind, the ego must die. So, based on Jesus' Communion (the Eucharist or Last Supper), we can equate "wine" with "blood." "Blood" means "death." So, "wine" in the context of the "wine-press" means death-- egodeath. Also, another, more indirect, meaning of the "press" is egodeath.

priest-- any thought or thoughtgroup that serves the holy, spiritual, or Love fulltime.

Prophecy (noun)-- a prediction or precognition of changes likely to occur during the processes of the Mind's full enlightenment.

prophesy (verb)-- to predict what events are likely to occur in the Mind during the process of enlightenment.

prophet-- a thought that creates, discovers, or shares prophecy.

Purple-- most noble and elevated spirituality. Love.

queen-- ego as false and illegitimate ruler of mindfactors.

rain-- Unconscious, refreshing, life supporting thoughts from higher or deeper Mind, Lovemind, or Coremind.

rainbow--the entire physical cosmos, created by the "white Light" of the One, but manifesting as the many, in diversity and multiplicity. Mind's dream of all "external and material" things. Also, according to the *chakral* system, a variety of Mindfunctions, but this meaning is very secondary.

red-- the first and lowest of the energies of the full energy-spectrum. It is bio-energy. Under the pressure of suffering (see "fiery red"), it is pushed upwards through the other *chakras* or energy-centers to become mental, and later, spiritual, energy. (See "jasper, red," and "sard.")

reed-- psychometric (Mind-measuring) attempts to understand the Mystery of Spirit, and to explain it in human (psychological) terms.

reign--to control the whole Mind.

rejoice-- to taste, or to come into, the state of bliss.

repent-- to turn away from unproductive, harmful, ignorant pursuits, and to devote Mindenergy to the good, constructive, healing, and positive.

resurrection-- bringing back to life thoughts or thoughtgroups once believed to be, or that actually were, "dead." (See that.)

Reuben--all parts of Mind that recognize the "son of God" as the deeper parts of the Self.

revelation--an "un-covering" or "dis-covering" of a Reality already existent within the deeper Mind.

Rich-- descriptive of imaginative and creative Mindfactors.

riches-- mental or spiritual abundance of inner resources.

righteous-- acting in harmony with law is the lower octave; living in alignment with cosmic Law or Love the higher.

right foot-- conscious use of Unconscious forces to create movement or progress.

right hand-- an action or expressed idea, practically implemented, and directed by volition, deliberation, or personal will.

River--flood of conscious and Unconscious thoughtstream that empties into the "sea" (greater Unconscious).

robe, white--purity of selfimage, bestowed by grace.

rock-masses--stubborn dogmas, behind or "under" which the mind wants to hide.

sackcloth--mourning and repentance, but still in darkness.

sailors-- thoughts not affiliated with a strong will or idea, but simply accommodating.

sard-- a red stone, hence, basic bioenergy, or Mindenergy applied to bioprocesses. (Compare "jasper, red" and "red.")

salvation-- rescue from ignorance and the terrible lower nature.

Sardis-- the mind's collection of beautiful and stable ideas.

sardius-- primal earthforces (bioforces) at the very beginning of the spiritual journey inward.

sardonyx-- bionatural Mindforces exposed to, and altered by, Spiritforces.

sapphire--insight or inner sight; the awakening of inner vision to inner realities.

satanmind-- the mind in utter abject slavery to fear. Sometimes, equivalent to "dragon, or "serpent." (See those.)

Saw-- was given insight. (Compare "see.")

scales-- the inner Unconscious Observermind, which records everything that you do, in order to make sure that it comes right back to you. Secondarily, indecision through overanalysis.

scarlet-- basic bioforces; the lower mindenergies of biosurvival.

Scarletmind-- all the pathological aspects of lower mind that support the Love-starved biosexdrive.

scented wood-- primitive bionatural thoughts moving towards Lovemind.

Scorch-- the effect that Spirit has on the fragile, unprepared human psyche when it first encounters It. Its gigantic, massive Power can create pain-- purifying pain-- despite the fact that It is Love.

Scorpion--primitive, dangerous, harmful, toxic thoughts of unforgiveness.

Sea-- the Unconscious.

Seal (noun)-- a mental block, preventing conscious access to a memory. Also, conscious suppression or Unconscious repression of a memory.

seal (verb)-- to mark a thought or thoughtgroup for identification (often, as a "slave" of Lovemind.) (See "slave.") Also, to bury so deeply in the Unconscious or subconscious ("abyss") as to make a thought or thoughtgroup completely inaccessible to conscious memory or recognition.

Seal of God--an identifying mark (behavior) that identifies intellectual thoughts ("forehead") as serving Lovemind.

Sea-workers-- thoughts and thoughtstructures derived from the subconscious or Unconscious.

Second beast-- Hypocritemind; an animal part of the psyche still burdened by dualism. It appears to be surrendermind, but expresses as dragonmind, and so, is a fraud. (Compare "idol.") It serves fearmind.

second death-- a deactivation of a thought or thoughtgroup after it has already been deactivated once, and then, stored in the subconscious/Unconscious.

See-- to gain insight. (Compare "saw.")

Serpent-- the free will, separated conceptually from the will of Love, behaving independently, making constructive errors ("sins"), and even serving fearmind ("satanmind"; see that).

seven-- in archetypal apocalyptic numerology, a holy or spiritual condition or state; potential enlightenment.

shaking-- a terrific, gigantic shift of Mind, particularly the bionatural ("earth").

Shame--a state of mind without awareness of inner purity; destructive absence of selfesteem.

Shepherd (verb)-- gently to guide thoughts and thoughtgroups into surrendermind.

sickle-- the mindfunctions which organize stray, minor, undeveloped, primitive earthly thoughts (compare "vegetation") into useful, nourishing forms (crystal-clear ideas). The mind's natural ordering and processing mechanisms.

signs-- indications of the activity of Power from the Mind, which can be either real or illusory. In the latter case, pretensions made by the subconscious mind.

Silence--the mindstate of stillness or crystalmind.

Silk-- very fine selfimage.

Simeon--the Mind's entire collection of thoughts and thoughtgroups that obey the will of Lovemind.

sin-- processing error; mistake; creative or constructive learning-experience. Also, disastrous crisis and/or horrible mistake.

six-- state or condition of transition between the human ("five") and the divine, spiritual Lovemind ("seven").

Six hundred sixty-six-- the "number" (conscious thought) of a "beast" (lower nature) and a "man" (intellect). Thus, use of intellect to examine lower levels of the mind. Also, by factoring, it is movement through duality and wholeness to the perfect state of oneness or Unity.

Slaughter-- to create "death" (see that) or deactivation of thoughts or thoughtgroups. Some "dead" Mindcomponents, when they go into the Unconscious, actually enrich the psyche by giving up their personal agendas, thus contributing to surrendermind. (Compare "altar" and "lamb".)

slaves--thoughts that are absorbed in the service of greater ideas. Also, thoughts that actively serve Love and Lovemind.

small--insignificant thoughts. (Compare "great.")

Smyrna-- states of Mind creating or supporting sadness.

Snow-- thoughts or thoughtgroups of the Unconscious.

Sodom-- Unconscious mindprocesses that secretly purify through suffering.

son of God-- the deep interior divine nature of Love.

son of man-- the human nature or conscious mind. But, when seen in glorified form in the vision, a being "like" the "son of man" is the human mind transmogrified or metamorphosed by interaction with holy Lovelight, and so, represents the much greater human Soul.

song-- expression of inner joy.

Spirit-- God, Coremind, Lovemind, the Supreme Goal, the Eternal, Immutable, Ineffable, Immeasurable, and Illimitable.

spirits-- cohesive Mindforces that display high-intensity Power for either good or negativity

stab (verb)-- to harm any thought or thoughtgroup viciously, even to the point of death.

staff-- thoughts and thoughtgroups that unite bionature with Lovemind, based on its verticality.

star-- the Light of Love and wisdom, from Coremind, especially in an area of mind ruled by darkness (ignorance; the subconscious). Equated, in 1:20, with "angel," as a strong Loveforce in Mind, drawing its Lovelight from Coremind (Spirit).

stealing--an invalid or immoral attempt to find a shortcut to Lovemind.

Steersman--guiding thoughts in the Unconscious mind, known to the conscious mind.

Sting-- mental pain and agony, created by unforgiveness.

Stone--lower biomind, analogous to "clay" (see that), but with added implications of rigidity, even petrification. But still it has higher potentials (for polished, it is quite beautiful.) Also the Christnature.

strength--tenacity, determination, endurance.

strike (verb)-- to injure through clashing, as in resistance.

sulfur-- intellectual thoughts or thoughtgroups that support growth through suffering.

sun-- the great Lightsource at the Center of being; the interior Sourcemind of Light; Coremind; Lovemind.

Sunrise--the state of mind at the beginning of enlightenment.

sunset-- darknight phases during the eternal journey inward.

supper-- spiritual nourishment.

sword-- thoughts, thoughtfeelings, and thoughtgroups used as weapons of attack against other Mindareas. Also, intent to conflict and/or destroy. (Compare "two-mouthed sword.") Also, attitude of belligerence.

synagogue of satan-- an organized, perhaps even religious, fearsystem within the Mind; a collection of antiagapic (counter-Love) thoughts and thoughtgroups.

tail-- the subconscious mind, the garbage-dump of Mind.

Tears-- sorrow.

Teeth-- assimilation, often violently forced upon a thought or thoughtgroup.

temptations-- the mind's collection of egodesires and sensual desires. Inclinations and attractions of lower mind, including materialism, hypersexuality, and hypersensuality.

ten-- in archetypal apocalyptic numerology, the state or condition of earthly completeness, wholeness, or closure. It is enlightenment within the sensory or earthly mind, hence, not fullest enlightenment.

Tent-- the mobility or portability of Lovemind's mental indwelling.

testifier-- A part of Christmind, or of the inner Christspirit. The inner "observer." (See that.)

testimony-- giving positive accounts of the benefits of serving Love.

thanksgiving--a recognition and acknowledgment that great spiritual wealth exists within your own mind, creating the attitude of gratitude.

thief-- Mindenergy of quiet imperceptibility (Unconscious). Also, hiding, guilt, negative selfimage.

Thigh-- expressed power of the lower nature, involved in making progress.

things sacrificed to idols--thoughtenergy which should be devoted to Lovemind, but is wasted instead on "false gods," such as money, materialism, lustful inappropriate sexuality, sensual overindulgences, etc.

thirst-- longing for Union with the perfect Lovemind. (Compare "hunger.")

thousand years-- see "one thousand years."

three-- in archetypal apocalyptic numerology, wholeness (or holiness), completeness.

three and a half-- mental conflict between wholeness ("three) and duality ("one-half").

"thrown down"-- created, in reference to the creation of earth. Implies creation by a "higher" Mind.

thunder-- intuition of a coming psychic or spiritual "Mindstorm."

Thyatira-- the Mind in its worship-mode, or in worshipful attitude. The mind's collection of elevated, Love-owned thoughts and thoughtgroups.

Tongues-- the largest thoughtgroups mentioned in Revelation, above "peoples" in size. Contains millions of thoughts.

topaz-- mindenergy halfway between intellect and Love.

torment-- the mind's response to Unconscious disapproval, and to confusion. Also selfcreated suffering.

Traveling merchants-- the mind's thought-distribution and -arrangement mechanisms.

tree-- all mindmechanisms and processes that change thoughts into actions. Also, strong, natural thoughts or thoughtgroups transforming themselves into actions or activities. Also, the potential for any thought to become action or activity, to express itself as practical reality in the world.

tree of life-- "Paradise" or the state of undiluted, unadulterated Love.Fullest enlightenment through complete Unity with Lovemind. Also, enlightenment through action. (Ga 5:22)

tribe-- a thoughtgroup or thought-constellation, smallest of the tribes, nations, peoples, and tongues. Contains thousands of thoughts.

tribulation-- a major period of trial, trouble, and challenge, designed for learning. In context, a period during the darknight of the Soul, or that darknight itself.

"true"-- real, Reality or the Absolute.

trumpet-- alert, especially regarding war or conflict between/among Mindareas.

twelve-- the celestial number; heavenly order. Also, the human heartmind's potential for full enlightenment.

twelve squared-- discovery that your mind is Lovemind.

twelve cubed-- penultimate inner cosmic order; your mind in perfect arrangement or enlightenment; final closure and wholeness, complete satisfaction, fulfillment, and contentment in Lovemind.

twenty-four-- the Mind, divided into two arrangements or orders ("twelves")-- conscious and Unconscious. Also, wholeness finally achieved after passing through two or more states of delusion (illusion; dualism). (2x2x2x3)

Two-mouthed sword--Ignorant, careless expressions of duality or dualism that create inner conflict in the psyche.

two witnesses-- a divided mind, trying to serve Love, but still locked in ignorance (dualism). (See "bymartyrian mind" and "bimind".)

ulcer-- anxiety/depression. Specifically, mental pathology that includes anger and depression, and arises from resisting Lovemind.

unbelievers--thoughts that support common or popular views, and that reject mystical views.

Unclean spirits-- mental and spiritual pathologies.

under-- the subconscious, a small area of the Unconscious that serves as the dust-bin of Mind.

Under the altar-- the subconscious area of Mind where the idea of surrender and selfsacrifice is first generated.

Up the middle--at the Center, in the very place of Lovemind, the utter Ruler of Mind.

vegetation--primitive, undeveloped thoughts, very low on the scale of spiritual evolution.

Vengeance-- perfect balance created by thc outworking of the cosmic Law of karma.

Vessel-- the empty, waiting human mind as cognitive "container" for supercognitive contents from Lovemind.

Vine-- Lovemind.

Virginity-- inner mental purity, uncontaminated by betrayal of Love.

voice-- communication/expression between or among any parts of Mind.

"voice of the mill"-- assimilation and processing of inner nutrition, spiritual food.

walls-- thoughts or thoughtgroups that serve as challenges, tests, or barriers to Union with inner Lovemind.

war-- any major conflict between thoughtgroups, ideas, or concepts, or between the forces of good and the illusions of "evil."

"washed...robes"-- purified and cleansed selfimage through grace, and through death or selfsurrender into Lovemind.

Water-- the Unconscious mind.

weeping--great sadness.

wheat-- spiritual nourishment.

white-- pure, clean, spiritually or mentally pristine, uncontaminated, or unpolluted.

Wild beast-- the great thoughtgroup that creates dangerous, wild, unregulated thoughts, often based upon hypersensuality, violence, hypersexuality, greed, materialism, fear, egocentricity, etc. The sum of dangerous, violent, selfdestructive thoughts in the conscious human mind and in the subconscious. It is irrational and impulsive. In one of its forms, it is "animalmind." It is similar in some ways to dragonmind.

wine-- essence or distillation of bionatural thoughts ("grapes" from "earth"). Thus, *in the context of the winepress, in which bionatural egothoughts die,* wine means death to the egonature. For the "wine" of Communion is the "blood" (death) of the ego (Jesus). It makes possible the resurrection of the inner eternal Spirit of the Christ. Also, in other contexts, confusion and disorientation.

Winepress-- see "press."

wings-- the ability of a thoughtgroup to transcend or rise above the normal or usual thoughtpatterns.

wisdom-- mental or spiritual discernment. Spiritual uses and applications of knowing (gnosis).

Woman-- mother; goddess. Wellspring of nature, fertility. Creativity, tenderness, gentleness. The feminine or *yin* side of cosmic Mind. Goddessmind. But in another context, the whore, the biosexdrive stripped of Love ("Babylon the great")

Woman's hair--The *yin* side of the inside of Mind. The gentler, more nourishing, supportive, soft, attractive, nurturing side of human nature. Tenderness, kindness, compassion, expressed in thought.

Wood--a stage or phase of Mind. It once was alive, but under human direction, lost its life. But it still has potential, for it can be made to be very beautiful. (Compare the famous "uncarved block" of Taoism.) (See also "scented woods").

Wool-- warmth or protection whose origin is surrendermind.

word-- perfect expression of Lovemind. (Compare "Logos.")

Work of their hands-- the transformation of thoughts or ideas into actual activity (behavior) or objects.

Worship-- to bestow the honor of the mind upon.

Write-- to impress upon or commit to memory.

Zebulun--all thoughts and thoughtgroups that recognize that the human mind is the "dwelling place" of Lovemind, the "Lord," or "God."

Zion-- spiritual thirst for Unity with the One (Lovemind) amplified and recognized at a conscious level.